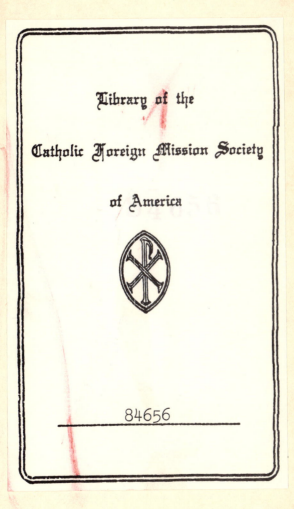

SOCIETY FOR NEW TESTAMENT STUDIES

MONOGRAPH SERIES

General Editor: R. McL. Wilson F.B.A.
Associate Editor: M. E. Thrall

37

KERYGMA AND *DIDACHE*

Kerygma and *Didache*

The articulation and structure of the
earliest Christian message

JAMES I. H. McDONALD
Lecturer in Religious Studies
Moray House College, Edinburgh

CAMBRIDGE UNIVERSITY PRESS

CAMBRIDGE
LONDON · NEW YORK · NEW ROCHELLE
MELBOURNE · SYDNEY

Published by the Press Syndicate of the University of Cambridge
The Pitt Building, Trumpington Street, Cambridge, CB2 1RP
32 East 57th Street, New York, NY 10022, USA
296 Beaconsfield Parade, Middle Park, Melbourne 3206, Australia

First published 1980

Printed in Great Britain by
Redwood Burn Limited
Trowbridge and Esher

Library of Congress Cataloguing in Publication Data

McDonald, James Ian Hamilton.
    Kerygma and *didache*.

    (Monograph series - Society for New Testament
Studies; 37)
    A revision of the author's thesis, University of
Edinburgh, 1974.
    Bibliography: p.
    Includes indexes.
    1. Kerygma. 2. Theology - Early church, *ca.* 30–600.
I. Title. II. Series: Studiorum Novi Testamenti Societas.
Monograph series; 37.
BS2545.K43M23 1979   251   77-95446
ISBN 0 521 22055 6

TO JENNY

CONTENTS

Contents

PREFACE

This book originated as a thesis presented to the University of Edinburgh in 1974 for the Degree of Doctor of Philosophy. Since then it has been substantially revised and rewritten. At all stages in its development, I have been indebted to the advice and encouragement of Professor Hugh Anderson of the University of Edinburgh. I am grateful to the editors of the S.N.T.S. Monograph Series for accepting the work for publication: to Professor Matthew Black, Principal of St Mary's in the University of St Andrews, for initial guidance, and to Professor R. McL. Wilson, of the same University, for much help while the manuscript was being prepared for the publishers; and to Dr David Hill, of the University of Sheffield, for the benefit of his criticism at an earlier stage. My indebtedness to the world of scholarship is, however, much wider than I can readily identify here. I can only hope that the acknowledgements in the notes and bibliography go some way towards indicating the extent to which I have relied on the labours of others. For any omissions and misinterpretations I crave the reader's indulgence.

I acknowledge the help I have received from many modern translations of the Bible, and while I have sometimes translated from the Greek myself and have not used any one version consistently, I am aware of having used the Revised Standard Version (1952) more frequently than any other.

From the time this work was in its earliest stages, my wife has been a constant source of strength and encouragement, and her contribution has included the typing of several drafts of the entire manuscript. To her the end product is affectionately dedicated.

Finally, it is a pleasure to acknowledge the friendly helpfulness and efficiency of the staff of Cambridge University Press.

Edinburgh　　　　　　　　　　　　　　　　　　　　　　　　I.McD.
St Andrew's Day, 1977

ABBREVIATIONS

A & G	W. F. Arndt and F. W. Gingrich, *A Greek-English Lexicon of the New Testament*, 1957
A.N.C.L.	*Ante-Nicene Christian Library*
A.N.E.T.	J. B. Pritchard (ed.), *Ancient Near Eastern Texts relating to the Old Testament*, Princeton, N.J., 1950
B.A.	*Biblical Archaeologist*, Cambridge, Mass. (now Missoula, Montana)
B.A.S.O.R.	*Bulletin of the American School of Oriental Research*, New Haven, Conn.
Beginnings	F. J. Foakes-Jackson and K. Lake (edd.), *The Beginnings of Christianity*, London, 1920-33
B.F.P.S.	C. Westermann, *Basic Forms of Prophetic Speech*, Eng. tr., London, 1967
B.J.R.L.	*Bulletin of the John Rylands Library*, Manchester
B.Z.	*Biblische Zeitschrift*, Paderborn
B.Z.A.W.	*Beihefte der Zeitschrift für alttestamentliche Wissenschaft*
C.B.Q.	*Catholic Biblical Quarterly*, Washington, D.C.
D.B.S.	*Supplément au Dictionnaire de la Bible* V, Paris.
Ency. Bib.	*Encyclopaedia Biblica*, London, 1899-1903
E.R.E.	*Encyclopaedia of Religion and Ethics*, Edinburgh, 1908-26
Ev. Th.	*Evangelische Theologie*, München
Exp. T.	*Expository Times*, Edinburgh
F.G.T.	V. Taylor, *The Formation of the Gospel Tradition*, London, 1933, r.p. 1964
H.J.	*Hibbert Journal*, London
H.N.T.	*Handbuch zum Neuen Testament*, Tübingen
H.S.T.	R. Bultmann, *History of the Synoptic Tradition*, Eng. tr., Oxford, 1963, 2nd ed. 1968
H.T.R.	*Harvard Theological Review*, Cambridge, Mass.
H.U.C.A.	*Hebrew Union College Annual*, Cincinnati

I.C.C.	*International Critical Commentary*, Edinburgh
Int.	*Interpretation:* a Journal of Bible and Theology, Richmond, Va.
Int. Bib.	*Interpreter's Bible*, New York, Nashville, 1952–7
I.T.Q.	*Irish Theological Quarterly*, Dublin
J.B.L.	*Journal of Biblical Literature*, New Haven, Boston, Philadelphia
J.E.H.	*Journal of Ecclesiastical History*, London
J.J.S.	*Journal of Jewish Studies*, Cambridge
J.Q.R.	*Jewish Quarterly Review*, London, Philadelphia
J.R.	*Journal of Religion*, Chicago
J.S.S.	*Journal of Semitic Studies*, Manchester
J.S.J.	*Journal for the Study of Judaism*, Leiden
J.T.S.	*Journal of Theological Studies*, Oxford
Mélanges M. Goguel	M. Goguel (Festschrift), *Aux sources de la tradition chrétienne*, Neuchâtel, 1950
Mélanges B. Rigaux	B. Rigaux (Festschrift), *Mélanges bibliques en hommage au R. P. Béda Rigaux*, Gembloux, 1970
M.M.	B. Gerhardsson, *Memory and Manuscript, Oral Tradition and Written Transmission in Rabbinic Judaism and Early Christianity*, Lund, 1961
N.C.E.	*New Catholic Encyclopaedia* , New York, 1967–74
Nov. T.	*Novum Testamentum*, Leiden
N.R.T.	*Nouvelle Revue Théologique*, Paris, Louvain
N.T.S.	*New Testament Studies*, Cambridge, Eng.
O.C.D.	*Oxford Classical Dictionary*
Peake	M. Black and H. H. Rowley (edd.), *Peake's Commentary on the Bible*, London, 1962
P.G.	J. P. Migne (ed.), *Patrologia Graeca*, Paris, 1857–64
Rab. Anth.	C. G. Montefiore and H. Lowe (edd.), *A Rabbinic Anthology* , London, 1938
R.d'H.E.	*Revue d'Histoire Ecclésiastique*, Louvain
R.G.G.	*Religion in Geschichte und Gegenwart*, Tübingen
S.J.T.	*Scottish Journal of Theology*, Edinburgh
S.M.R.	C. F. D. Moule (ed.), *The Significance of the Message of the Resurrection for Faith in Jesus Christ*, London, 1968.
S.O.T.P.	J. H. Robinson (ed.), *Studies in Old Testament Prophecy*, Edinburgh, 1950
S.S.M.	W. D. Davies, *The Setting of the Sermon on the Mount*, Cambridge, 1964

St. Th.	*Studia Theologica*, Lund
T.D.N.T.	*Theological Dictionary of the New Testament*, ed. G. F. Kittel (Eng. tr. of *Theologische Wörterbuch zum Neuen Testament*), Grand Rapids, Michigan, 1964–76
T.L.Z.	*Theologische Literaturzeitung*, Leipzig
T.T.	B. Gerhardsson, *Tradition and Transmission in Early Christianity*, Lund, 1964
T.U.	*Texte und Untersuchungen*, Berlin
V. Chr.	*Vigiliae Christianae*, Amsterdam
V.T.	*Vetus Testamentum*, Leiden
V.T.S.	*Vetus Testamentum* Supplement
Z.A.W.	*Zeitschrift für die Alttestamentliche Wissenschaft*, Berlin
Z.N.W.	*Zeitschrift für die Neutestamentliche Wissenschaft*, Berlin
Z.T.K.	*Zeitschrift für Theologie und Kirche*, Tübingen

INTRODUCTION

The problem of *kerygma* and *didache*

The dawn of modern, kerygmatic theology broke upon the slumbering
world in 1892 with the publication of a work by Martin Kähler[1] which
decisively challenged the historical relativism of the nineteenth-century
'lives of Jesus'[2] and redirected attention to the Christ of the apostolic
preaching. 'The real Christ is the preached Christ, and the preached Christ
is the Christ of faith.'[3] The high noon of the movement was marked by
the ascendancy of Barth and Bultmann, blood brothers of the *formgeschichtliche Schule* but diverging sharply, as brothers sometimes do, in
the very manner in which they developed their inheritance. The post-
Bultmannians still walk in the afternoon sunlight of kerygmatic theology,
even if the lengthening shadows suggest that the darkness of the night will
not be postponed indefinitely. The twentieth-century day, thus illumined
by the sunlight of the *kerygma*, has had its own share of diurnal difficulties,
many of them still unresolved as the working day draws towards its close,
but it has always claimed the advantage of locating clearly the genuine
source of light and power: the *kerygma*, the preaching which has characterised and enshrined the Christian faith from the beginning. Yet this basic
nuclear concept presents a concatenation of problems, a further examination of which is essential to any appreciation in depth of the nature of
Christian utterance.

The meaning of *kerygma* in the New Testament

The term *kerygma*, like the English word 'preaching', possesses inherent
ambivalence. It may refer to preaching as an activity or as the content of
proclamation, and sometimes it is not easy to decide which meaning predominates. When Paul comments that 'it pleased God through the foolishness of the *kerygma* to save those who believe' (1 Cor. 1: 21), is he referring to the folly of the activity of preaching or the folly of the message
itself? With G. Friedrich,[4] one may note Paul's desire to underline the
content of preaching (1: 23, 'we preach Christ crucified', and perhaps also

1

1: 18, 'the word of the cross'): the *kerygma* in 1: 21 is then the content of the message, which is mere foolishness to the sophisticated Greek.[5] But in 1 Cor. 2: 4, where Paul again dissociates his *logos* (speech) and *kerygma* (preaching) from the plausibility of worldly wisdom, he is clearly referring to the act of preaching which has an eschatological dynamic,[6] so that the faith of those who responded to his preaching was born not of human wisdom but of the power of God. This nuance can hardly be absent in 1: 21. C. F. Evans strikes a delicate balance in his interpretation: 'The content of the activity corresponds with the activity itself, "Christ crucified" being the apparently foolish content of the foolish activity of preaching.'[7] If one were to assess where the weight of meaning falls generally, one would conclude that *kerygma* almost invariably contains the primary notion of the dynamic activity of preaching, but no context excludes the idea of content,[8] which must therefore be included within the general connotation of the term.

A further ambivalence is illustrated by the difficulty of interpreting a phrase such as 'the *kerygma* of Jesus Christ' (Rom. 16: 25). If the construction is taken to be an objective genitive, the meaning is 'the preaching about Jesus Christ', the whole phrase being a summary, perhaps, of Rom. 10: 8-12.[9] If the phrase is modelled on the corresponding expression 'according to my gospel', the meaning is 'the message which Jesus Christ proclaimed'.[10] This allows a direct parallelism between the *kerygma* of Jesus and the *kerygma* of the early church, but New Testament usage is frequently more sophisticated and ambivalent. Thus 'Christ' is often the content of the *kerygma*: 'we preach Christ crucified' (1 Cor. 1: 23); but additionally and at the same time Christ is the agent in and behind the activity of preaching, as is clearly shown in Paul's understanding of his commission (Gal. 1: 16). This eschatological dimension has been rightly stressed by R. Bultmann.[11] In the Pastorals, *kerygma* can also denote the office of preaching with which the apostle is entrusted and which is the means of manifesting eschatological truth (Titus 1: 2f.; cf. 2 Tim. 4: 17). But, as will be subsequently illustrated, when the content of *kerygma* is examined in a more detailed way, no agreement exists as to its precise constituents.

Some modern uses of kerygma

That kerygmatic theology in general has attempted to remain faithful to this complexity of central concern may readily be admitted. Bultmann treats the *kerygma* as 'eschatological event'; his hermeneutic is directed to the problem of the meaningfulness of the *kerygma* to 'modern man'; and if he plays down the delineation of its content in terms of explicit formulae, he emphasises that it always has to do with God's action in Christ.[12] But the brand of kerygmatic theology which exercised considerable influence in Britain and beyond in the mid-twentieth century can hardly be credited with maintaining a similar equilibrium. The publication of C. H. Dodd's attractive and influential book, *The Apostolic Preaching and its Developments*, had the unfortunate effect of encouraging an inflexible understanding of the *kerygma* in terms of supposedly primitive and relatively stereotyped confessional formulae. It became a commonplace in English theological circles to assume the existence of 'a common pattern of *kerygma* in early speeches in Acts, in several passages of St. Paul, and in Mark's summary of Jesus' preaching in Galilee'.[13] Such widespread acceptance of a hypothesis that was by no means exhaustively argued suggests that it spoke to some psychological need on the part of the English-speaking theological public. A century or so of critical scholarship that had left the old dogmatic orthodoxy threadbare and discredited had also presented the New Testament as a conglomerate of oddments dazzling in their variety and fascinating in their peculiarity but reflecting many different historical and doctrinal milieux. The rediscovery of the primitive, kerygmatic pattern suggested that the vital clue to the unity of the New Testament and the location of its true focus had been uncovered.[14] The consequence of the inherent rigidity of this position was that the dynamic and fluid activity of preaching was caught and stopped as by a still camera. The electric shock of the eschatological 'now', the moment in a man's experience in which the living word of preaching strikes home more sharply than a two-edged sword, was neutralised by the intrusion of the concept of a timeless and eternal kingdom, a Platonic form[15] to be detected in the process of realisation, if not wholly realised, amid the temporal and ephemeral.

Fortunately, the element of aberration in this understanding of the *kerygma* has become much clearer in more recent discussion. If the film is temporarily stopped to allow analysis of the sermons of Peter and Paul in Acts, it must be recognised that such sermons, even if they do represent an authentic summary of what Peter and Paul actually said on the occasions in question, are the products of a fluid process of development in thinking and interpretation within the Christian community from its earliest stages onwards. Besides, the credal formulae abstracted from the film clip are themselves wholly time-conditioned, and in consequence have their limitations as vehicles for the wealth of insight, experience and faith which they strive to bear. Such desiccated formulae have little point of contact with Paul's preaching 'in demonstration of the Spirit and of power'. In more flamboyant vein, T. G. A. Baker invites the modern reader to study again the kerygmatic formulae abstracted as described and to ask whether, on their own, they 'would ever convert a fly – even a first-century Palestinian fly – let alone one of the twentieth-century European variety'.[16] In other words, such formulae are no longer kerygmatic in operation.

How biblical is modern usage?

The use of the Greek word *kerygma* as a technical term in modern theology carries an implicit claim that biblical usage is thus perpetuated. Yet the word *kerygma* is not particularly prominent in the New Testament, and the term *euangelion*, occurring nearly ten times as often, would appear to be more representative of biblical practice.[17] Not only does *euangelion* express the note of joyfulness, but it is also more satisfactory as a holistic term for the Christian message.[18] The limitations of the term *kerygma* have led to several disquieting terminological developments in modern biblical theology. Even in the heyday of the 'objectifying' view of the *kerygma* so strongly advocated by C. H. Dodd, its monolithic structure was rendered questionable by the failure of its advocates to agree upon the precise composition of the ancient message.[19] Its holistic inadequacy has led to the use of *didache* as a supplement to *kerygma*; and while this may appear to echo biblical usage – 'preaching and teaching' is a recognised biblical formula – it is not clear in practice that modern usage follows or preserves the biblical meaning.[20] A more recent development has been to use the plural term *kerygmata* to express the variety of ways in which the central message is communicated: 'it would be better to speak of "*kerygmata*" than, too confidently, of "*the kerygma*" '.[21] However valid this insight may be and however preferable to the uniform, monolithic structure indicated above, misgivings abound in relation to terminological concerns. To use the plural form is to depart even further from New Testament usage.[22] And the original object of *kerygma* terminology was to express the unity of the Christian proclamation, which is now apparently dissipated in a plurality of forms. Two conclusions are indicated: first, 'the term *kerygma* is more a technical term of modern biblical theology than of the Bible itself';[23] and, in the second place, in studies of Christian origins relating to the emergence and early articulation of the Christian message, the term *kerygma* can be used only with the greatest caution, and if it can be replaced by a terminology more representative of New Testament usage and practice, this alternative terminology should be adopted.

The relationship between kerygma and didache

If *kerygma* was the solar centre in the universe of kerygmatic theology, *didache* was sometimes represented as a lesser satellite whose function was entirely governed by the greater sun and whose light was no more than a lunar reflection. C. H. Dodd writes: 'It was by *kerygma*, says Paul, not by *didache*, that it pleased God to save men',[24] although a glance at 1 Cor. 1: 21 indicates that Paul said nothing of the kind. Elsewhere, Dodd writes:

> It is evident from the whole New Testament that the message of the church was conceived as having two main aspects: the Gospel of Christ, the theme of preaching (*kerygma*), and the Law or Commandment of Christ, the theme of teaching (*didache*)... The two are intimately united, though distinguishable.[25]

This inner dualism is worked out at several levels: for example, between the proclamation of salvation in Christ and the teaching of Christian moral practice; and between the proclamation to the non-Christian world and the instruction of those within the community. G. Wingren commented:

> It is surprising that Dodd, who in the whole New Testament sees the manifestation of one and the same oft-repeated *kerygma*, can be tempted by such a distinction. The Epistles that preach the *kerygma* most clearly, for example, 1 Peter and others like it, were sent to Christian congregations in trouble... It is false intellectualism to separate those who belong to the church from the missionary *kerygma*.[26]

In somewhat similar terms, C. F. D. Moule writes:

> if we maintain the familiar distinction between *kerygma* and *didache* too rigidly, we shall not do justice to the real nature of all Christian edification, which builds, sometimes more, sometimes less, but always at least some of the foundation material into the walls and floors.[27]

That there is a broad distinction between preaching and teaching,[28] in the ancient and the modern world, must be allowed. W. D. Davies is justified in underlining Matthew's didactic vocabulary in his introduction to the Sermon (Matt. 5: 1), but one notes that the distinction lies in the informality of the situation and the posture of the teacher rather than the substance of the message: indeed, Luke and presumably Q tend towards a sermonic rather than a didactic presentation of essentially the same material (cf. Luke 6: 17–20).[29] Further, preaching and teaching are properly regarded as being broadly complementary and as denoting the whole process of communicating the appropriate message. This operates equally for the ministry of Jesus (cf. Matt. 4: 23; 9: 35; 11: 1) and the apostolic mission (Acts 28: 31). The extent to which the terms overlap and integrate makes it difficult to separate them except in general terms.

Thus, Friedrich's contention that those who heard Jesus' preaching are different from those who heard his teaching[30] would be difficult to maintain in any rigid sense; and he goes on to show that Jesus, exercising his distinctive *exousia* (Matt. 7: 29), preached in the synagogue (the normal place for 'teaching') as he proclaimed the advent of the kingdom (cf. Luke 4: 21). In fact, the terms are so interrelated that they can be used virtually as synonyms: the disciples, sent out in Mark 3: 14f. to *'preach* and . . . cast out devils', return in Mark 6: 30 to 'report to him all that they had done and all that they had *taught'*. Equally, the attempt to distinguish between them in terms of content – the usual assumption being that *didache* represents ethical teaching – is shattered by Rom. 2: 21, where, as J. J. Vincent has put it, 'the "content" of the preacher's preaching (κήρυγμα) is good, solid ethical διδαχή!'[31] 'While you *preach* against stealing, do you steal?' Such distinction as exists between them must be sought in less tangible features.

An important contribution to this debate was made by K. Stendahl.[32] He distinguished between *kerygma* as a formal, functional activity (*Formalbegriff*) – roughly what Bultmann means by 'address' – and *kerygma* as content (*Inhaltsbegriff*), usually related to 'the things concerning Jesus' and taken by Dodd as *Heilsgeschichte*. He argued that preaching in the first sense may be 'kerygmatic' without however presenting *kerygma* in the second sense. Conversely, if *kerygma* in the latter sense is presented as no more than a recital of events or a string of propositions, it is not in fact kerygmatic: it is *unkerygmatisches Kerygma*. And what is in effect *didache* operating in a particular situation may be profoundly kerygmatic: this is, in Stendahl's terminology, *kerygmatisches Nicht-Kerygma*. Bearing this insight in mind, J. J. Vincent examined the synoptic gospels[33] in order to identify their kerygmatic elements and emerged with the conclusion that the key to the intrinsic synoptic *kerygma* lay precisely in its *didache*, which related to the whole story of Jesus: 'the only κήρυγμα of which we are entitled to speak on the basis of the Synoptics is "a didactic kerygma"'.[34] In relation to Jesus' teaching on the way of the cross, for example, 'the radical διδαχή is the κήρυγμα of God'.[35]

What are we to conclude from such evidence? *Kerygma* and *didache* can still be used as complementary terms to denote the central complex of Christian utterance but because of their peculiar interrelatedness they cannot provide a basis for a proper operational analysis of Christian communication. It is not enough to attempt to identify given material formally as *kerygma* or *didache*, for it might have both kerygmatic or didactic characteristics to a greater or lesser degree and at the same time possess other features which signify its nature and intention in a more useful way. Our aim in this work, therefore, is to identify and classify forms of Christian communication according to their nature, intention and operation. Such a task involves the elucidation of the broad hinterland of Christian communication of which the form critics were well aware but which in practice was subordinated in their work to the analysis of particular forms of the gospel tradition. Hence we propose to lay more, not less, stress upon the *Sitz im Leben* of early Christian utterance, for it was within the *koinonia* of the early communities that Christian meaning and insight found articulation and took on appropriate formal structures (cf. Acts 2: 42).

Towards a structural analysis of *kerygma* and *didache*

Before attempting to formulate our own hypothesis, we must take note of relevant research already carried out by Roman Catholic and by Scandinavian scholars in particular.

Formal analysis in Roman Catholic debate

Roman Catholic discussion, recognising a 'crisis of preaching' in the modern situation, has moved the subject into a position of central concern.[36] J. A. Jungmann has pointed to the biblical model of the proclamation of the gospel as the key to dynamic preaching with strong pastoral and kerygmatic concern. For him, *kerygma* is the christocentric message that comprises the essential content of Christian teaching and is designed for proclamation. It is to be distinguished from *catechesis*, which consists of practical religious training, teaching the history of redemption as in the scriptures, and systematic instruction in doctrine.[37] A. Rétif, in his more detailed historical research on the subject, emerged with a three-fold distinction: *kerygma*, the proclamation of the kingdom of God in Christ for evangelistic purposes; *catechesis* (or *didache*), the teaching that introduced converts to Christian doctrine and moral practice; and *didaskalia*, the more advanced instruction in the faith.[38] D. Grasso discerned yet another triple structure: evangelisation, *catechesis*, and homily, all of which have their focus in the person of Christ the Saviour.[39] Evangelisation, which is supremely kerygmatic, includes the proclamation of salvation history, centred on the cross and resurrection, and calls for decision. *Catechesis* follows evangelisation and is instructional, presenting the message of salvation with a view to initiating the convert into the Christian life and the mystery of Christ, either before or after baptism. Homily takes place in a liturgical context, within the family of the faithful, as 'a means whereby the liturgy realizes its proper goal, the union of the faithful with Christ', and is aimed at the will.[40] There is, however, an overriding unity in preaching, no one form being totally independent of the others.

These triple structures in particular represent a clear advance beyond the formal two-fold distinction between *kerygma* and *didache*. One difficulty in the Roman Catholic debate, however, is that frequently formal analysis is insufficiently related to the study of New Testament forms and is much influenced by the 'reading back' of church practice into the apostolic period.[41] The interdependence of the different forms, though recognised,[42] is not fully developed, and the more instructional forms lack the dynamic they appear to possess in the New Testament.

Scandinavian approaches to formal analysis

Bo Reicke[43] found his starting point in form criticism and comparative folklore – disciplines which indicate that early Christian preaching, like other types of cultural development, cannot have been without set forms at any stage. While the apostolic message was admittedly new and *sui generis*, historical research yields no support for the hypothesis of *creatio ex nihilo* as far as external forms are concerned. Since the apostles were the representatives of the Lord, 'an extension and multiplication of His person',[44] the comparison of their preaching with the models offered by the teaching of Jesus is particularly illuminating, but further prototypes may be sought in Old Testament prophecy and the messianic proclamations of the inter-testamental period.[45] It will be part of our strategy to explore, however briefly, this hinterland of Christian communication.

Reicke is less successful when he turns to a consideration of the main aspects of the divine messenger's activity, which he identifies as (i) conversion, including admonition and invitation, (ii) instruction and edification, (iii) testament, and (iv) revelation. Each of these categories is open to objection. 'Conversion' cannot properly describe a category of preaching. In any case, conversion is not in itself a function of the divine messenger: to claim that it is so would be theologically unsound and linguistically inaccurate.[46] A better description of what Reicke intends might be derived from the functions and activities of prophets, evangelists or missionaries. His term 'instruction and edification' is much too wide and requires to be broken down into its constituent elements, i.e., into the identifiable forms of communication which it embraces. *Catechesis* and homily have already emerged as possibilities. By contrast, Reicke's third category, 'testament', is much too specific. It refers to a particular type of rhetorical discourse, the 'farewell speech', which is perhaps better classified as a distinctive expression – often literary – of a broader paraenetic or homiletic form.[47] Finally, his use of the term 'revelation' to denote a form of preaching requires to be challenged. On the one hand, it is essentially a theological term, denoting the unveiling of the mystery of God in human history and therefore the concern, to a greater or lesser extent, of all Christian communication. On the other hand, 'revelational' utterances in the New Testament are regularly attributed to 'prophets',[48] and the question must be raised whether this kind of communication should not be classified with the prophetic preaching as a whole.[49] Certain forms of apocalyptic, however, seem to belong to some kind of teaching category, even if they form a singular strand of it.

Among other valuable Scandinavian contributions, a special place must be given to the work of H. Riesenfeld.[50] Concerned with the pre-history and origins of the gospel traditions, with the *Sitz im Leben* of the tradition of the words and deeds of Jesus, Riesenfeld is critical of the one-sidedness and dogmatism of at least latter-day form criticism.[51] A comparison of various examples of preaching in Acts with the gospel material indicates that 'mission preaching was not the *Sitz im Leben* of the Gospel tradition'.[52] The proclamation of the gospel within the Christian communities possessed a strong instructional and moral emphasis – the latter in the form of *paraenesis*. In this community preaching reference was undoubtedly made to the gospel tradition (e.g., 1 Cor. 7: 10f.; James *passim*). Yet, since such preaching did not so much transmit the gospel tradition as assume a knowledge of it on the part of the hearers, the *Sitz im Leben* of this tradition is not to be found in this communal instruction either. Such negative findings clear the way for Riesenfeld's main thesis, subsequently corroborated in large measure by B. Gerhardsson's study in depth of the transmission of tradition in the Jewish world in particular,[53] that the gospel tradition belongs to a category that is *sui generis* and is to be designated as *paradosis*. In the transmission of this material, the apostles had a particularly important role: they were the witnesses to and guardians of the holy tradition of the words and deeds, the life and work, of Jesus, which form 'a holy Word, comparable with that of the Old Testament':[54] 'the New Torah', 'the Word of God of the new, eschatological covenant',[55] recited in Christian public worship and communicated to a wider circle by a growing Christian ministry. Its special character is explained by the fact that 'this tradition, *qua* tradition, was derived from none other than Jesus. Hence our thesis is that the beginning of the Gospel tradition lies with Jesus himself.'[56] This thesis is supported by a consideration of the rabbinic methods of instruction which Jesus, as a teacher, used within the circle of his disciples and which can still be traced in such stylistic features as poetic constructions, in Aramaic echoes and in parabolic forms. Even parts of the passion narrative are referred back to Jesus' own interpretation of the events that were about to happen, as are the essential constituents of christology and ethics. Equally, the Johannine tradition is referred independently to the discourses and meditations of Jesus in the circle of his disciples.[57] The picture is completed by the assumption of messianic consciousness on the part of Jesus:

> Jesus is not only the object of a later faith, which on its side gave
> rise to the growth of oral and also written tradition, but, as Messiah
> and teacher, Jesus is the object and subject of a tradition of authoritative and holy words which he himself created and entrusted to his
> disciples for its later transmission in the epoch between his death
> and the *parousia*.[58]

Riesenfeld's preoccupation with the gospel tradition distinguishes his approach from that of our thesis, which is concerned with the structure of early Christian communication as a whole, but in the background a structural analysis is discernible in his work in terms of mission preaching, community preaching (with strong instructional and paraenetic overtones), and the transmission of tradition or *paradosis*. His great achievement was to secure the place of the last mentioned in its own right within the complex of early Christian communication. His other categories are less satisfactory. Community preaching appears an amalgam of several elements: preaching in the homiletic sense, *catechesis*, more advanced doctrinal and theological instruction, and ethical *paraenesis*. His understanding of mission preaching utilises the notion of a 'compressed summary of the saving work of Christ' and he sharply distinguishes such kerygmatic preaching to an outside audience from proclamation within the community. Both of these points we have already found less than satisfactory. Even more serious is his flight from genuinely creative elements in the early church, such as *propheteia* inspired by the Spirit. Even if he is justified in pillorying the excesses of the form critics in this respect, he is in imminent danger of ending up with as one-sided a view as that of his opponents.[59]

An operational model for early Christian preaching and teaching

The above brief survey of selected contributions to the debate has prepared the way for the articulation of our own thesis. To begin with Riesenfeld's startling omission: prophets and *propheteia* occupy a position of considerable prominence in the New Testament.[60] Prophets appear closely associated with apostles in the foundation of the church, and with teachers and evangelists in the work of its ministry.[61] *Propheteia* has to do with the reception and articulation of revelation, with the proclamation of the divine message as in the Old Testament tradition (cf. Rom. 10: 13ff.), and with pneumatic and other elevated experiences in worship and devotion.[62] What distinctive prophetic forms, structures or *Gattungen* can be discerned in the New Testament?

A second important category evident in the New Testament is *paraclesis,*[63] exhortatory preaching at home in liturgical or community circles and dependent upon midrashic tradition, which was also of service to Christian apologetic in a Jewish milieu.[64] If *paraclesis* is the foundation of the church's homiletic tradition, the later term 'homily'[65] should probably be associated with it since the Christian homily may be held to be represented seminally in New Testament *paraclesis.*[66] Once again, the question of discerning recurring or evolving forms of Christian *paraclesis* is of prime concern in this study.

Typically didactic structures within early Christian discourse would appear to be well represented by *paraenesis*[67] and *catechesis,*[68] which therefore provide the third main structure to be investigated. Finally, the importance of *paradosis* has already emerged in our review of H. Riesenfeld's work.[69]

In following up this four-fold hypothesis, it must be emphasised that the over-all aim is not so much an in-depth study of each of the structures in isolation as an investigation of their interdependence and integration as basic elements of early Christian communication. Since an element of continuity or similarity may be presumed between Christian forms of communication and those of the religious and cultural traditions upon which the Christian communities were dependent, the hinterland of these forms in Judaism particularly and in the wider international scene must be investigated. A particular concern will be to ask how far Christian forms were anticipated by Jesus' own practice. A perspective of great importance is provided by the *Sitz im Leben* of the early churches, by their *koinonia,* their worship and their mission, within which and for which the Christian forms of communication were developed. Such forms were closely associated with the ways in which the meaningfulness of the event of Christ was realised and articulated within the believing communities themselves. This study, therefore, necessarily involves coming to terms with basic problems of Christian origins. On the other hand, it also investigates, however briefly, the earliest essays and achievements in the field of Christian hermeneutics.

1

PROPHETEIA

Surely the Lord God does nothing,
  without revealing his secret
  to his servants the prophets.
The lion has roared;
  who will not fear?
The Lord God has spoken;
  who can but prophesy? (Amos 3: 7f.)

The phenomenon of prophecy

To study the fascinating variety and richness of the prophetic traditions –
from Zoroaster, the archetypal prophet of the Iranian tradition,[1] to
Muhammad, the Prophet of Islam,[2] and from the Hebrew *nabi'* to the
oracle prophets of Delphi or Dodona[3] – would involve a lengthy digression
at this point. Let it suffice to note that the precise meaning of the term
'prophet' is determined by the context and tradition in which it operates.[4]
No two prophetic traditions were more unlike than those of Greece and
Israel, yet some degree of linguistic compatibility was eventually arrived
at. When Alexander had effected the marriage of East and West, and
Hellenism had invaded the jealously guarded precincts of Judaism, the
question of the appropriateness of the Greek word *prophētēs* as a translation of *nabi'* was settled by the practice of the translators of the Septuagint, who made precisely this identification. No doubt they found the
flexibility of the Greek term something of an asset.[5]

Whatever cultural cross-fertilisation took place at certain points, the
basic forms of Christian *propheteia* inevitably derived in the main from the
prophetic tradition of Israel. In this context, importance attaches to the
function of the prophet as messenger (cf. Jer. 26: 15).[6] The prophetic
message is frequently introduced by the so-called messenger formula, of
which 'thus says Yahweh' is the most common form;[7] and it has been
claimed that an understanding of the procedure of message transmission
gives access to 'the structure of the event that we call prophecy'.[8] Essential
to the whole process is the prophet's commissioning and his reception of
the message – two elements which relate to the prophetic consciousness
and to the theological problem of revelation. Many scholars have pointed
to the importance of ecstasy in this connection,[9] and it undoubtedly
occurs at various levels of prophetic experience as well as in what may be
called 'primitive' prophecy (cf. 1 Sam. 10: 5f., 10–13). H. W. Wolff,

however, has argued that the I–Thou type of relationship is more congruous with, for example, the vision of Isaiah (Is. 6), in which the consciousness of the prophet remains alert, and that in any case it is impossible to explain the formation of prophetic speech in terms of ecstasy itself.[10]

To take message transmission as the sole criterion of 'the event of prophecy' would, however, be an oversimplification and distortion.[11] If the constraints of oral transmission placed a premium on brevity and precision, intelligibility and memorability, a combination of other factors, including intensity of prophetic feeling and the numinous aspect of the divine message, lent a poetic form and flavour to prophetic utterance that survived the editorial labours that shaped the prophetic books. Prophets invariably underwent considerable anguish of spirit. There was the difficulty of differentiating their message from that of the false prophet who also claimed to speak in the name of Yahweh[12] and from prophets of other religious traditions who were encountered in certain periods and situations.[13] In face of rejection and apparent failure, they had their own inner conflicts with despair and self-doubt – experiences which affected their concepts of servanthood and mission as well as the form of their utterances.[14] It is to the question of form that we now turn.

Basic forms of Old Testament prophecy

A comprehensive review of the investigation conducted by modern scholars into the basic forms of Old Testament prophecy is beyond the scope of this study.[15] An important contribution to it was made by R. B. Y. Scott,[16] who identified four primary forms of the prophetic oracle: reproach or cry of woe, threat, promise and exhortation.[17] C. Westermann criticised Scott's use of the term 'threat' and substituted 'judgment'. The basic form of the *announcement of judgment against an individual* comprises the complaint or accusation (either as accusing question or declaratory statement) and the statement of judgment, usually preceded by the messenger formula.[18] The *announcement of judgment against the nation* follows the same general pattern but is more complex.[19] The reproach or cry of woe Westermann regards as a variant form of the judgment speech,[20] in which the accusation exhibits the most stable form and sometimes includes synonymous parallelism (cf. Is. 5: 21ff.). Woes usually occur in series and have a social accusation.[21]

Scott is less successful in developing his third form, the *promise*. 'The structure of the salvation-speech', observes Westermann, 'has not yet been found.'[22] A more hopeful starting point is provided by J. Begrich's discussion of the so-called priestly salvation oracle in Deutero-Isaiah.[23] An examination of a number of passages[24] suggests a common pattern, fully exemplified by Is. 41: 8–13. Generally, it includes an exhortation not to fear (cf. 41: 10a, 13b), the naming of the addressee and his relationship to God (cf. 41: 8f.), an assurance of Yahweh's presence as helper and upholder, often in the first person (cf. 41: 10, 13), and an announcement of the action God will take on their behalf (cf. 41: 11f.). This form corresponds in a remarkable way to some of the laments found in the prophets and the psalms.[25] The supplicant cries 'My God, my God, why hast thou forsaken me?' (Ps. 22: 1).[26] When an answer is given (cf. Is. 54: 7f.), he cries in gratitude:

> Thou didst come near when I called on thee;
>   thou didst say, 'Do not fear!' (Lam. 3: 57)

In a separate article, Westermann carried out what he has called a preliminary survey of the salvation speeches.[27] He distinguished three broad categories: the assurance of salvation (*Heilszusage*), the announcement of salvation (*Heilsankündigung*) and the portrayal of salvation (*Heilsschilderung*). The first contains a statement of assurance in the perfect tense, with Yahweh as subject, as in Is. 43: 1 – 'Fear not, for I have redeemed you'; or in the call of Jeremiah (Jer. 1: 8ff.) – 'Behold, I have put words in your mouth'. The second is related to history as men experience it and requires the future tense. Is. 43: 2 is an example which is an integral part of a more complex oracle. In Jer. 32: 15 the announcement stands by itself. Confirmation of the announcement may be provided by a prophetic sign (e.g., Is. 7: 14; Jer. 28: 10). In the third type, the portrayal of salvation, the present condition is contrasted with the picture of a totally different reality that transcends the historical (cf. Is. 11: 6–9). The vivid detail of such portrayal was well adapted to the apocalyptic presentation of salvation that blossomed in ancient Judaism, yet imagery of this type also occurs early, in the blessing of Jacob (Gen. 49: 11f.) and the oracles of Balaam (Num. 24: 5ff.).[28]

Prophecy in Israel, whether orientated specifically to judgment or salvation, was concerned to relate Israel anew, in her changing historical circumstances, to the basic symbols and central themes of her faith.[29] Prophetic insight extended not simply to the meaning of such symbols and themes in themselves, so to speak, but also to Israel's historical position – her relationship to past, present and future – and to the dynamic interaction of all these elements. Thus, two themes prominent in the message of the unknown exilic prophet are the exodus, which the prophet employs 'as the essential image of his vision and proclamation about the future',[30] and the creation tradition, used 'to proclaim the work of Yahweh as an arch stretching over creation, history and eschatological fulfilment'.[31] The need to intensify and reapply the basic symbols was made all the more urgent by the traumatic course of Israel's history and particularly by the catastrophe at the hands of Babylon. The failure of the house of David to embody the covenantal ideal expressed in 2 Sam. 7 led Isaiah to depict the future king and kingdom in which it would be realised (Is. 9: 1-7; 10: 33 - 11: 9).[32] The impending collapse of Israel provided the occasion for Jeremiah to speak of the making of a new covenant between Yahweh and his people (Jer. 31: 31–4).[33] As defeat and exile signified the death of Israel, Ezekiel proclaimed his vision of the resurrection of the nation through the life-giving spirit of God (Ezek. 37: 1-14).[34] The experiences of God's people suggested to Deutero-Isaiah that suffering – representative or vicarious – was the inevitable lot of the servant figure in Israel.[35] In the midst of the Maccabean struggle, the writer of Daniel saw the overthrow of the beasts and the giving of everlasting dominion to 'one like a son of man' (Dan. 7: 13f.).[36]

The question of how this intensification and reapplication of basic symbols was achieved within the crucible of the prophetic consciousness is extremely complex. The influence of a number of factors can, of course, be indicated: the engagement of the prophet both with the empirical situation, to which he had a deep sensitivity, and with Israel's tradition from which he drew his major religious symbols; extreme concentration upon certain creative tensions in the situation and a heightened perception and imaginative awareness of them in the context of a spiritual exaltation which could sometimes pass into ecstasy; and a communing of the spirit of man with the Spirit of God.[37] But this kind of summary gives an inadequate account of the essential mystery at the heart of the process: the apperception of the will of God in relation to the particularities of the situation; or the reception of the divine revelation in the consciousness of the prophet and its subsequent articulation by him. R. B. Y. Scott speaks of the ' "Word" which burned itself into the prophet's mind':[38]

> If I say, 'I will not mention him,
>> or speak any more in his name',
> there is in my heart as it were a burning fire
>> shut up in my bones,
> and I am weary with holding it in,
>> and I cannot.[39]

This 'Word' given to the prophet may present itself to his consciousness as a single word, name phrase, or puzzle sentence,[40] all of which evince certain common features: 'they are brief, striking, enigmatic and marked by strong rhythm, verbal symmetry, paronomasia, assonance, and a preponderance of sibilant and guttural sounds'.[41] These first articulations of the 'word from beyond' serve as embryonic oracles to be expanded and expounded in the fuller prophetic forms discussed above and also in sermons, exhortations, *paraenesis* and other borrowed forms.[42]

After the watershed of the exile, the disastrous history of Israel impressed itself on the prophetic consciousness as a chastening lesson and the *call to repentance* became a characteristic of later prophetic discourse. 'The Lord was very angry with your fathers. Therefore say to them, Thus says the Lord of hosts: Return to me, says the Lord of hosts, and I will return to you...' (Zech. 1: 2f.). Repentance was, of course, always inherent in the message of the prophets.[43] Isaiah recalled Israel to God in memorable words later termed the 'nine norms' of repentance (Is. 1: 16f.), and Hosea has been called 'the great exponent of the doctrine of repentance'.[44] However, the exile served to emphasise the importance of both national and individual repentance, so that penitential utterances[45] and the specific call to repentance (cf. Is. 55: 7; Ezek. 18: 21f.) became features of post-exilic Judaism and inter-testamental literature.[46] Again, the centrality of written scripture meant that prophets like Daniel engaged in scriptural exegesis and reinterpretation (cf. Dan. 9: 2, 24), an extension of the procedure of earlier prophets who used and reapplied older biblical tradition.[47] In Daniel, the message of God is conceived in two halves – the mystery and the interpretation; the latter usually being granted to the prophet.[48] The exegetical concern is closely linked with what is to happen 'in the latter days' (Dan. 2: 28), even to fairly precise predictions of the approaching end.[49] Thus the call to repentance and exegetically based eschatological concern characterise the prophetic tradition in its latest pre-New Testament stage.

The prophetic forms had inevitably changed, even disintegrated, as the prophets met the changing circumstances of the nation.[50] After Malachi (and apart from Daniel), the living prophetic voice was commonly thought to have ceased,[51] although various people – like John Hyrcanus I – were held by some to evince prophetic characteristics.[52] The emphasis upon written scripture in Judaism encouraged the predominance of the scribes and the ascendancy of the casuistical over the pneumatic. Yet through this scripture the old prophetic voices still spoke, and the old prophetic symbols lay open to interpretation. From such materials came Israel's variegated expectations of the future.[53] Whether a messenger in the old prophetic mould, not to speak of 'a prophet like unto Moses' (cf. Deut. 18: 15; 34: 10), would arise in Judaism, whether he could act as the catalyst to unleash the inherent dynamic in Israel's religious symbols for the contemporary nation and bring its history and expectations to comprehensive fulfilment, and what forms such prophetic dynamism would assume – these questions were as yet mysteries in the mind of God.

The formal structure of the preaching of John

After the eclipse of Old Testament prophecy, the first prophetic figure of prime importance to emerge from ancient Judaism was John the Baptist.[54] Our focus is upon his place within the prophetic tradition of Israel and the way in which he appropriated and reapplied major prophetic symbols and themes to the situation that confronted him.

An *announcement of (messianic) salvation* is apparent in Matt. 3: 11f.; Luke 3: 16f.; Mark 1: 7f.; and also Acts 1: 5 and 11: 16. This logion is essentially a prophecy of the Coming One.[55] But what was its earliest form in the tradition?

Mark's version has the more convincing opening: 'There comes one mightier than I after me...' The usual time-scale of salvation prophecy – 'behold, the days are coming when...' (cf. Jer. 31: 27, 31, 38) – is telescoped to one of imminence: 'after me' could refer even to a disciple of John.[56] Thereafter, the picture of the Coming One is built up by means of a comparison with John: he is inestimably mightier and will baptise, not 'with water' but 'with the Spirit'.[57] Wind and fire form a traditional grouping in Jewish teaching about judgment.[58] Wind or breath (*ruach, pneuma*) is the instrument of the Messiah, who will slay the wicked 'with the breath of his lips' (Is. 11: 4). Fire is also linked with judgment and punishment in Israel.[59] But the couplet in Mark 1: 8 should not be taken as a simple contrast of symbol and substance: rather, it would appear that the onset of messianic times brings a triple test by means of water, wind and fire. The tests that the Messiah himself will apply are essentially complementary to John's water baptism, which is the prelude to them.[60]

This salvation utterance was subject to reinterpretation within the Christian communities. Its history can be traced in terms of the development of christology.[61] Yet behind all this, the nature of John's work is clear enough. As the messenger of the Messiah, he announces his coming and, by the prophetic act of baptism, inaugurates his work (cf. Matt. 3: 10; Luke 3: 9). His utterance is not imitative but shaped by the inner constraints of his message and situation. The form he uses is neither typical of the announcement of judgment nor of the salvation oracle, but combines elements of both.[62] A new form is thereby produced: the announcement of imminent messianic salvation.

A typical, eschatologically orientated *summons to repentance* is found in Matt. 3: 7-10; Luke 3: 7-9. From the formal point of view, it consists of an introduction which comprises a rebuke; the main part of the message – 'therefore, bring forth fruit(s) worthy of repentance';[63] the supplementary message, anticipating an appeal to Abrahamic descent; and a final proclamation of the in-breaking of the eschatological crisis. It stands in the tradition of Zech. 1:2f., but with the eschatological element intensified. In Judaism it could be held that the coming deliverance was delayed because of Israel's slowness to repent. Repentance, some held, would bring the day of salvation nearer.[64] In John's preaching, the crisis of messianic judgment is imminent and inevitable and men must come to terms with it as a matter of extreme urgency.[65] His message is directed to the people of Israel, who were in breach of the covenant.[66] His summons followed the general tendency in Judaism to individualise religious responsibility,[67] and he heightened this aspect with eschatological urgency.

An alternative Matthaean form of the summons to repentance is found in Matt. 3:2. It consists of the summons itself and a causal clause which sets forth the imminent eschatological crisis of God's reign as the grounds for giving heed to the summons. It could be restated as: the kingdom is at hand; therefore ('thus says the Lord') repent![68] Two features are remarkable: Matthew places the same utterance on the lips of Jesus (Matt. 4:17); and Matthew alone ascribes the proclamation of the kingdom (as opposed to the Coming One) to John.

Theological factors are paramount in appraising this utterance. All the evangelists in their own way suggest that the presentation of the gospel begins with John.[69] Matthew's theological perspective places John not at the climactic conclusion of the period of promise but at the inception of the fulfilment.[70] Matthew therefore allows a close affinity between the message of John and Jesus, who both proclaim salvation before they pronounce judgment,[71] and the message of the kingdom is set in this context.[72]

Luke, on the other hand, sets the nearness of the kingdom severely in the context of the *parousia* (Luke 21:31). Luke's theology is fully stretched to take account of John, and a certain ambivalence within it indicates the tension between the tradition the evangelist received and his adaptation of it. The focus of his interpretation of the kingdom lies in the future – indeed, the distant future at the close of the epoch of the church – and consequently John's relationship to it is 'ruptured'.[73] Luke 16:16 has become something of a *cause célèbre* in New Testament debate. H. Conzelmann took it to mean that John belongs wholly to the earlier epoch of the law and the prophets, but retains a significance for the new epoch that immediately followed him (cf. 16:17). There is, however, 'no preparation before Jesus for the proclamation of the Kingdom of God'.[74] The good news of the kingdom of God is preached 'from then on'. H. Flender noted that this phrase expressed not merely the separation of but also the continuity between John and the preaching of the kingdom of God,[75] and he consequently modified Conzelmann's version of Luke's pattern of redemptive history. W. Wink noted that in Luke's gospel John is in fact included in the era of fulfilment though excluded from the period of Jesus' ministry. He therefore suggested that the first part of the era of fulfilment is the ministry of preparation carried out by John the Baptist (3: 1–20); the second part is Jesus' Galilean ministry, of which John is not part (3: 21 – 9: 50).[76] Moreover, when Luke 16: 16 is set beside its difficult Matthaean counterpart (Matt. 11: 12) – 'from the days of John the Baptist until now...' – its secondary nature becomes apparent, and indeed Matt. 11: 12 'has a very strong claim to authenticity'.[77] John the Baptist stands in close relation to the activity of God as king.[78]

This conclusion does not, of course, establish the authenticity of Matt. 3: 2.[79] Indeed, scholarly opinion has leant heavily towards regarding this verse as editorial. From the point of view of its form, however, there is no need to do so: it is an eschatologically grounded prophetic summons to repentance. In terms of theological content, while Luke had his own reasons for not attributing to John the preaching of the kingdom, he did ascribe to John the 'good news' (Luke 3: 18) of the coming king (3: 16). Yet from the phenomenological point of view one can hardly differentiate between the coming king and the coming kingdom, for 'kingdom' denotes not a static condition but the exercise of kingly sovereignty. Luke's theological sophistication led him to tie the concept of the kingdom to christology[80] and the *parousia*[81] but as far as the Baptist tradition is concerned, perhaps Matthew got it right – at least in spirit, if not in the letter.

The formal structure of the preaching of Jesus

A formidable obstacle to this type of enquiry is presented by *formgeschichtliche* problems, which were apparent in the discussion of the Baptist and are particularly acute in relation to Jesus. The procedure adopted here will first identify prophetic structures in the tradition and then proceed to a brief discussion of the *formgeschichtliche* issues raised. It may be observed that if Jesus, in some of his utterances and procedures, spoke and acted as a prophet in the Jewish tradition, the *formgeschichtliche* argument that material common to the Jesus tradition and that of Judaism is to be discounted as a Christian borrowing from Judaism is seen to possess a certain circularity! Yet some criterion of differentiation must be sought. If we allow that Jesus did on occasion use Jewish material *simpliciter*, it is appropriate to enquire whether he had a specific or distinctive reason for doing so. Again, utterances that reflect his prophetic awareness may be distinguished from christological statements coinciding exactly with post-resurrection church teaching. While attestation by several sources is a

factor to be noted, the general consistency of the elements that make up
the total picture is even more important. The overriding factor is not that
of preserving what may be called the principle of scepticism – assuming
the historical tradition to be guilty of inauthenticity, as it were, until it is
proved innocent! – but that of phenomenological appropriateness. Is a
given utterance, in form and content, appropriate to the general religious
and social milieu, to the particular situation to which it is reported to have
been addressed and to the speaker to whom it is attributed?

Jesus was, not infrequently, called a prophet by 'the people' or 'the
crowds' and by certain individuals, including the disciples.[82] Yet there is
something of a conspiracy of silence both on the part of the evangelists
and possibly also on the part of Jesus concerning his prophetic role, although some scholars suspect that Jesus may have spoken of it more often
and more explicitly than the records suggest.[83] Again, while it is likely
that he had an initial experience analogous to prophetic commissioning,
the overlay of christological teaching appears to have obscured its precise
elements beyond hope of recovery.[84] The starting point must lie, therefore, with the identification of prophetic forms in his message.

The first form, the *summons to repentance*, is found in Matt. 4: 17 and
Mark 1: 15, where the dominant imperative is 'Repent'. Matthew retains
the eschatologically orientated prophetic form: repentance in view of the
impending advent of the kingdom.[85] Both evangelists testify to the main
thrust of the message. The essential prerequisite for establishing a positive
relationship with God as king is that total reorientation which 'repentance'
denotes.[86] The fact that this summons duplicates that already ascribed by
Matthew to the Baptist does not in any way impugn its authenticity. It is
phenomenologically essential to both ministries.[87]

Governed as it is by the concept of *shubh*, the *announcement of
(imminent) salvation* has necessarily a conditional element and an obverse
in the judgment of the unrepentant. The proclamation of the kingdom –
'the kingdom of God is at hand' – is the basic announcement in the gospels.[88] The future aspect of salvation prophecy is replaced by imminence,
and the note of comfort by urgency. Both are reflected in the call to
repentance by which the announcement is prefaced. The question of form
cannot, however, be completely divorced from that of content. The form
itself underlines the fact that the total reorientation of man to God is a
prerequisite of 'entry' into the kingdom (cf. Matt. 18: 3).[89]

Closely associated with the proclamation of the kingdom is the
announcement of the time of fulfilment (Mark 1: 15).[90] A parallel to this
theme can be found in Luke's programmatic synagogue homily on the text
of Is. 61: 1ff. (Luke 4: 18ff.), with its announcement, 'Today this scripture

has been fulfilled in your hearing' (4: 21).[91] The theme of fulfilment, however, is open to the charge of being part of the post-resurrection exegetical effort, or *midrash*, of the church. Matthew in particular comments throughout on the fulfilment of scripture.[92] Is it legitimate to claim this type of announcement as a prophetic utterance of Jesus?

Is. 61: 1ff., which forms the text of Jesus' homily in Luke 4, plays an important role in the tradition concerning Jesus' ministry, for with Is.35: 5f. and perhaps 29: 18f., it provides the substance of the reply given to John's enquiry about whether Jesus was 'he who is to come' (Matt. 11: 3ff.; Luke 7: 20, 22). In Q, therefore, this saying represented the quint-essence of Jesus' ministry, which possesses strongly prophetic motifs.[93] But an even more telling factor, and one particularly relevant to this study, is 'the importance of Is. 61 as the inspiration of the beatitudes',[94] which rank among Jesus' most distinctive sayings.[95] A beatitude such as 'blessed is he who takes no offence at me' (Matt. 11: 6; Luke 7: 23) expresses Jesus' total personal identification with his message. He himself belongs, through his mission and message, to 'the time of fulfilment', which – whatever else it means – suggests that the hopes and expectations of Israel are acquiring reality through him and his work.[96] According to the criteria of multiple attestation and general consistency, the announcement of the present as the time of Israel's fulfilment and thus the time for ultimate decision is a distinctive mark of Jesus' proclamation of salvation.[97]

Jesus' prophetic message, however, was by no means confined to the oracle of salvation. Even the prophetic figure in Is. 61: 1ff. had ascribed to him a double-edged function:

> to proclaim the year of the Lord's favour,
>   and the day of vengeance of our God.[98]

A remarkable feature of Jesus' judgment prophecy is the recrudescence of the *unconditional announcement of judgment*, which had lapsed about the time of the exile.[99] A good example is provided by the woes[100] on the cities of Galilee (Matt. 11: 21–24; Luke 10: 13ff.). The woe is addressed to a specific target: Chorazin, Bethsaida and Capernaum respectively. The reason for the unconditional announcement of judgment is given: the failure of their citizens to repent when the works of God were done in their midst. This kind of announcement[101] operates in the tradition as a standard form of unconditional judgment upon those who reject the preaching of the kingdom (cf. Matt. 10: 15; Luke 10: 12).[102] The woes in Matt. 23: 13–29 and Luke 11: 42–47, directed against the scribes and Pharisees, are derived from a Q tradition but have been subjected to editing by both evangelists. In form they consist of the cry of woe and the reasons for the judgment, although the actual announcement of judgment is simply assumed, apart from the editorial conclusions in Matt. 23: 36 and Luke 11: 51.[103] Clearly, paraenetic material (cf. Matt. 23: 16–22) has been attracted into this prophetic form, which has been built up in the church for polemical purposes. But while Matthew introduced Pharisees and Sadducees into the Baptist tradition as the objects of prophetic invective (Matt. 3: 7), the same cannot be said here, for the woes were already directed to these groups in Q before the evangelists interwove their own interpretation. It is therefore possible, to put it no higher, that these woes represent a strand in the historical encounter of Jesus with the Pharisees.[104] A somewhat similar form to the 'woe' occurs in Luke 23: 28–31, which seems to reflect traditional martyr motifs.[105] It includes an announcement of judgment which employs a beatitude (v. 29) as a kind of inverted woe (cf. 21: 23). In fact, Jesus appears to have used both the *unconditional* and the *conditional announcement of judgment* according to the situation, as his sayings against 'this generation' indicate. The saying about 'the sign of Jonah' (Matt. 16: 4) is a case in point. A prophetic sign makes a proclamation in a particularly powerful way, although it is open to interpretation and therefore may have about it an element of puzzle.[106] The original logion was probably given without *midrash* (Matt. 16: 4) and referred to Jonah's preaching of repentance. If this is so, then the implied judgment on the wicked generation is conditional. The people of Nineveh did, in fact, repent![107]

The *prophetic action* or *sign* illustrates the double emphasis of salvation and judgment in Jesus' ministry. The *announcement of salvation* underlies Luke 11: 20 (Matt. 12: 28), a well-known *crux interpretationis*,[108] in which Jesus' acts of exorcism are interpreted as prophetic actions:[109] i.e., as signs which confirm the verbal proclamation of the kingdom.[110] The kingdom is indeed 'at hand' when the action of the prophet is seen to be, at one and the same time, the action of God as king. Jesus' table-fellowship with tax-collectors and sinners is also a powerful proclamation of one aspect of the kingdom (cf. Luke 15: 1f.). On the other hand, the cursing of the fig tree is a *prophetic sign of judgment*, though variously interpreted in early church *paraenesis*.[111] In Mark's narrative it introduces Jesus' powerful action of judgment against the temple (Mark 11: 15ff.). Two actions in particular are related to Jesus' expectation of his death, at least in the latter days of his ministry. One is the anointing at Bethany, which Jesus interpreted as symbolic;[112] the other is the last supper.[113]

Prophetic actions are frequently called 'parabolic' actions. The parable itself is a paraenetic form well adapted to prophetic discourse since its linguistic mechanism is designed to conduct the hearer to a deeper level of meaning and awareness.[114] The parables attributed to Jesus provide a useful commentary on the facets of his prophetic ministry. The *summons to repentance* is reflected in, for example, the parable of the ten virgins (Matt. 25: 1–12) or the thief at night (Matt. 24: 43f.; Luke 12: 39f.). One's response to the crisis of God's approach must be that of preparedness so that the critical encounter is joyful rather than tearful. This possibility, of course, presupposes the *announcement of salvation*, symbolised by the wedding, the new garment and the new wine (Mark 2: 18–22) and reflected in the great parables of divine mercy: the lost sheep, the lost coin, the so-called 'prodigal son' (cf. Luke 15 *passim*), and the Pharisee and the tax-collector (Luke 18: 9–14), to take only a sample.[115] The *announcement of judgment* has its place in the parables of Jesus, as is evident in the children playing in the market place (Matt. 11: 16f.; Luke 7: 31f.) or the rich fool (Luke 12: 16–20).[116]

Both prophetic actions and parables indicate Jesus' awareness of suffering and death as an integral part of his ministry.[117] Jesus could hardly have avoided identification with the prophetic motif of rejection and suffering as the inevitable consequence of the proclamation of judgment (cf. Matt. 5: 12; 23: 37).[118] He could hardly have been unaware of the probable consequence of his prophetic action in the temple.[119] His encounter with the scribal realm of discourse was hardly less traumatic (cf. Mark 2: 23 – 3: 6). Almost every facet of his ministry, from exorcism (cf. Mark 3: 22 par.) to parables like the good Samaritan, operated amid controversy and carried possible offence.[120] His words and actions were sustained by an acute exegetical concern, a distinctive *midrash* that brought the immediacy of prophetic insight to the exegesis and resulted in a radical reinterpretation and intensification of meaning.[121] Certain specific passages filter through the tradition very clearly. Is. 61: 1ff. and 35: 5f., even when expounded by Jesus as an oracle of salvation, arouse antipathy! One of his typical procedures seems to have been to regard the scriptures as providing a broad canvas in which the sufferings of those faithful to God's call provide a basic motif. 'The prophets' were persecuted, and faithful disciples can expect the same fate at the hands of disobedient Israel.[122] If he selected a particular *locus classicus* for this theme, it was almost certainly not the servant songs of Deutero-Isaiah.[123] The two New Testament passages which cite Is. 53 give no support to the idea that Jesus found in the concept of the servant the clue to the positive value of suffering as vicarious sacrifice.[124] A more persuasive case can be made out for regarding Dan. 7: 12f. as an important text which Jesus may well have 'peshered' to show his disciples that the sufferings of the faithful will be vindicated in the end. Out of his dialogue with the scriptures in the light of the historical experiences of his ministry and the sense of vocation which it inevitably presupposes there may well have come a firm expectation of rejection at the hands of Israel and a violent death; and certain memorable sayings underline the notion that a divine necessity governs the course of his ministry: the inescapable cup (Mark 10: 38; 14: 36) and the baptism with which he must be baptised (10: 38).

Jesus' expectation of the future is notoriously difficult to ascertain.[125] To be sure, Jesus used the symbol of the kingdom in relation to a total fulfilment of God's purpose, as in the petition, 'may thy kingdom come'. Similarly, he used the symbol of the messianic banquet. A number of parables (e.g., on the theme of seed growing to harvest, or eschatological discrimination) and many proclamations of salvation and judgment assume an element of futurity in connection with vindication and judgment.[126] He probably drew upon Dan. 7: 12f., 'a classic passage of vindication',[127] to interpret his eschatological mission and the suffering it entailed.[128] For Jesus, the future – God's future – was not simply an extension of linear history but the *eschaton*, the goal and consummation of the purpose of God. Through prophetic action, this future encounters men in their historical situation, so that the latter becomes a time of decision and opportunity for the service of God. But as N. Perrin points out, no definite form can be discerned in Jesus' statements about future expectation.[129]

Yet such observations hardly do justice to the scope of the problem. If Jesus understood his ministry to include suffering and death, what expectation did he have beyond death? The attribution to him of a prediction of his resurrection, as in the passion predictions, can hardly be other than a *vaticinium post eventum*; but he may have related his work to the prophetic notion of faithful Israel who suffers much but is finally vindicated.[130] His riddle-saying about the temple,[131] which the Johannine tradition takes as a symbol of his body (John 2: 21) and the Markan possibly of the church (Mark 14: 58), may well indicate that he identified himself (i.e., his mission and his personal fate) with the compound notion of the death-and-resurrection of the true Israel by the power of the Spirit.[132] And if he used Dan. 7: 13f., his identification with the Son of man symbol would have led to his use of the *portrayal of salvation* to denote the fulfilment of God's purpose for which his own work was of decisive significance. The precise forms he used are obscured by the post-Easter community's fondness for apocalyptic portrayal.[133]

Earlier, it was suggested that the baptism epiphany story, by its very nature, afforded little insight into the spiritual experience of Jesus. Does the prophetic material itself shed any more light on the subject? The precise operation of the I–Thou relationship between the prophet and the God who commissions him always has an element of mystery about it, and this is obviously even more crucial in the case of Jesus, in view of the messianic claims made for him and the christology subsequently built upon him. It is also related to the problem not only of the self-understanding of Jesus as it may be deduced from the structure of his message and mission, but the self-consciousness of Jesus, which has presented New Testament scholarship with endless difficulty![134] A beginning may be made with the prophetic prayer form which occurs in Matt. 11: 25f. and Luke 10: 21f. It is made publicly in the presence of the disciples; it celebrates the divine revelation[135] to the child-like (*nēpiois*) rather than the wise; and it is interpreted by Luke as an utterance made in exaltation of spirit. Above all, it contains an address to God as *pater*, which may well represent the Aramaic *'abba*.[136] Such an utterance is congruous with some of the most distinctive strands in the ministry of Jesus, and even Bultmann admits that he can find no compelling reason for denying it to Jesus.[137] How far, then, does *'abba* afford us access to the nerve-centre of Jesus' religious awareness?

The fatherhood of God (i.e., God as Father) is yet another of the major symbols of the Old Testament. It belongs particularly to the covenantal realm of discourse. Repentant Israel cries: 'You are our Father' (cf. Is. 63: 16; 64: 8). In reply, God speaks of his yearning for 'Ephraim, my dear son' (Jer. 31: 20). The inner meaning of the covenant, for prophets such as Hosea, Jeremiah and Deutero-Isaiah, found expression above all in the father–son relationship of God and Israel: an intimate relationship based on the gracious authority of God and the thankful obedience of Israel but characterised in practice by the unfaithfulness of Israel, which deserved God's judgment but was ultimately overwhelmed by his mercy. This symbol, combining as it did reverence and intimacy, was available for appropriation by men of devotion and insight.[138] Rabbinic liturgies produced the address, 'Our Father, our King'.[139] The connotation of familiarity has almost certainly been overstressed by J. Jeremias in relation to Jesus' use of *'abba*.[140] Jesus, in his own prophetic consciousness and ministry, realised the full dimensions of this major symbol of Israel's religion.[141]

Appended to the prophetic prayer discussed above is a difficult but important logion (Matt. 11: 27 and Luke 10: 22, the former being clearly the more authentic version).[142] The question is whether there can be discerned, behind the existing logion, a prophetic utterance in the tradition of Israel and congruous with Jesus' ministry. Consider Amos 3: 7 –

> For the Lord God does nothing
> without giving to his servants the prophets knowledge of his plans.

Notice the sweeping language: 'God does *nothing* without...' In Matt. 11:

27, 'everything' is 'handed down'.[143] The next statement expresses the reciprocity of intimate understanding, which J. Jeremias renders as follows:

> And as only a father knows his son
> so also only a son knows his father
> and he to whom the son wants to reveal it.[144]

He goes on: 'the text neither speaks about a mystical union (*unio mystica*) brought about by mutual knowledge nor does he use the christological title 'the Son'. Rather, Jesus' words simply express a plain, every-day experience: only father and son truly know each other'.[145] One must admit that, in terms of the text of Matthew (and Luke, for that matter of it), Jeremias' rendering is strained and cannot readily be taken as the evangelists' primary meaning, which is christological. But he may well have unveiled the underlying structure of Jesus' I–Thou relationship with the God of the covenant, viz., the analogy of the father–son relationship (Jesus having identified, as it were, with the true Israel which knows God as Father).[146] It is a misunderstanding to say, as a modern commentator does, that Jeremias' version is 'hardly memorable' and 'only of doubtful truth as a general proverb'.[147] The logion makes the cardinal point that the father–son relationship is one which can only be known from the inside. This is the key to 'all' knowledge of God (line 1), while the revelation others can receive from the 'son' who already knows the 'father' (line 3) is not 'knowledge' in the gnostic sense but insight into and help towards entering the filial relationship:[148] i.e., the analogy is deliberately stretched to include the notion of helping another to realise what it means to be a 'son'. Jeremias may also be right in pointing to this relationship as the germ of much Johannine christology.

Unfortunately, Jeremias does not make the all-important distinction between the prophetic realm of discourse, to which his rendering of Matt. 11: 27 is particularly appropriate, and the christological stance of the early church. Consequently, he proceeds to make sweeping claims about 'a unique revelation and a unique authority' vested in Jesus, 'something new and unheard of which breaks through the limits of Judaism'.[149] Influential though his exegesis has been, it is dangerously exposed to a whole range of philological, philosophical, hermeneutical and phenomenological objections.[150] The case for ascribing to Jesus the proprietory rights of the term *'abba*, meaning *'my* father', is almost certainly misguided. Greek phrases such as 'my father', 'our father', 'his father', 'the father', may well be renderings of the one Aramaic word, *'abba*: a term of address used by all the children of God (cf. John 20: 17). It is dangerous to apply the term 'unique' to a usage that is not, in fact, without parallel in contemporary writing (cf. 3 Enoch 48: 7) nor in the Hebrew tradition;[151] nor can it reasonably be claimed that Jesus' use of *'abba* is 'foreshadowed only within the context of messianic expectation'.[152] More to the point is Jeremias' claim that 'it represents the centre of Jesus' awareness of his mission'.[153] Yet even that statement requires some qualification, for with the 'father' symbol Jesus used, among others, those of 'king' and 'judge', and with the 'son' symbol he associated the 'servant' and, of course, the 'messenger'. A right appreciation would require both to balance such symbols and to take account of their inherent tensions. Perhaps Jeremias would have been justified in pointing to the father–son analogy as the strongest clue to the I–Thou relationship at the core of Jesus' prophetic awareness but, as with prophets generally, the modern interpreter soon meets the *temenos* within which he may not set foot, for the ground is holy.

But if no single symbol nor analogy used by Jesus is itself adequate to lay bare his prophetic self-consciousness to our human gaze, his followers clearly felt a similar inadequacy in the term 'prophet' as applied either to his ministry or his religious awareness. 'Not any imminent end of the universe, not any principle of creation, not any casuistry, led Jesus to his understanding of God's will. He passed beyond all principles he had inherited, beyond the light of Law and Prophet, to what we can only call an intuitive awareness of the will of God in its nakedness.'[154] To make this crucial point, W. D. Davies resorts to rhetoric – and Christian rhetoric at that. One would not expect an orthodox Jewish rabbinical scholar, for example, to speak thus: at most, he might allow that Jesus stood in some sense in the prophetic tradition, although Judaism did not, and could not, acknowledge him. By the intensity of his vision and insight, Jesus tended to break the constraints of Judaism on almost every side (Christians would say he transcended them), and therein lies the phenomenological appropriateness of at least the general tenor of Davies' remarks.

The importance of this observation is considerable, for it implies that Jesus stood in tension with his background: i.e., in a relationship of continuity and discontinuity with his own tradition. Initially, he was closely associated with John's movement, yet he developed his ministry on different lines.[155] Initially, he was part of the Galilean scene – associated, perhaps, with the charismatic Judaism of the early Hasidim or Devout;[156] yet his ministry is not characterised by charismatic phenomena of the more ecstatic type (and the early church would have lacked the motive to erase them from the tradition if they had been there).[157] He lived and acted as a prophet, yet according to a Q logion,[158] he regarded the title of prophet as inadequate to describe even John the Baptist. C. K. Barrett endorses C. H. Dodd's view that Jesus followed the practice of Amos and Jeremiah, who did not speak of themselves as prophets or 'men of Spirit'; but it is difficult to engage in this type of argument without reading back Christian theological interpretation into the life of Jesus.[159] One might suggest, however, that as a general rule Jesus seems to have avoided making claims to traditional religious titles.[160] He did not *claim* to be a prophet; he *acted* as a prophet when occasion demanded. He did not *claim* to be Spirit inspired; he *acted* in the power of the Spirit when it was appropriate and necessary to do so. The totality of his words and actions, his appearing and his dying, is the vehicle of his message and mission. On this basis, a further point can be made. C. Westermann has made it clear that a prophet is commissioned only to deliver the message with which he was entrusted; even the commonly used description of him as 'the mouthpiece of Yahweh' is to be rejected as overestimating and misunderstanding the prophetic role.[161] But Jesus' historical mission appears to have developed far beyond the confines of such a concept – so far, indeed, that the question, 'Who do you say I am?' could not be answered by any unqualified term from the common stock of Judaism.

Prophecy and the origins of early Christian preaching and teaching

To turn from the situation of Jesus' ministry to that of the early church is to enter what is in some important respects a different world. Externally, the world is much the same. No cataclysmic event of world history marks it off as a new era. It is within the community of Jesus' followers that the paradox of continuity and discontinuity is acutely expressed. The presence and experience of the disciple-apostles established a degree of continuity with the earlier period, but the renewed community enshrined elements of discontinuity and novelty not only in its physical aspects – geographical spread, multiracial membership, organisation and so on – but, above all, in its inner life; for Jesus, who had so recently been himself an experiencing subject, had now become the object of religious experience[162] and the content of proclamation.[163] The apostles had been admitted to an awareness of and even participation in this christological revolution as it was taking place, and they emerged as the witnesses, guardians and interpreters of its truth. The church was a *koinonia*[164] of memory and the Spirit.[165] If, once again, 'memory' underlined the links with the past, the operation of the Spirit on the memories tended to impart to them such richness of meaning and dimensions of understanding as to effect at least a partial transformation of them; while diverse phenomena such as dreams, visions, revelations, ecstasies, glossolalia, interpretations, healings, miracles – these and others suggest *prima facie* that the floodgates of prophetism and pneumatology were thrown open in a way that never characterised the circle round Jesus. Indeed, the unleashing of such psychic power, with its inherent enthusiasm and its tendency towards exaggeration and extravagance, carried a threat to the coherence and order of the community; but on the other hand its creative energy, when properly harnessed to the eschatological crisis with which the early Christians found themselves involved, could bring new form and substance to 'the faith that was in them'.

The apostolic witness

Whatever difficulties may attach to the term 'apostle' in New Testament studies,[166] Paul seems to have acknowledged the centrality of the Twelve and the Jerusalem apostles, all of whom were eyewitnesses of the risen Christ (1 Cor. 15: 5ff.); and to the tradition of their testimony Paul added his own. Beyond the admitted differences of emphasis and operation, Paul and the apostles of Jerusalem were united in their witness to the special event by which the followers of Jesus had been reconstituted as the community of God's people, viz., the resurrection of the crucified Messiah.[167] Thus, apostolic tradition (*paradosis*)[168] encapsulated their witness (*martyria*) both to Jesus' ministry and death and also to his resurrection.[169]

The language of 'resurrection' itself implies the story of a prior death. On the other hand, the disclosure of the risen Christ to his disciples is related in terms of 'appearances' which stimulated in the disciples the response of faith. The verb *horao* is used here, as in the Septuagint, for 'seeing with the eye of faith'.[170] It is the language of epiphany, which points to a disclosure of God in action for those who have eyes to see.[171] Thomas, because he had 'seen', believed (John 20: 29): believed, that is, in the crucified Christ as Lord. The apostolic *martyria* points to the primal, apostolic response of faith as a seeing–believing–understanding in relation to the whole event of Christ. Only in this sense does the unfortunate but frequent description of the resurrection as 'a fact' have validity.[172]

In the tradition of Israel, the classical mechanism for receiving divine revelation, including that which might enter the tradition as an epiphany, is the heightened perception, spiritual intensity and religious sensitivity of the prophet, at the heart of whose ministry stands the commission he has received in the mystery of the I–Thou encounter with God. If, as is reasonable, the resurrection experiences are understood in terms of *propheteia*, not only does the element of transcendent mystery retain its importance in any account of them but the I–Thou relationship central to them is also underlined. The disciples encountered the one whom they had known, loved and confessed as the Christ, and whom they last remembered in the dereliction of the cross. It was he who now invaded their consciousness not as one 'among the dead', imprisoned and terminated by the past, but as one 'raised up', 'glorified', 'victorious': pointing to the future with that hope, vitality and assurance that had characterised his former life and infecting them with this outlook as he had done before. But this relationship is inseparable from the mystery. It is not 'to be understood as an unambiguous theophany... an exercise of arbitrary power on the part of God. The mystery in which God clothes his condescensions towards man is not set aside in the resurrection.'[173] There was about it a sense of the ineffable, the overwhelming, the numinous; yet inherent in it was the awareness of a renewed relationship, imbued with dazzling possibility.

Three central elements emerge from the complexities of such experience. First, there is the one who encounters the disciples: the content of the epiphany is Jesus himself. The encounter, which centres on their recognition of him,[174] releases a powerful dynamic which enables the disciples to articulate the experience,[175] to reappraise and reinterpret his ministry and death,[176] to relate him in new ways to the scriptures and initiate a many-sided, creative midrashic interpretation or Christian *pesher*,[177] and to explore the eschatological implications of his completed work.[178] In the second place, there were those who encountered the risen Christ. The dominant feature in this connection is their sense of being commissioned as apostles of Jesus Christ.[179] The third feature is the feelings of the experiencing agents: fear, awe, amazement, joy. Here, Paul objectifies through theologising: the overwhelming experience points to the incomparable grace of God (Gal. 1: 15).

The creative consequences of the apostolic experiences are important. The witness of the apostles was instrumental in creating a formalised Christian *paradosis*, as is evident in 1 Cor. 15: 3–8, in the sermon summaries of Acts and even in its literary introduction (Acts 1: 3f.).[180] Beyond the actual summaries, the resurrection faith supplied the dynamic for the new hermeneutic which enabled the death and resurrection of Christ to be interpreted as 'according to the scriptures' (1 Cor. 15: 3f.) – a hermeneutic, which made possible further developments in christology and eschatology. A narrative form was created to transmit a concise description of the apostles' experiences and their significance,[181] thus providing material which the early preachers, teachers and missionaries may well have used as paradigms or illustrative examples;[182] and a more circumstantial narrative form or 'legend' is also found (Luke 24: 13–35; John 21: 1–14).[183] But since it has been argued here that the resurrection experiences can be understood in terms of *propheteia*, one final point may be made about the resurrection tradition. A prophet of Israel might quote his initial experience to throw light on the nature of his mission and vocation (cf. Is. 6: 1–13; Jer. 1: 4–10); otherwise, he simply delivered the message given to him. A Christian apostle might cite his experience of meeting the risen Christ in defence of his own apostleship (Paul does so several times), but the focus of the experience is objective: it proclaims the crucified Jesus whom God has made 'both Lord and Christ' (Acts 2: 36). The resurrection tradition preaches Christ.

Prophetic phenomena in the early church

The narrative of Pentecost in Acts 2 provides a striking description and interpretation of apparently ecstatic phenomena.[184] The writer clearly presupposes an organic connection between the reception of the Spirit and the inception of Christian preaching. Yet such spiritual intensity belongs more typically to the religious sect or pneumatic cell than to missionary confrontation with and conversion of thousands (cf. Acts 2: 41).[185] Consequently, it may well be suspected that Luke has foreshortened the perspective by connecting Christian missionary preaching too immediately with Pentecost.[186] However, his narrative testifies to the prominence of prophetic and pneumatic phenomena in at least some churches in Luke's time and to the presumption that they were an early feature of Christian communal experience.

In 1 Cor. 14, Paul's distinction between the prophetic, which is expressed in intelligible utterance,[187] and the pneumatic, which tends to incoherence, possibly reflects the emergence of a highly esteemed 'Spirit-endowed' group who claimed to possess pneumatic gifts of a high order.[188] While Paul is prepared to recognise a variety of spiritual gifts, to contrast 'spiritual' and 'unspiritual' in the church (1 Cor. 2: 13 – 3: 3; cf. Gal. 6: 1) and to accept that some are 'mature' and others not (Phil. 3: 15), the basis of his view is that the Spirit is given to the church as a whole and that the individual must strive to realise the potentialities that are thus presented to him.[189] When, however, this striving becomes boastful or is not made to operate for the edification of the community, it is inadmissible. Paul evidently sharply reverses the popular evaluation when he puts intelligible preaching before tongues, but he does so with an openness which testifies to the delicate nature of the issue. All this suggests that he is dealing with a phenomenon which, despite its more recent extravagances, had long been established in the church. His aim is the correction of more recent aberrations and the refining of its essential constituents: expressions of pneumatic inspiration, interpretation and intelligible proclamation.[190] That this is a typically Pauline procedure is seen from the similar refinement he effects in the concept of the Spirit.[191]

Prophets and prophecy in the early church

Despite the fact that Paul never explicitly calls himself a prophet[192] nor does he apply the term to any of his colleagues,[193] prophecy is for him the supreme *charisma*.[194] The gift of prophecy could manifest itself throughout the community of believers. Paul encouraged *all* to prophesy (1 Cor. 14: 5), and while he claimed to 'speak in tongues more than you all' (14: 18), the whole tenor of his argument is that he also excels them in prophecy – i.e., in intelligible utterance.[195] Prophetic forms manifest themselves at many points in Paul's preaching. What is virtually the text of a major sermon to the Romans (Rom. 1: 16f.)[196] is in effect the prophetic *assurance of salvation* to all who have faith in the gospel, be he Jew or Greek. In the same sermon, he balances the *announcement of judgment* (2: 1–6, 8f.) and the *announcement of salvation* (2: 7, 10), while emphasising that God's kindness is meant to lead one to repentance (2: 4b). His prophetic insight into the present and future – heavily dependent as it is on Christian *midrash* – is illustrated in his *announcement of Israel's salvation* (11: 25ff.). At least two clear examples of the *portrayal of salvation* occur, in 1 Cor. 15: 51–54 and 1 Thess. 4: 15ff. In other words, to proclaim God's action in Christ for the salvation of mankind Paul adapts traditional prophetic forms to the Christian proclamation, which in turn can be conveyed in scriptural language, complete with the 'messenger formula'.[197] Thus, in prophetic fashion, he builds up, encourages and comforts the Christian communities (cf. 1 Cor. 14: 3), or convicts them and calls them to account (14: 24), while affording them insight into the mystery of God in Christ (13: 2; cf. Eph. 3: 4f.).[198]

The writer of Acts,[199] while highlighting the gift of the Spirit to the whole church, singles out a number of leading men as prophets.[200] An illuminating instance of an early Christian prophet in operation is provided by Agabus.[201] M. E. Boring's analysis is perhaps worth quoting in full:

(1) He is a member of a group of prophets, not a solitary individual.
(2) He functions within the church, not outside of or over against it.
(3) His word is not sought by the community, but it comes of his own initiative. (4) He does not use any manipulative techniques in order to secure the revelation. (5) His work is heard as authoritative.
(6) The authority in which his word is held is not limited to a single congregation or community but embraces (at least) Jerusalem, Caesarea, and Antioch. (7) He seems to have no 'official' authority within the church structure; e.g., when he comes from Jerusalem to Antioch, he is not 'sent' or 'commissioned'. (8) The community is called to exercise some discernment in response to his oracle; while

the revelation possesses an authority acknowledged by all, one's own response to it is a matter of one's own discernment. (9) He predicts a this-worldly historical event, which in fact soon takes place. (10) He engages in symbolic actions in the manner of Jeremiah and Ezekiel. (11) He introduces his oracle with τάδε λέγει τὸ πνεῦμα τὸ ἅγιον and is described as speaking διὰ τοῦ πνεύματος.[202]

Boring has suggested, on the basis of *Redaktionsgeschichte*, that 'originally Agabus claimed to speak the word of the risen Lord',[203] but this must be regarded as speculative. Whether or not they have had visions and revelations of the Lord (2 Cor. 12: 1), prophets characteristically spoke by the Spirit. More to the point is Boring's second observation, that Luke has de-eschatologised the prediction, and that it originally referred to the imminent eschatological drama in which famine was a stock element.[204] If this is so, Agabus' oracle is an *announcement of eschatological salvation*, inherent in which were elements of warning on which the community acted. His prophetic *symbolic action* (Acts 21: 10f.) may belong to a similar context (i.e., the woes prior to the End). On the other hand, prophetic utterances guided the community (cf. 13: 1ff.); 21: 10f. operated also in terms of warning and guidance, to which Paul had to make his own response (21: 13ff.).[205] The *announcement of judgment* occurs in Acts in several forms: against an individual (13: 11), against the Jews (28: 25-28), and as part of Christian preaching (10: 42f.; 17: 31), sometimes with heavy reproach (7: 51ff.). The recital of the mighty acts of God and the announcement of judgment are frequently capped by the call to repentance (2: 38ff.; 3: 19ff.; 17: 30).

If it is correct to say of the prophet author of Revelation that, in some respects, 'he stands closer to Jewish prophecy than to what we know of New Testament prophecy',[206] one would expect Old Testament motifs to dominate his prophetic utterances in a manner uncharacteristic of his Christian prophetic brethren.[207] The initial experience he describes, however, is not his call to be a prophet but his commissioning to write this prophetic book: 'now write what you see, what is and what is to take place hereafter' (Rev. 1: 19).[208] He is addressed by 'a great voice like a trumpet' (1: 10), has a vision of 'one like a son of man' (1: 13-16)[209] and is overcome by its momentousness (1: 17).[210] In this state of terror, he receives from the divine figure what is in effect an *oracle of salvation*,[211] complete with the introductory formula 'Do not fear' and a direct statement of assurance that the figure who addresses him is 'the first and the last',[212] who has known death, is alive now and for ever, and holds the key that unlocks the gates of death and the grave.[213] The prophet is thoroughly

Christian in that the figure who addresses him is indisputably the glorified Christ, but he is like an Old Testament prophet in the authority he claims and the unswerving obedience he expects for his message.[214]

The range of prophetic forms he uses may be illustrated first from the letters to the seven churches.[215] A prominent form is the *announcement of judgment*, complete with accusation;[216] the *call to repentance* is a recurring feature,[217] and the prophet characteristically gives a *conditional promise of salvation* to 'him who conquers'.[218] Salvation is in the future; it is reached only after patient endurance and faithfulness in the eschatological struggle with evil, and means that one will not be 'hurt by the second death' (2: 11). Elements of the *portrayal of salvation* are readily discernible.[219] The prophetic I-saying in 3: 20 represents an *assurance of salvation*, combining a statement of the present position ('behold, I stand...') with the promise of full communion if the door is opened. Each message begins with the assurance, given in the first person, that the glorified Christ 'knows' intimately the particular situation and performance of the church addressed. This is covenantal language, expressing the intimate concern and involvement of the divine power and introducing utterances of rebuke, encouragement and assurance as appropriate.[220]

It is impossible to make a detailed study here of the prophetic forms which occur throughout Revelation. The prophet author 'has the witness of Jesus',[221] which he declares throughout the book by means of the *portrayal of salvation*, which includes other prophetic forms within itself. The remarkable eighteenth chapter, 'the doom-song of Babylon', is in fact a salvation prophecy, for the overthrow of God's enemies is an ancient way of conceiving the vindication of God's people;[222] hence the hallelujahs of chapter nineteen. The whole revelation is grounded in what Christ has already done,[223] and looks to the consummation of universal salvation in him.[224] The *call to repentance* is therefore central to the church's mission.[225] The writer appears to assume that all Christians are potentially prophets (cf. 19: 10), although those designated as prophets in fact fulfil this ministry.[226] As for himself, he claims an even more exalted status as mediator of the revelation of Christ to his brethren; he attempts to give a definitive interpretation of the present and the future in the light of the victory of Christ.

Prophecy and tradition

The prophet does not work in a vacuum; he functions within a tradition. The data of his visionary experience, the religious concepts with which he works, the language in which he proclaims the message he received, and his role in the community are all influenced, even partly determined, by his tradition. Yet he also claims a freedom in relation to it[227] – the freedom of inspiration, to speak and act in accordance with the revelation given to him, and as the Spirit moves him.[228] Hence between the prophet and elements of his tradition there emerge creative tensions and a dialogue of considerable importance for the development of the tradition and faith wherein he stands.[229]

The relationship of the Christian prophet to tradition was complex.[230] In the churches *dominical tradition* (i.e., tradition stemming directly from Jesus) was recognised as particularly authoritative,[231] yet the prophet, through the intimacy of his I–Thou relationship with the Lord, was admitted to an immediate awareness of some aspects of 'the mind of Christ' in relation not only to himself (cf. 2 Cor. 12: 9) but to community concern also (cf. 1 Thess. 4: 15); and he might be the means by which Christ addressed the community in the first person.[232] Such statements are usually easily identified as Christian prophecy, but in certain circumstances they could be associated with or absorbed into gospel tradition as utterances of Jesus. This process was more probable in situations such as community worship, where gospel tradition was transmitted in a context in which the sense of the presence of the Lord could be intensified by prophetic utterance (cf. Matt. 18: 20); where, on the basis of gospel tradition, whole dimensions of christology could be opened up by prophetic revelation, and shared and absorbed by the community through 'psalms and hymns and spiritual songs';[233] and where intense eschatological longing – 'Come, Lord Jesus!' (Rev. 22: 20) – was informed, and indeed controlled (cf. 2 Thess.), by prophetic portrayals of salvation and eschatological admonitions (cf. Mark 13). That there was a feed-back into gospel tradition in these areas – i.e., christology[234] and eschatology[235] in particular – is very probable; yet the precision with which Paul distinguished dominical tradition from other forms of utterance remains impressive.[236] Generally speaking, there is no question of prophetic logia swamping the logia of Jesus and making the two groups of sayings completely indistinguishable.[237]

Closely related to dominical tradition is *kerygmatic tradition* – i.e., the basic *paradosis* of the Christian faith[238] – which provided firm guidelines which no utterance claiming to be Christian could abrogate. When a pneumatic in the community, for whatever reason,[239] cried 'Jesus be cursed' (1 Cor. 12: 3), the guidelines were broken and the Spirit of God was known not to be in operation. The cry 'Jesus is Lord' was prompted by the Spirit since it was in accord with basic Christian proclamation. But, as has been indicated above, the apostolic experiences which led to the articulation of fundamental Christian *paradosis* were themselves prophetic in nature.[240] Prophetic insights of a fundamental character thus provided guidelines for discriminating between subsequent pneumatic utterances. This principle is reflected in two types of authority to which prophets were subject. One was the *discipline of the Christian prophetic tradition* (1 Cor. 2: 13), which seems already to have built up its own rubrics and precedents necessarily related to basic *paradosis* as well as to prophetic practice (14: 32). The second was the *discipline of apostolic authority*, on which the *paradosis* rested to a very considerable extent (cf. 1 Cor. 15: 5ff.) and to which the prophets were undoubtedly subject (14: 37f). To these, two further principles may be added. The prophet had to contribute to the *edification of the community* (cf. 1 Cor. 14), and he had to exhibit in the quality of his living his acceptance of the *norms of Christian behaviour*, expressed above all in *agape*.[241]

Perhaps most important of all, there developed in the early communities a *Christian hermeneutical tradition*, which used the scriptures of the Jews as testimony to the Christian understanding of Jesus as the Christ, and which was probably founded on the midrashic practice of Jesus himself.[242] Christian hermeneutical procedures were characterised by an eschatological stance which was defined by the event of Christ, related to the situation of the early Christians, and in continuity with the ancient prophetic quest (cf. 1 Pet. 1: 10ff.). Yet even this eschatological stance was arrived at with the help of a scriptural hermeneutic, for the articulation of the resurrection faith – even the realisation of the truth that the crucified Jesus was risen – was inseparable from a scriptural understanding of the suffering and death of the Christ.[243] Once the scriptures were seen to testify to Christ (cf. John 5: 39), they were brought into dynamic relation with the disciples' recollections of Jesus and so helped to shape the gospel tradition which provided the ground level of the edifice of Christian belief and practice.[244] Prophetic activity was involved both in the fundamental resurrection experiences[245] and in the on-going hermeneutical work, in which prophets, through the insight given them, were uniquely able to 'spark the gaps' and set in motion new dimensions of understanding. The celebration of the birth of the Messiah is a case in point.[246] A further example is the development of the Son of man symbol: in the moment of his martyrdom, Stephen had a prophetic vision ('full of the Holy Spirit'; Acts 7: 55) of 'the Son of man standing at the right hand of God' (7: 56).[247] At the same time, the prophetic consciousness, so to speak, was so nourished in scripture that the articulation of visions and pneumatic experiences was largely dependent on scriptural language and conceptuality.[248]

Special procedures were evolved in more advanced exegetical circles, of which St John's gospel is an outstanding example. The influence of prophets and *propheteia* on the fourth gospel has been noted by a number of writers.[249] Several factors coalesce to form John's distinctive approach. One is the liturgical tradition shared by John and those whom he addresses in his gospel; many sections of it have a liturgical setting. Another is that familiarity with synoptic-type tradition appears to be taken for granted, and this material provides the basis of Johannine reinterpretation which sometimes involves the ascription of notable I-sayings to Jesus. This situation suggests that

> a leading member of the Ephesian Church, possessed of very vivid traditions about the words and deeds of Jesus...might weave into his extempore eucharistic '*propheteia*' – his prayer and discourse – an extended meditation on the mission and work of Christ, in a form in which he as it were (though with complete reverence) impersonated Christ. Christ was the unseen Celebrant, and the disciple or elder, uttering the eucharistic prayers and praises and discourse, drew upon the very words which had come down in the living traditions as Christ's own words on the eve of His betrayal. The whole Gospel may have grown up round such worship.[250]

The 'raw material' of such discourses, however, comprises not only vivid synoptic-type traditions and sayings of Jesus but also Old Testament and other relevant traditions reshaped and reprocessed, as it were, in the crucible of John's prophetic consciousness and in accordance with his distinctively Christian hermeneutic. Such a position is consonant with a situation in which the synoptic tradition has already become relatively fixed.

To conclude briefly: there is no reason to deny that prophecy made a genuinely creative contribution to the articulation and evolution of the Christian message, although prophetic tradition would assign the creativity to the power of God through his Spirit or to the risen Christ. The articulation of basic Christian *paradosis*, the exploration of new levels of meaning and the sharpening of spiritual awareness were all directly related to *propheteia*; yet it operated within and upheld the necessary constraints of the *koinonia*. By its nature, *propheteia* cannot operate *in vacuo* or *ex nihilo*. It found its data in the scriptural tradition of Israel, the event of Christ, and the hermeneutical principles of the new faith, which indeed it helped to shape. The insights it provided into the Christian understanding of the scriptures and the impetus it gave to the forging of basic symbols, christological and eschatological, figure among its most important and creative contributions. As far as the synoptic tradition is concerned, however, its influence was for the most part indirect, and mediated through the hermeneutical skills and theological expertise of its redactors. It is misleading, to say the least, to suggest that the early Christians failed to distinguish between the utterances of Christian prophets and the words of Jesus in the synoptic tradition. Paul's practice alone is sufficient to raise serious objections to such sweeping assumptions.[251]

It was in the growth areas of christology and apocalyptic that Christian prophetic utterances were attributed to Jesus, although the practice of John is to be distinguished from that of the synoptists.[252] Only occasionally do the latter allow a suspect I-saying, for example, to become attached to the tradition of Jesus' teaching, often by way of expansion of meaning or commentary.[253] As for apocalyptic – that most 'open-ended' of early Christian concerns – Jesus' teaching to the disciples about the future appears to be caught up in Christian concern for the *parousia*, with all its disquieting and lengthening preliminaries. In Mark 13, for example, around the nucleus of a dominical tradition that his followers will be persecuted for his sake but nevertheless need have no fear, there has gathered a conglomerate of apocalyptic and other related utterances (many of traditional Jewish origin) in which the paraenetic intention is of overriding importance.[254] Only in this way can the teacher or evangelist adequately convey the word of the Lord to an anxious community.

2

PARACLESIS AND HOMILY

> After the reading of the law and the prophets, the rulers of the
> synagogue sent to them, saying, 'Brethren, if you have any word
> of exhortation (logos paracleseōs) for the people, say it'. (Acts 13: 15)
>
> Bear with my word of exhortation (logou tēs paracleseōs). (Heb. 13: 22)

Popular preaching in the Graeco-Roman world

With *paraclesis*, 'exhortation', and *homilia*, 'familiar converse', we enter the
world of popular preaching. The hinterland of *paraclesis* is permeated with
religious meaning: 'comfort', 'consolation', 'asking for help'; and as 'exhortation' the word can denote both summons to decision and encouragement
to persevere.[1] The ethos of *homilia*, the term later applied to popular
preaching, is one of intimacy and familiarity, of friendly converse and
persuasive argumentation, with overtones of serious intent and instruction.[2] The world of the first century was as open to moralistic discourse
as the modern world is closed to it. The church began in a cultural environment in which preaching was a basic mode of communication.

Behind this cultural phenomenon stood centuries of development and
preparation, the roots of which were embedded in the Greek situation
bequeathed to posterity by Alexander.[3] The soil was the international
culture, based on Hellenism. Yet such hellenistic internationalism contained
within itself immense tensions. It had killed the city state and the order of
things which it symbolised; yet it was from the age of the city state that it
drew its inspiration. Its focus was upon the past; its present was derivative,
imitatory. Hence the hellenistic age was wracked with problems: problems
of identity, amid the depersonalisation of the huge unit; of freedom in a
tyrannical state; of values, now that the meaningfulness of the city state
democracy was gone; of religion, now that the gods of the city state were
dead; of security in a world shaken to its foundations. Amid such confusion
and fearfulness, the man who was listened to was the one who entered into
dialogue with his audience in familiar terms and retained throughout his
discourse a firm pragmatic concern as he recommended to his hearers a
particular life-style as an antidote to the perplexities and confusion of their
life situation. Among the proliferation of philosophical tendencies which
addressed themselves to a greater or lesser extent to this situation were the
Cynics, who evolved the form of discourse known as the diatribe, which

was to be of great consequence for Christian homiletics and which will now be illustrated briefly in its two major phases.

The Cynic diatribe

The early Cynics[4] discovered that traditional philosophical methods, however appropriate to the leisured milieu of Athens, made no impression upon the type of hellenistic audience with which they were usually confronted. Both Diogenes and Crates attempted traditional methods, but without success. Diogenes observed that 'when he spoke seriously about weighty subjects, noone stayed to listen, but when he began to whistle a crowd soon assembled'.[5] Here we discern what was to become one of the most distinctive Cynic characteristics – the art of communicating at a popular level.[6] In its hinterland, however, stands the conviction that goes back to Socrates, viz., that virtue is communicable.

The credit for perfecting the Cynic diatribe must be given to the third-century preacher, Bion of Borysthenes.[7] In his hands it became 'un dialogue monologué',[8] a discourse on a moral subject, given by a preacher before an audience but retaining the mannerisms and devices of animated conversation.[9] Here is Bion in full flood:

> Therefore we should not try to alter circumstances but to adapt ourselves to them as they really are, just as sailors do. They don't try to change the winds or the sea but ensure that they are always ready to adapt themselves to conditions. In a flat calm they use the oars; with a following breeze they hoist full sail; in a head wind they shorten sail or heave to. Adapt yourselves to circumstances in the same way. Are you old? Do not long for youth. Again, are you weak? Do not hanker after the prerogatives of the strong... Are you poor? Do not seek the ways of the wealthy.[10]

Bion was the prototype of the wandering preacher, who was to become so important a few centuries later. He personifies the ideal of the *kosmopolites* who practised what he preached by travelling from city to city rather than adopting Athens as his fixed point. His own adaptability is illustrated by the fact that, unusually for an early Cynic, he became a court philosopher and once more anticipated later developments within the Cynic movement.[11]

The Cynic diatribe was both satirical and amusing, but possessed at the same time a deeper moral earnestness than is sometimes apparent at first glance. Its purpose has been summarised as 'to put across ethical teaching in a popular way by sugaring the pill with a strong element of parody'.[12] Its persistence for many centuries and its influence both on Roman literature[13] and Christian preaching testify to its usefulness and effectiveness.

The Stoic-Cynic diatribe of Imperial times

Zeno,[14] the founder of Stoicism, imbued his philosophy[15] and his life-
style[16] with a characteristic moral earnestness and propagated his views
through popular preaching. Four great Stoics acquired prominence in
Imperial times: Seneca,[17] Musonius Rufus, Epictetus[18] and Marcus
Aurelius. For reasons of brevity and convenience, Epictetus alone is
discussed here as the exemplar of this later diatribal usage.

On the style of Epictetus – a subject which has received careful scrutiny
from modern scholars[19] – a few brief comments must suffice. His style is
predominantly colloquial, avoiding the periods of highly stylised prose and
using short sentences in the cut and thrust of debate, real or imaginary.
This is 'paratactic diction', which characterises the diatribe.[20] Rhetorical
questions, for example, are relentless; question and answer are frequently
used: conditional clauses are a common device for advancing the argument;
and repetition is used to drive the point home.[21] The flow of the diatribe
is vigorous and arresting. The attention of the listener is not allowed to
wander. He cannot easily disengage. The result is a discourse that is relentless but colourful, startling and lively.[22]

The form of the diatribes is more important for our purposes. While
flexibility is a necessary characteristic, a general pattern is discernible.
Take Epic. 1.18 as an example – a discourse about not being angry at the
errors other people make. Epictetus begins, not unusually, with a quotation from the philosophers, followed by a question to his audience. We
may paraphrase thus:

> If what philosophers say is true, viz., that everyone possesses basic
> convictions on which he acts..., why do you express anger against
> so many people when they are doing precisely that?

This dilemma is expanded diatribally to give a microcosm of the whole
discourse.

> 'Because they are thieves and robbers', you may say. What do you
> mean by 'thieves and robbers'? Surely they are people who hold
> wrong convictions about good and evil. Why then be angry with
> them? Shouldn't we rather pity them? Show them their error!
> You will see them abandon their mistakes. If they don't recognise
> that they are wrong, then they have failed to improve upon their
> present standpoint.

The central part of the diatribe explores various aspects of the theme.
First, there is, as so often, a negative argument directed against the proposition that thieves and robbers should incur capital punishment. Next, he

raises the question why people do in fact show anger or hate towards them. Is it, he asks, because we value so highly the things of which these men rob us? So the philosopher advances the familiar theme of detachment – from clothes, wife, possessions. If these possessions represent your values, pity yourself! Spelling the matter out in detail, he shows that the thief's convictions are exactly the same as his audience's: the good life consists in possessing goods. A personal anecdote adds immediacy and colour. Epictetus had an iron lamp which a thief stole – as was to be expected, for a man only loses what he possesses. Finally, the philosopher points out that the one thing that no-one can take away – not even a tyrant – is the will. Self-knowledge is essential, as is discipline. 'If you have a headache, don't say, "Alas! I have a headache." Don't say "Alas!"' If you have this attitude to life, you are free, you are invincible. And so to the peroration, strikingly parallel in form to Romans 8:[23]

> Who then is invincible? It is he who is disturbed by no outside
> influence. Take an athlete. He has won the first round. What about
> the second? What if there should be exceptional conditions – a
> heat wave? What if the event should be at Olympia? ... What if
> you put a young girl in his path – what will happen then? What
> about the temptations of darkness? What about the effects of
> fame or abuse? What about praise, or death? In all these things
> he is victorious...

Bultmann concludes that the diatribe, generally speaking, has three parts: the positive exposition of the ideal, followed by the negative presentation of it or the chiding of the audience for not living up to it, and finally a concluding statement of the philosopher's meaning.[24] The above example illustrates this general form, within which considerable variation is possible. The concern for formal unity is illustrated by the fact that the opening statement can be reflected in the conclusion. Thus, the opening sentence of Epic. 2:1 – 'the opinion of the philosophers perhaps seems to some to be a paradox' – is picked up at the end: 'So this paradox will no longer appear either impossible or indeed a paradox at all' (2:1.40). At other times, this device is used to round off a particular section of the discourse.[25] The introduction to the discourse can be effected in various ways. Some concrete circumstances may prompt it. 'I am sick here,' said one of his pupils, 'and I want to return home.' (3:5) This is the prelude to a diatribe on having a right attitude of mind, concluding: 'If you possessed it, you would be content in sickness, and in hunger, and in death.' A foppish rhetorician comes to see Epictetus (3:1), and earns a diatribe on finery in dress. Normally, the discourse either begins with a philosophical statement or speedily leads up to it, thus setting out the theme of the whole speech.[26]

Popular preaching in the Jewish tradition

Whatever cultural cross-fertilisation may have taken place during the hellenistic period in particular,[27] two major factors differentiate popular preaching in the Jewish tradition from the Graeco-Roman homily. Jewish preaching was related to a scripture-using tradition which evolved its own distinctive hermeneutic;[28] and it operated within the tradition of the synagogue, which by the first century had developed into 'a virile full grown and firmly established institution'.[29]

The central concern of Jewish preaching was in fact the interpretation and contemporisation of the scriptural message.[30] Midrash[31] – the technical term for this hermeneutical process – denotes, at least by the time of the Destruction, an interpretative and paraphrastic commentary on the scriptures which proceeds by comparing one text of scripture with a variety of others –'expliquer la Bible par la Bible'[32] – and by relating the biblical meaning to the contemporary situation. Essential to it is 'the reciprocal relation between personal experience (or event) and text'.[33] 'Has not after all "every word of the scripture seventy aspects"? These aspects were latent; and as generation after generation found expression for some or other of these aspects, they revealed again and anew the Torah which Moses received on Sinai.'[34] Such midrashim are traditionally divided into two recognised types: *midrash halachah*, designed to elucidate the fundamental principles of the legislative parts of the Torah; and *midrash haggadah*, providing homiletic commentary on scripture. Generally speaking, midrashic procedures occur relatively early in Judaism and can be detected within the scriptures themselves as earlier texts are reinterpreted by later ones.[35] '. . . midrash is in fact the way in which our whole Old Testament grew up. Deuteronomy is a midrash on the ancient Israelite laws, the Priestly Code is another; our book of Isaiah is the monument to centuries of midrash.'[36] 'Implicit'[37] or 'covert'[38] midrash is found both in canonical writings and in the Apocrypha, the Genesis Apocryphon and the Palestinian Targum, as well as in the glossing of Septuagint texts: procedures which amount to a virtual rewriting of the Bible.[39] By contrast, 'explicit' or 'overt' midrash proceeds by citing a scriptural text (the lemma) and appending interpretative commentary to it.

Explicit midrash, albeit of a distinctive type, is well illustrated by the *pesher* commentaries of Qumran, although a variety of midrashic forms are found in the sectarians' writings.[40] The midrashic nature of the *pesher* technique is unmistakable, although it is probably unnecessary to labour the

point with even clumsier jargon such as *midrash pesher*.[41] Its verse by verse
paraphrasing, probably used in a liturgical setting in the community, suggests a parallel with the targums.[42] But above all, its eschatological intensity
indicates that it is essentially a prophetic type of midrash, not only because
it is derived from the Teacher of Righteousness 'to whom God made known
all the mysteries of the words of his servants the prophets',[43] nor because
it is usually (but not exclusively) based on the prophetic books, but because
it gave the community the sense of living in the final eschatological crisis
and made the scriptures speak to their situation.[44] Thus, in Qumran exegesis
the Old Testament citation, which can itself be subject to implicit midrashic
emendation,[45] is followed by an exposition – usually introduced by 'interpreted, this concerns...' or a similar phrase – designed to reveal the eschatological mystery to the elect community.

Next, by a kind of hermeneutical shorthand, a body of *testimonia* is
assembled,[46] bringing together key passages for the purposes of Qumran
exegesis and presupposing the application of the *pesher* technique to the
individual passages in their scriptural context.[47] Important though the confirmation of the existence of *testimonia* at Qumran is for New Testament
studies, there is no case for supposing that they represent the source of
Qumranic scriptural teaching. They are a product of it, an important stage
in the development and defence of the sectarian position.[48]

Midrash, whether in its traditional or its eschatological form, is broadly
homiletic in its approach.[49] It was therefore basic to the homiletics of the
synagogue, which was geared to the reading and exposition of scripture and
thus had to resort to the use of targum (since some did not understand
Hebrew)[50] and of homily (so that the message of scripture could be understood in contemporary perspective). Surviving homiletic midrashim[51] indicate two broad types. The *yelammedenu* homily – a form in use in Hillel's
time – is distinctive in that it starts with a question put by leaders of the
congregation (*yelammedenu rabbenu*: let our teacher instruct us).[52] The
teacher's answer followed customary midrashic practice and might include
an appeal to *halachah*. The *proem* homily, on the other hand, begins with
a *proem* or introductory text, chosen with care in order to interpret and,
in a sense, bind together the readings of law and prophets (*seder* and
haftarah). Although the text was not selected from either, it usually linked
with the *haftarah* by means of word-play or other linguistic form, and the
evidence suggests that the preacher kept the *haftarah* constantly in mind.[53]
In both forms of homily, the theme was developed by means of a string of
cited texts (*haruzin*: 'pearl stringing'), affording a characteristic 'list' structure to the homily. Considerable substance, however, was introduced by
means of appropriate stories, parables or other illustrative material which

formed part of the homiletic convention. As a well-known saying of R. Johanan put it: 'When R. Meir used to deliver his public discourses, a third was *halakah*, a third *haggadah*, and a third consisted of parables'.[54] The over-all unity of structure was secured by the fact that the preacher controlled the interpretative development so as to lead to a conclusion related to the *seder*. To quote an admirable summary, based on the *proem* form:

> the homilies in a sense move from the circumference of a circle to its centre. They start from a proem-text outside the *seder* and the *haftarah* of the day, but linguistically related to the *haftarah*; they proceed by *haruzin* which implies the *haftarah* and may perhaps quote from it; and the *haruzin* leads directly to a text from or pointing to the *seder*.[55]

One rabbinic example from pre-Destruction times is that of Eliezer ben Hyrcanus of Jamnia, who is described as giving the sermon in the school of R. Jochanan ben Zakkai at Jerusalem. It is clear from the very brief outline we possess that he opened the homily with the phrase, 'This is what the scripture says', cited a *proem* text from Ps. 37:14f. and linked it with the opening passage from the day's *seder* (he specifically related it to Gen. 14: 1, and 12-15) by means of 'pearl stringing'.[56] J. Mann held that the *haftarah* implicit in the whole sermon was Is. 41:2.[57] From other examples which abound in the homiletic midrashim but are, of course, later,[58] the rabbinic proneness to the use of antithesis can readily be seen (cf. Taanit T 1:8).[59]

The literary products of ancient Judaism suggest that Jewish homiletics were broader than the synagogue homily *par excellence* and developed in the direction of thematic speeches while retaining some synagogal characteristics. For example, a lyrical address on a homiletic theme and pattern occurs in Sir. 44: 1 - 50: 24. Structurally, it consists of an introduction (44:1-15), develops by means of recital and historical retrospect (44:16-50: 21) and has a brief conclusion to pick up the invitatory note of the introduction (50: 22ff.). It is impossible to identify a central text with any assurance; the address is based on a wide range of written scripture ('as it is written', 48:10), including the Torah, the prophets and a number of the writings.[60] An example of a testamentary speech is found in 1 Macc. 2: 49-69. After an indication of the context ('the days drew near that Mattathias should die'), the theme statement exhorts his children, in these ruinous times, to show zeal for the law and the covenant of the fathers (v. 49f.); the development is by enumeration (cf. 'pearl stringing') of the fathers' deeds, from Abraham to Daniel (vv. 51-60), and teaches that they should put their trust in God (v. 61), be courageous and grow strong in the law (vv. 61-64). The conclusion contains specific commendations: Simeon, for his counsel;

Judas, for his military qualities: rally round the law and avenge the wrong done to your people (vv. 65–68)! Finally, the passage returns to the setting: Mattathias blessed them and died (v. 69f.).[61] H. Thyen[62] found that while such addresses were closely related stylistically to the Cynic–Stoic diatribe, they were distinguishable from the latter in several respects. Their style is heavier, lacking the vivacity of the Greek preachers. Genuine dialogue tends not to occur; and in keeping with the more solemn tone the witticisms and humour of the exponents of the diatribe are also lacking. Yet almost all the devices of the diatribe recur in Jewish preaching, and it must be remembered that the diatribe itself underwent changes not unlike those which are found in the Jewish form.

The homiletic pattern discernible in the Qumran writings is related to the eschatological standpoint of the community and its founder. In the so-called *Damascus Rule*, a prominent place is given to an exhortation or sermon in which the preacher, probably a 'Guardian of the Community',[63] encourages his flock to remain faithful and develops the theme that faithfulness is rewarded and disobedience punished. In the introduction the theme of the discourse is clearly stated, with its inherent antithesis between the stubbornness of the wicked, who incur God's wrath, and the faithfulness of the remnant, whom God spares. The sermon, developing by self-conscious steps,[64] is structured antithetically and makes use of 'pearl stringing' for biblical illustration. These two motifs are used in conjunction. Thus, the 'heavenly watchers' (rebel angels), their sons ('giants'), the generation of the flood, the sons of Noah – all these went astray and incurred God's anger. By contrast, 'Abraham did not walk in this way' and was accounted the friend of God, a status also conferred on Isaac and Jacob, partners in God's covenant. By contrast again, the sons of Jacob strayed and were punished; and this leads to a recalling of the sins of Israel in Egypt, for which they were inevitably punished. Yet there was always a faithful remnant, with whom God made good his covenant (cf. 3:12ff.). And so the preacher proceeds, with specific reinforcement of the obligations of the covenant in later sections (cf. 6:11ff.). The conclusion of the sermon is strongly eschatological (cf. 7:9ff.) and is built around antitheses, as the fate of the disobedient is contrasted with that of the faithful.[65]

Philo of Alexandria has been called 'the founder of the art of preaching as we know it' and 'perhaps the greatest philosophic preacher that has ever lived'.[66] The evident background of Philo's writings is the synagogue homily.[67] His writings echo the diatribal technique and topics while retaining the midrashic character of Jewish exposition. In sharp contrast to Qumran, Philo's exegesis is directed to the Torah or Pentateuch only, and these books give him the texts for his philosophical ramblings. A characteristic device is to express his philosophic concepts in language and imagery derived from scripture.[68]

Although some have suggested that Philo has so integrated the homiletic patterns with his entire discourse that it is impossible to disentangle them,[69] the outline of a synagogue-type homily on the theme of heavenly bread has been convincingly identified in two passages: *Legum Allegoriae* III, 162-68 and *De Mutatione Hominum*, 253-63.[70] The Old Testament text that provides the theme of the homily – Ex. 16: 4 in the former instance, Gen. 17: 19ff. in the latter – recurs in straightforward or paraphrastic form throughout the discourse: a fact which suggests that the liturgical reading of this passage took place prior to the delivery of the homily. In developing the theme, Philo uses the practice of 'pearl stringing' but restricts his material to the Pentateuch.[71] In his peroration he returns to consider the main text in the light of his exposition. Such examples indicate that Philo approximated to Palestinian midrash in some of his most characteristic discourse.[72]

On the other hand, Philo seems to have adapted his approach to the type of audience or situation which confronted him.[73] The discourse which has been plausibly identified as *De Benedictionibus et De Exsecrationibus*[74] represents a more popular approach to a less sophisticated audience.[75] It has been described as 'a thorough Deuteronomic address',[76] although it draws considerably upon Lev. 26 also. The theme of the first part is that careful observance of the law will be rewarded with many blessings. Scriptural quotations abound, introduced in the Greek rhetorical manner, and here and there vividness is added by the use of rhetorical questions, hypothetical dialogue and imaginary interruptions. Briefly, the blessings promised are victory over enemies, successes in war, the achievement of peace with all its blessings, the honours that accrue to the successful and, on a slightly lower plane, good bodily health (XX, 118). In the second part, the curses which fall on the unfaithful are vividly portrayed: famine, with all its attendant horrors and miseries; enslavement, total failure in all undertakings, disease, and many kinds of terror. By contrast, the proselyte will be exalted, for he came over to God's side and won the highest of all prizes. But after a time, God will renew the nation. The general outline of the talk is built around a simple antithesis. The language is characterised by a vivid realism – the blessings are very solid blessings, the curses very horrifying.

Philo, therefore, made use of thematic structures based on antithesis. While he also used many Greek rhetorical devices his discourses differ from the diatribes of the Cynics and Stoics in their exegetical emphasis and in the extent of their philosophising. He also makes extensive, though not consistent, use of allegory.[77] His failure to achieve consistency is attributable to the fact that his basic procedures are homiletic. Allegorical interpretation can hardly be made into a scientific system; it is an art rather than a science, and it is a tool which preachers of all ages have thankfully accepted.

The homily in the preaching and teaching of Jesus

Jesus preached and taught in the synagogues of Galilee,[78] yet evidence of specific homilies he delivered is very restricted. In Luke 4: 16-30, in which the synagogue setting is described in some detail (vv. 16-20), Is. 61: 1ff., quoted with overtones of midrash or *pesher* (cf. 4: 18f.), possibly represents the *haftarah* in a *proem* type homily. While the eschatological element in Jesus' hermeneutic suggests a comparison with the *pesher* of Qumran, Luke underlines the fact that the decisive and fulfilling event is taking place in Jesus' own ministry. The *redaktionsgeschichtliche* perspective is important throughout.[79]

But can more be said about this homily? J. Mann[80] has pointed out that Is. 61: 1ff. is a possible *haftarah* to Gen. 35: 9 in which God appeared to Jacob and blessed him. If Gen. 35: 9 is taken as part of the *seder* and Is. 61 (possibly vv. 1-7) as the concluding lection from the prophets (thus providing the *proem* text), a *pesher* type of interpretation may be assumed in the body of the sermon, applying the *proem* text to Jesus' mission. Luke 4: 18 then represents the gist of the conclusion of the homily. A. Finkel goes further. The beatitudes, as we have previously noted,[81] appear to derive precisely from Is. 61: 1-7; at the same time, they connect neatly with the theme of blessing in Gen. 35: 9. The common source from which Matthew and Luke derived the beatitudes was an account, however partial, of a synagogue homily of Jesus; and the hermeneutic which Jesus applied to scripture was radically prophetic (or eschatological) in its orientation.

The reconstruction is impressive, although complete assurance cannot be attained. If anything, the solution is almost too neat. Why was the homily so dismembered by the evangelists?[82] Besides, Jesus' midrashic procedures were possibly much more comprehensive and convoluted than is suggested here. Is. 61: 1ff. is also related to 'the midrash complex for which Dan. 7: 13 and 14 forms the point of departure':[83] in other words, to the great themes of the kingdom of God, the defeat of evil, the Son of man and the glory of the one anointed by the Spirit. These may well have had a place in Jesus' message in the synagogues: the technique of 'pearl stringing' was well able to accommodate them.

A second passage is John 6: 31-58. The starting point is the comment of the evangelist at 6: 59 – 'This he said in the synagogue, as he taught at Capernaum'.

The unity of the discourse has become a crux of Johannine exegesis, hinging to a considerable extent on the interests of the exegete. Thus, some have tended on the whole to detach vv. 51c–58 from the context given to it by the evangelist.[84] But on strictly literary criteria the contrast between this passage and its context is very slight;[85] the entire sequence is thoroughly Johannine, and the interpolation theory at best doubtful.[86] The most significant studies for our purpose are those by P. Borgen, in which he suggests that the key to the understanding of the discourse lies in its midrashic character.[87] The *seder* for the day seems to have included Ex. 16: 4; the *proem* text was Ps. 78: 24: 'and he gave them bread from heaven to eat' (cf. John 6: 31); and the *haftarah* probably included Is. 54: 13. The reference to the eating of the manna recurs in vv. 49 and 58, thus indicating that the whole section is midrash. The theme of 'bread from heaven'[88] is followed throughout the whole passage and the term 'eating', reintroduced at v. 49, becomes the centre of the debate thereafter. The text itself is developed according to the familiar midrashic pattern of contrast: 'not (Moses)... but (my Father)... for ...' (v. 32f.). There is initially a positive response from the congregation (v. 34), enabling Jesus to expound the theme in *pesher* fashion, with specific reference to his own ministry (vv. 35–40). Then the first objection, which repeats Jesus' words (v. 35), is raised by the congregation (v. 41f.) – part of the objection coinciding with the Jews' comments in Luke 4: 22b and highlighting the paradox of Jesus' personal position. Jesus' response is to state even more vigorously (vv. 43–51) the meaning of his interpretation, citing Is. 54: 13, repeating the theme (vv. 48ff.) and sharpening the paradox. A second objection (v. 52), concerning the concept of 'eating the flesh', follows a similar pattern, the response once more presenting the concept in uncompromising terms and ending (v. 58) with a total recapitulation of the theme.

The passage as it stands is so thoroughly Johannine that one must allow for the evangelist's reworking of the material in total fashion.[89] K. P. Donfried has questioned whether it is possible to go further than to suggest that the evangelist used for the purposes of the dialogue 'certain exegetical principles common to those of Jewish background';[90] and the relationship of a literary pattern, such as is discernible here, to the historical situation in which the discourse is ostensibly set frequently presents a problem to which only a tentative answer is possible. Nevertheless, the evangelist explicitly indicates a synagogue setting (6: 59) and, as P. Borgen has indicated, it is a tenable hypothesis that the structure of the discourse reflects the form and procedures of the synagogue homily.[91] Even if this hypothesis is treated with caution, the passage invites comparison with Luke 4[92] and suggests that in his synagogue exposition Jesus reached a critical point at which his personal involvement in God's work of fulfilment and salvation broke the constrictions of rabbinic practice, taking him into

the realm of the prophetic and pneumatic and revealing the eschatological
basis of his 'peshering' of the scriptures.[93]

The *yelammedenu* form and procedures[94] are found in a number of
gospel passages, concerned with sabbath or other halachic practices. Thus
in Matt. 12: 9–13 (and par.), the question put to Jesus is: 'Is it lawful to
heal on the sabbath?' (Matt. 12:10). In reply, Jesus instances the admitted
necessity to help an animal in distress,[95] and concludes with an assertion
of human value (12:12). The versions of Mark and Luke (Mark 3:4; Luke
6:9) record Jesus' citation of accepted *halachah*,[96] a device frequently
used in *yelammedenu* procedures. Another example occurs in the pericope
concerning plucking the ears of corn on the sabbath (Matt. 12:1–8, par.),
where the question is implied in the Pharisees' criticism of Jesus (12:2).
In Jesus' reply, the use of the phrases 'Have you not read what David
did...?' and 'Have you not read in the law...?' gain point if 1 Sam. 21:
1–10 was the *haftarah* and Num. 28: 9f. the *seder* on that day.[97] In yet
another instance (Luke 13:10–17), the head of the synagogue couches his
question in a rabbinic argument based on Ex. 31:15, forbidding work on
the sabbath. Jesus' reply makes use of a simile based on the permitted
action of releasing an ox or an ass so that it can find water to drink: so
Jesus unties the constraints of the sick.[98] Apart from sabbath questions,
Jesus is requested (Mark 10:1–15; Matt. 19:1–12) to speak on the matter
of divorce, often discussed in rabbinic circles.[99] He bases his reply on Gen.
1: 27 and 2: 24, propounding the dictum: 'what God has joined together,
let no man put asunder'. It is possible that overtones of other homilies,
both *proem* (or *pericope*) and *yelammedenu* in type, can be detected in
the gospels.[100]

Paraclesis and homily in the early Christian church

What homiletic forms can be identified by means of a structural analysis of
early church material? Two factors are important: one is the predominantly
Jewish background of the early Christian preachers – which leads one to
expect to find in their discourses some affinities with Jewish homiletics;
the other is the radical, eschatological stance of the early Christians. How
far did their practice follow that of Jesus himself, and how far did the
eschatological factor lead to distinctive homiletic forms?

Basic forms of Christian 'paraclesis'

If a Christian address can approximate in form to a synagogue homily, then
it surely must be Paul's reported *logos parcleseōs* in the synagogue at
Antioch in Pisidia (Acts 13:15–41).[101] J. W. Bowker,[102] partly building
on the work of J. Mann and J. W. Doeve, has indicated 1 Sam. 13:14 as the

proem text, tallying sufficiently closely in Hebrew with 2 Sam. 7: 6–16 as
to suggest that this latter passage was probably the *haftarah* underlying the
homily. A fitting *seder* reading can be found in Deut. 4: 25–46, while the
characteristic *haruzin* or 'pearl stringing' method is evident. Yet some features seem to puzzle Bowker. The *proem* text, it is deduced, must have
been derived from the Targum[103] – which is, to say the least, unusual.
Again, Bowker describes Acts 13: 22–41 as 'a typical *proem* homily',[104]
but it is not clear whether he regards 13: 17–21 ('an introduction, linking
the *seder* reading with the *proem* text')[105] as wholly appropriate in a
formal sense. He admits that 'to some extent the evidence is contradictory'
and that it would appear 'that the speech in Acts cannot be claimed as a
true *proem* homily'; and he concludes: 'the evidence is perhaps just sufficient to warrant the suggestion that it was a sermon in origin, and that at
the time that it was delivered the *proem* homily form was very nearly fixed
and stabilised, but there was still some slight room left for manoeuvre
within it'.[106]

The curious form of 1 Sam. 13: 14 (whether or not in combination with
Ps. 89: 21 and Is. 44: 28) may be explained by the fact that the verse is well
and truly 'peshered'.[107] The whole introduction, therefore, while no doubt
relating to the synagogue lections as is fitting in a synagogue setting, is
governed by the eschatological standpoint of Christian belief and reaches
its climax not with David at v. 22 but with Jesus the Saviour in v. 23. This
fact must be recognised in any attempt at final analysis. The introduction
(16–23) forms, in effect, a theme statement, in which God's purpose for
his people is traced from the Exodus (v. 17f.), through the Settlement (v.
19f.) and the Kingdom (v. 21f.), to Jesus (v. 23). Then comes the witness
of John to Jesus (v. 24f.), which is probably an extension of the theme
statement. There follows a somewhat sonorous transition to the major
thesis of the address: 'to us has been sent the message of this salvation'
(v. 26): a message centred on the mission, death and resurrection of Jesus
(vv. 26–33) and elucidated by specific *testimonia*,[108] with midrashic
commentary (v. 34–37). The conclusion (vv. 38–41), with inherent appeal,
is the proclamation of the meaning of Jesus' work for the hearers, together
with a warning couched in the words of Hab. 1: 5. The formal structure of
the sermon is thus:

Theme statement	:	13: 16–25
Theme development	:	13: 26–37
Conclusion	:	13: 38–41

As a Christian address delivered in the fashion of a homily in a Jewish
synagogue, its procedures are necessarily sophisticated. It probably passed,

in the synagogue setting, as a sectarian address, which might be expected to strain the conventions – sometimes to breaking point: the backlash came the following sabbath (13: 44f., 50). An approximation was made to the form and procedures of the *proem* homily, with *proem* text and reference to *seder* and *haftarah*; but the conventions were broken by the power of Christian *pesher*, which radically reorientated the form and substance of the address. The apparent starting point in scripture permitted the preacher to preserve the conventional Jewish development from scripture to current event, but in fact his thinking was dominated by his Christian eschatology which provided the implicit starting point and impetus. As the Jewish preacher kept the *haftarah* constantly in mind,[109] so the Christian preacher constantly related his Christian standpoint, implicity or explicitly, to the scriptures he was using.

Acts 13: 16–41 thus represents the prime example of the formal transition from the *proem* type synagogue homily to Christian *paraclesis*, consisting of a thematic address or sermon. The form that is adumbrated may be characterised as follows: a unity of theme is discernible throughout; a leading theme statement, encapsulating a basic Christian standpoint (it might therefore be 'peshered' scripture or contemporary experience), is developed by means of a recital of revelatory events and 'peshered' texts, the relevance of which tends to be spelled out to the hearers; and a conclusion, related to the initial theme statement and marked by eschatological intensity and existential concern, usually includes the notes of appeal or admonition (or, alternatively, it might be doxological). The genius of Acts 13: 16–41 lies in the fact that it takes the use of the law seriously before showing the ultimate insufficiency of the law. It also demonstrates the use of the kind of recital which had an Old Testament pedigree and an intertestamental expression,[110] and was now becoming a stock Christian homiletic device.

The pattern of Acts 2: 14–36 is analogous. Here the address begins explicitly with the current event, viz., the Pentecostal phenomena (vv. 14ff.), to which is applied explicit Christian *pesher* procedure: 'this is what was spoken by the prophet Joel' (v. 16). The form in which the citation of Joel 2: 28–32 occurs indicates interpretative rewording, as the inserted phrases 'in the last days' and 'God declares' suggest.[111] The *theme statement* (vv. 14–21) therefore consists largely of Christian *pesher*. Thereafter, the *theme development* (vv. 22–34) contains a recital of Jesus' ministry, death and resurrection, including further *pesher* on Pss. 16: 8–11; 132: 11 and 110: 1. The main body of the address thus amounts to a validation of the *pesher* standpoint expressed in the theme statement. The *conclusion* is a proclamation of Jesus as Lord and Christ (v. 36): i.e., as 'eschatological event', the call to repentance (vv. 38ff.) being implied by the nature of the proclamation.

It is virtually a commonplace of New Testament criticism that the speech of Stephen in Acts 7: 2–53 does not belong to the context of his martyrdom but is essentially a hellenistic synagogue sermon,[112] perhaps recalling the kind of recital given in the synagogue on feast days,[113] but presenting Christian *kerygma*. And, indeed, it is feasible to identify Gen. 12: 1 as a possible *proem* text, Ex. 33: 12 – 34: 9 as the *seder*, and Is. 65: 22 – 66: 5 as the *haftarah*.[114] But this is no synagogue homily. With its long exposition of Jewish history[115] and its concern with the 'fathers',[116] it is clearly directed to a Jewish audience but from a minority standpoint which is defined by the Christian 'peshering' of the scriptures[117] and resembles in some respects that of the sectarians of Qumran.[118] Formally, its most notable feature is that the *theme development*, with its long recital (7: 2–50), precedes the *theme statement* ('you always resist the Holy Spirit. As your fathers did, so do you': 7: 51; cf. 7: 53), which is held back to increase its ultimate impact. The *conclusion* is then speedily reached: like their fathers who killed the prophets, they have murdered and betrayed the Righteous One (v. 52). The eschatological significance of such an action is self-evident. It would appear that Luke has made use of a typical pattern of Christian preaching in the mission to the hellenistic Jews[119] – probably one associated in the tradition with the Hellenists if not with Stephen himself – and adapted it to the dramatic situation of Stephen's martyrdom.[120]

From the rich diversity of Diaspora Judaism[121] the Christian missionary preachers had much to gain. The Areopagus speech (Acts 17: 22–31), which draws considerably from the hellenistic ethos (cf. vv. 24–29),[122] has been described as 'a typical exemplar of the first Christian sermons to the Gentiles'.[123] Its setting is that of encounter in disputation both with Jews and God-fearers in the synagogue (v. 17) and, more immediately, with Stoics, Epicureans and others in the Agora (v. 18) – the Christian missionary thus of necessity playing the role of the wandering preacher and presumably resorting to the methods of the diatribe.[124] The starting point of the discourse is engagement particularly with the 'unknown god' of Athenian religiosity and generally with idolatry (cf. the speech at Lystra, 14: 15ff.). Its development makes use of the notion of the religious quest of mankind (17: 26ff.; cf. Rom. 1: 19f.) and God's 'overlooking' of the 'times of ignorance' (cf. Acts 17: 30; cf. 14: 16). Up to this point Jewish propaganda had probably prepared the way for the Christian preacher.[125] The climax of the discourse, however, proclaims the divine summons to repentance in an eschatological context described in specifically Christian terms. The theme is the revelation of the God hitherto unknown (17: 23b), or the necessity to 'turn from the vain things to a living God' (14: 15b). Even the condensed version of the Areopagus speech in Acts suggests systematic and progressive development, including the *introduction* and *theme statement* (v. 22f.), the *theme development* (vv. 24–29), and the *conclusion* implying God's action in the present ('but now') and embracing the call to repentance (v. 30) with its eschatological and christological undergirding (v. 31): thus God is known through his revelation of himself in Christ.[126]

A remarkable example of 'pearl stringing' in a Christian discourse occurs in Heb. 11, where the theme (11: 1–3) is developed by a catena of examples, in scriptural order (vv. 4–31), concluding with a generalised summary (vv. 32–40).[127] It may well be that Heb. 11 is part of a larger homiletic structure incorporated in the epistle.[128] Thus, a homiletic theme on 'faith and endurance' (cf. 10: 32, 36, 39) seems to begin towards the end of chapter 10.[129] The 'peshered' form of Hab. 2: 3f. (cf. Is. 26: 20) in Heb. 10: 37f. may be held to correspond to the *proem* text in synagogue homiletics:[130] the 'vision' (made concrete as 'the coming one') is slow to be realised, but the righteous man lives by faith – a faith that includes patient waiting and quiet endurance inspired by examples of the faithful. Thus chapter 11 exemplifies the faith that involves the assurance and conviction of things not yet seen or realised in the visible world – the 'not yet' of the writer's eschatology;[131] chapter 12 develops the 'not yet' in terms of *hypomonē* (v. 1) and *paideia* (vv. 9ff.). Throughout, the exegesis is based on 'Jesus the pioneer and perfecter of our faith, who for the joy that was set before him endured the cross, despising the shame, and is seated at the right hand of the throne of God' (v. 2). The conclusion is extensive (vv. 12–29), exhorting the hearers in the immediate task of Christian living, illustrating the glory of the heavenly Jerusalem by means of a contrast with the revelation at Sinai and culminating on a high eschatological note. In short, Heb. 10: 32 – 12: 29 reflects a model of Christian preaching which has developed from procedures derived from synagogue preaching but which is acquiring Christian sophistication as it is organised to express deep insights into Christian existence.[132]

One general observation may not be without importance. The recital form is appropriate to the *magnalia* both of ancient Israel and of the early church (cf. 1 Cor. 15: 3–8) because their focus is historical events which must be communicated and interpreted through narrative. Such procedures, involving a high degree of selection and imaginative insight, spring not so much from systematic theology as from homiletic practice. That is as true of the covenantal recitals of the Deuteronomist as it is of early Christian preaching; equally, it is an appropriate medium for the psalmist. In approaching the study of biblical material through such perspectives, allowance must always be made for 'the preacher's awful licence'. A strong element in *Heilsgeschichte* is homiletics![133]

More elaborate thematic forms of Christian 'paraclesis'

Paul's letters provide evidence of the more strictly thematic type of *paraclesis*. Though not written as sermons, some of his letters are clearly intended to convey a message which he would have delivered personally in a sermon to the assembled community had the opportunity been given him (Rom. 1: 10f.; cf. 15: 23, 32). It would therefore be surprising if in composing such a letter he did not, consciously or unconsciously, reflect his homiletic procedures, even if necessarily in condensed form.

Rom. 1: 1–15 is epistolary, like 15: 14–33 and 16 *passim*.[134] Apart from the introductory remarks (1: 1–15) which, however, conclude with Paul's assertion that he is 'eager to preach the gospel to you also who are in Rome', the substance of the letter begins with what looks like a statement of homiletic theme in vv. 16f., which can be subdivided into four parts: 'I am not ashamed of the gospel. It is the power of God for salvation to everyone who responds in faith (a), to the Jew first and also to the Greek (b). For in it the righteousness of God is revealed through faith for faith (c); as it stands written: "He who is righteous through faith shall live." ' (d). But if this is a theme statement, how do we identify the homily which develops it?[135]

Rom. 1: 18–32 is antithetical to the theme statement (part (a)) in that it deals with the wrath of God as opposed to the salvation he offers, but as in the theme statement (a) salvation is available to everyone who has faith, so in the subsequent passage the judgment of God falls on 'all ungodliness and wickedness of men', who are without excuse because of God's revelation of his nature in the created order – without excuse, indeed, *whoever they are* (2: 1; cf. (b)). Here, the area of discourse is subtly extended to include Jews (the Gentiles having borne the brunt so far) and to open up the possibility of salvation to all: God's forbearance and kindness is not to be presumed upon but is meant to lead men to salvation (2: 4). Judgment and salvation therefore concern all, the Jew first and also the Greek, the theme words (1: 16c) being repeated at 2: 9 and 2: 10. At this point, the discourse has established that 'God shows no partiality' (2: 11; cf. Deut. 10: 17) either in judgment or salvation.[136]

This confident and, to some, startling thesis receives necessary expansion in 2: 12–29, in which it is demonstrated how the Gentiles can be 'doers of the law' (vv. 12–16) and how the Jew, instructed in the law and circumcised, may be totally disobedient (vv. 17–24). Thus, when true circumcision is understood in terms of total obedience to God, Jew and Gentile are once again seen as being in a comparable, if not equal, position in the sight of God (2: 25-29).

The obvious objection is anticipated: 'Then does the Jew not have any advantage? Has circumcision no value?' (3: 1) – to which Paul gives a strong affirmative. The Jews received 'the oracles of God' (3: 2), and God does not break his pledge (3: 3ff.). But the Jew cannot complain of God's unfaithfulness or injustice if God pronounces judgment against his unfaithfulness, nor can he draw any antinomian conclusions from it. Therefore, in relation to the question of obedience, Jews are in fact no better off than Gentiles. All, both Jews and Greeks (3: 9 again repeats the theme), are under the power of sin, a point illustrated by *haruzin* exposition (3: 10-18). Thus the law effectively shows the plight of all men, made aware of their sinfulness by the law and helpless to remedy it (3: 20). Parts (a) and (b) of the theme statement have thus been fully discussed.

Then comes the positive solution (cf. part (c)), which is given by the grace of God as a gift (3: 24) to all, *without distinction* (3: 22b).[137] The divine grace, manifesting itself on the cross and capable of reception only by faith (3: 25), shows the extent of God's righteousness and forbearance. In a series of rhetorical questions, human 'boasting' is eliminated, not on the principle of works of the law but on that of faith, by which alone man is accepted by God as just (3: 28). And – repeating the (b) motif once again – this applies to *all* mankind, Jew and Gentile alike (3: 29f.), without abrogating the authority of the law (3: 31).

Chapter 4 is closely related to the foregoing argument, not only because 'here the scriptural evidence is marshalled for the theme of the righteousness of faith which has been expounded in 3: 21-31',[138] but also because it provides the exposition of the remaining part (d) of the initial thematic statement, 'he who through faith is righteous shall live' (1: 17b). Abraham is the prototype of the believer, and is the model for uncircumcised and circumcised alike (4: 10ff.). His true descendants are those who share his faith (4: 16b). Despite all the odds, he never wavered in the trust he put in God and his promises (4: 20f.) – in the God 'who gives life to the dead and calls into existence the things that do not exist' (4: 17b). Thus, 'belief in God's power of resurrection is identical with belief in justification',[139] the first being both the presupposition and the ratification of the latter. The basis of Abraham's faith was the promise. The Christian has before him the reality of the cross and resurrection of Christ (4: 23ff.).

It can hardly be disputed that 1: 18 – 4: 25 gives a closely reasoned exposition of the theme stated in 1: 16f.[140] Structurally, it falls into two main parts: (i) 1: 18 – 3: 20, and (ii) 3: 21 – 4: 25. The development is by antithesis: (i) stands in antithesis to the theme statement, which is positively developed in (ii). (i) and (ii) are thus antithetical to each other. This love of antithesis in homiletic structure is a rabbinic characteristic. The antithetical sub-themes are skilfully interrelated, however, as in 2: 6-10. Another structural unifier is the insistence on the fundamental similarity of Jew and Gentile, in the thematic statement (1: 16), the first main section (2: 1, 9ff., 26, 28f.; 3: 9), and the second (3: 22, 29f.; 4: 9-12, 16f.). This unifier is absent from chapters 5-8, thus underlining the structural homogeneity of 1: 16 - 4: 25 and differentiating this structure from that of the four subsequent chapters.[141]

That Paul is at least reflecting his homiletic style in the early chapters of Romans has been widely admitted. C. H. Dodd, while not suggesting independent composition, commented that this section 'seems to follow the lines of a sermon or sermons which Paul must often have had occasion to deliver, probably when he was debating in the synagogue'.[142] W. L. Knox said of the earlier part: 'the form is a deliberate parody of the portentous grandiloquence with which the synagogue preacher encouraged his Jewish hearers to thank God that they were not as other men are and to encourage the Gentiles among them to become proselytes'.[143] We have argued further that Rom. 1: 16 - 4: 25 is in fact a coherent unit, a thematic homily antithetical in structure and expounding systematically the initial statement of theme (1: 16f.).

Briefly, two further examples may be taken from Paul's correspondence. As in Romans, Paul's opening remarks in 1 Corinthians lead him to emphasise his preaching mission (1 Cor. 1: 17; cf. Rom. 1: 15); and he then proceeds to advance a theological proposition which, in conjunction with a scriptural quotation (Is. 29: 14)[144] and the succeeding discourse, appears to operate as a theme statement (1: 18f.; cf. 3: 19f.): 'the word of the cross is folly to those who are perishing, but to us who are being saved it is the power of God'.[145] The first part of the discourse (1: 20- 2: 5) takes up the question of divine and human wisdom in highly rhetorical vein and with much use of antithesis, reaching a climax in the gospel statement at 1: 23f., which serves to restate the theme. After further rhetorical development (vv. 25-31), Paul rounds off this part with his personal testimony (2: 1-5), corresponding to the halachic digression of rabbinic practice.[146] The second main part (2: 6 - 3: 17), standing in antithesis to the first, focuses upon the 'wisdom' Paul does preach (2: 6): the hidden wisdom of God, revealed by the Spirit, totally different from 'the spirit of the world'.[147] Using the images of the gardener and the master builder, Paul emerges with the notion of the church as the temple of God (3: 16f.) and brings his argument to a rhetorical and eschatological climax in 3: 18-23. On this analysis, 1 Cor.

1:18 - 3:23 is seen to reflect the structure of thematic *paraclesis*, developed systematically and by antithesis on a stated theme (1:18).

The second example is provided by Rom. 9-11, a self-contained unit as many commentators have noted.[148] Structurally, 9:1-5 is a statement of theme (although highly personalised): and the theme is Israel, whom God called 'My son, my first-born' (Ex. 4:22). Paul pours out his anguish at the present plight of Israel, with whom he is identified by race, a plight that is all the more deplorable when contrasted with their great religious heritage.

The first main section (9:6-29) picks up the natural response to the antithesis between Israel's sacred role and its present position, viz., the suggestion that God has not kept his word (9:6). By *haruzin* exposition, Paul demonstrates the outworking and implications of God's election (vv. 7-13).[149] This evokes two further objections: is God unjust? (vv. 14-18); and, how can God find fault with man, if his will is irresistible? (vv. 19-29). Paul's response to both objections relies once more upon *haruzin* from both law and prophets. Here Hos. 1:10 and 2:23 and the doctrine of the remnant in Is. 10:22f. are particularly important: if this address was ever given in a synagogue setting, it is possible to imagine it linking well with *haftarath* which included Is. 10:20-23. In the next part of his argument, introduced in typically diatribal style, Paul counters the apparent arbitrariness of election by affirming the principle of faith (9:30 - 10:21). No sooner has he accounted for the rejection of the Jews on this score than he reintroduces the note of intense personal concern in his prayer for them (10:1ff.) and leads on to a Christian *pesher* on Christ as the end of the law (10:4-13). Finally a series of rhetorical questions and *haruzin* establishes that 'faith comes from what is heard, and what is heard comes by the preaching of Christ' (v. 17), but Israel remains disobedient. Yet another diatribal device marks the transition to the third main section of the thematic development, in which the faithful remnant is identified (11:1-6). The fact that the rest of Israel is disobedient has become the providential occasion for the enrichment of the Gentiles, who may stand in awe before the graciousness of God but who have no grounds for pride, for they too could fall from grace. And the door is not finally closed on the Jews themselves: 'For if you have been cut out of a naturally wild olive tree and grafted unnaturally into a cultivated olive tree, how much more readily will these natural branches be grafted back into their own tree?' (11:24). And he spells out this *mysterion*: the hardening of Israel until the full number of the Gentiles comes in (v. 25), and then the salvation of all Israel, as scripture says (v. 26). Even when disobedience seems to prevail, the mercy of God is reaching out to men. A doxological conclusion is a fitting climax (vv. 33-36), corresponding to the intensity of feeling with which Paul began the discourse.[150] Thus, when the

theme suggested itself as appropriate within the total structure of this
letter, Paul introduced his well-used material with only a slight abruptness
at 9:1 to betray his mental switch.[151]

Outside the Pauline corpus, we have already identified a homiletic structure in Hebrews which followed the rabbinic 'pearl stringing' practice. From
the point of view of form, Hebrews is a peculiar document,[152] with an
epistolary conclusion but no epistolary introduction and a high degree of
exhortation throughout.[153] A. C. Purdy commented: 'Hebrews as a whole
can hardly be called a homily. It is rather a writing produced by a preacher
and teacher who weaves into the whole materials he has often used'.[154]
Such judgments can only be tested by formal analysis.

Heb. 1: 1–4 has the hallmark of the theme statement: God who has
previously spoken through the prophets has now spoken to us in his Son;
and this final revelation is superior to earlier revelations (1:1) just as its
bearer is superior to lesser divine beings (1:4). The theme development
includes a precise exposition of the theme statement: the Son is greater
than the angels (1:5-14), therefore attend to him (2:1-18); his gospel is
greater than the law of Moses (3:1-6), therefore rejection of Christ is
worse than rejection of Moses (3:7-4:13). Like Israel of old, we may fail
to enter the 'rest' God has provided for his people. This discourse relies
heavily on midrashic 'pearl stringing' and Christian *pesher*: particularly Ps.
8:4ff. (Heb. 2:6ff.), which is the hub of the theme development in the
first two chapters, and Ps. 95:7-11 (Heb. 3:7-11) which is the mainspring
of the remainder of the development (3:1-4:10).[155] Yet the over-all
unity of the discourse is secured both by its own inner logic and by the
balance of introduction (1:1-4) and peroration (4:11ff.). As God has
spoken in past and present, so now the hearer is reminded that the word
of God is living and active (4:12), and before him no creature is hidden
(4:13). The formal structure is that of a thematic homily, developed by
means of antithesis and chiasmus.[156] Thus, if we take the theme statement
as comprising two positive theses about the Son ('A' – he is the heir of all
things (1:2), and 'B' – he reflects the glory of God (1:3)), together with
two corresponding antitheses ('a' – the earlier revelations are secondary
(1:1), and 'b' – angelic beings are inferior (1:4)), then the argument proceeds with a scriptural base as follows:

> An examination of 'b' points to the truth of 'A', therefore
>   hold to 'A'.
> An examination of 'a' points to the truth of 'B', therefore
>   beware of rejecting 'B'.

Although simpler, this structure possesses some similarity to Rom. 1:16 –

4: 25. It is also parallel with the Romans passage in that the theme statement of Hebrews (1: 1–4), like Romans 1: 16f., provides both the theme
for the entire epistle and that of the succeeding argument. It seems reasonable to conclude that the writer is here recalling a homily which he has
previously used, the structure of which is discernible in 1: 1 – 4: 13.

The theme statement (4: 14ff.) for the next part of the homiletic
development (4: 14 - 10: 25) has to be accommodated to the continuing
flow of the epistle as a whole. It has to link specifically with what has
gone before (cf. 4: 14a), and has to maintain the explicit homiletic concern (4: 14b, 16). The theme is the great high priest, Jesus the Son of God
(4: 14b; cf. 10: 21), who endured the temptations of humanity without
succumbing to them (4: 15) and who thus inspires believers with confidence as they approach the 'throne of grace' (4: 16, cf. 10: 22).[157] The
central text is Ps. 110: 4,[158] with which Ps. 2: 7 combines (cf. 1: 5). The
discourse is described as *polus* and *dysermeneutos* (5: 11).

The development of the theme is carried out by a series of antitheses,
with accompanying exhortations. The first is 5: 1–10, where the contrast
is between the 'high priest chosen from among men', and the high priesthood of the Son. This adumbrates the next antithesis, but the matter is of
such intrinsic difficulty (5: 11) that the preacher must prepare his hearers
by means of extensive exhortation (5: 11 - 6: 20), at the close of which he
brings them back precisely to the place where he left off (cf. 5: 10 and 6:
20b). The antithesis now developed is between the priesthood of Melchizedek and that of Aaron (7: 1–28), Christ being 'a high priest for ever
after the order of Melchizedek' (6: 20). The third and culminating antithesis takes up the point that Christ ministers in the heavenly rather than
the earthly sanctuary and consequently the old covenant and the old sanctuary are superseded by the new covenant and the mediatorial work of
Christ whose sacrifice is perfect and unrepeatable (8: 1 - 10: 18). His argument completed, he concludes the discourse on the note of eschatological
exhortation (10: 19–31).

This theme clearly approximates to a type of structure which we have
already met: the progressive theme, antithetically developed. The coherence
of its structure, together with its intense homiletic concern, creates the
strong possibility that it was originally an independent homily[159] which
the author has incorporated skilfully into his written document and made
the hub of his argument.[160]

2 Peter and Jude are related to one another closely enough to justify a
joint consideration of them. The thought and some of the phraseology of
Jude 4–18 are found in a slightly different but easily identifiable form in
2 Pet. 2: 1–18 and 3: 1–3.[161] 'The best assumption is that both epistles

derive from a common tradition which may well have been oral rather than written. Very possibly there was a sermon pattern formulated to resist the seducers of the church. This would explain both the similarities and the differences in a satisfactory fashion.'[162] The correctness or otherwise of this conclusion must be put to the test of formal analysis. Taking the shorter first, does the epistle of Jude lend itself to such an analysis? Can the supposed sermon pattern be identified in it, and is it similar to those we have claimed to identify elsewhere?

The form of the discourse enshrined in the letter may be illustrated as follows:

Theme statement : exhortation to true believers, in view of the enemies within, doomed as they are (3b, 4).

Main body
Introduction : the gracious God also acts in judgment against his enemies, with examples (5–7).

First section : the enemies of God today and the judgment of scripture against them (8–15).

Second section : the enemies of God and the true believers whom the preacher addresses and exhorts (16–23).

The discourse is thematic, beginning and ending with an exhortation to true believers but being concerned primarily with the judgment of God against the enemies and disrupters of the faith. It might well have followed readings from Genesis reflected in the introduction to the main body (5–7). The discourse develops systematically, employing the traditional Jewish pattern of listed examples and making use also of strong contrast or antithesis (cf. 8f., 16ff., 19ff.). Its admonitory note is strengthened with one 'Woe to them', reflecting prophetic admonition. The ascription of praise may be epistolary, although a spoken discourse intended for community use could have ended in this way.

The conclusion that we have here a homiletic outline or pattern can hardly be resisted;[163] it probably represents anti-heresy or apologetic preaching. The writer also preserves something of the warm, friendly yet serious manner in which it would usually be delivered.

From the formal point of view, the interest of 2 Peter lies in the use the writer makes of the apologetic homily so well utilised in Jude[164] and in his adaptation of it to a slightly different purpose.[165] The writer's overriding concern is to urge the recipients of the letter to remain steadfast in the eschatological faith, expressed in terms of the coming of the Lord Jesus at 1:16 but elsewhere as the coming of the Day of the Lord (or of God: cf. 3:12). It is this faith that is under attack from the false prophets and

teachers, and in reply the writer stresses the cosmic nature of the eschatological drama and the urgent need for godly living in face of the Day of
the Lord.[166]

After the epistolary introduction[167] the beginning of a homily is discernible, 1:16–21 representing a slightly extended *theme statement*: the
proclamation of the *parousia* rests not only on myths but on personal
testimony (cf. transfiguration) and on prophecy inspired by the Holy Spirit.

The first part of the main body of the discourse is largely derived from
the apologetic tradition used by Jude. In 2 Peter, it is introduced in antithesis to the last part of the theme statement:[168] There are false prophets
who mislead many, as opposed to the true prophets who speak by the
Spirit. This part may be divided into three sub-sections:

(i) false prophets, their success and impending condemnation
     (2:1–3).
(ii) how the judgment of God operates against the unrighteous,
     especially those who 'indulge in the lust of defiling passion
     and despise authority' (2:4–10).
(iii) denunciation of the unrighteous troublers of the church, the
      'slaves of corruption', whose latter state, having once known
      Christ, is worse than ever (2:10b–22).

The second part of the main body, introduced by an epistolary note,
returns to the main theme by an appeal to 'the prediction of the holy
prophets' (as opposed to the false ones), reinforced by the 'commandment
of the Lord and Saviour through your apostles' (3:2), together with a
renewal of the eschatological emphasis (3:3f.). The remainder of the discourse (3:5–10) is devoted to a defence of traditional eschatology, in
which the 'scoffer' has always figured (3:3f.), and to the ethical consequences of such belief (3:11–18).

It would appear that, after allowance has been made for literary and
epistolary elements, 2 Peter discloses a classic Jewish homiletic structure,
in which the three main parts stand in antithesis to each other in such a
way that the third or concluding part resumes and presses home the leading theme of the first part or introduction.

None of the remaining books of the New Testament appears to be essentially a homily. The epistle of James is sometimes described as such,[169] but
its structure is much too loose and it is preferable to describe it as paraenetic:
'a collection of wise instruction from a highly competent Christian
teacher'.[170] 1 Peter is another epistle which some commentators have cate-
gorised perhaps too precipitately as a sermon – in particular, a baptismal
sermon extending to 4:11, where a break is generally recognised. While a

baptismal concern is evinced at various points (1:2; 3:21), a homiletic or sermonic structure is difficult to identify. There is no theme statement, nor is there a systematic development of thought.[171] The epistle does not correspond to a homily either as a total entity or in most of its parts. The final part (4:12-5:11), taken by some to be addressed to the whole congregation, has perhaps the best claim to be of homiletical derivation. Thus, 4:12f. may well be the theme statement: persecution must be expected and accepted in fellowship with Christ and in an eschatological perspective. The first main section (4:14-19) expands upon the Christian attitude to suffering; the second (5:1-10) is a charge to elders and congregation, highly rhetorical in places (5:2), to carry out their duties in the right spirit, 'knowing that the same experience of suffering is required of your brotherhood throughout the world' (9b). The last note, which might be a condensed conclusion, is the assurance of God's restorative work after suffering endured (10).[172]

Finally, one important consequence of the development of the thematic homily in the early church should be indicated. It provided the framework for a new *Gattung*, the written gospel. Mark, we may assume, had no earlier model on which to fashion his work. He had an abundance of material, provided by church *paraenesis* and *paradosis*. His problem was to weld it together in a coherent whole which would adequately present the gospel of Jesus the Messiah, for his concern was kerygmatic and didactic. One hesitates to characterise Mark's work *simpliciter*, with W. Marxsen, as a *Predigt*.[173] It is not a sermon or homily as it stands; it is a new literary form, which came to be called a *euangelion*. But its framework or structure, like its intent, is unmistakably derived from the thematic homily. Consider the following possible outline:[174]

Theme statement	:	Mark 1:1 (the gospel of Jesus the Messiah).
Part 1		
Introduction	:	Mark 1:2-13 (including the disclosure of the Messiah and his confrontation with evil).
Main body	:	Mark 1:14f. (programmatic) - 8:26 (the ministry of the veiled Messiah, actualising the kingdom).
Part 2		
Introduction	:	Mark 8:27 - 9:8 (confession of Messiah; Messiahship and the cross).
Main body	:	Mark 9:9 - 15:47 (the way to the

cross, the crucifixion of the King,
death, burial).

Conclusion and climax   : Mark 16: 1–8 (the resurrection).

The more lyrical homily

Many commentators have seen 1 John as not so much a letter, more a tract
or homily.[175] To seek confirmation of such judgments by means of formal
analysis is by no means easy, because the author adopts a peculiar, convoluted style which develops by means of its inherent gyrations and consequently yields only with great difficulty to any superimposed pattern.

The document begins with a clearly defined prologue or exordium (1:
1–4) enshrining the theme, which is no other than the original *kerygma* of
the church, rooted in the beginnings of things (cf. Gen. 1: 1; John 1: 2).
'What is proclaimed as tangibly experienced is the primal divine reality
manifested both as life and truth.'[176]

The contours of the rest of the discourse, however, can be discerned
only by close analysis.[177] A unit of importance is the tightly constructed
1: 5–10.[178]

God is light; (a)
in him is no darkness at all. (b)

If we say we have fellowship with him and walk in darkness, (a)
we lie and do not do the truth. (b)
But if we walk in the light as he is in the light, (a)
we have fellowship with one another (b)
and the blood of Jesus his son cleanses us from all sin. (c)

If we say that we have no sin, (a)
we deceive ourselves and the truth is not in us, (b)
If we confess our sins, (a)
he is faithful and just, so that he will forgive our sins (b)
and cleanse us from all unrighteousness. (c)

If we say that we have not sinned, (a)
we make him a liar and his word is not in us. (b)

This appears to be a hymn or poem,[179] which may well have been composed and in use before the writing of this epistle.[180] 1 John 2: 1–17,
which includes commentary on the hymn, has all the marks of being composite. Its unity derives mainly from the intimacy of the epistolary address
which the writer adopts, although the individual groupings have their own
integrity of structure. R. Bultmann has suggested the possibility of discerning a source which the author has broken up to suit his purpose as com-

mentator.[181] Reconstructed, it reads as follows:

> He who says 'I know him' but disobeys his commandments
> is a liar, and the truth is not in him;   (2:4)
> but whoever keeps his word,
> in him truly love for God is perfected.   (2:5a)
> He who says he is in the light and hates his brother
> is in the darkness still.   (2:9)
> He who loves his brother abides in the light
> and in it there is no cause for stumbling.   (2:10)
> But he who hates his brother is in the darkness
> and walks in the darkness.   (2:11a)

These five couplets, introduced with one exception (5a) by *ho* and the present participle, present a remarkable counterpart to five of the couplets of the 'hymn of light'.[182] It may well be that the basis of the first section is the 'hymn of light' containing eleven couplets in all. The source would appear to emanate from a highly rhetorical and poetic milieu, probably to be associated with prophecy.

The next section of the epistle is both polemical and eschatological (2:18-25).[183] E. von Dobschütz anticipated Bultmann's source criticisms in a study of 2:28 – 3:12, in which he identified as basic, prior material four couplets containing antithetical parallelism, which are surrounded in the text by commentary.[184]

> Every one who does right is born of him.   (2:29)
> Every one who commits sin is guilty of lawlessness.   (3:4)
> No one who abides in him sins;
> No one who sins has ever seen him.   (3:6)
> He who does right is righteous.   (3:7b)
> He who commits sin is of the devil.   (3:8a)
> No one born of God commits sin.   (3:9a)
> No one who does not do right is of God.   (3:10b)

As well as the formal unity of each couplet, this grouping can appeal to a common ethical concern presented in a common religious perspective. The total unity, however, is not quite so convincing as that of the 'hymn of light'. This is probably due to the way the author has split up the couplets, varying their contents slightly in the process. Besides, other material makes a fair approximation to those listed above; for example, 2:23:

> No one who denies the Son has the Father.
> He who confesses the Son has the Father also.

Sometimes, a line gives the impression of being one limb of such a couplet: 'Everyone who has this hope in him purifies himself' (3: 3a). The conclusion must be that there is evidence here of a source in the form of balanced couplets, probably related to the 'hymn of light' source, but worked over much more severely by the author, so that it is reflected here rather than cited.

1 John 4: 1-6 is another polemical section which recalls the tenor of 2: 18-25. The object of attack is the false prophets, whose pneumatic exercises are, however, no guarantee of their validity. There is considerable formal pattern to the warnings against false teachers, both in 2: 18-25 and 4: 1-6,[185] the author once again making use of church *didache*.

In 4: 7-21, there is also a strong impression that sources of some kind are in use, but they have been worked over to such an extent as to defy precise reconstruction. A number of couplets is visible.[186] Perhaps, however, there is in the background a 'hymn of love', embodying the essence of Johannine teaching and employing the shorter line for maximum effect:

Love is of God.
He who loves is born of God
and knows God.
For God is love.   (4: 7f.)

No man has ever seen God.
If we love one another,
God abides in us,
and his love is made perfect in us.   (4: 12)

God is love.
He who abides in love
abides in God,
and God abides in him.   (4: 16)

This suggestion helps to explain the repetitiveness and circularity of this section - excessive even for this writer. Around the hymn, the writer constructs his commentary, using homiletic exhortations (4: 7, 11), definitive statements (4: 9f., 13, 17) and didactic material, including material of a confessional nature (4: 14ff., 18-21).

The chapter division at 5: 1 is artificial, for there is no essential break in the narrative. Beginning with a couplet followed by a definitive statement (5: 1f.), the writer once again links faith and love. A catechetical pattern may be discerned at 5: 5. In his final paragraph (5: 6-12), he is concerned with testimony - not least with the testimony of the Spirit (5: 7f.) - and his climactic point is once again a couplet:

He who has the Son has life;
he who has not the Son of God has not life.   (5: 12)

The remainder of the chapter is clearly epistolary (5:13), structured around the theme of knowledge.[187]

To conclude our survey of the document as it stands, the following outline analysis might be offered:

1:1-4		Introduction to letter
1:5-2:17	(A)	The children of God - the 'hymn of light', with appropriate commentary.
2:18-27	(B)	The children of God and of antichrist (polemical).
2:28-3:24	(A)	The children of God - their way of life.
4:1-6	(B)	The children of God and of antichrist (polemical).
4:7-5:12	(A)	The children of God - the 'hymn of love' with interspersed commentary, and the divine witnesses.
5:13-20		Conclusion of letter.

The document as it stands is in epistolary form though lacking the usual kind of epistolary formulae in the introduction and conclusion. Despite its apparent meanderings, repetitions and recapitulations, its structure follows the lines of simple antithesis, corresponding to the antithetical characteristics of the author's style and material. In what other ways can it be described? Rhetorical? Very much so - in the introduction, the rhetorical elaboration is almost painful. Homiletic? Yes, indeed, although in its present form it is a letter - however peculiar. The strongly kerygmatic and didactic notes indicate that, despite its epistolary form, 1 John reflects the kind of discourse the author might give orally and is therefore close to a lyrical type of homily, to be compared to the 'interpretation' that expounds prophetic utterance. At least the 'hymn of light' and the 'hymn of love' should be assigned to Christian prophecy, and the author himself suggests this debt in his reference to the testimony of the Spirit.[188] 1 John appears to enshrine in its innermost being several elevated poetic passages, not unintelligible in themselves but requiring elucidation and commentary. That the writer handles the original utterances with a certain freedom, interleaving didactic commentary, suggests that they may well be the creations of his own exalted experiences or that they have become wholly integrated with his own thinking.[189]

To attempt here even a brief summary of the findings of this chapter would be superfluous. Broadly speaking *paraclesis* proceeded on the basis of the fundamentals of Christian *pesher* and *paradosis* and contributed directly to the building up of the Christian exegetical tradition. It was always contemporary, related to the situation of the hearers (and therefore, like so much Greek preaching, an essentially popular medium of communication). Closely associated with *paraenesis*, it helped to define the Christian way of life. It took its place in the developing liturgy of the church, contributing directly to its language and structure; and it put to the service of the church the resources of creative imagination and of rhetoric, recital and antithesis being two leading aspects – all of which became landmarks in the articulation and clarification of Christian meaning.

While the New Testament uses the term *paraclesis*, such preaching occurs as *homilia* in Justin (*Apol.* 1: 67); after the fourth century, *sermo* (or *sermo popularis*) was common.[190] The *Gattung* under discussion is undoubtedly one of the most characteristic and persistent phenomena in Christendom.

3

PARAENESIS AND *CATECHESIS*

So it is not a piece of *paraclesis* that I have produced for your benefit, but rather *paraenesis*. (Isocrates)[1]

I would rather speak five words with my mind, in order to instruct others, than ten thousand words in a tongue. (St Paul)[2]

Paraenesis in the Graeco-Roman world

The *paraclesis* which Isocrates rejected as an adequate vehicle for the moral education of his young acquaintance Demonicus consisted of the kind of exhortatory discourse beloved of the sophists, those virtuosos of the art of eloquence and persuasion, whose aim in lecturing was primarily to give instruction to students on how to succeed in public life.[3] Though not without skill in this type of oratory, Isocrates adopted a more direct, instructional model for moral teaching: *paraenesis*, in which exhortation was intimately concerned with the practical problems of living.[4]

This enthusiasm for moral teaching was, of course, shared by more authentic philosophers than many of the paraenetic teachers actually were themselves: by Socrates, for instance, whose view that virtue is knowledge of the good presupposes that it can be taught. Living, like Plato and Aristotle after him, in what has been called 'the glow and the afterglow of the Periclean age in Athens', Socrates was able to bring a certain optimism to his view of the world which was alien to later teachers but which provided the essential grounds of his teleology. Those later teachers, whether Stoics, Cynics or others, rejected what seemed to them the weighty and tortuous intellectualism of the Academy and sought for instant solutions. Yet such popular teachers did not entirely reject the work of the great philosophers, however impatient they were with their successors and imitators; but their philosophic concerns and their methods[5] were adapted for the popular market, and certain of the great philosophers themselves were taken as symbols of the philosophic quest and of virtue: Socrates, with what A. H. Armstrong calls 'his straightforward and simple moral rectitude, his ease in well-doing';[6] Plato, with his theory of forms and *anamnesis,* his hints of other-worldliness, his myths and his recognition of the importance of emotions; Aristotle, with his analysis of ethics, his concern for teleology, his careful study of this-worldly phenomena and his relating of them to the transcendent, his stress upon disposition and contemplation. Examples from their careers, stories they told, and *dicta* which had become virtually fixed, philosophical tradition were the stock in trade of the teachers of the market place. The great fourth-century philosophers represented a kind of reference library from which a teacher could abstract whatever material he wished; and the library was extended by the accretion of the leading teachers of the popular schools, such as Diogenes and Zeno.

Paraenesis itself, unlike the diatribal procedures which characterise *paraclesis*,[7] tends to brevity and to a simple succession of imperatival units. Moreover, it is concerned with intimate, personal counsel on moral and spiritual issues, with down-to-earth practical advice as part of the education of the recipient. According to Aristotle, it was the kind of teaching appropriately given only by the more elderly teacher, on matters of which he has some experience.[8] Its dominant characteristic is its adherence to the popular, gnomic wisdom, passed on from generation to generation and frequently embodied in ancient poetry and other traditions.

A brief résumé is given below of the leading formal characteristics of *paraenesis*, which will help to structure the present discussion and facilitate comparisons of paraenetic forms in different cultural settings.

The paraenetic topic

The word *topos*[9] is used in rhetoric to denote a commonplace – the proper subject of dialectical and rhetorical syllogisms – which may deal with such questions as justice or politics and may be of various, identifiable types.[10] In relation to *paraenesis*, it denotes a particular topic of moral concern. Xenophon gives a list of such *topoi* in the teaching of Socrates: courage, wisdom, prudence, justice, madness, envy, leisure, kings and rulers:[11] together with a string of aphorisms on less momentous matters.[12] In Isocrates, the subject matter ranges from the ideals of honour, virtue, self-control and healthful enjoyment to the problem of correct dress and prudence in public life.

A minimal *topos*[13] may consist only of a sentence or so, devoted to one subject and including an imperatival or gnomic sentiment.[14] Isocrates on the whole follows the imperatival type of topic. 'Fear the gods; honour your parents; show respect to your friends; obey the laws.'[15] 'Act towards your parents as you would wish your children to act towards you.'[16] The *topos* may be extended by various devices, such as an adverbial clause of reason: 'Don't take delight in violent laughter and don't engage in brazen talk, for the one is foolish and the other senseless.'[17] Further extensions by means of antitheses or contrasts, illustrations, similes, proverbs or quotations bring the *topos* up to the dimensions of a paragraph. Here is a typical example, on 'material possessions':

'Do not make your aim the excessive acquisition of material goods, but the moderate enjoyment of them. Despise those who are eager for wealth yet are not able to make good use of what they already have, for they are like a man who has obtained a fine horse but is himself too wretched a horseman to ride it. Try to make your wealth something that is for use rather than a mere possession. It is something for use when people know how to enjoy it, but a mere possession to those who are able only to acquire it. Treasure what you possess for two reasons: so that you can withstand a great emergency, and so that you can help a friend in dire straits. Otherwise, strive after wealth in moderation but not excessively.'[18]

The cohesion of the unit is sealed by the repetition in the last line of the sentiment of the first line. Otherwise, one notes the continued use of imperatives, the causal extensions and the use of the simile. Other devices frequently used include questions, rhetorical or otherwise, sometimes providing a framework for the build up of the *topos*; and conditional clauses, allowing discussion of hypothetical circumstances. Occasionally, the *topos* may be introduced by the preposition *peri*; Marcus Aurelius has three such *topoi* in succession: 'About death', 'About pain', and 'About glory'.[19]

One limitation of *topoi* is their generality. Ethical teaching of any value, however, must be related to the real world where the ideal is not always practical and where accommodations have to be made and tensions accepted. The *topoi* have a formula for dealing with the principle of relativity. 'Avoid banquets given by strangers or ignorant people. But if ever you find that you must take part, concentrate carefully on not adopting the manners of the vulgar.'[20] In the event of one's being involved in less desirable situations, a particular course is recommended to obviate the worst ills that may result.

The advantage of the *topos* lies in the direct, practical advice that it offers with clarity and a marked lack of equivocation. It assumes not merely a basis of authority – although the teacher's authority is a fundamental assumption – but also rational procedures; and by using figurative devices it can tease the mind into active thought. It also assumes the unity of thought and action, and is therefore a useful vehicle for the educationist like Isocrates and the philosopher like Epictetus or Marcus Aurelius. In short, the *topos* in hellenistic usage is an extremely flexible unit of *paraenesis*, capable of great variation of subject matter, treatment and tone, and related to practical and fundamental issues of living.

Topical figures

The *topos* frequently includes various figures, such as simple or extended

similes and metaphors, parables, allegories, fables and myths. The most
common is the simile, the usefulness of which is not confined to mere
illustration; it can also stimulate the mind to explore the image further
in search of illumination.[21]

A well-known example occurs in Livy, who describes a historical situation in which Menenius Agrippa used the parable of the limbs of the body
to help quell a revolt and reconcile the dissidents to the state.[22] In this
case, it is essential that the parable uses an acceptable image: viz., the interdependence of the members of the body and their essential coherence.
Thereafter, it must suggest a relevant analogy with the situation which has
polarised the antagonistic parties. It can then be instrumental in reconciling
the dissidents by inducing them to accept another dimension of reality as
of overriding concern. To achieve that end, it has to bring them to the
point of decision.

The 'two ways'

The simple antitheses so common in the *topoi* as well as in the homily lead
to a distinctive motif in paraenetic teaching which is singled out here because of the frequency with which it appears in the various traditions and
its correspondence to a deep-set dualism in ethical teaching.[23] The implication of this dichotomy for *paraenesis* is that the teacher must attempt to
give his pupils an understanding of the ethical issue and to encourage them
to come to a decision about it.

Catalogues of virtues and vices

The rhetorical practice of cataloguing virtues and vices can be traced, at
least in its negative form, to the Pythagorean and Orphic societies.[24] The
Stoics, clinging to the notion that virtue is based on knowledge and vice on
ignorance, listed the virtues as intelligence, bravery, justice and self-control.[25]
Similarly, passion could be analysed as grief, fear, desire or pleasure.[26] The
basic procedure can be seen in Aristotle, who makes restrained use of the
catalogue method in establishing the mean between the extremes of excess
and deficiency.[27] A popular expression of it is to be seen in the game of
draughts in which the individual counters bore the name of a vice.[28]

The 'Haustafeln'

The term *Haustafeln*[29] denotes a type of *paraenesis* which not only occurs
in the New Testament but has pagan and Jewish antecedents as well as a
persistent role down through Mediaeval Christendom.

No *Haustafeln* in the strictly formal sense occur in the Graeco-Roman
world, but some approximations to them are found and their general spirit

is well represented. The accepted basis of them is the unwritten, moral law, 'the unwritten and sure requirements of the gods', in Antigone's words;[30] and among these the Xenophontic Socrates highlights reverence for the gods and honour to parents, the sacrosanct nature of family relationships and the obligations of friendship.[31] Epictetus has a famous passage in which the aspiring pupil comes forward and says: 'Speaking as a man of piety, philosophy and diligence, I want to know what my duty is to the gods, to my parents, to my brother, to my country, to strangers'.[32] With the 'honouring' included in such obligations goes an ethic of submission. 'Is someone a father? My teaching is that you should care for him and yield to him in all matters, submitting when he reproaches you and when he inflicts corporal punishment.'[33] The emphasis varies as the 'unwritten laws' of Greek custom are transmuted into the *kathēkonta* of Stoic ethics and as the philosophical schools themselves evolve. In early Stoicism, gods and parents are given the leading honours. In middle Stoicism, the state is dominant and the gods have dropped out, while family relationships continue to command considerable attention.[34] By the time of Epictetus, the gods are back and slaves have made an appearance. There is, by the time of the Roman Empire, a tendency to assume a list of duties centred on husband–wife, father–children, and master–slave relationships.[35] This is not to say, however, that the prototype of the New Testament *Haustafeln* is to be located in this hellenistic form.

The farewell discourse

The farewell discourse, which acquires particular weight and poignancy from the situation in which it is delivered, is probably best described as a special form of *paraenesis*, although it can evince a close affinity with other forms such as *paraclesis* and *propheteia*.[36] Examples include the speech of Oedipus, in which he gives specific instructions affecting the future of the city and takes farewell of his friends;[37] and that of Cambyses, in which he lays his last injunctions upon the Persians and reinforces them with blessing or curse.[38] In the Greek tradition generally, the elements of the farewell speech include the recognition by the dying person that death is imminent; a farewell to his friends; a retrospective summary of his life, with or without the element of conscience-searching; and the giving of instructions or transmission of authority to his successors, including directions about his funeral; but not all of these elements occur in any one speech.[39]

Paraenesis in the Jewish tradition

The Jewish tradition is differentiated from the Graeco-Roman in a number of ways, including its longer and closer contacts with the ancient cultures

of Babylon and Egypt to which it owed, among other debts, the beginnings
of its scribal class, but above all it is made unique by the distinctive religion
that informed its every aspect and by the Torah which exerted a determinative influence on the total life of the nation. Thus in moral and religious
education the learning of the Torah and the religious practices of Israel are
of central concern (cf. Deut. 6: 6f.).

With the fixing of the Torah (and later of prophets and writings as well)
in written form, the inherent danger of the apparent irrelevance or inadequacy of ancient prescriptions in relation to contemporary conditions underlined the need for rigorous interpretation to bridge the situational gulf. The
nature of the resultant midrashic interpretation and Jewish hermeneutics
has already been discussed.[40] But apart from specifically exegetical teaching
traditions, there is in Jewish *paideia* a relatively independent paraenetic
tradition that has many points in common with its Graeco-Roman counterpart without being antagonistic to exegesis. Indeed, at certain points – the
later part of Proverbs, for instance, or Sirach – *paraenesis* and exegesis are
effectively fused. By the time of Sirach, however, the wisdom type of
popular instruction had become ingrained in Jewish *paideia*. To this type
of *paraenesis* we now turn.

The paraenetic topic

The emergence of the paraenetic topic in the Jewish world is closely bound
up with the development of the wisdom tradition. The so-called 'Proverbs
of Solomon' (Prov. 10: 1 - 22: 16) consist largely of paraenetic topics of the
short, gnomic variety: for the most part, 'independent sentences, each of
which is intended to be a well-considered and definitive observation on a
particular topic'.[41] According to McKane's classification, three types are
to be distinguished.

> A son who gathers in summer is prudent,
>   but one who sleeps in harvest brings shame. (10: 5)

This kind of saying is related to old wisdom and is concerned with the
moral education of the individual. The use of the indicative mood and the
impersonal but concrete nature of the observation are to be noted.

> Hatred stirs up strife,
>   but love covers all offences. (10: 12)

In this couplet, emphasis is placed on social concern and the harmful
effects of certain kinds of behaviour on the community.

> The Lord does not let the righteous go hungry,
>   but he thwarts the craving of the wicked. (10:3)

Here the saying has taken on the colour of Yahwistic piety and represents a later stage of the tradition. Below this level of reinterpretation lies a saying of the first type.[42] For the study of *paraenesis*, however, more significance must be attached to the subsequent grouping of such gnomic forms. The proverb, however brilliant when an intuitive hermeneutic is properly applied to it, can be pedestrian, puzzling or intellectually limiting if taken literally or improperly understood. It was inevitable that sooner or later proverbs should be built up into larger groupings and amplifications or qualifications added. One type of grouping which uses word jingles[43] and *Stichwörter*,[44] seems designed largely for mnemonic or artistic purposes; but identifiable units, formed by congruity of content, finally emerge as embryonic topics.[45]

Yet the full development of the topic was dependent upon the influences of a second form of wisdom statement, the instruction genre, which eliminated the elusiveness of the gnomic saying by replacing the indicative with the imperative and justifying its commands or exhortations in subordinate clauses expressing motive, purpose or consequence.[46] The instruction sentence in itself does not constitute a full paraenetic topic, although it often contains the germ of one; but when a grouping occurs around a central theme, then the *topos* may be said to have emerged.

> Hear, my son, and be wise,
> > and direct your mind in the way.
> Be not among winebibbers,
> > or among gluttonous eaters of meat;
> for the drunkard and the glutton will come to poverty,
> > and drowsiness will clothe a man with rags.[47]

The rather severe imperatival form can, however, undergo modification. In Prov. 7, there is an instructional sequence at the beginning (1–5) and at the end (24–27), but the centre of the chapter is taken up with a delightfully descriptive passage on the 'adventuress with her smooth words'.[48]

The later wisdom book, Sirach, provides many examples of the paraenetic topic at a point of greater maturation, when hellenistic influence had made its contribution to Jewish *paideia*. In Sirach, the topics range from basic obligations to the poor through a variety of precepts about everyday life to specific counsel for magistrates and rulers (Sir. 10). The characteristics of this type of *topos* include the use of the imperative to impart authoritative counsel, supported by a subordinate clause of reason; but in general there is more flexibility and openness about its use than in the earlier instructional models. There are general statements of a gnomic order, rhetorical questions, antitheses and comparisons, all of which contribute to the 'intuiting' of the *topos* and to the possibility of its throwing light upon one aspect of the human situation.[49]

Topical figures and illustrations

The 'pure' *mashal* or proverb *par excellence* uses particular imagery or material from the concrete world to present a statement that is potentially meaningful for human existence.

> A son who gathers in summer is prudent,
>> but one who sleeps in harvest brings shame. (Prov. 10: 5)

Such a saying is open to interpretation; it can erupt into meaningfulness in a flash of inspiration in which the truth of the proverb, springing from the particularity of its own situation,[50] is seen as applicable to another, comparable situation, i.e., that of the interpreter. It can then be further generalised or universalised: 'it is the testing or critical situation which constitutes the sifting process and provides a reliable indication of ability and character'.[51]

The further development of the didactic tradition leads in a number of directions. In the embryonic *topos* in Prov. 7, the warnings against becoming involved with the immoral woman are reinforced in two ways: first, by an extended and evocative description in the most concrete terms of the woman's contrivances; and second, by a series of similes describing the total doom of any who becomes involved with her (Prov. 7: 22f.). In this *topos* we note the place given to illustration, as well as the continuing use of similes in which the *tertium comparationis* is of a typical, non-controversial nature. The extension of this type of simile leads to the similitude, the kind of parabolic language which relies on a typical situation or recurring event.[52] By contrast, the 'parable proper', i.e., considered as a more precise category, focuses upon one specific case that possesses intrinsic point. 'There were two men in a certain city, the one rich and the other poor. The rich man had many flocks and herds; but the poor man had nothing but one little ewe lamb.' Nathan's parable (2 Sam. 12: 1-4) is the beginning of a paraenetic topic which achieves its impact by bringing David into active participation in the situation (v. 5f.); and after the analogy between the parabolic situation and his own had been brought home to him (vv. 7-12), he realises he has passed judgment on himself and sees his own conduct in a new light (v. 13).[53] The parable, therefore, depends upon the appropriateness and attractiveness of its narrative, carefully prepared and subtly developed by the narrator.[54]

The collection of rabbinic anecdotes in the Mishnah and Talmud[55] tends to divorce rabbinic parables from their original context and to set them alongside other anecdotes recording significant sayings or actions of the rabbis. In other words, they are caught up in a secondary, didactic medium. Clearly, in their original setting they contributed directly and decisively to the topic - frequently of a paraenetic nature - in which they were introduced. They occur in exhortatory contexts, and in scholarly arguments, disputations or controversies.[56] Allegory is also used for paraenetic purposes and represents an elaboration of the riddle (cf. Ezek. 17: 2), veiling the underlying reality while hinting at it and requiring a key to unlock its secret.[57]

The 'two ways'

'Two ways has God given to the sons of men, and two inclinations...all things come in twos, the one over against the other. There are two ways - of good and evil; included in these are the two inclinations in our hearts, discriminating them'.[58] This passage points to the deep-set duality in Jewish ethical thinking, which becomes even more pronounced with the intensification of eschatology and apocalyptic. It is linked to the inherent antithesis between 'the way of righteousness' and 'the way of the wicked'.[59] The 'two inclinations', the *yetzer ha-tov* and the *yetzer ha-ra*,[60] are of course fundamental to rabbinic anthropology. The rabbis gave priority to the question of choosing the right way,[61] and one rabbi described the choice as between 'the way to Eden and the way to Gehinnom'.[62] The community of Qumran also reflected strongly this dualistic interpretation of life.[63]

The 'two ways' type of teaching is all too open to oversimplified ethical teaching and to instant, automatic judgments of a sweeping or obtuse kind. Yet, as Kirk well illustrates, the writer of the Testament of Asher shows an acute awareness of the sophistication of ethical issues, such as the deceptiveness of appearances and the equivocal nature of human actions.[64] People can combine the 'two ways' in their own persons and actions: like the 'merciful oppressor' or the 'fasting adulterer'. There is therefore a necessity to discriminate far more precisely than in terms of the broad, general categories; yet, when all allowances have been made, a basic duality remains in which the positive element is ultimately ascendant:

> Observe then, my children, the basic duality in the universe: the one thing standing in opposition to the other, the one hidden by the other. Death succeeds life, dishonour glory, night day, and darkness light. But the universe is under the sway of the day, and justice is under life; that is why eternal life waits upon death. And it cannot be said that truth is falsehood, or that justice is injustice, for all truth is under the light, just as the whole universe is under God.[65]

Catalogues of virtues and vices

Long before hellenistic influence affected Judaism, cataloguing was an accepted device in Israel, as in Jeremiah's temple sermon (cf. Jer. 7: 9f.). In later literature, the native Jewish and the imported hellenistic catalogue styles merged without difficulty.[66] Thus, in the Testament of Benjamin the seven evils of which the sword is mother are catalogued (8: 2), while a positive catalogue is found in the Testament of Issachar (ch. 5). The liturgy for the Day of Atonement included a catalogue of twenty-two vices resembling those found in the Didache and in Romans.[67] A notable example occurs in the Community Rule of Qumran in association with the 'two ways' motif.[68] Again, the fifth chapter of Pirqe Aboth is built up essentially on the catalogue model, and the sixth catalogues not only the virtues of the man who busies himself with the study of the Torah but also the forty-eight steps in the learning of it.[69] The catalogue method in Israel is thus used for a variety of teaching functions, but usually to commend certain actions and dispositions or to warn against the dangers of their opposites.

The 'Haustafeln'

The germ of the 'household code' is apparent in the Torah (e.g., in the fourth commandment); and doubtless behind this stands the ancient tribal respect for family ties, hospitality and other social obligations that is reflected also in the wisdom tradition and its sources. This gains clear expression in Sirach[70] and in the fourth chapter of Tobit in particular. Philo offers a full allegorical commentary on the fifth commandment – 'for old and young, for rulers and ruled, for benefactors and beneficiaries, for slaves and masters'.[71] Josephus reflects the familiar sequence of relationships in his defence of the Jewish law.[72] A poem falsely attributed to Phocylides and Graeco-Jewish in flavour contains sections devoted to husbands and wives, parents and children, and masters and slaves.[73]

How far is this kind of teaching typically Jewish, and how far is it affected by cultural cross-fertilisation? That Philo and Josephus were influenced to some extent by Greek models can hardly be disputed. Philo not only uses the Stoic term *kathēkon* but also cites lists of duties related to it when commenting on the scriptural text.[74] Even the passage from the *De Decalogo*, of which a brief excerpt was cited above, is indebted to Stoicism. J. E. Crouch, however, notes that the form of the code Philo uses does not correspond closely to the traditional Stoic listing. With its emphasis on the principle of reciprocity and concern for the duties of inferiors, it stands nearer to the *Haustafeln* of the New Testament than to the *kathēkon schēma* of the Stoics.[75]

Within Judaism itself, the rabbis understood the 'Noachian' laws, which ante-date the book of Jubilees in which they appear (cf. 7: 20, 28), to be valid for the whole human race.[76] The duties set out in Jubilees include blessing the Creator, honouring father and mother, and loving one's neighbour. This universal aspect of Judaism's world-view gave rise to the Gentile mission beloved of the Pharisees in Jesus' day. It is likely, therefore, that hellenistic Jewish teachers such as Philo seized the opportunity to combine this Jewish tradition with that of the Stoics; and from the fusion of the two they developed a code which had a distinctive inner logic and was of considerable value for the purposes of propaganda and apologetic in the Gentile world.

The farewell discourse

Apart from some notable examples in the Old Testament itself,[77] the farewell discourse occurs frequently in the literature of ancient Judaism and even determines the structure of certain books.[78] Since E. Stauffer has made a detailed analysis of valedictions and farewell speeches,[79] it is unnecessary to duplicate his work here. It is sufficient to note that there must be, as the primary formal requirement, a speech of farewell by one who is aware that he is about to die or to be carried off to heaven[80] – a speech normally addressed to his family or close associates and including some weighty injunctions, warnings or advice.[81] Reinforcement is often given by a prediction of the consequences of obeying or disobeying these behests.[82] Other prominent features can be personal reminiscences, reviews of history and revelations about the future, particularly in relation to the destiny of the people. The discourse can also be accompanied by memorable actions (cf. prophetic actions) such as a last meal, footwashing, or blessing.[83]

Paraenesis in the ministry of John

The paraenetic topic in John's ministry

In Luke 3: 10–14[84] there occurs a block of three topics dealing with questions raised by the crowds, or by groups within the crowds, concerning the appropriate response to the imminent Day of the Lord. To the crowd in general John commended a radical openness to one's neighbour, a total sharing of the basic human requirements of food and clothing (cf. Luke 6: 29). The form of the *paraenesis* follows the model of the instructional wisdom saying, the content being typically Jewish.[85] Similarly, the taxgatherers or customs men are advised to 'collect no more than is appointed you': a policy which at its lowest forbids exploitation, and which if taken radically would make tax-gathering impossible under the system in operation at that time. Soldiers on active service are given the three-fold counsel:

no oppression, no extortion, and let their wages suffice them.

A not uncommon Christian evaluation of this *paraenesis* is given by
T. W. Manson. 'John's positive teaching serves to mitigate the worst evils
of an evil system; but it does not and cannot transform the system. It could
relieve the sickness of society; but it was not the radical cure.'[86] But is this
not pure Christian apologetic? *Paraenesis* is frequently practical rather than
radical, but it is possible to argue that John's teaching is in fact a radical
application of the law to the situation in question.[87]

Topical figures and illustrations

Under paraenetic figures, we may list the image of the vipers (Matt. 3:7;
Luke 3:7) fleeing for safety before a wilderness fire.[88] The figure of the
felling of the tree (Matt. 3:10; Luke 3:9) may have been suggested by the
timber operations in the Jordan valley (cf. 2 Kings 6:1–4) but, like many
of John's images, was also stock Old Testament usage (cf. Is. 10:33f.).
John, like the later Jewish literature,[89] applies it specifically to the judgment to come upon the Jews. The metaphor of winnowing also combines
the everyday-life element with biblical imagery (Is. 41:15f.) to suggest the
eschatological separation of righteous and unrighteous. Both chaff and fire
imply familiar religious images in the Jewish milieu, as does 'bearing fruit'.
These examples give sufficient indication of a skilful teacher sensitive to
the power of appropriate imagery, and borrowing freely the traditional
images of the prophets and other religious teachers of Israel.[90]

Other paraenetic features

Indications in existing material are slight. A 'two ways' motif is implied in
the eschatological separation of the righteous and sinners. There are no
lists and nothing corresponding precisely to the *Haustafeln*, although the
paraenetic topics in Luke 3:10–14 are addressed to discernible groups.

Paraenesis in the ministry of Jesus

Since the *paraenesis* of Jesus is available to us only through the *paradosis*
of the church, familiar *formgeschichtliche* puzzles demand the attention of
any serious investigator of Jesus' teaching.[91] A full examination of such
issues would be out of context here. Where the perspectives of form or
redaction criticism are essential to the understanding of a paraenetic passage, this fact will be duly noted. In general terms, however, much of the
paraenesis ascribed to Jesus may be regarded as integral or supplementary
to his prophetic ministry: an instrument he used to elucidate the antinomies
and polarities of faith and life. The echoes of his teaching in the tradition
are, of course, confined within an alien structure – whether it be that of the

gospels themselves, or of collections of logia,[92] parables[93] or traditional pericopae.[94] To some extent, therefore, the form of some of Jesus' utterances may have been lost along with their contexts – the Sermon on the Mount, for example, owes its total form to Matthew rather than Jesus;[95] but in other cases the tensile strength of Jesus' paraenetic constructions – especially in the smaller units – may well have withstood the pressures of transmission, editing and application to new situations.

The paraenetic topic

The basis of the paraenetic topic in Jesus' teaching, as in all its manifestations, is the gnomic utterance, the observation of practical wisdom such as:

'Out of the abundance of the heart the mouth speaks' (Matt. 12: 34b; Luke 6: 45b).
'Sufficient for the day is the day's own trouble' (Matt. 6: 34b).
'The labourer is worthy of his hire' (Luke 10: 7b; cf. Matt. 10: 10b).
'Those who are in good health do not need a doctor, but those who are ill' (Mark 2: 17).

These sayings are uttered in contexts which enable them to come to life; new light is shed on their meaning and application. Thus the above examples, while in themselves mere pieces of popular folklore, acquire particular pungency and meaning in relation to explosive or delicate themes related to the life of God's covenanted people and their religious practices, such as the congruity of outward act and inward disposition, detachment from worldly security and worldly cares, the disciple's way of life, and Jesus' concern for publicans and sinners. The gnomic form[96] can be applied even more directly to a specific, religious theme:

'No one who puts his hand to the plough and looks back is fit for the kingdom of God' (Luke 9: 62).
'Whoever will not receive the kingdom of God as a child will not enter into it' (Mark 10: 15).

Following McKane's analysis of Old Testament wisdom sayings, we identify a second main group as instructional in form:

'Doctor, heal yourself' (Luke 4: 23).
'Let the dead bury their dead' (Matt. 8: 22b; Luke 9: 60).
'Be wise as serpents and innocent as doves' (Matt. 10: 16b).

Again, the situation which they address contributes to their interpretation. Characteristically, the instruction form is built up into a fuller type by various additions, such as a reason or purpose clause (cf. Matt. 6: 34).

Various devices such as parallelism, repetition, antithesis and the collocation of positives and negatives contribute to a slightly more extended topic, often perfectly balanced and employing the full rhythmic quality of elevated Semitic speech.[97] Other devices include the use of conditional clauses[98] and temporal clauses.[99] But after the long evolution of the wisdom tradition in Israel, there ceases to be a sharp distinction between the gnomic and instructional genres.[100]

This wisdom type of *paraenesis* is closely associated with the logic of the parable, the germ of which is contained in such maxims as 'look at the birds of the air...', or 'consider the lilies of the field...', or in vivid pictures of typical behaviour in the observable world.[101] Rhetorical elements are caught up naturally into the paraenetic type, whether or not designed for the purposes of *reductio ad absurdum*.[102] Jesus employs a whole range of devices to enable the mind of his hearers to search for the radical answer, the deeper truth. A typical structure for the extended topic may therefore be as follows:

(i)   Instructional sentences, sometimes repeated for the sake of parallelism or strophic balance.
(ii)   A statement of reason or purpose, subject to similar strophic adjustment.
(iii) Rhetorical question or questions.
(iv)   A conclusion or 'punch line'.

A beautifully balanced example of this typical structure occurs in Matt. 7: 7-11 (cf. Luke 11: 9-13): 'ask the Father'; and another example is Matt. 7: 1-5;[103] 'judge not...'. But, editorial and transmissional variations apart, the paraenetic topic is essentially flexible, and comparisons and antitheses in particular may supplement or replace the rhetorical questions or the subordinate clause. Antithetical topics include the cultically orientated passages on giving alms (Matt. 6: 2ff.), prayer (6: 5f.) and fasting (6: 16ff.).[104]

Such paraenetic topics, clearly discernible despite editorial manipulation of various kinds, point to the distinctive *paraenesis* of Jesus; the distinctiveness lying not in the astonishing novelty of his materials but in the way in which he brought them to life for his hearers, so that a new light was shed upon some aspect of their living, opening up new possibilities for them and imparting a share, however fragmentary, of Jesus' own flashing prophetic insight. This same insight, however, also probed to the radical depths of the scriptural and hermeneutical tradition in which Jesus stood; for whereas in the Jewish tradition there was a tendency for scriptural exegesis to be syphoned off from *paraenesis* and reserved for the concentrated study of sectarian groups, Jesus assimilated it within the astonishing unity of his procedures. It is, however, by no means unlikely that much of Jesus' *parae-*

nesis was specifically directed to the community he had gathered round him, the righteous community whose standards and quality of life were markedly different from the world's: 'it shall not be so among you' (Mark 10: 43). Such an interpretation would be compatible with the contemporary, Judaistic background, consonant with prophetic practice and congruous with the content of his teaching.[105]

In these exegetical topics designed to interpret the law (cf. Matt. 5: 21–48), a scriptural passage replaces the gnomic or instructional sentence; and the process of interpretation is inaugurated by advancing to the scripture sentence an antithesis to open up the deeper issues of meaning in radical fashion. What is new and arresting is not the formal method but the quality of the interpretation, which contrasts sharply with some of the additions to the original antitheses – additions which illustrate 'the tendency to depress enthusiastic demands to the level of a bourgeois morality'.[106] Jesus appears to have applied similar antithetical procedures to prohibitions (e.g., 5: 21, 27, 33).[107]

The paraenetic topic was 'tailor made' for Jesus' didactic requirements. He was no systematiser of theological thinking, no purveyor of ethical principles or legislative provisions. His procedure was aimed at giving insights into the real state of things, at engineering, so to speak, moments of truth that put his hearers under the necessity of decision. Hence his technique was to pick up a particular issue from life – a wisdom saying or scriptural quotation was frequently the opener – and the illumination came through the examination, comparison or discussion of it in concrete detail. His own insights have been compared in their operation to 'gull-like swoops' or 'lightning flashes'.[108] The paraenetic topic was eminently adaptable as a means of helping his hearers to participate in this experience.

Topical figures and illustrations

Such is the sophistication of New Testament usage that distinctions have been felt necessary between similitudes, parables, illustrations and allegories.[109] Such distinctions possess a certain usefulness and validity, but a measure of confusion arises because they in fact overlap in operation and the term 'parable' is itself used both in a specific and in a comprehensive fashion.[110] Thus the similitude (e.g., a comparison with the operational characteristics of leaven, mustard seed, grain) is certainly parabolic, though the so-called 'parable proper' has to do with what one man did (e.g., 'there was a man who held a great feast'); again, if the illustrative story of 'the good Samaritan' were to be denied the title of parable, one would be forced to stop and enquire whether one were not talking nonsense; and although the distinction between parable and allegory is much firmer than in the other cases, some parables show a strong tendency to develop into allegories.

All parables and related forms are topical figures – devices having a natural, spontaneous role within the paraenetic topic. This spontaneity arises from the fact that they are themselves extensions and expressions of wisdom teaching, and in their operational variety they reflect the flexibility and adaptability of the paraenetic topic itself.[111] Do the parabolic categories that have been detected correspond to the types of wisdom teaching we have noted?

The gnomic saying, which includes the riddle in its hinterland, moves at the level of the general and the typical and rests upon observation and insight, producing an image which can open up a new and meaningful perspective for the participant. This corresponds in the main to the similitude, which can also operate in such a way that the *tertium comparationis* becomes part of the insight-giving process. Inevitably this means that there is an element of puzzle about the similitude. Its meaning unfolds only to those 'who have ears to hear'.[112] It is designed to tease the mind into active thought.[113] It seems to me that the allegory is similarly related to the riddle, where the puzzle element is even greater.[114]

The instructional saying possesses a concreteness and directness, as against the generality and allusiveness of the gnomic utterance. The element of comparison which it often contains is capable of development as the so-called 'parable proper', which relies on the strength of a well-formulated narrative about a particular person or incident to make its point with force. Operationally, the illustration is separated from the 'parable proper' by no more than a hairsbreadth. It is a narrative stage-managed to exemplify the actual issue in question (e.g., 'the rich fool', Luke 12: 16–21). The instruction saying which it illustrates might be formulated thus:

Do not lay up for yourself treasures upon earth...
But lay up for yourself treasures in heaven (cf. Matt. 6: 19f.).

The 'parable proper' is a narrative stage-managed to set an individual instance before the hearer as an indication of a general law to which he must submit.[115] The meaning of the 'great supper' for the original hearers might be paraphrased thus:

Come quickly to the feast when you are invited,
lest your host invite others in your place and you be left outside.

Or, theologically interpreted:

Now is the acceptable time (cf. 2 Cor. 6: 2).[116]

The parables, indeed, give strong support to the contention that Jesus' paraenetic topics were not restricted to a traditional wisdom base but included prophetic and conceptual data of prime concern to Jesus' ministry. This is shown by the many parables designed to afford some insight into the nature of God's kingly activity or into his grace or judgment, but always in relation to the historical situation, not as timeless truths. For example, they might arise out of his discussion of major issues in his ministry, such as his table-fellowship with 'publicans and sinners',[117] to which are related among others the so-called 'prodigal son' (Luke 15: 11–32), 'the labourers in the vineyard' (Matt. 20: 1-16), and 'the unmerciful servant' (Matt. 18: 21-35). Every parable, like every wisdom saying, enshrines a 'cosmic disclosure' which may be brought to light through the interaction of the speaker, the hearer and the situation or picture of reality which the parable or wisdom saying evokes. Parabolic discourse is, in fact, so patterned as to have a certain direction-finding mechanism to locate the area of potential disclosure, and this area may sometimes be specifically designated, as in the parables of the kingdom. At all events, the disclosure is cosmic: it has universal significance.[118]

The 'two ways'

The 'two ways' motif is an integral part of the construction of many parables, especially of those which operate on the basis of contrast.[119] The use of this motif was a basic procedure of Jesus' *paraenesis*, probably for several reasons. It is characteristic of the prophetic call for decision;[120] it is also part of the peculiar nature of religious insight to operate by means of antitheses and contrasts.[121] The 'two ways', however, represent not an ultimate dualism but the duality of obedience and disobedience, radical acceptance or effective rejection of the total demand of God.[122]

Catalogues of virtues and vices

An instance of the catalogue procedure is found in Mark 7: 21f., where Jesus is reported to have listed the vices which 'come out of a man' and defile him;[123] but since this is an isolated instance in the Synoptics, it raises the question of whether the catalogue has simply been ascribed to Jesus by the teachers of the church. It is just possible that Jesus did use this form in controversy with the Pharisees or even the Essenes, to whose teaching it is closely parallel,[124] but the prosaic monotony of cataloguing would appear less typical of his teaching method than the insight-seeking procedures indicated above.[125]

The 'Haustafeln'

The gospels do not record any instance of Jesus' use of a household code in his teaching. In fact, his attitude to the family had about it a disconcerting duality fully in accord with the polarity that characterised his thinking. On the one hand, the command to honour one's father and mother is radical-ised[126] and is caught up in controversy with the Pharisees. On the other, radical obedience to God may mean departing from family groups and loyalties (Matt. 10: 37f.; Mark 10: 29f.; Luke 14: 26), which may be a barrier to discipleship, and the disciple may expect hostility from family groups thus divided (Matt. 10: 35f.; Luke 12: 53). This latter teaching in particular may be coloured or created by early Christian experience but the creation of a group of disciples whose service to God took precedence over any other relationship appears authentic (cf. Matt. 12: 46-50, and par.). In these circumstances, it is not likely that Jesus found it incumbent upon him to initiate or reinforce social codes relating to the family, although the full sophistication of his position must be appreciated, for he is not hostile to the family unit as such. Family sequences appear in the teaching attribut-ed to him (Matt. 12: 50 par., as well as Mark 10: 29f.), but they are not related to *Haustafeln*.

The farewell discourse

The gospel traditions reflect the form of the farewell discourse both in their account of Jesus' passion and in the resurrection narratives. For example, Luke's passion narrative contains an account of Jesus' final meal with his friends (Luke 22: 14-19),[127] an indication of his awareness of approaching death (22: 21), warnings and exhortations addressed specially to those close to him (22: 22-28), sayings on the theme of succession (22: 29f.), a prayer for those left behind (22: 32), an element of 'flash-back' or reminiscence (22: 35), and sundry predictions or solemn warnings (22: 22, 34) – all of which are paralleled elsewhere in farewell situations and speeches.[128] John's lengthier narrative also reflects the form of the farewell discourse. Jesus, knowing that his hour has come (John 12: 23, 28; 13: 1; 17: 1, 27), calls together 'his own' (13: 1ff.), takes a last meal with them (13: 2) and washes their feet (13: 5). The continuing story avails itself of the farewell motif in a variety of ways, including: the commandment to love (13: 34) and other solemn instructions (14: 21, 23f.), words of comfort and assur-ances of continuing divine help (14 *passim*; 15: 26; 16: 5-11, 20-24), indi-cations of future glory (14: 28f.; 16: 28), the sorrow of those bereft (16: 20ff.) and the world's hatred they must endure (15: 18-25; 16: 1-4), prayer for those left behind (17 *passim*) and intercessory prayer (14: 13f., 16), and the bestowal of blessing (14: 27).

In assessing this material, three perspectives must be kept in mind. In general, the perspective of *Formgeschichte* indicates that the early Christian teachers fashioned and understood the tradition of Jesus' passion at least partly in terms of the farewell discourse and associated motifs. *Redaktionsgeschichte* points to the contribution of the evangelist. John, for example, places the whole sequence of events in a setting that is more properly described as eschatological[129] rather than apocalyptic. Mark, on the other hand, introduces a strongly apocalyptic type of *paraenesis* at this point (cf. Mark 13). But a phenomenological perspective on Jesus' situation in the closing phase of his ministry suggests the probability – almost the inescapable conclusion – that Jesus himself was aware of his impending death and therefore of his own involvement in what we may call a 'farewell situation'. The gospel narratives appear to be compounded of all three elements. The passion narrative – the primacy of which in the evolution of gospel tradition was firmly indicated by source criticism – represents *paradosis* with very strong overtones of *paraenesis*. In the last analysis, it is a commentary on the cross for the Christian: in Markan terms, an exposition of what it means to take up one's cross and follow Christ (cf. Mark 8: 34f.).

Farewell motifs are also evident in the resurrection narratives. In Luke 24: 36–53, the pericope includes an account of the risen Christ's identification of himself as the crucified Jesus in the presence of his astonished disciples (vv. 36–39); the meal of fish he ate in their presence (vv. 41ff.); his recollection of words he once uttered to them concerning the fulfilment of the scriptures in himself (vv. 44ff.); the commissioning of the disciples as witnesses (v. 48); instructions about the reception of the promised Spirit (v. 49); his blessing upon them as he departs (vv. 50f.); and their subsequent joy (vv. 51f.). Similar motifs can be found, for example, in Matt. 28: 16–20[130] and John 20: 19–23.[131]

Paraenesis in the early church

The early Christians inherited a tradition of *paraenesis* from Jesus. Much of their teaching was carried out in a milieu in which paraenetic forms were already well defined. However, the fundamental feature of Christian *paraenesis* is that it is wholly governed by God's act of salvation in Christ. It is designed to spell out, both for the neophyte and for the mature, the implications and consequences of faith in Christ. With its concern for nurture and discipline, it attempts to give expression to the characteristic motifs of the Christian faith in the life of the believer and the believing community. It elucidates the imperative implied in the indicative of God's action in Christ. It describes the way followed by those who truly know Jesus Christ as Lord.

An approach to the study of *paraenesis* raises a whole range of questions. Does Christian *paraenesis* consistently evince certain prominent and characteristic motifs of Christian faith, as one would expect it to do; and, if so, how integral are such motifs to the *paraenesis* itself? Are there different types of *paraenesis*? What paraenetic forms operate in early Christian teaching? These three questions are selected for discussion here.

Among the motifs which recur in Christian *paraenesis*, the following may be said to possess particular importance:

(i) *Paraenesis* is closely associated with baptism, which marks the watershed in the life and experience of the convert[132] and can be related meaningfully both to the central symbols of salvation (the *Glaubensformel*) and to the indicative-imperative combination which characterises the new life in Christ.[133] In baptism, the Christian has 'put on Christ' like a garment (cf. Gal. 3: 27),[134] just as he has put off all that is evil.[135] Again, in Rom. 6 Paul interprets baptism in terms of identification with the death and resurrection of Christ. The Christian, having died to sin (vv. 6ff.), is set free from bondage to the power of sin, which is the lot of fallen humanity; but his participation in the resurrection of Christ, his 'rising again with Christ', appears to combine the notions of reality and of possibility: it is set in a teleological perspective (cf. vv. 4, 22) and governed by recurring imperatives (cf. vv. 12ff., 19).

(ii) *Paraenesis* is orientated towards an eschatological *telos*, which is summed up appropriately in terms of Christ himself, the love of Christ, his *parousia* or some traditional symbol of the last judgment. Acknowledging that he is not yet *teleios* (cf. Phil. 3: 12f.), Paul describes himself as 'straining forward to what lies ahead' and pressing on 'toward the goal for the prize of the upward call of God in Christ Jesus'.[136] The Ephesians are urged 'to grow up in every way into him who is the head, into Christ' (Eph. 4: 15); and the writer spells out this course in terms of the distinction between the Gentile way of life and the way of those who have 'learned Christ' (4: 20), as well as by applying the put on/put off paraenetic motif (4: 17–23). Paul tells the charismatic Corinthians, 'Make love your aim' (1 Cor. 14: 1); and this is the basis on which he reassesses spiritual priorities for the believing community. In the Pastorals, paraenetic metaphors such as the fight and the race include the notion of the 'crown of righteousness' awarded by the righteous Judge on judgment day (cf. 2 Tim. 4: 7f.). A similar teleology is associated with perseverance in the Christian calling in face of suffering.[137] The Christian makes it his aim to please the Lord, 'for we must all appear before the judgment seat of Christ, so that each one may receive good or evil, according to what he has done in the body' (2 Cor. 5: 10).[138] A by-product of this type of teleology is a devaluing of worldly goals. The Christian does not love the world or the things in it (cf. 1 John 2: 15f.).[139]

(iii) *Paraenesis* has a fundamental concern with 'the new life in Christ'. To describe it and commend it, teachers had recourse to contrasting life

prior to Christian faith (whether 'under the law' or 'as Gentiles live') with
the way of Christ (or 'under grace' or 'in the Spirit'); and for this purpose
the 'two ways' model and catalogues, separately or in conjunction, proved
useful. Another device is to relate the Christian life to the commandment
to love one's neighbour (or brother). 'The early Church', wrote W. D.
Davies, 'confronted the world with a body of moral teaching, a Messianic
law.'[140] Paul speaks paradoxically of the 'law of Christ' (Gal. 6: 2), James
of the 'law of liberty' (James 2: 12). The element of paradox is made
necessary by the fact that the paraenetic use of conventional models
(whether catalogues, codes, commandments or 'laws') is justifiable only if
they can be related to the Christian's response to God in Christ: i.e., to the
fundamental motifs of the gospel, which may be expressed in terms of
God's grace, the working of his Spirit, *agape*, the example of Jesus, or the
motifs of incarnation and atonement.[141]

(iv) Some *paraenesis* in the church appears to have been developed on
the basis of Old Testament scripture: whether from the Torah itself, psalms,
prophets or wisdom sayings. In such cases, however, the intention is not to
bypass the christocentric area of paraenetic concern. The Old Testament
was the sole scriptural authority in the church for a considerable time, and
a Christian 'peshering' of the scriptures is to be assumed whenever such
paraenesis occurs – even when the *pesher* is not immediately obvious (cf.
Rom. 12).

The second question raised at the beginning of this discussion was: are
there different types of *paraenesis*? Broadly, two specific types can be distinguished. The first may be described as 'traditional *paraenesis*' (i.e., *paraenesis* explicitly based upon *paradosis*, or upon general paraenetic themes);
the second type is 'situational *paraenesis*', sometimes termed 'contemporary'
or *aktuell*, which consists of 'exhortation on an *ad hoc* basis, using no, or
only very few, traditional paraenetic elements since traditional elements
cannot always deal with certain new and unique situations (e.g., 1 Corinthians)'.[142] To these two broad categories we shall append a third, 'ecclesiastical *paraenesis*', which combines both traditional and situational elements
but is related directly to the institutional needs of the church and the
ministry.[143]

Thirdly, the study of paraenetic form relates to the overall pattern, the
distinctive paraenetic *Gattung* within which both the motifs and varieties or
types of *paraenesis* are embraced. Since the topic or *topos* remains the most
characteristic form, our investigation proceeds by noting some features of
its use in Christian circles.

The paraenetic topic in the early church

Traditional paraenetic topics The purpose of this type of topic is to give guidance to Christians in the areas of belief and conduct. Weight is placed on *paradosis*, cited specifically for the purpose.[144] Thus in 1 Cor.15, the *paradosis* is introduced by explicit phrases of recapitulation (vv. 1ff.) which also emphasise the transmission and reception of authoritative church tradition.[145] The basic datum of the faith, comprising the central doctrinal symbols, interprets the life and fate of Jesus of Nazareth as messianic and of prime significance for salvation. The symbols include within themselves the testimony of the apostles as eyewitnesses to the historical events of the death and burial of Jesus and as experiencing subjects of the para-historical resurrection appearances; together with the testimony of interpreted scripture and the positive interpretation of the death 'for us'. The symbols themselves are thus complex and compound, but the assent of faith to precisely this complexity of interpretation is essential to entry into the church. Thus, 'if you confess with your lips that Jesus is Lord and believe in your heart that God raised him from the dead, you will be saved' (Rom. 10: 9).[146] This formula as it stands could be the answer to a catechetical question, such as: 'What must I do to be saved?'[147] Thus, the traditional paraenetic topic might well have functioned as part of the catechetical preparation for baptism. On the other hand, 1 Cor. 15 is designed to correct doctrinal aberrations and misapprehensions in the church (vv. 12ff.); and while the extended passage (vv. 12–58) combines the characteristics of *paraclesis* and *paraenesis*,[148] it concludes on a clearly paraenetic note.[149] 'Therefore, my beloved brethren, be steadfast, immovable, always abounding in the work of the Lord, knowing that in the Lord your labour is not in vain' (v. 58). Perhaps the underlying paraenetic or catechetical concern makes it all the easier for Paul to add his own commentary to the *paradosis* (vv. 8–11). However, this concern was perhaps never wholly absent in his handling of tradition, and his procedures here may well approximate to his usual method.

A striking example of Paul's use of traditional *paradosis* occurs in 1 Cor. 9: 4–18 (concerning support for the apostles), where Paul alludes to a command of the Lord (v. 14) without actually quoting it. The point of his paraenetic exposition, however, is not to elucidate the meaning of that command but to relativise it – i.e., to show how he might or might not obey it according to the requirement of his ministry and situation.[150] Thus traditional *paraenesis* can virtually become situational or ecclesiastical in the hands of Paul. In his discussion of divorce, he does cite the command of the Lord (1 Cor. 7: 10f.) and proceeds to extend and apply it to analogous situations, such as marriages with unbelievers (1 Cor. 7: 12–16); he had already discussed the situation of the unmarried and the widows (vv. 8f.), and the question of marriage in general (vv. 1-7) – all of which may be described as authoritative, apostolic *paraenesis* or, in Jewish terms, binding *halachah*.[151] Inevitably, such *paraenesis* involves a measure of casuistry, as he shows when he argues, in effect, that the dominical command in 1 Cor. 7: 10f. does not apply to the case discussed in 7: 12-16.[152]

A characteristic feature of one type of Pauline *paraenesis*, therefore, is the traditional symbol or principle, which provides the focal point of reference for the teaching of the apostle. From the formal point of view, there is usually an introductory phrase of some kind[153] or a statement of recall (1 Cor. 15: 1), assurance (7: 32) or commendation (11: 2). The focal statement of principle or tradition is then given,[154] its meaning, extension and application being developed by means of various rhetorical devices. Thus 1 Thess. 4: 1-8, introduced on a recapitulatory note (v. 2), focuses on 'the will of God, your sanctifier' (v. 3a). Strong emphasis is placed on sexual morality (vv. 3f.), avoiding unbridled lust in the manner of 'the heathen who do not know God' (v. 5), and respecting the rights of one's brother (i.e., other people v. 6). The theme of v. 7 – 'God has not called us for uncleanness, but in holiness' – picks up vv. 1ff. The writer reinforces this principle with a solemn warning (v. 8; cf. v. 6b).

P. Carrington and E. G. Selwyn justly point to the law of holiness (Lev. 17-26, esp. 17-18) as the ultimate basis of this kind of teaching, not least since it was connected in Judaism with the initiation of a proselyte.[155] The key verse – Lev. 19: 2: 'Say to all the congregation of the people of Israel, You shall be holy; for I the Lord your God am holy' – is reflected in 1 Thess. 4: 3, 7 and is explicitly cited in 1 Pet. 1: 15f., a paraenetic passage of considerable interest.[156] A comparison of the two passages, however, does not fully substantiate the hypothesis of a common source, operating in a fixed formula at baptism or in catechetical instruction. It suggests rather common themes or motifs, the main points of which tend to recur in such *paraenesis*. These include, as an immediate consequence of the concept of holiness, a 'separation' motif (as in 1 Thess. 4: 3 and 1 Peter 2: 11), called by Carrington and Selwyn the *'abstinentes* clauses'.[157] There is consequently a somewhat negative emphasis in basic ethical *paraenesis*, with the positive side present largely by implication.[158] When this kind of *paraenesis* is put against the background of paganism, the reason for this emphasis becomes clear, for a precondition of Christian discipleship is detachment from the former ethos.[159]

Three typical paraenetic topics, incorporating a hellenistic form of introduction, are to be noted: 'concerning brotherly love' (1 Thess. 4: 9-12), 'concerning those who are asleep' (vv. 13-18), and 'concerning the times and seasons' (5: 1–11). In the first, the central religious symbol is the command to love one another (4: 9); in the second, the resurrection of Jesus (4: 14a); and in the third, the coming of the Day of the Lord 'like a thief in the night' (5: 2). Such *topoi*, in their concern for a specific subject, their constant notes of admonition and counsel, the predictability of their construction and the consistency with which they revolve around, interpret or at least reflect a focal point of religious authority or revelation, represent *traditional paraenetic procedures*, easily reproduced by less experienced Christian teachers without recourse to the mere repetition of fixed formulas.[160] There is some evidence that general *paraenesis* tended to accumulate in the hands of early Christian teachers as material from diverse sources was used to expand and strengthen earlier paraenetic units. Rom. 13 is a case in point. D. G. Bradley found here a block of four *topoi*, 'each of which could stand alone, and each of which gives a teaching on a problem of Christian life and thought',[161] although vv. 1–7 are well integrated in the passage as it stands in Romans. What is remarkable about these verses is their extreme generality and the ascription of total authority to the state.[162] It would appear that the injunctions of vv. 1–7 have been attracted into the Pauline letter by a process which we may describe as paraenetic assimilation.[163] In the topics which follow, the central religious symbol is more in evidence.[164]

Situational paraenetic topics The Corinthian correspondence indicates that Paul related his paraenetic procedures to the particular situation which confronted him. Dealing with the reported case of immorality at Corinth he 'lays down the law' in no uncertain terms:[165] at this point, the situational and the ecclesiastical types of topic merge. His introduction uses ironic reproach and rhetorical question (1 Cor. 5: 2a, b), and he expands the topic by means of the figure of the leaven which is developed in such a way as to include the symbol of Christ the Paschal Lamb, sacrificed for us (vv. 6ff.). When dealing with the question of litigation against a fellow Christian (6: 1–8), he sustains his topic by means of a series of rhetorical questions, into the first four of which he inserts the major symbol of the saints judging the world (vv. 1ff.).

When he turns to the subject of their correspondence with him – 'concerning the matters about which you wrote' (7: 1)[166] – he is able to relate many of their problems to general or traditional *paraenesis*. But when he begins to speak 'about food offered to idols' (8: 1), he provides not only a model of situational *paraenesis* but a description of the process by which such *paraenesis* was formed. Chapter 8 represents the situational topic *par excellence*. From the situation it picks up the emphasis on 'knowledge', contrasts it with the love of God through which one is known by God (v. 3), and works out this contrast in terms of eating food offered to idols. What matters in this instance is not so much to know that 'an idol has no real existence' (v. 4) – despite the fact that idolatry was a cardinal sin in Christian eyes! (cf. 10: 14) – but to be aware that the 'weaker brother' may be harmed by a thoughtless exercise of Christian freedom. Not to be aware of that fact is to sin against 'the brother for whom Christ died' (v. 11) and so to sin 'against Christ' (v. 12) – the central symbol of the topic.[167]

Paul's situational *paraenesis* is designed to help the church members to work out individually and corporately what the 'law of Christ' (9: 21)[168] is for them in the midst of their predicaments. 1 Cor. 12–14 is also situational and deals with pneumatic disorders at Corinth. Yet while Paul would have his churches acquire moral insight and sensitivity, he also points them towards relevant traditions, scriptural statements and dominical words; and in the last analysis, if all else fails, Paul's ruling is firm: 'if anyone is disposed to be contentious, we recognise no other practice, nor do the churches of God' (11: 16). 'Situation ethics'[169] need not mean that the trumpet gives forth an uncertain sound.

Ecclesiastical paraenetic topics Paul's situational *paraenesis* in particular approximates to ecclesiastical *paraenesis*.[170] This kind of topic arises out of the institutional needs of the church and its ministry and is in evidence particularly in the Pastorals, where topics deal with bishops (1 Tim. 3: 1ff.); deacons (3: 8–13; and their wives presumably: cf. 3: 11); widows (5: 3–16) and elders (5: 17–22). In relation to teaching elders, a scriptural principle is adduced concerning their maintenance (5: 18).[171] However, because the writer exercises personal oversight of his presumably younger ministers, the distinction between ecclesiastical and personal advice is a very fine one.[172]

The second part of the Didache[173] consists largely of ecclesiastical *topoi* most of which are introduced in the formal topical manner. The first major one is 'about baptism' (Didache 7: 1–4), and contains precise instruction for the preparation and execution of the rite. 'About the eucharist' (9: 1 – 10: 7) includes an order of service for the sacrament, although concession is made to the spontaneity of the prophet (10: 7). Between these topics, shorter injunctions are given about fasting (8: 1) and prayer (8: 2f.), in both of which the curious rigidity of the Didache is apparent.[174] To distinguish Christians from 'the hypocrites', the former should fast on Wednesdays (the day of Jesus' arrest?) and Fridays (the day of crucifixion), not Mondays and Thursdays. They should not 'pray like the hypocrites' (8: 2) but should say the Lord's Prayer three times a day (8: 3). Counsel is also

offered concerning the treatment of itinerant teachers (11:1f.), and there
is a full topic 'about apostles and prophets' (11:3 - 13:7) which handles
with considerable delicacy the vexed question of distinguishing the false
from the true. Further topics deal with the assembly on the Lord's Day
(14:1-3), with the election of bishop and deacons (15:1f.), and with
reproof and discipline within the community (15:3f.), while a concluding
series of exhortations is eschatological in tone (16:1f.). Thus Didache 6-16
provides the best example we possess of ecclesiastical topics, of which it
consists almost entirely, and the probability that these topics made up an
originally independent paraenetic tract must be considered strong.[175]

Topical figures and illustrations

Topical figures in early church instruction tend to be less frequent, less
consciously rhetorical or literary, than their non-Christian counterparts;
and the parable, familiar in the Jewish world particularly and characteristic
of Jesus, is no longer frequently used, at least in its pure form.

When the simile, extended simile and metaphor do occur, they are
integral to the purpose of the topic and are not merely decorative. Thus
the simile in 1 Peter: 'Like newborn babes, long for the pure spiritual milk'
(2:2),[176] and Paul's extended simile in 1 Cor. 15:36-44 are crucial to the
respective arguments. An extended metaphor used for paraenetic purposes
is 'the whole armour of God', in Eph. 6:10-17.[177] Such figures are close
to allegory and typology in their mode of operation. Thus in 1 Cor. 15:44
the figure is followed by the typology of the first and last Adam, while the
metaphor of Ephesians is interpreted throughout in the allegorical manner.[178]

The fate of the gospel parables in the early church provides a useful indication of what was happening. The parables of Jesus were part of the *paradosis*
and operated according to paradotic principles. The paraenetic function[179]
in the early church was complementary to the transmission of the *paradosis*,
which exerted a measure of control on the material. Thus a parable like the
sower is found in the tradition in a double form, viz., the parable in concise
form (Mark 4:3-8) and an expanded form with allegorical features
(4:14-20).[180]

The writer to the Hebrews uses *parabolē* to denote a symbol or figure: the
debarring of Israel from the inner sanctuary in the temple, while the latter
existed, 'is symbolic for the present age' (Heb. 9:9; cf. 11:19). Barnabas uses
it twice in relation to scriptural interpretation.[181] The Old Testament scriptures contain many riddles which must be interpreted allegorically if meaning
is to be found in them for contemporary Christians. The latter need enlightenment, or at least as much as they can bear, for some deeper mysteries are
beyond them, 'since their meaning lies in parables' (Barnabas 17:2).[182]

The reason for this important shift of emphasis in the use of topical figures is to be found mainly in the eschatological position of the church. Jesus' use of parables was a discovery method of an open type, in which a *rapprochement* between the experience of the speaker and the hearers was established as the starting point of an exploration which could lead to 'disclosure'.[183] But the early Christian teachers, on the basis of their shared experience, recognised in the total event of Christ the central symbol of the mystery of life and the universe; and it was to this central symbol that they had to direct their hearers. Sometimes they use a straightforward paraenetic image, such as the 'whole armour of God' which the writer to the Ephesians uses to illustrate the 'put on' motif (Eph. 6: 11-17). Sometimes allegory and symbolism are used to convey the sense of the deeper mysteries of God. The meaning is not open to all (cf. Mark 4: 11 par.); hence the emergence of a gnostic motif.

The fourth gospel is the *locus classicus* of the gospel allegory, placed on the lips of Jesus.[184] A good paraenetic example occurs in 1 Cor. 12: 12-31. The figure used is the familiar one of the body.[185] The key to the analogy is given at the outset: 'Christ', we have to discover, is a corporate entity sustained by the 'One Spirit' (12: 13). The argument is designed to show the interdependence of members and the 'varieties of service' (cf. 12: 5), and this type of paraenetic analogy appears to have been frequently used in the early church (cf. Eph. 4: 11ff.; Rom. 12: 4-8). The use of typology is likewise stimulated by the centrality of the Christ symbol. Thus the wilderness wanderings of Israel are to be interpreted typologically (1 Cor. 10). The rock from which they drank was Christ (10: 4), and the whole episode provides warnings to us (10: 6) and was written down for our instruction (10: 11). Such typological procedures thus show 'how past events disclose the pattern of events to come'.[186] They enable Paul to indicate typological patterns embracing both Old Testament data and Christ as Saviour or the church as the New Israel; and in so doing he looks at the Old Testament 'as it were with prophetic eyes'.[187] His overriding purpose, however, was the edification and enlightenment of the Christian community.

The 'two ways'

'There are two ways, one of life and the other of death; and there is much difference between the two ways.' The first part of the Didache is the outstanding example of the important 'two ways' motif in early Christian *paraenesis,* but before examining it more closely we note that New Testament ethical instruction made use of this motif also, even if in a more muted form. The ethical dualism which it expresses in its more uncom-

promising form is not the absolute dualism of Zoroastrianism but the
dualism of ethical choice. As such, it is implicit in conversion from one
way of life to another, in the reorientation involved in moving from
Judaism to Christianity and in adherence to spiritual rather than worldly
values.[188]

As has already been noted, when the major concern is with separating
oneself from the ways of the ungodly, the negative side of the dualism is
stressed, sometimes exclusively.[189] It may well be that these passages
represent only part of the motif that was actually in use.[190] Full expression is given to the 'two ways' motif by the formula of 'put away'[191]
followed by 'put on', which is strongly reflected in Col. 3: 8–12, Eph. 4:
22ff. and Rom. 13: 12ff. That these two motifs (i.e., *abstinentes* and
deponentes) were brought together for instruction purposes is obvious
from Col. 3 and Eph. 4, and their connection with baptism is borne out
by the imagery used.[192] Nevertheless, since no *explicit* reference to baptism occurs in the 'two ways' passages themselves (in contrast to, e.g., Gal.
3: 27),[193] the argument that they are essentially 'baptismal catechisms'
falls short of proof.[194] They have, in fact, more to do with on-going
Christian nurture than they have with baptismal instruction. Another motif
which occurs in similar contexts is that of darkness and light.[195] Yet
another, closely associated with the put away/put on motif and with the
death and resurrection motif, is the contrast between the old man and the
new man.[196]

There is therefore a whole series of 'two ways' motifs, interlaced and
crisscrossing, in early Christian *paraenesis*, but it was left to the writer of
the Didache to spell it out with unrelieved explicitness:

> The way, then, of life is this: first, you must love God your creator;
> second, your neighbour as yourself; and whatever you would not
> have others do to you, you must not do to them...
>
> The way of death is this: first, it is wicked and accursed... (there
> follows an extensive catalogue of vices).

With the Didache, the 'two ways' motif operating on the 'life and death'
model can be described as codified.[197] The situation was obviously thought
to demand a direct, authoritative *paraenesis,* giving a clear answer to the
enquirer and the convert as to what the Christian life involved in practice.
Separated from Judaism, the church had to show that it had no less an
ethical concern. Confronted with the Gentile world, it used well-tried and
accepted paraenetic categories. The 'two ways' motif lay ready to hand,
exploited by Judaism, used in the gospels and represented in various ways
in early Christian teaching. It was but a short step to formalise it and

present in successive, imperatival topics what the Christian way of life involved and what it excluded.[198]

Catalogues in early Christian paraenesis

Paul apparently found catalogues useful as concise summaries or examples of his meaning or sometimes for elucidating a 'two ways' motif.[199] The latter usage is well illustrated by Gal. 5: 19–21, where the basic contrast is 'the works of the flesh' and 'the fruit of the Spirit'. Here the conventional catalogue is combined with characteristic Pauline flair and insight. But Paul can also apply it to a single motif, usually the sins of the flesh as in Rom. 1: 29f., 1 Cor. 5: 10f., and 2 Cor. 12: 20.[200] He is undoubtedly using conventional ethical concepts and didactic practices from both Jewish and Greek worlds,[201] and the catalogues are probably whole or partial citations of commonly accepted groupings. A particular link with the Greek tradition is his frequent use of *to kalon* and *to agathon*, recalling the *kalokagathia* of the Greek moralists.[202] Even the formula 'faith, hope and love' is a brief catalogue, which the Gnostics may well have developed later into a catalogue of their own: 'faith, hope, knowledge and love'.[203] Titus has 'faith, love, patience' (2: 2). Other catalogues are concerned with the trials of an apostle (1 Cor. 4: 11ff.) and the afflictions of the faithful (2 Cor. 6: 4–10), and the convention can have considerable rhetorical appeal (cf. Rom. 8: 35–39; 2 Cor. 11: 22–29). That its use was not confined to Pauline circles is illustrated by 1 Pet. 2: 1 – a typical 'put away' catalogue – and James 3: 15–18.[204]

The 'Haustafeln'

The so-called *Haustafeln* are found in several paraenetic passages in the epistles and later Christian literature.[205] The background to this form lies partly in the popular philosophy of the Graeco-Roman world[206] but much more immediately in hellenistic Jewish circles which were concerned to relate the Christian message to the human situation which they found meaningfully presented in terms of the basic *schema* of the *Haustafeln*, viz., duties to wives, children, and slaves. Hence it is probable that converts to Christianity from among the God-fearers, the 'Greeks' of the synagogues, contributed directly to the development of the *Haustafeln* as a Christian paraenetic topic. Thus, if we take Col. 3: 18 – 4: 1 as the earliest Christian example, several features suggest that it represents an earlier paraenetic form adapted for use in this context.[207]

Why was such material regarded as valuable for church *paraenesis*? The *Haustafeln* occur in the context of *paraenesis* directed to the church community. The fact that exhortations to women and slaves are common

factors in all New Testament *Haustafeln* suggests that these groups stood
near the centre of paraenetic concern. At Corinth, Paul had to deal particularly with the problem of women enthusiasts (1 Cor. 14: 34f.); slaves
appear to have been less of a problem (7: 21f.). At Colossae, however, it
would appear that, under the impulse of (possibly heretical) *enthusiasmos,*
slaves were not simply claiming the equality of the pneumatic in the church
but threatening to assert equality in society: hence the appropriate clause
in the *Haustafeln* is expanded in order to make their duties clear (Col. 3:
22-25). In Eph. 5: 21 - 6: 9, the framework of the *Haustafel* is identical
but is subjected to intense theologising by means of a Christian midrash
which inserts appropriate christological symbols in each section to complete
the christianisation of the *paraenesis.*[208] A similar kind of procedure is
applied to the form in 1 Pet. 2: 11 - 3: 7, although only three of the units
which appear in Colossians and Ephesians are found here (slaves, wives,
husbands) and the theological flavour is distinctive. A notable feature is
the extension of the 'ethic of submission' to 'every human creature,
whether it be to the emperor as supreme, or to governors' (2: 13ff.).[209]
The succession of imperatives, common in Graeco-Roman *paraenesis,* is
another distinctive item (cf. 2: 17).[210] J. E. Crouch found the *Sitz im
Leben* of the Christian *Haustafel* to be the tension between enthusiastic
and nomistic elements in the early hellenistic Christian communities: 'the
Haustafel represents the nomistic tendency of Pauline Christianity. It was
created to serve emerging orthodoxy as a weapon against enthusiastic and
heretical threats to the stability of both the church and the social order.
It is no accident, therefore, that *Haustafeln* appear only in "orthodox"
works and that they increasingly serve the interests of the emerging church
order.'[211]

The farewell discourse

Paul's speech to the elders of Ephesus (cf. Acts 20: 17-38) corresponds
fully to the form of the farewell discourse.[212] The occasion is an intimate
gathering at Miletus of the elders who have been summoned from Ephesus
(vv. 17f.). Beginning with a recapitulation of the apostle's ministry (vv. 18-
21), the speech proceeds to indicate that his journey to Jerusalem under
the compulsion of the Spirit[213] brings the certainty of suffering (vv. 22-24)
and that the present audience will never see him again (v. 25). The speaker
protests his innocence of any charge of shirking his responsibilities to them
in the past (vv. 26f.); exhorts them to pastoral care of the church (v. 28) in
view of the subsequent arrival in their midst of false teachers (vv. 29f.);[214]
emphasises the need for watchfulness (v. 31); commends them to God (v.
32) and holds up the example of his own ministry as a model for them to

emulate (vv. 33ff.). The concluding thrust comprises a proverbial utterance described as 'the words of the Lord Jesus' (v. 35) and an act of prayer (v.36). The scene ends with the sorrow of the assembled company as they bid him farewell and escort him to his ship (vv. 37f.).

In the Pastorals the motif of the farewell discourse is also evident.[215] Of 2 Timothy in particular Johannes Munck wrote: 'Cette lettre est donc elle aussi un discours d'adieu'.[216] To some extent a similar claim may be advanced for 2 Peter. The elements of recollection and the 'departure' of the apostle[217] are found in 2 Pet. 1: 12-15, and his followers receive weighty instructions about how to deal with the scoffers who will arise in the last days (3: 3-12). There tends to be a shift of emphasis in the early Christian farewell speech, which distinguishes it from the typical Jewish form. While both speak of the last days, the Christian apostle is concerned with what will happen in the *interim* between his death and the return of Christ: evil times will come on the church; an escalation of the activity of antichrist will put upon the faithful the necessity of guarding against false teaching, enduring persecution and maintaining the true apostolic traditions.[218]

Finally, is there a distinction between *paraenesis* and *catechesis*? In the New Testament, *katecheo* tends to emphasise basic instruction in the content of faith.[219] Thus *catechesis* was particularly appropriate to baptismal candidates,[220] but care must be taken to ensure that later catechetical procedures are not simply read back into the apostolic age. The concept of spiritual development that appears to underlie much of the New Testament is richer and more flexible than the *catechesis* of the Didache,[221] for example; and since instruction was continued after baptism within the *koinonia* of the church (cf. Heb. 5: 12ff.; Eph. 4: 13-16), it would seem unlikely that preliminary teaching was markedly different in quality from later instruction. Both probably drew upon the resources of prophetic preaching (cf. Acts 2: 14ff.), Christian midrash (8: 27-39) and *paraenesis* in the broad sense (cf. Eph. 4 *passim*) as well as upon church life in general. At the same time, certain emphases were particularly appropriate to those preparing for baptism: for example, basic *paradosis* which had to be handed down 'as of first importance' (cf. 1 Cor. 15: 1ff.); basic christological material which supplied the motif for the Christian way of life (cf. Phil. 2: 1-11);[222] the Christian interpretation of scripture (cf. Acts 17: 2f.); and ethical teaching of the 'two ways' type which related well to the decisive change which baptism signified.[223] As far as a distinctive formal *catechesis* is concerned, the New Testament yields no specific evidence. Perhaps it is just possible to discern the evolution of a catechetical method through dialogue and liturgy in the story of the Ethiopian eunuch (Acts 8: 30ff.).[224] And perhaps basic, doctrinal *catechesis* is detectable in 1 John, with its characteristics of brevity and antithetical parallelism,[225] but catechisms of the more formal type properly belong to the post-apostolic age, which lies beyond the scope of this study.[226]

Even if it is permissible to distinguish *catechesis* in the New Testament as instruction in the basics of the faith,[227] it is important to realise that this is no more than a convention which enables the focal elements in *paraenesis* (as well as in other forms, such as *propheteia* and *paradosis*) to be selected for systematic study, memorisation and appropriation: i.e., such *catechesis* operates with data in abstraction from any particular context.[228] A mastery of such data is only one stage of Christian training. The goal of the training is not that the catechumen may become a theologian (the church is not an army of theologians) but an informed and committed Christian.[229] For this to happen, the data of *catechesis* must be related dynamically to the situation of the catechumen. Thus *catechesis,* in so far as it represents basic instruction, is properly effective only when it is put to work in the applied area of *paraenesis* and of Christian living and discipleship.

4

PARADOSIS

'I commend you because you... maintain the traditions even as
I have delivered them to you' (1 Cor. 11: 2).

'So then, brethren, stand firm and hold to the traditions which you were
taught by us, either by word of mouth or by letter' (2 Thess. 2: 15).

Tradition in the hellenistic world

Greek culture differs from Hebrew in that it has no overriding concern with
a paramount revelation given and received historically. Tradition nevertheless operates within the culture in relation to ancient epic and gnomic poetry
and is held to be an essential part of moral education. After the pupil had
mastered the alphabet and could understand the written word, he was confronted by 'the works of good poets to read' and compelled to learn them
by heart with a view to moral improvement. His teacher chose 'such poems
as contain moral admonitions, and many a narrative interwoven with praise
and panegyric on the worthies of old, in order that the boy may admire and
emulate and strive to become such himself'.[1] Rote learning was the basic
way of receiving and absorbing such tradition, which was presumed to have
important implications for moral improvement. Nicerates is reported as
saying: 'my father, designing to make a virtuous man of me, ordered me to
get by heart every verse of Homer; and I believe I can repeat to you at this
minute the whole Iliad and Odyssey'.[2] The important Socratic qualifier is
that mechanical recitation by itself is of little avail: it must be accompanied
by understanding and by close attention to meaning. Although Plato was
dissatisfied with the moral content of the poets,[3] Socrates is sometimes
represented as championing traditional values, and he speaks of 'the ancients'
who 'handed down the tradition' as 'our betters and nearer the gods than
we are'.[4] Here we may have no more than a rhetorical device, but it does
illustrate an awareness of tradition in operation.[5]

Tradition was of importance in other areas too. In rhetoric, elementary
books called *Progumnasmata* contained examples of the *chreia*, defined by
Theon, a teacher of rhetoric of the first or second century A.D., as 'a concise and pointed account of something said or done, attributed to some
particular person'.[6] The focal element in rhetorical (i.e., 'persuasive') discourse was thoroughly memorised. It was received as tradition well tried in
the heat of contention. When known and understood, it was then put to

work in new ways. Theon observed:

> Students give themselves practice on *chreias* by reproducing, by
> varying, by adding, by inverting. We expand them and compress
> them. As well as this we construct and reconstruct them. The
> method of reproducing is obvious. Someone has uttered a *chreia*:
> we try, to the best of our ability, to convey the meaning in the
> most telling form whether by using the identical words or others.[7]

R. O. P. Taylor comments that the *chreia* is primarily a historical statement, and thus avoids the use of mythological data.[8] It is therefore
genuine tradition but is designed for flexible use. Although received
memoriter, it may be re-presented in such a way as to underline its
intrinsic truth or convey that truth with maximum impact in a given
situation.

By contrast, in the milieu of the mystery religions a much less flexible
understanding of tradition emerges, for the 'mysteries and solemn rites'
(Wisd. 14:15) are transmitted as a sacred trust to be kept inviolate and
observed scrupulously.[9]

Tradition in Israel

It has rightly been said that Judaism is 'torah-centred'.[10] An essential part
of this *torah* is written (scripture), itself compiled during and after the
Exile of manifold traditions which recorded and interpreted Israel's history
and faith from the foundations of the nation and from creation itself. But
a fixed authoritative tradition requires explanation, interpretation and
application to new situations – in fact (though this verbalisation may be
avoided) supplementation. Precisely how this was done depended on the
tendency within Judaism with which one was identified; for at least from
the Greek period onwards a certain fissiparous tendency was evident in
Judaism, and such incipient fragmentation is important for a study of
Jewish *paradosis*.

There was priestly *paradosis* – at the turn of the ages, Sadducean. The
ritual and sacrificial requirements of the *torah* (as in Lev. 1 and 3) fell far
short of providing detailed instructions for every aspect of the rites.[11] Oral
tradition directed the priestly rites and the performance of priestly duties.[12]
The Samaritans also were the perpetuators and exponents of ancient ob-
servances and practices, the self-styled 'Keepers of the Truth'.[13] Whether
in connection with their distinctive calendar, Mount Gerizim, the use of
the tetragrammaton, the technique of sacrifice or marriage and divorce,
the Samaritans understood themselves to adhere to traditions handed down
by the elders and their forefathers, the 'Pure Ones'.[14] For example: 'accord-

ing to Samaritan tradition, the secret of the calculation of the new moon was first given by God to Adam, and was transferred from generation to generation until it came to Moses, who passed it on to Phinehas; he was the first to establish the Samaritan calendar according to the astronominal calculation of the meridian of Mount Gerizim'.[15]

The Qumran sectaries were forced by the nature of their movement to be supremely conscious of their immediate historical tradition, stemming from their founder and the events which brought the community into being, and the traditions of Israel, which were understood as relating to themselves in a unique, eschatological fashion. The nature of their distinctive 'peshering' of the scriptures has already been indicated.[16] Possessing written documents which may have been both official and 'secret' in that they were authoritative in and the private concern of an intimate community, they resembled both Sadducees and Samaritans in certain respects in relation to tradition.[17]

The Pharisaic-rabbinic tradition, which was to be predominant after the fall of the temple and the Qumran sectaries, reached back to Maccabean times and largely took over from that point the scribal tradition that had been evolving at least since the Exile in Babylon. To be sure, there is a certain difficulty in working back from Mishnaic times (not to mention Talmudic) to the period before the fall of the temple,[18] yet there is impressive consistency in the rabbis' handling of and general attitude to scripture and tradition.[19]

Underlying this concern for tradition were common educational presuppositions, techniques and emphases. The parental teaching function had long been supplemented in Israel by a scribal tradition related to international culture and taking root in Israel from the time of David and Solomon. But first-century Judaism had absorbed much Greek and cosmopolitan influence while preserving its distinctive Jewish ethos, and accordingly Jewish educational presuppositions and procedures were not unrelated to or inconsistent with those of the wider international circle. The scribes – who are by no means limited to Pharisaic circles[20] – shared a common professional and educational standpoint.

The principal characteristics of this educational milieu are neatly summarised by Gerhardsson:

the learning by heart of basic texts; the principle that 'learning comes before understanding'; the attempt to memorise the teacher's *ipsissima verba*; the condensation of material into short, pregnant texts; the use of mnemonic technique, which was fairly simple in early Tannaitic times, but which by the end of the Amoraic period had become highly complex; the use of notebooks and secret scrolls; the frequent repetition of memorised material, aloud and with melodic inflexion, the retention of knowledge by these methods – not to mention the idea of the teacher as 'pattern' and the pupil as 'imitator'.[21]

That the transmission of tradition was governed by these presuppositions can hardly be questioned, the rabbis mechanising somewhat the process of reflexion and systematisation. Yet their object was to avoid the 'woodenness' of inferior education, such as *mere* memorisation. Their aim was to promote insight and discover new truth. Accordingly, 'to describe the way in which oral Torah is transmitted is to describe a complicated interplay between basic solidity and complementary flexibility'.[22] *Halachah* statements could in fact be formulated by pupils according to the teacher's basic position, and the actions of a rabbi could be used as paradigms for teaching purposes. Tradition is thus seen as a living organism, constantly growing under carefully regulated conditions around a living heart.

Jesus and tradition

Two questions are to be distinguished: (i) Jesus' involvement with Jewish *paradosis*, and (ii) Jesus as the fountainhead of a new, Christian *paradosis*. In practice, these questions overlap to a certain extent.

Paradosis is the immediate issue at stake in Matt. 15: 1-20 (cf. Mark 7: 1-23). As it stands, this passage is no doubt composite, deriving its precise form from early Christian teaching and editing. But from the phenomenological viewpoint, the issue was inevitable in the context not merely of the Palestinian Christian churches[23] but of the ministry of Jesus and the disciples' community; for the issue is directly related on the one hand to the paramount question of the interpretation and practice of the Torah and on the other to the distinctive life-style of Jesus and his disciples. The halachic question of handwashing indicates Jesus' lack of sympathy for the 'tradition of the elders',[24] at least on this issue. V. Taylor rejects Bultmann's criticism that the scribes' question is not answered: the answer in Mark, based on Is. 29: 13,[25] is 'a devastating answer' and 'comes to grips with the main issue and answers with a decisive "No" '.[26] Mark understands Jesus' position to be a rejection of 'the traditions of men' which effectively obscure the real demand of God (Mark 7: 8; cf. v. 13). This is consonant with the radical nature of Jesus' *paraenesis* discussed in the previous chapter and with his prophetic activities. Matthew is essentially in agreement with Mark's point (Matt. 15: 3) but elects to illustrate it by means of Qorban (15: 4-9; cf. Mark 7: 9-13).[27]

Did Jesus then act as a rabbi? Here again, one must be aware of the inherent polarity in Jesus' procedures, for the failure to recognise this has led to much critical confusion and acrimony. B. Gerhardsson argued that Jesus taught as a rabbi and that his disciples were instructed as students of a rabbi and subsequently formed what was virtually a rabbinic academy.[28] To maintain such a position, he tended to play down the importance of Mark 1: 22 (Matt. 7: 29): 'he taught them as one with authority, and not as their scribes'. Even if this is an editorial 'frame' passage,[29] it is also an important interpretative clue which the writers are offering their readers. Like the scribes, Jesus taught; but he did not teach as the scribes did: he was distinguished from them by that which identifies him rather with the prophetic, pneumatic or charismatic, with what A. N. Wilder calls 'immediacy, directness and spontaneity'.[30] Yet Wilder fails to preserve Jesus' characteristic polarity when he denies that he had a conscious concern with catechetics – a statement difficult to reconcile with the evidence surveyed in the last chapter. And M. Smith, in his sweepingly negative review of Gerhardsson's work, shows a certain insensitivity to the refined nuances of Jesus' position when he claims, against Gerhardsson, that the New Testament demonstrates 'the loss of any reliable record as to Jesus' attitude towards the Law' and speaks of 'the mess of contradictory scraps of evidence which the gospels preserve'.[31] Subsequently, Gerhardsson sought to retrieve the balance:

> There must be a middle way. We need not represent Jesus and the early Church as more *unique* or more *conforming* than they were. To regard Jesus as a Jewish Rabbi among many Jewish Rabbis and the early Church as a Jewish sect among many Jewish sects is certainly as far from the historical truth as to call Jesus '*völlig allein in seiner Zeit, sterneneinsam in seinem Volk*'.[32]

Something of this creative tension is seen in practically every aspect of Jesus' life. He ceases to act typically of a rabbi precisely at the point where he appears to act as a prophet and vice versa. He is much concerned with the law of God, yet the flashing insights into its full implications and the spelling out of its meaning in radical fashion, whatever form the individual parts of his teaching may have taken, defy any total categorisation such as 'rabbinic'. He tends to transcend or qualify any one category that is offered as a description.

The recognition of this fact renders difficult any attempt to characterise Jesus' relationship with his disciples as *simply* that of a rabbi and his pupils. At least, that is not the only possibility open to us: a prophet also tended to be the leader of a group of disciples. Structurally, the group will be ordered according to the character of its leader. If Jesus did not teach as the scribes did, his community was not simply a scribal one. If Jesus emphasised radical penetration into the religious issue in question, his disciples were instructed in such a way that it became possible for them to share the insight and develop the faculty of discernment. That the disciples were able to remember many of Jesus' sayings – unforgettable as they must have appeared – is extremely likely. That they were, as Gerhardsson implies, drilled in the technique of repetition is unlikely, despite the pervasive educational practice; for such a practice would fit awkwardly with the intentionality of Jesus' teaching. Thus in Matthew, Jesus' teaching on religious devotion is characteristically set over against the misuse of religious practices (cf. Matt. 6:1-18), and the type of prayer he commends is set over against mechanical repetition (6:7). The disciples, therefore, appear to have received not a set model but a specimen of brief, meaningful prayer and to have been exhorted to pray after that fashion. Thus the prayer pattern is not given primarily as *paradosis* but as *paraenesis*, designed certainly to be a guide for religious practice but also to be part of the insight-giving process into which Jesus was admitting his disciples and which might be frustrated by mechanical methods. And this remains true even for the context Luke provides, in which Jesus inducts the disciples into the practice of prayer in response to their request.[33]

What is evident is the tendency for Jesus' *paraenesis* to become *paradosis* in the hands of the disciples engaged in their mission. It is true that the much edited versions the gospels present of the mission of the Twelve[34] concentrate attention on the proclamation of the kingdom in word and action: the mission is essentially prophetic,[35] an extension of Jesus' own ministry. But the transmission of the *paraenesis* of Jesus would appear incidental to it. It is Jesus rather than the Twelve who is 'teacher'. Mark relates that the 'apostles' (*sic*) reported to Jesus on their preaching and teaching (Mark 6:30), but apart from the overlay of later vocabulary and interpretation the reference to 'teaching' in this context appears to be the work of healing and exorcism for which the disciples had been commissioned (cf. 1:27). In other words, a teaching ministry involving the transmission of Jesus' *paraenesis* as Christian *paradosis* belongs to the period after his death. There is no suggestion that the intimate discussions Jesus had with his disciples were primarily directed to the establishment of such a *paradosis*. Such evidence as we possess is directed to the encouragement of deeper insights into the mysteries of God's ways or the meaning of Jesus' teaching and mission or the momentum of historical events. The disciples' questions about parables are not directed to the clarification of their external form but to the elucidation of their meaning and purpose – or so the evangelists understood them to be.[36] Questions dealt with in this way are concerned with the disciples' failure to cast out an evil spirit (Mark 9: 28; cf. Matt. 17: 19), with the Elijah expectation (Mark 9: 11; cf. Matt. 17: 10); with the interpretation of the marriage law (Mark 10: 10); with the end things (Mark 13: 3f.; cf. Matt. 24: 3; Luke 21: 7); and, above all, with the prospect of the cross – a prospect so unthinkable that the disciples are unable to comprehend it and their rapport with Jesus breaks down over the issue. That the teaching offered by Jesus on these points has been coloured by later church concerns is transparent, but that does not detract either from the contextual appropriateness of the issues to the ministry of Jesus or from the essentially paraenetic nature of his procedures (e.g., Mark 10: 23, 35–45). The later perspective is sometimes clearly indicated or expressly affirmed. The disciples 'did not understand the saying' (Mark 9: 32), which was only clarified by subsequent events. 'When . . . he was raised from the dead, his disciples remembered that he had said this; and they believed the scripture and the word which Jesus had spoken.'[37] Only when this latter step has been taken can it be said that *paradosis* has come into being. Christian *paradosis* would appear to consist, at least in part, of the words (*paraenesis*), actions and fate of Jesus, understood afresh in the light of the resurrection faith and formulated according to situational exigencies by the early Christian preachers and teachers.

Tradition in the early church

The early church is indicated as the crucible in which Christian *paradosis* was finally compounded. The final and only sufficient catalyst was the resurrection faith, as Luke effectively shows in his resurrection narratives in which the risen Christ instructs the disciples in the reinterpretation of the scriptures from a christocentric standpoint (Luke 24: 27, 44f.) – a reinterpretation which recalls his teaching 'while I was still with you'. Reinterpretation[38] and recollection[39] are thus two basic procedures: a point heavily underlined by John (cf. John 14: 25f.). Scandinavian scholars[40] have rightly emphasised the significance of Acts 2: 42 as indicating the didactic function of the *koinonia* which is itself characterised by its table-fellowship – a significant link with the former disciples' group presided over by Jesus[41] – and its intense devotional life. Here, as the apostolic teaching, now compounded of many elements, is corporately shared and explored, new insights emerge under the guidance of the Spirit and the manifold Christian *paradosis* is shaped on the anvil of didactic necessity. For, as Matthew makes clear, the apostolic ministry inaugurated by the risen Christ is characterised by a teaching mission (Matt. 28: 19f.), conducted in the paradoxical presence of the Christ who has been taken from them.

But while this outline of the origins of *paradosis* may thus be sketched in lightly, a bolder description of it is dependent upon a more detailed investigation of an area that is already something of a battleground of critical conflict. Some of the more important issues will now be reviewed.

It will be generally allowed that Luke presents a highly developed theology of salvation.[42] Gerhardsson, however, protests against the 'extremely tenaciously-held misapprehension among exegetes that an early Christian author must *either* be a purposeful theologian and writer *or* a fairly reliable historian'.[43] Gerhardsson may be justified in castigating the more extreme forms of this dichotomy: in rejecting the notion, for example, that Luke's work is no more than a magnificent piece of creative or imaginative writing directed to evangelical ends. But it appears that Gerhardsson is in some danger of confusing faithfulness to religious tradition with a historical concern to know the Jesus event *wie es eigentlich gewesen ist*. Christian *paradosis* inevitably contains a high degree of religious interpretation, including theological reflexion and prophetic insight. It is concerned primarily not with the Jesus event but with the Christ event, although the former may to a greater or lesser extent be found in the latter. Thus while it may be true that Luke's modifications of Mark's material are minor, his use of Mark indicates not a primarily historical judgment about the accuracy of his material but a theological and religious acceptance of it – through it one may 'see' and 'hear' Jesus the Christ (Luke 1:1). To enable one to do so to even greater advantage and reach an understanding of 'the truth' of the Christ event (Luke 1:4), Luke includes not only the teaching tradition of Q but also other traditions which underline the cosmic significance of Christ – from Adam to the Ascension, as it were. Gerhardsson rightly says that 'what we know as Lucan theology may have been common creed in early Christianity, or in parts thereof';[44] but he confuses the issue by talking of 'the reliability of Luke's account' or of its being 'a source of reliable information',[45] thus smuggling in what appears to be a simplistic view of religio-historical tradition.

Several particular issues call for comment at this point.

Jerusalem

To be sure, Jerusalem was the centre of the world for the Jews (as Mecca for the Muslims); Jesus' ministry reached its climax there (in the context of a Passover celebration, be it noted), and the early church had its original focus there (but also possibly in Galilee).[46] The Christian tradition therefore included a positive and negative attitude to Jerusalem: the city of God, and the city of rejection. In the highly critical times of the early church when 'the last hour' had come, Jerusalem with its rich religious and scrip-

tural import became inevitably the focus of much reinterpretation and
discussion in Christian circles. Thus there developed ideas of the church as
'the true temple' and of 'the new Jerusalem' as an eschatological concept.
It is in Luke's works that the stories of Jesus the Christ and of the church
are linked together with Jerusalem as the critical focus: a total structure
which presupposes a later standpoint and perspective. Gerhardsson appeals
to Luke 19: 28 - 21: 38 as 'built on an older collection of traditions concerning Jesus'.[47] This proves nothing: the gap to the original situation
remains. The hub of the passion story is at least equally early, yet Mark
does not end up with the focus on Jerusalem but on Galilee. Even in the
Lucan tradition, strong evidence is found of a later, accumulative tradition
rather than simply an early, monolithic one. Thus Luke 19: 39–44 (peculiar
to Luke) contains a prediction of the destruction of Jerusalem which is
partly derived from the *pesher* activity of the early Christians on scriptural
texts[48] and also appears to reflect knowledge of the event itself. Luke is
doubtless faithful to his traditions; but those traditions come through a
community in which intensive reinterpretation was constantly taking place
'in the Spirit' (cf. 1 Cor. 14), and in consequence the traditions he uses do
not necessarily lead one back by an uncomplicated historical route to the
self-understanding of Jesus or the *earliest* community.[49]

The Twelve and the church in Jerusalem

The Twelve play a significant part in Luke's account (Luke 6: 13; 9: 1f.),
being maintained by the election of Matthias (Acts 1: 15ff.). They are
essentially witnesses to Jesus in his life, death and resurrection. It is worth
noting, however, that they bear witness particularly to the resurrection (cf.
Luke 24: 36–53), which marks the point at which their minds were open
(24: 45), so that all their memories of Jesus are filtered through this new
understanding. Therefore, the disciples' witness - and the *paradosis* which
came from them - concerning the life and teaching of Jesus from the days
of the Baptist onwards cannot be regarded as a matter of simple transmission on the rabbinic model. Their principal role is to 'preach the word'
or 'preach Christ', especially his resurrection. That commission certainly
includes teaching; and it is readily conceded that some of their teaching
was related to that given by Jesus - effectively turning his *paraenesis* into
Christian *paradosis*. Matthew, who stresses the apostolic teaching mission
launched by the risen Christ, is particularly concerned to include a mass
of Jesus' own teaching as the Sermon on the Mount.

But Gerhardsson is anxious to give the Twelve a role in church order
and unity which is hard to sustain on the evidence of the New Testament.
Luke may be reasonably consistent in his use of the term 'apostle', but it

is strikingly different from Paul's;[50] and while Paul's can by no means be taken as normative in the church, Luke's has all the appearance of being governed by a rigid concept of salvation history: Paul does not qualify as an apostle in terms of Acts 1: 21f.[51] Allowance must therefore be made for variations of viewpoint in the church – Luke is not wholly representative.

Nevertheless, the Twelve have a symbolic role in the church: this Paul accepts as much as anyone (1 Cor. 15: 5). The symbol, current in Judaism, would appear to have been employed by Jesus in relation to the group he formed around him. But was it any more than a symbol in the early church? As M. Smith observed, 'We have thirteen or fourteen names for Jesus' reportedly twelve apostles'.[52] Did the Twelve in the church form an ecclesiastical, administrative or collegiate entity? It appears highly doubtful. Paul recognises a Jerusalem authority, headed by James (the Lord's brother), Cephas and John (Gal. 2: 9); but this does not accord with the list in Acts 1: 13, for which James, of course, would not qualify.[53] Yet James appears to have been the presiding authority in Jerusalem and to have attempted to exercise some oversight over the churches of Judaea and beyond (cf. Gal. 1: 19; 2: 12). The Twelve therefore is at best a shadowy entity, doubtful in composition and obscure as far as later history is concerned.[54] It was an emotive term, useful for later writers indulging in the grand sweep.[55] Consequently, the symbolic Twelve does not provide Gerhardsson with the base he needs to meet the demands of his hypothesis on the transmission of tradition through a unitary central agency.[56] This symbol apart, however, the Christian community at Jerusalem undoubtedly possessed influence and authority.

The early Christian churches and their traditions

Even if, for the modern scholar, 'the temptations are to a greater elaboration of the supposed background theologies than the amount of evidence really justifies',[57] it will be conceded that the early churches embraced a variety of emphases within the overarching unity of their Christian faith. Without arguing a case such as *quot sententiae, tot ecclesiae*,[58] one may nevertheless point to a certain variety of groups in the church, some representing distinctive environments and cultural traditions though none of them existing in isolation from the other. Important among such groups were the 'Hebrew' Christians, based in Jerusalem and Judaea (cf. Gal. 1: 22f.) and combining their messianic faith with profound respect for messianic Torah.[59] They were distinguished by the writer of Acts from the 'Hellenists' or hellenistic Jewish Christians, who had a foothold in Jerusalem but existed in strength in the Diaspora, and whose position seems to have been strongly christocentric.[60] The Samaritan Christians could hardly but represent a distinctive tendency, although apparently enjoying close relations with the hellenistic Jewish mission.[61] The Galilean Christians may well represent yet another early grouping,[62] characterised by pneumatic experiences including encounters with the risen Lord, an intense eschatological expectation related to their own area (cf. Mark 16: 7) and a strong attachment to the memory of Jesus in Galilee. Again, the Gentile mission was an important offshoot of the christocentric Diaspora mission. Tensions between such groups could, on occasion, be considerable; yet the groups themselves appeared to overlap to such an extent that any attempt to resort to relatively separate operation was doomed to failure (cf. Gal. 2). Nevertheless, the picture at Corinth – 'I belong to Paul', 'I to Apollos', 'I to Cephas' and perhaps even 'I to Christ' (1 Cor. 1: 12) – probably becomes more and more representative of the church situation in which Diaspora Jews and Gentiles make up the total community. The mention of Apollos (cf. Acts 18: 24) is symptomatic of a greater fragmentation than has often been recognised.[63] In addition gnostic tendencies, both within and outside the church, are to be reckoned with. Paul knows well that the problematic element in the church is the safeguarding of its unity (cf. 1 Cor. 1: 13ff.). In face of this evidence, Gerhardsson's argument for a monolithic ecclesiastical system centred on Jerusalem as the seat of the highest doctrinal authority[64] is doomed to failure. The partial parallels he draws between Acts 15 and the general sessions at Qumran[65] or the Sanhedrin or other rabbinic assemblies provide a commentary on Luke's understanding of how such a session might have operated, rather than on a given historical occasion.[66]

How do these considerations affect the traditions current in the diverse sectors of the early Christian communities? Possibly the Galilean churches, with their pneumatic and eschatological emphasis, contributed to the build-up of traditions in aretalogical fashion around the 'miracles, portents and signs' (Acts 2: 22) that characterised much of Jesus' ministry in those parts and indicated the divine *exousia* with which he acted. The Markan passion story[67] is narrated in the context of a pilgrimage to Jerusalem (Mark 10: 33) with Galilee as base (8: 27; 9: 30f.; 10: 1, 32) and the expected return of Jesus to Galilee (16: 7); it is therefore also likely to reflect traditions current in that church, or at least a combination of the Galilean and Hellenist traditions, for Galilee had good communications with the Diaspora to the north-west and north-east as well as with Jerusalem itself.[68] Matthew's passion story appears largely dependent on Mark's, apart from his own paraenetic additions[69] – the Galilean base was obviously acceptable to Syrian Christians. The Lucan story in which localities lose their geographical significance and acquire a symbolic meaning[70] is more or less dependent[71] on Mark: perhaps a variation on the Galilean hellenistic tradition, with more emphasis on the hellenistic and compatible with Caesarea as its location. Luke's interest in Samaritan figures suggests that he might well have been in touch with Samaritan sources (included in source L), and this also appears to be true of the fourth gospel. However, the degree to which the Johannine tradition diverges from the others at many points suggests a virtually independent tradition,[72] characterised by the theological teaching and interpretation of the evangelist or his sources and assigned variously by scholars to a hellenistic, Palestinian or Samaritan origin.[73]

The diversity of the passion narrative provides a useful commentary on the nature of tradition. In all churches, there was a variety of reasons, all of them basically paraenetic, for telling the story of Jesus' death. There was an *exegetical* reason: its narration accompanies the searching of the scriptures for prophetic testimony to such an event, and on occasion the two processes influence each other. There was a *didactic* reason, aiming to develop the atoning significance of his death - e.g., he 'died for our sins' (1 Cor. 15: 3); he 'gave himself a ransom for many' (Mark 10: 45). There was an *apologetic* reason, for the cross was a stumbling block to Jews and foolishness to Gentiles (1 Cor. 1: 23): the telling of it in a restrained and meaningful way could contribute to the overcoming of such difficulties. There was a *liturgical* reason: so central was the cross in the Christian faith that a recitation of the passion story was required in worship - not least as a Christian focus in the liturgical celebration of the mighty acts of salvation wrought by God, corresponding to the Exodus story in the Passover.[74] Hence the transmission of this *paradosis* of the passion was qualitatively different from a semi-mechanical process within a small, quasi-rabbinic community. It was a lively, creative process, conserving the memory of the past, not as inert data but as *gospel*, presenting to the contemporary hearer the gospel of Jesus through a specific aspect of his life and ministry.[75] Thus *paradosis* was valued because of the authentic witness it bore (cf. 1 Cor. 15: 1ff.) and its paraenetic and homiletic usefulness.

Paul and tradition

Paul, the erstwhile scribe steeped in the traditions of his people (Gal. 1: 14),[76] had come to write off all such assets for the sake of Christ (Phil. 3: 5ff.).[77] Consequently, there is an ambivalence in his attitude to Christian tradition. Inevitably, something of the rabbinic attitude to tradition was transferred to his new milieu. In Paul's epistles, O. Cullmann observes, 'we find the whole Jewish *paradosis* terminology, and, what is more, we find it used in a definitely positive way'.[78] On the other hand, the focus of his new faith was Christ, through whom came his calling as an apostle without human mediation (Gal. 1:17). In his preaching, teaching and every other aspect of his ministry, Paul must remain true to that calling, not least in face of any traditions, no matter how authoritative they may appear to be, which contradict or are incompatible with that primary revelation. When Paul withstood Peter to his face at Antioch, he was rejecting the table *halachah* which had proceeded from Jerusalem and which Peter and Barnabas were prepared to accept.

Such ambivalence should put the modern critic on his guard against forcing Paul's use of the vocabulary of *paradosis* into a preconceived mould or otherwise failing to appreciate the nuances of his expressions. What is significant is not *that* Paul uses this vocabulary but *how* he uses it. A brief discussion of certain key passages is necessary to throw light on this problem.

(i) 1 Cor. 15:3ff. represents a classic instance of Paul's use of tradition. It has been studied so frequently that we may confine our observations to a minimum:

(a) It has long been recognised that 1 Cor. 15:3ff. represents an early formula which was part of the primitive Christian tradition[79] - perhaps a tradition which Paul received at Damascus soon after his conversion[80] or at least at Antioch, the base of his mission.[81] It is also reasonable to suppose that he discussed its data at Jerusalem[82] although this suggestion neither proves nor even indicates a Palestinian as opposed to a hellenistic, origin for the formula.[83]

(b) The received formula, apart from some insertions (possibly by Paul), is carefully balanced, as can be seen in the focal section (vv. 3b-5a):

> that Christ died / for our sins / in accordance with the scriptures/,
> that he was buried /
> that he was raised / on the third day / in accordance with the
> scriptures /,
> that he appeared to Cephas / then to the twelve/

The basic kerygmatic statement - the irreducible content of Christian *paradosis*, even if it is, as here, only partially stated - is that Jesus is the Messiah, that the Messiah died and rose again (or was raised), and that this event was accomplished as part of God's saving purpose for mankind, as attested by scripture. These elements, although articulated with a certain flexibility of expression, are inseparable: here is the bedrock of Christian *paradosis*. There can be little doubt that *kata tas graphas* belongs to an early stage of tradition and refers in v. 3 to 'Christ died'.[84] As for the phrase 'for our sins', the idea that the sufferings and death of the righteous have vicarious, expiatory value is not unfamiliar to ancient Judaism.[85] Paul's use of *hilastērion* and the 'blood' of Christ probably reflects early tradition.[86] Hence the two prepositional phrases in 1 Cor. 15: 3 serve to indicate two distinct approaches to the interpretation of the cross – both of them early, and both expanding, deepening and interrelating as the theology and hermeneutics of the church matured.[87] A similar pattern of construction is to be discerned in the resurrection statement (v. 4).[88]

(c) A further possible parallelism can be detected in the tradition about the resurrection.

> he appeared to Cephas / then to the twelve (v. 5)
> he appeared to James / then to all the apostles (v. 7)

U. Wilckens has argued that these lines were originally legitimation formulae on which rested the special authority of the people concerned;[89] and this one may accept without necessarily also accepting Wilckens' entire position on the history of early Christian tradition.[90] While primacy is given to the appearance to Peter, that to the Twelve, though clearly subsequent, need not be regarded as necessarily derivative from his.[91] Together, these appearances authenticate the mission of Peter and the Twelve as witnesses to and proclaimers of the message of the Messiah crucified and risen. Peter's group provided the *essential* link between the ministry of Jesus and the preaching of the risen Christ.[92] The appearance to James, 'the most significant of the early recruits to the young church'[93] and subsequently the leader of the church at Jerusalem, may be said to parallel that to Peter; but the phrase 'then to all the apostles' is much more difficult to handle. Although it is a formal parallel to 'then to the twelve' (v. 5), it may not be parallel in substance (which would involve a complete contrast between 'the twelve' and 'all the apostles'). Probably Paul is using a comprehensive phrase to denote the view that every apostle derived his commission from the risen Christ. It is also possible that this was originally a Jerusalem tradition which claimed that all the apostles were commissioned from Jerusalem, as in Luke–Acts:

> For out of Zion shall go forth the law,
> and the word of the Lord from Jerusalem (Is. 2: 3).

(d) The appearance 'to more than five hundred brethren at one time' (v. 6) is not clearly corroborated in any other tradition. The temptation to relate it to the Pentecost occurrence in Acts is strong,[94] even if the case falls short of proof.[95] Coming as it does between the parallel formulae in v. 5 and v. 7, it would seem to reflect either yet another resurrection tradition,[96] probably not directly connected to those in v. 5 or v. 7, or a summary form which Paul was accustomed to use.[97] The qualification entered in v. 6b is clearly a Pauline comment.[98]

(e) To the traditions which he received Paul adds the experience which made him apostle to the Gentiles (cf. Gal. 1:15f.) and which thus becomes Pauline tradition. Attention centres on the term *to ektrōmati*.[99] While the connotation of his former persecution of the church is operative (v. 9), that of his apostleship is dominant. Hence this Pauline tradition suggests that Paul has been, as it were, hurried into the world, sadly deficient though he might be, in order to perform the eschatological role of leading the mission to the Gentiles. By God's grace he was enabled to work 'more abundantly than all the others' (v. 10). The Gentile churches, like the Corinthians, were his 'workmanship in the Lord', the seal of his apostleship (9:2).

(f) The claim that all the apostles believe and proclaim the same message presumably refers to the basic formula in vv. 3-4 and possibly v. 5a.[100] The list of witnesses is secondary, since various groups of churches clearly emphasised their own tradition of witness and there is no corroboration of Paul's list as a fixed and universally accepted formula. The claim implicit in 1 Cor. 15:1ff. is that the tradition cited here is operative in Paul's churches and that its central content is both endorsed by all the apostles and derived from them.

It is also appropriate to distinguish between this *paradosis* and the *euangelion* which is the immediate content of Paul's preaching: e.g., Christ crucified, the power and wisdom of God (1 Cor. 1:18, 24), or the grace of God in Christ through whom by faith comes justification and peace (Rom. 1:16f.; 5:1). His initial invitation to recall the *euangelion* is subsequently modified by the phrase 'with what discourse (with what form of words)[101] I preached the gospel to you' – the anacoluthon and repetition of the main verb making clear what Paul actually wants to talk about. Remember, he says, what was involved in my presentation of the gospel: the tradition of the cross and resurrection that I myself received and passed on to you. The Corinthians had no intention of deserting the gospel, of 'believing in vain'; but they had – so Paul had heard – seriously and indefensibly modified part of the tradition which was inseparable from the preaching of the gospel, viz., the concept of resurrection (cf. 15:12ff.; 35). The *paradosis*, therefore, is not the gospel itself but the essential accompaniment and presupposition of the gospel. It presents data which must be conveyed to and grasped by the hearer if he is to understand the basis on which the gospel can be proclaimed. Doubtless Paul was aware of much of this *paradosis* when he persecuted the church, when it appeared to him to undermine the foundations of Judaism, elevating Jesus above Moses and deserting 'the traditions of our fathers'. His conversion involved the revelation of the gospel of God's grace to him; and in that light the *paradosis* took on a different complexion.

1 Cor. 15:1-11 reveals the concept of *paradosis* operating in the Gentile

mission a considerable time before the evangelists committed such traditions to the written form of a connected narrative (cf. Luke 1:1-4). The passage underlines the place of biblical *pesher* and theological interpretation in the *paradosis*: an interesting point in view of the fact that the gospels are seen today, more clearly than in earlier stages of criticism, to possess a corresponding emphasis.

(ii) A number of paraenetic passages in Paul contain ostensible claims to dominical origin. These are now briefly reviewed:

(a) 1 Thess. 4:15 - 'this we tell to you by the word of the Lord'. The context is eschatological expectation and apocalyptic *paraenesis*, in which the major symbol of the death and resurrection of Christ has already been adduced (4:14). The dominical reference in 4:15 seems to be designed to emphasise the meaning of that symbol in relation to the particular problem of 'those who have fallen asleep' (v. 15b; cf. v. 14b).

What is meant here by 'the word of the Lord'? One suggestion is that it is a saying of Jesus, an *agraphon* otherwise unrepresented in the gospel tradition.[102] Another is that it is an apocalyptic quotation mistakenly ascribed to Jesus;[103] or, perhaps better, a presentation by Paul of general Christian apocalyptic symbolism which was believed to express the mind of the Lord concerning the future and which does eventually impinge on the gospel tradition in Mark 13.[104] The mechanics whereby disparate traditional material, including that from the scriptures and possibly from the teaching of Jesus, was sifted and remoulded into a convincing whole which carried dominical attestation are doubtless to be ascribed to prophetic circles in the churches,[105] though not necessarily to a private revelation of a visionary type.[106] A fairly complex process is indicated here.[107] Paul's own prophetic experiences - as well as his reflexion on such data as came his way through the tradition - may have served to confirm or correct a wider prophetic consensus in the church about the *parousia*. The phrase 'the word of the Lord' may be deliberately ambiguous in order to hold certain nuances in tension: the word of Jesus and the word of Christ,[108] apocalyptic traditions in the church, the prophetic word, and the word of scripture.[109] Most weight should probably be placed on the last two.

A comparison of Mark 13 and the book of Daniel shows that Mark draws heavily upon a midrashic tradition at this point.[110] The *Sitz im Leben* of such teaching is clearly the early Christian community.[111] The *parousia* of the Son of man (v. 26f.) 'is painted in the colours of a theophany, such as those used in the Old Testament in connection with the day of Yahweh'.[112] In 1 Thess. 4:16f., the apocalyptic picture of the Lord's coming is similar in general type but draws from a wider range of

scriptural imagery. When allowance is made for Pauline adaptation, however, it does not appear to derive immediately from the tradition on which
Mark drew, although it is clearly related to it. Other features of the Daniel/
Mark tradition are reflected more convincingly in the Thessalonian letters
(esp. 2 Thess. 2) – antichrist, the abomination of desolation, false prophets,
the sufferings of the righteous in the last days, evil attempts to deceive the
elect – all of which have a connection with Daniel's blasphemous king.[113]
Again, the theme of watchfulness in 1 Thess. 5: 1ff. bears some relation to
the tradition of Luke 21: 34ff. A feature of New Testament eschatological
passages is their strongly paraenetic tone.

Thus it is both possible and proper to speak of an early Christian eschatological *paradosis*. It was not stereotyped, nor was it formulated with the
precision of the kerygmatic *paradosis* of 1 Cor. 15: 3ff. Its content and
development were related to the continuing dialogue with the eschatological
symbolism and expectations of scripture, interrogated and 'peshered' from
the standpoint of faith in Christ; with the tradition of the teaching of Jesus
himself;[114] and with the changing situation of the church. Prophetic insight
may well have acted as the catalyst.[115] Thus when Paul expounds his 'word
of the Lord', he can relate the essence of Christian eschatological *paradosis*
directly to the particular problem that confronts him or his churches and
expand it, if necessary, with further material from its scriptural source –
Daniel, in particular, a veritable treasure-house of eschatological symbolism
and ideas. From such the Thessalonians drew comfort and encouragement.

(b) 1 Cor. 9: 14; cf. 9: 4. This strongly rhetorical passage is confessedly
an *apologia* for Paul's apostolic practice (v. 3). Its focus is a statement that
the maintenance of the apostolic ministry is a right which is endorsed both
by the Torah (v. 9) and by the Lord (v. 14): a right which remains even if
Paul chooses not to exercise it.[116] But the *halachah* Paul wishes to establish
by his practice at Corinth[117] is not based on the command of the Lord nor
on Paul's waiving of apostolic privilege but on the necessity to avoid putting
an obstacle in the way of the gospel of Christ (v. 12). For this he will 'endure
anything' – including waiving privileges that are his according to dominical
paradosis.[118] Thus the Lord's command is undoubtedly viewed in an oblique
perspective.

Prima facie, the received practice of the apostles rests on an utterance of
the Lord's which Paul paraphrases rather than cites. His allusiveness is often
taken to presuppose 'a well-known commandment of Christ'.[119] Can this
be pin-pointed in gospel tradition? Many scholars point to Luke 10: 7[120] –
a tradition which requires investigation.

The Lucan account of the sending out of the disciples is complicated by
the fact that the evangelist has incorporated two different versions,[121] of

which the second (ch. 10) is clearly integral to his theological concern:[122]
it is 'a paradigm for the mission of the Church in the world'.[123] Thus Luke
10: 7 established for the Gentile mission the principle that the prophet-
missionary or apostle (in the wider sense) should be maintained[124] by those
to whom and on whose behalf he ministers. In the Gentile mission itself the
principle was extended to the ruling elders of the community, especially
those who preach and teach (1 Tim. 5: 17). In 1 Timothy the scriptural
basis for it is Deut. 25: 4, to which is added the logion as found in Luke 10:
7.[125] Since Paul also cites Deut. 25: 4 before alluding to the dominical
logion, two possibilities present themselves: either the Paulinist author of
1 Timothy is copying Paul at this point,[126] or both he and Paul himself
reflect the same church tradition and similar hermeneutical procedures.[127]
But whereas Paul is particularly vague in his handling of the logion, the
Paulinist is precise in his use of Luke 10: 7. It is likely, therefore, that this
hermeneutical tradition did not originate with Paul but was current in the
hellenistic Jewish Christian and Gentile Christian circles to which Paul,
Luke and the Paulinist belonged.[128]

Luke 9: 1–6 is part of the complex web of synoptic relationships which
includes also Mark 6: 7–13 and Matt. 10: 1–16.[129] Certain features of the
Christian Palestinian mission perhaps influence the Markan narrative: two
exceptive clauses permit staff (v. 8) and sandals (v. 9), prerequisites of
practical missionary activity.[130] Matthew and Luke appear to follow early
tradition (Q?) in incorporating the command to proclaim the kingdom
and to heal.[131] Matthew, however, includes and attributes to Jesus two
sayings on the subject of maintenance: 'you received without pay, give
without pay' (Matt. 10: 8);[132] and 'the labourer deserves his food' (10:
10). The first – almost certainly a Matthean insertion, reflecting opposition
to a paid apostolate in the church – rules out any question of salary. The
second speaks of receiving hospitality (cf. Luke 10: 7).[133] Here we seem
to have reached the bedrock of the Palestinian situation in which Jesus
worked. But even if the logion is ascribed to Jesus, it is not in any sense a
command to his disciples. It is a gnomic utterance which not only presupposes Jewish hospitality but is also in context with the theme of total
dependence upon God: 'no gold, no silver, no copper, no second tunic, no
sandals, no staff...you will be given your food, and you will have earned
it!' The importance of the passage lies in the fact that it shows the attitude
of Jesus to the maintenance of the disciples by those whom they serve. It is
little wonder that Paul paraphrased the 'command'! The *halachah* of Jesus
did not consist of a formal logion which might be interpreted as messianic
torah: it was implicit in Jesus' entire attitude. Since *paradosis* operates
verbally, however, the attitude and practice of Jesus are transmitted in

narrative tradition which included a gnomic instructional saying (sometimes cited independently) encapsulating the principle on which he bade his disciples act. Scholarly effort is thus misdirected when it tries to determine whether Paul is dependent on Matthew rather than Luke, or vice versa.[134] He fully accepts the Luke - 1 Timothy tradition; his practice is nearer the Matthean but depends on characteristically Pauline reasoning. It is unnecessary as well as misleading to presuppose that the *gnome* is the product of Christian prophecy speaking for Jesus.[135] *Paradosis* within the churches supplied all the data required. In that *paradosis*, hermeneutical practice played as important a role as the transmission of logia and narratives.

(c) 1 Cor. 7: 10f. (cf. vv. 1-16). The prohibition of divorce is ascribed with impressive emphasis to the Lord as distinct from Paul: i.e., a dominical source is expressly affirmed to strengthen apostolic teaching. For paraenetic purposes, the dominical verdict (or central symbol) is represented as wholly unambiguous;[136] yet Paul appears simply to give the 'clear meaning' of Jesus' teaching rather than a formal logion. In related paraenetic topics, Paul makes the concession[137] that marriage is commendable even in the time of eschatological crisis[138] but he relates his teaching both to celibacy (vv. 1, 7) and to sexual abstention for spiritual purposes (v. 5) as well as to the cases of the unmarried, the widows and mixed marriages. But what was the dominical tradition?

Mark 10: 1-31, to which the Markan version of this tradition belongs (vv. 2-12), appears to be an assemblage of catechetical material, not unlike the *Haustafeln* discussed in the previous chapter.[139] The question the Pharisees ask in v. 2 is inconceivable in the Palestinian setting of Jesus' ministry.[140] The argument of the passage does not follow a convincing sequence[141] although by v. 6 it reaches what appears to be the nerve-centre of Jesus' position – to which we shall return in due course. After a break at v. 10, which is typical of Mark's editorial practice, two statements occur: the first (v. 11) is contrary to Jewish custom, while the second (v. 12) is possible only in a Graeco-Roman milieu where the woman can take the initiative in divorcing her husband.[142] The Markan tradition has clearly been modified by church catechetical and polemical activities and seems to have its *Sitz im Leben* in the hellenistic Jewish (perhaps even Gentile) mission.[143]

The question of the Pharisees in Matthew's account (19: 3) is much more credible, since the phrase *kata pasan aitian* focuses attention upon the grounds for divorce. The progression of the argument is also more convincing. Jesus counters the question at once by citing the creation story (Gen. 1: 27; 2: 24) and establishing the concept of marriage as 'one flesh'. The Pharisaic reply involves Deut. 24: 1ff., to which Jesus responds by suggesting that such procedures are but concessions to the hardness of the human heart. They are not the sum and substance of the issue (v. 8). There follows a repudiation of divorce and re-marriage as adulterous, with the exceptive clause *me epi porneia*: a tradition also recorded in Matt. 5:32.[144] Luke 16:18 has a similar prohibition but without the exceptive clause.

If Mark's account is hellenistic Jewish, Matthew's belongs to the ethos of Christian scribalism and apologetic *vis à vis* rabbinic Judaism; for he relates the whole issue to the Hillel–Shammai debate.[145] Matt. 5:32, as G. F. Moore noted, contained a *verbatim* statement of the Shammaite position: unchastity was the sole grounds for divorce.[146] This aspect of the tradition is surely secondary, for as soon as Matthew has admitted that Jesus' main concern was a radical understanding of the institution of marriage in terms of God's creation, the whole issue is seen to be couched in eschatological rather than legal terms.[147] The exceptive clauses seem to belong, with the question of re-marriage, to subsequent casuistry.[148] It was of course essential, especially for the early Christians, to ask how this eschatological view might work out in practice; and it is *possible* that Jesus was involved in this question also.[149] Is divorce ever permissible (cf. Mark 10:2)? What about the Torah (cf. Deut. 24:1–4)? Is Jesus' position that of Shammai as opposed to Hillel (cf. Matt. 19:3)? Is re-marriage or marriage to a divorcee sinful (cf. Matt. 5:32; 19:9; Luke 16:18)? Would it be better not to marry at all (cf. Matt. 19:10)? Thus the 'dominical tradition' concerning marriage necessarily expanded – and at a relatively early date.

To return to Paul: the tradition which Paul solemnly affirms as dominical – 'not I but the Lord' (1 Cor. 7:10) – is presented in summary fashion in Paul's own words, together with a parenthesis also in Paul's own words. Once again, it is gnomic sentiment that seems to act as the catalyst for the whole tradition.[150] With Jewish precision, Paul indicates that the wife should not separate from her husband (if she does so, or already has done so, let her not re-marry; reconciliation with her husband is the only alternative to remaining single); and the husband should not divorce his wife. Here we have evidence that the expanding tradition that was to find written expression finally in Mark and Matthew was already accepted as *paradosis* – indeed, as *halachah* – as early as Paul's correspondence with Corinth.[151] The eschatological orientation is an authentic note which survived the changing times and was captured by written gospel tradition. The possibility of celibacy, as well as its unsuitability for everyone, provides a link between Paul's account and Matthew's. All this means that *paradosis* was a vital and creative force in the early churches. By means of *paraenesis* it interpreted the will of the Lord for believers. What is illegitimate is to conclude, even where Paul is most particular to separate the command of the

Lord from his own instruction, that he provides us with a transcript of the *ipsissima verba* of Jesus himself.

(d) 1 Cor. 11: 23–34. To correct the abuses evident among the Christians at Corinth, Paul appeals strongly to the traditions which he had handed on to them (v. 2). When he turns to the problem of the divisions in the community (v. 18f.) and to the abuses of the Lord's supper (v. 20),[152] the *paradosis* which he cites presents Jesus' words and actions at the last supper as a model (vv. 23–26), perhaps in more than one sense. The tradition recalls the night on which Jesus was 'handed over' – i.e., delivered up to death in accordance with God's saving purpose for mankind.[153] To the three actions which the head of the household normally performed at table Paul attached special significance in this context: taking a loaf, saying the blessing,[154] and breaking the bread (vv. 23f.). There follows the statement of meaning, the *hermeneia*, which is attributed to Jesus himself and which addresses the contemporary hearer directly, especially in its second part: 'do this...'. For the sake of brevity the description of the taking of the cup is curtailed, but the word formula is given in full,[155] again with the impression of contemporary address (v. 25). In what is presumably the final sentence of the *paradosis*, the remembrance includes not simply the recalling of a past event (still less, nostalgia for something that is no more) but a proclamation of the death of Christ as saving event and an anticipation of the *parousia*. There follows what appears to be a deduction of Paul's from the tradition concerning the consequences of eating and drinking 'in an unworthy manner' (vv. 27–32) – which allows him to express a prophetic admonition. He closes on a paraenetic note: when you come together for a meal, wait for one another! (v. 33).

The whole passage (vv. 17–34), essentially a paraenetic topic with an extended central symbol provided by *paradosis*, is directed to the problems of community. To 'remember' Jesus is to recall the act of sharing which symbolises the fellowship of his disciples – and prefigures the messianic banquet.[156] To this the liturgical paradigm which comprises the *paradosis* in question is subordinate; but liturgical overtones persist in the well-ordered procedure he commends – standing, as it does, in sharp contrast to the disorder of the Corinthian fellowship. Other motifs are also evident. He does not quote the *paradosis* primarily to expound the doctrine of atonement, yet this is integral to the notion of the self-giving of Jesus which is focal to his presentation. Nor does he speak explicitly of the church as the body of Christ, although the materials are ready to hand. Again, a prophetic motif is clearly discernible – certainly in the warning against 'profaning the body and blood of the Lord' (v. 27) and the judgment which that entails.[157]

Three terms are used in connection with the fellowship of the early church: the common meal, the breaking of bread[158] and the Lord's supper, the latter being closely related in Christian thinking and practice to the Passover. In time, the Lord's supper becomes, if not separated from the common meal, then at least a delimited part of it. The model which Paul supplies reflects not only his understanding of the tradition some twenty to twenty-five years after its inception but also the practice which he regards as desirable in his churches. Mark's version (14: 22–25) is very specific about the actions involved: 'he took bread, said grace over it, broke it, and gave it to them' (v. 22); 'he took a cup, gave thanks, gave it to them, and they all drank from it' (v. 23). The accompanying formulae show signs of doctrinal or theological development (esp. v. 24), which is even more obvious in Matthew (26: 28).[159] The eschatological dimension is apparent in all versions (Mark has it in the context of an 'amen' saying), and the use of the liturgical 'fruit of the vine' is also a feature in common.

The liturgical aspect of the gospel tradition can be illustrated in another way also. M. D. Goulder has argued that a gospel is a liturgical rather than a literary genre – 'a lectionary book... used in worship week by week in *lectio continua*'.[160] Matthew, a Jewish Christian *sopher*, expounded the Jewish scriptures in accordance with the festal cycle[161] and by means of Christian traditions: 'and as the Jews read the Law by *lectio continua* round the year so did he come in time to put together the elements of his new developed *paradosis* into a continuous book'.[162] Goulder's stimulating work has its controversial aspects, but one must admit that the structure of Matthew's passion narrative accords well at points with such a hypothesis. Thus two days before Passover the narrative would include 26: 2 – 'You know that after two days the Passover is coming, and the Son of man will be delivered up to be crucified'. The next evening, the anointing of Jesus for his burial would have been appropriate – a story told 'for a memorial of him' (26:13); and perhaps also Judas' bargain to betray Jesus (26:15).

26.17–25 ..., the preparation and eating of the Last Supper, would be read at the Christian Passover, at sunset; as it says, 'When it was evening...' (v. 20). 26.26–46, the Institution of the Eucharist, the closing psalm, and Gethsemane, would fall naturally at 9.00 p.m.: the Passover meal was a full-length occasion. 26.47–68, the Arrest and Trial, is marked off from the previous section by the threefold, 'Could you not watch with me one hour?', and would be read at midnight. Luke adds the apt comment, 'This is your hour, and the power of darkness' (22.53). 26.69 – 27.2, Peter's Denial and Jesus' delivery to Pilate would follow at cockcrow, 3.00 a.m. (26.74).

27.3-56, the whole story of the Passion from Judas' remorse to the women's watching of Jesus' death, would be taken at the one main service in the daytime of Passover. 27.57-28 would be the reading for Easter Saturday. The opening words, 'When it was evening...' assign it to sabbath; the opening words of 28, 'Now after the sabbath, toward the dawn of the first day of the week...' assign it to Saturday night. No doubt it was in practice divided between the two Saturday services. 28: 19f. supplies dominical authority for the Easter baptisms; and the whole of 28 would be repeated on the octave.[163]

A liturgical tradition such as this – even though the cultic action is modelled on the action of Jesus himself – does not relate easily to the pre-crucifixion scene. John is at variance with the synoptists on the day on which the last supper was held and, despite the extraordinary appositeness of his procedures for theological purposes (cf. 1 Cor. 5: 7), there have been advocates of the substantial historicity of his account.[164] It is doubtful, however, not only on what day of the week the supper was held but whether it was a Passover celebration at all, for the Passover motif could easily have been imported into the tradition by early Christian teachers for theological, interpretative and liturgical purposes. No overwhelmingly convincing arguments, however, can be adduced for alternative types of meal. Neither the *kiddush* nor the *haburah* type of observance is supported by strong evidence.[165] No doubt Jesus' observance at the last supper can be properly related to his practice of table-fellowship throughout his ministry.[166] The special nature of this meal can be explained in terms of his impending death and the 'farewell' situation,[167] while some otherwise puzzling aspects – e.g., the apparent absence of the lamb at the meal – no longer require explanation. Yet by itself, this solution to the problem of the last supper possibly deserves to be described as weak. Why was Jesus in Jerusalem in the first place? If the evidence is held to point to the celebration of the Passover, then the last supper can hardly be separated totally from that feast. The gospel accounts as they stand doubtless reflect subsequent theological interpretation and liturgical celebration of the event (the sequence of events being made to fit the orthodox Jewish calendar). Perhaps some of the strains and tensions of the passion narrative can be accounted for on the hypothesis that Jesus and his disciples followed unorthodox practice. Did they hold the Passover according to the solar calendar followed by some groups who diverged from the Pharisees?[168] In that case, Tuesday evening is the likely date for the last supper,[169] the gospels having telescoped the events immediately prior to the crucifixion in order to fit the traditions into a framework to which they did not originally refer.[170]

In view of this complexity, it is nothing short of astonishing that O. Cullmann should describe this *paradosis* as 'a factual account of the last meal of Jesus' and should suggest that it in no way represents 'a case of theological interpretation'.[171] Yet in other respects Cullmann's view is highly sophisticated. He rejects the commonly held view that 'from the Lord' in 1 Cor. 11: 23a refers to the historical Jesus as the first link of a chain, and opts for the exalted Christ, not however operating through a special vision or through the first 'conversion' experience but through the tradition. 'The formula of 1 Cor. 11: 23 refers to the Christ who is present, in that he stands behind the transmission of the tradition, that is, he works in it.' [172] But while Cullmann accepts the identification of the exalted Lord and the earthly Jesus, he does so in such a way as to appear to subordinate the latter to the former.

The difficulty lies in the fact that Cullmann telescopes several types of investigation into one impossible unity. A distinction must be made between the historical question of the form and development of Christian *paradosis* and the hermeneutical question about how such *paradosis* operates in a given situation. From the historical point of view, the pericope of 1 Cor. 11:23ff. involves a recollection of the last supper preserved and developed in relation to the common meals of the Christian community and overlaid with the language of Christian sacramentalism. From the hermeneutical viewpoint, it presents the contemporary demand of the Lord to the Corinthians. Paul has the freedom to make use of the *paradosis* for his own purposes, which are primarily paraenetic. On the whole, therefore, his use is more akin to the hermeneutical than the historical: the latter appears only as part of the dominical symbol on which his liturgical *paraenesis* focuses. Cullmann's error, if we may presume to call it such, arises out of his own desire to produce a theology of *paradosis*, thus introducing yet another perspective which confuses important procedural distinctions and linguistic or contextual nuances.[173]

Paradosis is a fundamental form of Christian communication. It is 'of first importance' (1 Cor. 15:1). It differs from our first three structures – *propheteia, paraclesis* and *paraenesis* – in that it provides them with basic data. The prophet, exegete and the teacher (and, in a more general sense, the theologian) stand in a position of dependence upon and dialogue with *paradosis*; hence *paradosis* is brought, as they are, into engagement with empirical situations and thus loses the rigidity that one might associate with a basic datum. Yet its centre, its substance, is inviolate. *Paradosis* transmits Christ (cf. Col. 2: 6) – and does so even when it does not enshrine a specifically dominical utterance or action. Its substance or focus is never 'man made' (cf. Col. 2: 8), which would imply a different self-understanding, so to speak, from that which God has given in Christ.[174] In the last analysis, all types of Christian communication – dependent as they are on *paradosis* – share with it the primary concern of transmitting Christ and the understanding of life which is given in him, and of summoning man to make the appropriate response of trust and commitment.

CONCLUSION

Through the many-sided experiences-within-community which we have noted in the foregoing chapters, the followers of Jesus came to conceive, articulate, communicate and develop their message. 'Their' message only in a paradoxical sense: for while they undoubtedly struggled towards understanding and articulating it, there was always a sense in which it was 'given' or a sense in which they were 'led into truth', for the object of their message transcended their full comprehension and 'blicks' or insights into reality came not by human contrivance but through openness to the transcendent. In the concrete reality of Jesus the Christ, the transcendent had been expressed in human terms, as 'good news' in word and action. The 'word' was largely the *paradosis* originating with Jesus, interpreting and interpreted by the word of scripture. The 'action' was many-stranded: the 'action' of the death of Jesus, of the resurrection experiences and the Spirit, of common meals and 'remembering', of searching the scripture, and of the *koinonia* as a whole. The proclamation of the Christ event as 'good news' was now to be accomplished in similar fashion, in word and action (cf. John 3: 18).

The experience of the Christian *koinonia* has to be translated into intelligible terms for the purposes of edification (cf. 1 Cor. 14: 1-19), evangelism and apologetic exposition (cf. Acts 2: 14ff.). The basic forms of such utterance have been examined in the foregoing chapters in terms of *propheteia, paraclesis* and *homilia, paraenesis* and *catechesis*, and finally the *paradosis* which informs them all and to the shaping and preservation of which they all contribute. There is, we must conclude, no brief formula, no list of items, which provides a neat summary of the *kerygma* (any more than the book called 'the Didache' provides a neat summary of Christian *didache*) that would allow us to assign the forms of articulation studied above to one or the other. *Propheteia* might seem primarily related to *kerygma*, the proclamation of the central event of revelation, yet the prophet is also concerned to teach, to explain the right understanding of that event, and he may adopt ethical teaching as the vehicle of his admonitions or apocalyptic

teaching as the means of relating future expectation to the present time of
crisis or decision. The homilist may be thought of as primarily a teacher,
an expositor with the practical aim of exhortation to righteous living or of
promoting understanding through the exposition of scripture. Yet in so
doing he is never far removed from the kerygmatic, from proclaiming the
summons to faith in response to the grace of God or in view of his judgment. *Paraenesis* is supremely didactic, yet related to a kerygmatic core,
which we have termed the 'major symbol' in the foregoing study. *Paradosis*
similarly might appear expressly didactic, yet in 1 Cor. 15: 3-11 Paul cites
paradosis as the basis of *kerygma*. Thus Christian utterance tends to be
both kerygmatic and didactic. Nor is one necessarily prior to the other.
The common view that *kerygma* is primary and *didache* secondary is un-
commonly wooden and imperceptive. It takes one possible model - that a
man first hears the *kerygma* and, having responded positively to it, is nur-
tured on *didache* - as the only or at least the regulative pattern. Yet *didache*
may be a *praeparatio evangelica*, whether unconsciously - as perhaps was
the case with Saul of Tarsus - or consciously, as was almost certainly the
case with the disciples in the immediate post-crucifixion period. In the
evolution of the Christian faith, *didache* in the form of *paradosis* stemming
from Jesus (and the world-view it implied) and in the form of scriptural
midrash informed by particular experiences of the earliest Christian communities was certainly the precursor of *kerygma* as Christian proclamation.

Does our understanding of *kerygma* and *didache* help to clarify the task
of communicating the Christian message today?

Kerygma as the address of God to man, as the proclamation of Christ,
as the invitation to a new understanding of the self and a new orientation
of the personality, as the setting forth of the possibilities of the Christian
way - *kerygma* in all these interrelated senses is vital and focal, and its
challenge must never be weakened. The church that lives on 'cheap grace'
is a church that has forgotten its kerygmatic basis. But *kerygma* is not a
sufficiently wide and flexible term to encompass the entire hermeneutical
task. This is where our appeal is to *didache*, which is in itself a more flexible and many-sided procedure than *kerygma* and which can reinforce the
latter so that it becomes more truly kerygmatic. Consider the following:

(i) One of the great problems in Christian communication today is to
find sufficient common ground on which to proceed. In the Jewish world
in which the message was first compounded, the concepts of God, religion,
judgment and salvation were in common coinage; and the Gentile world,
with the bankruptcy of its traditional religion and its search for individual
freedom and salvation, could relate easily to such language and conceptuality - the task made easier by the cultural exchanges that had in effect

married the Jewish and the wider worlds over the years. Today, a symptom of the so-called post-Christian society is the indifference towards or even the rejection of the linguistic and conceptual residue of 'Christendom'. Solutions advocated for the resolution of this problem have included the total acceptance of the 'biblical' world-view as the price of gospel truth, and the existentialist approach, stressing the notion of self-understanding. Neither is in itself satisfactory, for the former superimposes the ancient world-view and its linguistic and conceptual elements upon the modern – indeed it tries to replace the latter with the former – thus denying the integrity of contemporary understanding of the world and man's place in it; while the latter, the existentialist, though of great value, is in the last resort too restricted and one-sided.

A basic task of Christian *didache* is to establish a linguistic frame of reference in which Christian communication can occur in the modern age. This would include the clarification of what men mean – or might mean – when they speak of 'God', 'providence', 'good and evil', 'religion': in short, when they use religious language or even contemplate the puzzles it presents. It would also involve the discussion of terms not used in religious discourse but related to religious concern, such as the growth and development of the human personality, obsession, fixation or group therapy. The approach to ultimate questions – even the possibility of there being ultimate questions – is through human language and discourse. In fact, since language expresses man's thoughts about himself in his world, the transition to the discussion of human existence as such is readily made. Equally, the discussion will extend to the events which the *kerygma* proclaims, for they are always the central points of reference for the Christian. What has to be fought for is their relevance to the modern situation.

Thus, since we claim that the gospel presents a new way for mankind, we must recognise that there is in the experience of mankind a 'pre-understanding', an awareness of the human predicament which can be developed through dialogue and which the gospel must address and illuminate if Christian communication is to take place. The task of eliciting such a 'pre-understanding' is that of *didache*, but at some point in the discussion the *didache* will become kerygmatic.

(ii) Since the witness to the gospel is contained in the scriptures (and likewise the definitive expression of the gospel in Christ), hermeneutics in the narrower sense of scriptural interpretation comes into its own. The classic situation for the practical outworking of such procedures is within the Christian community, where there is a recognition of the value of attending to what the scriptures say; but since secularisation has its effects within the church as well as outisde it, and since we no longer live in a society where an auditory message is received with rapt attention, much more care has to be given to the elucidation of the meaning. Thus, in worship and in conjunction with the sermon or address, a modern Christian midrash is indicated. Proper study of the text and sympathetic understanding of what the ancient writer was trying to say to his own situation are essential steps. Next, the examination of the human, relational affinities which link the modern age to the ancient open the way for hearing the scriptural message with a new freshness and relevance to modern times; and this can be further applied to the human personality, situation and predicament, individually and communally, through the rationality and imagination of the exegete or the common resources of the discussion group. Basically, these steps are not incompatible with existentialist hermeneutics, although no claim is made for the particular validity of the existentialist analysis of human existence;[1] and they are also in line with the 'relational hermeneutics' of J. S. Glen.[2]

(iii) The aim of *didache*, whether as exploration of modern man's self-understanding or as midrash, is kerygmatic. At the heart of the process of Christian communication stands the *kerygma* proper, the proclamation of God's grace in Christ (it is capable, of course, of starting from a variety of points: e.g., incarnation or atonement). Here is that which encounters man, questioning the adequacy of his previous self-understanding and setting him in a transcendental perspective, though one expressed in human dimensions through Jesus Christ. But this means that the *kerygma* is inseparable from the *paradosis* which conveys the data necessary to the intelligibility of the proclaimed message. To be sure, *paradosis* may have a didactic function in filling out the proclamation through subsequent teaching, but *paradosis* is no less present in the proclamation itself and is in any case essentially kerygmatic. The matter may be expressed in this way. When *paradosis* is presented as something that must be learned, remembered and explored, it is essentially *didache*. In 1 Cor. 15 it operates in this way, for it is the specific object of recall (15:1) and is subsequently explored at depth in relation to its resurrection content. When it is presented as part of the proclamation designed to bring the hearers to the response of faith and the assurance of salvation, it is *kerygma*. It operated in this way on the occasion of Paul's original 'preaching of the gospel' at Corinth (15:1f.). Yet these two distinctive procedures are never wholly separate: the *kerygma* is implicit in the *didache*, and the *didache* is intimately associated with the *kerygma*.

Such a hub of preaching–teaching is central to all Christian communication, leading as it does to the exposure of the hearer to those events in time and space in which God has acted for the salvation of mankind.

(iv) *Paraenesis* is important both for introductory and nurtural purposes.

Various types have been analysed above. The most flexible and inherently valuable paraenetic procedure is possibly the situational, in which an analysis of the contemporary situation of the hearer is instrumental in relating him to the kerygmatic core of the faith and thus presenting him with an opportunity of revising his life-style accordingly. Here once again *didache* and *kerygma* coalesce, but it is worth noting that the effectiveness of the *kerygma* is here dependent on the thoroughness and appropriateness of the *didache*. General *paraenesis* also has its place, for the Christian needs to know the contours of the terrain he is traversing as well as the particular situation with which he is involved at any one time. Even general rules, like the *Haustafeln*, have a certain limited usefulness. By *catechesis* and *didaskalia*, on the other hand, one understands instruction in the basic elements of church faith and practice, directed in the first instance to catechumens and presenting in rudimentary form the core of didactic, kerygmatic, liturgical and practical concern. As this is the presupposition of Christian understanding, there must always be adequate reinforcing of such fundamentals within the Christian *koinonia*.

(v) We have suggested above that *propheteia* is in some respects the mother of articulated Christian utterance. Does it have a continuing role? On the one hand, it might be said of *propheteia*, as T. S. Eliot said (in the second of his 'Four Quartets') of the use of words, that each venture is:

A new beginning, a raid on the inarticulate,
With shabby equipment always deteriorating
In the general mess of imprecision of feeling.

What matters when the prophet has spoken is not that one should reproduce his experience, but that one should heed his message. Paul, with his plea for 'five words' spoken 'with the mind' in order to 'catechise' others (1 Cor. 14: 19), heavily underlines the point. Speaking with tongues may be no more than luxuriating 'in the general mess of imprecision of feeling'. Prophecy, however, contributes its articulated utterance to Christian *didache*, which then becomes the object of attention. On the other hand, the affective side of man has always been involved in the appreciation of religious meaning, whether in prophecy or mysticism or in the various levels of devotion, worship and prayer; and perhaps today when there is a reaction against arid intellectualism and academic abstruseness a greater attempt should be made to cultivate the spiritual gifts (1 Cor. 14: 1) as Paul recommends despite his awareness of how easily they can be misused. Certainly meditation and worship in all its aspects belong within this tradition, and Christian education and nurture have tended to be equated too exclusively with instruction. Moreover, the intellectual and the emotive

combine in creative imagination, without which the task of Christian communication is gravely impaired. *Propheteia* can point the way here, for out
of his sensitivity to man's total situation and the reservoirs of religious
meaning which lie within it the prophet struggles in thought and feeling
with the immense possibilities which by their very nature bid fair to defy
full comprehension and articulation until by a kind of supreme orgasm the
word that needs to be uttered is finally delivered as *kerygma* and as *didache*,
bringing the dimension of the transcendent into encounter with the human.
In the last analysis, such creativity and vision is required if the Christian
message is to have continuing relevance in a rapidly changing world.
Instruction in the catechetics of the past is not enough.

(vi) Our final paragraph takes us back to the *koinonia*, the common
fellowship within which the Christian message was originally fostered and
articulated. Behind that first message there lay common exploration of
meaning, discussion, study, argument, devotion – always under the guidance
of the Spirit, with an openness to the transcendent. The message, once
uttered, was always supported and lived out by the community, so that the
community in its common life was an instrument of evangelism as much as
its message. And its message was further developed – by Justin, Tertullian,
the Alexandrians, the later Fathers and many more. These two aspects –
living out the message, and its further development – are perennial. Learning by doing, by participation, by involvement is the most immediate form
of learning, and one particularly appropriate to such themes as discipleship
and commitment. The church is under constant obligation to respond more
fully to the gospel of Christ, so that it is more truly his Body, an extension
of his incarnation and instrument of his ministry of reconciliation. It is also
under obligation to be less of an institution, more of a community, in which
people can learn the freedom and support of the love of Christ. But a church
that is truly alive and led by the Spirit is also impelled to further exploration
of the meaning of its faith and way of life – and not merely through its theologians but through its common life and fellowship. *Koinonia* is intimately
associated with *didache* (Acts 2: 42). Despite the doctrine of the Spirit who
can teach the church 'all things' (John 14: 26), and despite the *reformata
semper reformanda* of the Reformation, there is always a tendency to rest
on the faith and formulae of the past and to take up defensive positions
against an aggressive modernity. I have tried to identify the sense in which
the past is always with us – whether as *paradosis* or as some other form of
historically conditioned *didache* or as *kerygma*, the proclamation down
the ages of the gospel event. I have also tried to indicate that the communication of the faith is not complete until the Christian community
allows its experience of life to be enriched and its insight quickened

by the Spirit so that it can give new utterance to what the Spirit is
saying to the churches (Rev. 2: 7).

NOTES

Introduction

1   M. Kähler, *Der sogenannte historische Jesus und der geschichtliche biblische Christus*, 1892 (Eng. tr., *The so-called Historical Jesus and the historic Biblical Christ*, 1964).

2   There were, of course, other reasons for the abandonment of the 'old quest'. In particular, W. Wrede's emphasis on the 'Messianic secret' in Mark pointed to the writer's theological and dogmatic concerns and, in this anticipation of *Redaktionsgeschichte*, undermined widely held assumptions about the overriding historical concern of Mark's outline: *Das Messiasgeheimnis in der Evangelien*, 1901 (Eng. tr., *The Messianic Secret*, 1971). Also A. Schweitzer's critical appraisal of the liberal enterprise in *Von Reimarus zu Wrede*, 1906 (Eng. tr., *The Quest of the Historical Jesus*, 1910), clearly demonstrated the degree of subjectivity involved in it and drew attention to the importance of the eschatological element, a point also insisted upon by J. Weiss, *Die Predigt Jesu vom Reiche Gottes*, (2nd ed.) 1900. A classic comment on liberal subjectivity is that of G. Tyrrell: 'The Christ that Harnack sees, looking back through nineteen centuries of Catholic darkness, is only the reflection of a Liberal Protestant face, seen at the bottom of a deep well': *Christianity at the Crossroads*, 1909, p. 44; cf. D. M. Baillie, *God Was In Christ*, 1948, p. 40.

3   M. Kähler, p. 63. Cf. P. Althaus, *The so-called Kerygma and the Historical Jesus*, Eng. tr., 1959, pp. 19–37; and I. Henderson, *Rudolf Bultmann*, 1965, pp. 11–16.

4   G. Friedrich, *T.D.N.T.* III, p. 716, n. 2.

5   C. H. Dodd, *The Apostolic Preaching and its Developments*, 1936, p. 3, simply assumes this interpretation in the opening paragraph of his book.

6   Cf. 'in demonstration of the Spirit and of power'.

7   C. F. Evans, 'The Kerygma', *J.T.S.* 7 (N.S. 1), 1956, pp. 25f., n. 5. Similar ambiguity surrounds 1 Cor. 15: 14. In Matt. 12: 41 and Luke 11: 32, the nuance of 'message' can perhaps not be eliminated from a context in which the act of preaching is primary.

8   The notion of content predominates in the shorter ending of Mark and the difficult, and secondary, Rom. 16: 25.

9   Cf. Sanday and Headlam, *Commentary on Romans (I.C.C.)*, 1895, *ad loc.*

10   Cf. G. Friedrich, *T.D.N.T.* III.

11   R. Bultmann, 'New Testament and Mythology', in *Kerygma and Myth* I, Eng. tr., 1954, pp. 41ff.

12 It is true that Bultmann stresses *kerygma* as 'address' and resists objectification of it in terms of a merely historical recital: cf. *Theology of the New Testament* I, Eng. tr., 1952, p. 307. But he also says that the *kerygma* is 'the word of Christ whose contents may also be formulated in a series of abstract propositions' (*Kerygma and Myth* I, p. 209), and that it 'necessarily assumes the form of tradition' (*ibid.*, p. 115).

13 This particular quotation is from R. P. C. Hanson, *Tradition in the Early Church*, 1962, p. 10. This kind of approach is reflected in numerous textbooks: cf. A. M. Hunter, *Interpreting the New Testament 1900-1950*, 1951, pp. 35f.; H. F. D. Sparks, *The Formation of the New Testament*, 1952, pp. 19-22; and in works of reference, exemplified by R. H. Strachan, 'The Gospel in the New Testament', *Int. Bib.* VII, 1951, pp. 3-31.

14 Compare and contrast E. F. Scott's *The Varieties of New Testament Religion*, 1943 (incl. the Preface), and A. M. Hunter's *The Unity of the New Testament*, 1943.

15 Cf. C. H. Dodd, *Parables of the Kingdom*, 1935, (3rd ed.) 1936, pp. 43ff., 53ff., 108. For a criticism of Dodd's Platonism, cf. M. Burrows, 'Thy Kingdom Come', *J.B.L.* 74, 1955, pp. 1-8; R. H. Fuller, *The Mission and Achievement of Jesus*, 1954, pp. 20, 33; G. Lundström, *The Kingdom of God in the Teaching of Jesus*, Eng. tr., 1963, p. 121; E. Jüngel, *Paulus und Jesus*, 1962, pp. 107-20; D. A. Templeton, 'A Critique of some Aspects of Kerygma as understood by R. Bultmann and C. H. Dodd', unpublished Ph. D. thesis submitted to the University of Glasgow, 1967, p. 38. It might be said that Dodd realised eschatology in the life of Jesus and Bultmann in the *kerygma*: Templeton, *op. cit.*, p. 43. In his later writings Dodd does appear to recognise that eschatology must have at least some concern with the future and to move from realised to inaugurated eschatology: cf. *The Interpretation of the Fourth Gospel*, 1953, p. 477, n. 1. Bultmann also appears to have modified his position slightly when he speaks of the in-breaking of the grace of God in Jesus' 'conduct': *Z.T.K.*, 1957, p. 224, and *Glauben und Verstehen* III, 1960, pp. 176f.: cf. J. M. Robinson, 'The Formal Structure of Jesus' Message', in *Current Issues in New Testament Interpretation*, Klassen and Snyder (edd.), 1962, p. 97.

16 T. G. A. Baker, *What is the New Testament?*, 1969, p. 20. For a survey of the use of *kerygma* in critical scholarship, from J. S. Semler in 1777 (where *content* predominates, though not in unchanging formulae) and J. G. Herder (d. 1807: in his usage of it, the oral nature of the gospel as *announcement* is stressed) to R. Bultmann (in whose work it acquires central hermeneutical significance), cf. G. Ebeling, *Theology and Proclamation*, Eng. tr., 1966, pp. 113-18.

17 Like *kerygma*, *euangelion* reflects the activity of a herald but stressed the 'good tidings' that are proclaimed. It has a worthy Old Testament pedigree (cf. Is. 40: 1-11; 52: 7f.), reflected in New Testament usage (cf. Mark 1: 3; Rom. 10: 15).

18 The preference for *kerygma* in modern theology may be explained partly by the fact that 'gospel' acquired other connotations in the post-apostolic age: e.g., as a literary term.

19 Thus W. Baird wrote: 'Hunter and Craig posit a three-point *kerygma*, but their three points are not identical. Filson lists five facts or doctrines, while

Glasson ardently contends for five slightly different elements. The Swedish scholar Gärtner suggests a *kerygma* of seven essential points': 'What is the Kerygma? A Study of 1 Cor. 15: 3–8 and Gal. 1: 11–17', *J.B.L.* 76, 1957, p. 182.

20 The problem is discussed below.

21 C. F. Evans, *J.T.S.* 7 (N.S. 1), p. 41.

22 The plural is used not infrequently in Philo as in classical Greek, but not in a theological sense: cf. *Agric.* 117; *Leg. Gaj.* 46.

23 W. Baird, *J.B.L.* 76, p. 184.

24 C. H. Dodd, *Apostolic Preaching,* p. 6.

25 C. H. Dodd, *The Johannine Epistles (Moffatt N. T. Commentary)*, 1946, p. xxxi.

26 G. Wingren, *The Living Word,* Eng. tr., 1960, p. 18.

27 C. F. D. Moule, *The Birth of the New Testament,* 1962, p. 130.

28 *Didache* in the New Testament usually indicates the totality of teaching, whether of Jesus (Matt. 7: 28; 22: 33; Mark 1: 22, etc.; John 7: 16f.; 18: 19; cf. 2 John 9f.), of the Pharisees (Matt. 16: 12), of the apostles (Acts 2: 42; 5: 28; 17: 19), or, for that matter, of 'Balaam' (Rev. 2: 14), of the 'Nicolaitans' (2: 15), or of 'Jezebel' (2: 20, 24). Paul adopts this holistic usage in Rom. 6: 17 (the 'standard of teaching') and 16: 17, but implies a particular expression of Christian *didache* in 1 Cor. 14: 6 and 26. Nevertheless, only in Heb. 6: 2, where *didache* refers to doctrinal formulae relating to cleansing rites, the laying on of hands, the resurrection of the dead and eternal judgment, and in 13: 9 ('diverse and strange teachings') is *didache* completely particularised, as it came to be in the apostolic fathers (Didache 2: 1; 6: 1; 11: 2; Barnabas 9: 9). Cf. Rengstorf, *T.D.N.T.* II, pp. 163f. It is therefore undesirable to use *didache* as a technical term to denote a particular form of Christian communication or even a group of forms.

Didaskalia seems to denote the activity of teaching (Rom. 12: 7; cf. Eph. 4: 14) and the teaching that comes through scripture (Rom. 15: 4). In the Pastorals it occurs in this sense (1 Tim. 4: 13, 16; 5: 17; 2 Tim. 3: 10; Titus 2: 7), but it also suggests Christian teaching in its totality, especially over against other teachings which have no authority and are harmful (1 Tim. 4: 6; 6: 1; in plural – 4: 1; Col. 2: 22; cf. Matt. 15: 9; Mark 7: 7). By this time, the teachers have come into their own as the transmitters and guardians of the apostolic tradition: cf. Clement of Alexandria, *Strom.* 7. 17. 108. It remains true, however, that the total Christian message is communicated by preaching and teaching in combination: 1 Tim. 5: 17; cf. 2 Tim. 4: 17.

29 W. D. Davies, *S.S.M.,* 1964, pp. 7f. For the Jewish practice of teaching in a seated position, cf. *Aboth* 1: 4; 3: 2, 6.

30 Friedrich, *T.D.N.T.* III, p. 713, the point being that *didaskalia* has to do with exposition of scripture to the pious in the synagogue, while *kerygma* is the herald's cry to the outsiders.

31 J. J. Vincent, 'Didactic Kerygma in the Synoptic Gospels', *S.J.T.* 10, 1957, p. 265.

32 K. Stendahl, 'Kerygma und Kerygmatisch', *T.L.Z.,* 1952, pp. 715–20.

33 J. J. Vincent found that the content of *kerygma* in the gospels '(1) is not

generally the kind of summary of *Heilsgeschichte* that we might have expected, (2) refers almost as often to repentance and forgiveness, not always in the context of a "therefore" after a *heilsgeschichtliche* statement, (3) can also be a testimony to a miracle': *S.J.T.* 10, p. 269.

34   *Ibid.*, p. 271.

35   *Ibid.*, p. 273.

36   Cf. D. Grasso, *Proclaiming God's Message: A Study in the Theology of Preaching*, 1965, pp. ix ff. In part a response to the problems inherent in the secularisation and dechristianisation of society, the debate has been influenced strongly by the modern *Verkündigungstheologie*, or kerygmatic theology, associated in R. C. catechetical circles with J. A. Jungmann in particular: cf. *Die Frohbotschaft und unsere Glaubensverkündigung*, 1936; and *Handing on the Faith: A Manual of Catechetics*, 1959, esp. Appendices II and III, pp. 387–405.

37   Cf. J. A. Jungmann, *Handing on the Faith*, pp. 92–7, and p. 387, n. 1.

38   Rétif, however, admitted the fluidity of New Testament usage: cf. 'Qu'est-ce que le kérygme?', *N.R.T.* 71, 1949, pp. 910–22.

39   D. Grasso, *Proclaiming God's Message*, pp. 222f. Similarly, J. Daniélou works with the three-fold structure: *kerygma*, homily, *catechesis*: cf. *La catéchèse aux premiers siècles*, 1968, pp. 13f.

40   D. Grasso, *Proclaiming God's Message*, pp. 230ff. Grasso is at pains to stress the difference between *catechesis* and homily. The former aims at the intellect, is systematic, didactic and rational, calm and static. The latter aims at the will and feelings, 'tends to see the affective element, more the heart than the mind of God', is lyrical and vivacious, dynamic and disturbing.

41   Cf. D. Grasso, *Proclaiming God's Message*, p. 243.

42   Cf. *ibid.*, p. 232, n. 13.

43   Bo Reicke, 'A Synopsis of Early Christian Preaching', in *The Root of the Vine*, A. Fridrichsen and others (edd.), 1953, pp. 128–60.

44   *Ibid.*, p. 129; cf. Matt. 10: 1ff. The apostles did not simply repeat what Jesus had said but performed an activity corresponding to Jesus' activity as the messenger of God.

45   The book of Enoch and the Testaments of the XII Patriarchs are cited in particular. Influences from outside the Jewish tradition are also admitted but regarded as weak at this early stage.

46   Theologically unsound, because while evangelist and teacher act as husbandmen it is God who gives the increase (1 Cor. 3: 6); linguistically inaccurate, because conversion describes a religious experience, not a formal category of preaching. The prophet was the messenger *par excellence* but frequently failed to make many converts; yet his mission was not thereby invalidated: cf. Is. 6: 9ff.; Matt. 13: 14f.; Mark 4: 11ff.; Luke 8: 10; John 12: 39ff.; Acts 28: 26f.

47   A. N. Wilder adds a cautionary note: the term 'testament' may well be a misleading modernisation: *Early Christian Rhetoric*, 1964, p. 43. In Chapter 3 *infra*, it is treated as a special form of *paraenesis: vid.*, pp. 73, 79, 86f., and 98f.

48   Acts 11: 27; 13: 1; 15: 32; 21: 9f.; 1 Cor. 12: 26f.; Eph. 4: 11.

49   Note that the Pentecost story with its ecstatic elements concludes with a call to repentance and the 'conversion' and baptism of a large number of people.

50 H. Riesenfeld, *The Gospel Tradition and its Beginnings: A Study in the Limits of 'Formgeschichte'*, 1957; also in *The Gospels Reconsidered: A Selection of Papers read at the International Congress on the Four Gospels in 1957*, 1960, pp. 131-53.

51 In particular, H. Riesenfeld attacked the ascription of the gospel tradition to an origin in early church 'preaching', 'catechetical instruction' or 'controversy', and the assumption of 'an extraordinary creative capacity in the first Christian generations', which he described as 'a truly miraculous and incredible factor in the history of the Gospel tradition': cf. *The Gospels Reconsidered*, pp. 134f.

52 *Ibid.*, p. 138.

53 B. Gerhardsson, *Memory and Manuscript, Oral Tradition and Written Transmission in Rabbinic Judaism and early Christianity*, 1961 (denoted henceforth in this work by *M.M.*).

54 H. Riesenfeld, *The Gospels Reconsidered*, p. 145.

55 *Ibid.*, p. 146.

56 *Ibid.*, p. 147.

57 *Ibid*, p. 151.

58 *Ibid.*, p. 153.

59 For a fuller review of the Scandinavian approach than is attempted here, cf. W. D. Davies, 'Reflections on a Scandinavian Approach to "The Gospel Tradition" ', in *S.S.M.*, 1964, Appendix XV, pp. 464-80.

60 Cf. E. C. Selwyn, *The Christian Prophets*, 1900; *The Oracles in the New Testament*, 1911; *First Christian Ideas*, 1919; E. G. Selwyn, *The First Epistle of St Peter*, 1946, pp. 260-8; H. Pope, 'Prophecy and Prophets in New Testament Times', *I.T.Q.* 7, 1912, pp. 383-400; J. D. G. Dunn, 'New Wine in Old Wine-Skins: Prophet', *Exp. T.* 85, 1973, pp. 4-8; *Jesus and the Spirit*, 1975.

61 Eph. 2: 20; 3: 5; 1 Cor. 12: 28; Eph. 4: 11; cf. Rom. 12: 6; 1 Cor. 12: 7-10; 13: 2; 1 Pet. 4: 10f.

62 Cf. 1 Cor. 14 *passim*; 2 Cor. 12: 1-4, 7; Col. 3: 16; Eph. 5: 19.

63 Acts 13: 14ff.; cf. 1 Tim. 4: 13; Heb. 13: 22; 1 Pet. 5: 12; Jude 3. Within the community itself there is a responsibility for mutual exhortation: 'a charisma of pastoral exhortation': O. Schmitz, *T.D.N.T.* V, p. 796. On *paraklesis* and *parakalein*, cf. O. Schmitz, *op. cit.*, pp. 794ff. As used here, *paraclesis* is the address or discourse, frequently exegetical, that has its *locus* as a rule in the worshipping community and contributes to its edification and encouragement (*paraclesis* in the wider sense). The aim of this kind of discourse thus partly overlaps that of intelligible *propheteia* (cf. 1 Cor. 14: 3) and that of *didache* (which appears to denote a 'lesson' or scriptural exegesis in 14: 26). It is thus obvious that *paraclesis* has both a kerygmatic and a didactic function.

64 Cf. Acts 17: 2; B. Lindars, *New Testament Apologetic*, 1961, pp. 251-86; B. Gerhardsson, *M.M.*, pp. 225-45. A comparison with the eschatologically orientated exegesis of Qumran suggests itself: to what extent did Jesus establish a distinctive exegetical tradition (cf. Luke 4: 16ff.)? And how did the early Christians relate to it?

65 *homilia* in classical usage has a social connotation ('company', 'intercourse': cf. 1 Cor. 15: 33); in hellenistic Greek it frequently means 'speech', and in

Justin it occurs as 'sermon': *Dial.* 28 and 85; cf. Ign. *Polyc.* 5: 1. It
denotes table talk at the community meal or *agape* at Troas: cf. Acts 20:
7; cf. 1 Cor. 11: 20ff. Other 'homiletic' occasions included baptisms (Acts
2: 40ff.), festivals (cf. Melito's Paschal homily), and even departures (Acts
20: 18–35), although the 'farewell speech' is probably to be classed as
paraenesis: *vid. infra*, pp. 197f; cf. E. Norden's well-known description of
homilia as preaching in which 'das lehrhafte Moment im Mittelpunkt stand':
Die antike Kunstprosa II, r.p. 1958, p. 541.

66   K. P. Donfried has observed that 'the term "homily" is so vague and ambiguous that it should be withdrawn until its literarily generic legitimacy has
been demonstrated': *The Setting of Second Clement in Early Christianity*,
1974, p. 26. While my concern is primarily with preaching as an oral form
(rather than with written sermons as a literary genre), caution needs to be
exercised in relation to terminology. Terminological confusion is apparent,
for example, in W. Barclay's 'A Comparison of Paul's Missionary Preaching
and Preaching to the Church', in *Apostolic History and the Gospel*, Gasque
and Martin (edd.), 1970, p. 170: 'Paul's letters are sermons far more than
they are theological treatises... They are sermons even in the sense that
they were spoken rather than written'. The precise question is: can we discern homiletic patterns in the letters? Again, Donfried is correct in insisting
on a differentiation of Christian forms from the diatribe on one hand and
homiletic midrash on the other: *op. cit.*, pp. 27ff.: we must attempt to
trace the development of inherently Christian forms, whatever their debt
to other models may be. But Donfried's position itself seems open to
criticism. (i) It is excessively cautious and might inhibit the use of readily
available terms simply because they have been misused by some scholars;
he does, at one point, admit the possibility of using the term 'homily' as
Justin and Ignatius did (p. 27). (ii) His description of 2 Clement as a
'hortatory address' (p. 35) is perhaps too wide to have much significance
for a formal study and suggests the conundrum: when is a homily not a
homily? Answer: when it is a hortatory address! (iii) His attempt to
identify a three-fold formal pattern – theology, ethics, eschatology – is
misconceived, for he has confused the search for inherent structural
development with areas of content which tend to appear in a certain
sequence.

67   *Paraenesis* comes from the root 'recommend', 'advise', and is typically
associated with ethical counsel and moral education, with a suggestion of
intimacy and practicality. Widely used in the ancient world, it tended to
produce distinctive forms which can be traced in Christian utterance also,
and paraenetic topics became a marked feature of Christian teaching. *Vid.
infra*, Chapter 3.

68   *Catechesis*, derived from *katēchein* meaning 'to tell about something', or,
as in Paul, 'to give instruction concerning the content of faith' (cf. H. W.
Beyer, *T.D.N.T.* III, pp. 638f.), comes to denote Christian instruction,
especially in the basics of the faith, and in due course provided the church
with the vocabulary of catechist, catechumen and catechism: cf. 2 Clem.
17: 1; Acts 18: 25; also P. Carrington, *The Primitive Christian Catechism*,
1940; E. G. Selwyn, *The First Epistle of St Peter*, Essay II, pp. 365–466,
esp. pp. 370f.; A. M. Hunter, *Paul and his Predecessors*, 1940; and A.

Seeberg, *Der Katechismus der Urchristenheit,* 1903.

69 Cf. also O. Cullmann, *The Early Church,* Eng. tr., 1956, p. 63.

Chapter 1. *Propheteia*

1 Cf. E. Herzfeld, *Zoroaster and his World* I, 1947; R. C. Zaehner, *The Dawn and Twilight of Zoroastrianism,* 1961.

2 Cf. W. M. Watt, *Muhammad, Prophet and Statesman,* 1961.

3 Cf. H. W. Parke, *Greek Oracles,* 1967; H. W. Parke and D. E. W. Warmell, *The Delphic Oracle* II, 1956; R. Flacelière, *Greek Oracles,* Eng. tr., 1965.

4 'προφήτης allein ist ein Rahmenwort ohne konkreten Inhalt': E. Fascher, ΠΡΟΦΗΤΗΣ, *Eine sprach- und religionsgeschichtliche Untersuchung,* 1927, p. 51. The application of the word is remarkable: there are prophets of the Muses, of nature, of public opinion, of truth and reason. The word was applied to the propounders of the viewpoints of philosophical schools, to interpreters or exegetes of philosophical writings, poetry or oracles: cf. H. Krämer, *T.D.N.T.* VI, p. 794.

5 In relation to *prophētēs* and its associates, the prefix *pro-* denotes 'forth' rather than 'fore'; and the term *phētēs* 'expresses the formal function of declaring, proclaiming, making known': H. Krämer, *T.D.N.T.* VI, p. 795; cf. E. Fascher, *op. cit.,* pp. 4–7. The word for a 'foreteller' is *mantis,* from which *prophētēs* is differentiated: it acquires this connotation only at a late date. *Prophētēs* is closely associated with *hypophētēs,* where the prefix *hypo-* suggests the impartation of deeper meaning or hidden truth: interpretation 'in depth': H. Krämer, *op. cit.,* pp. 784f.; E. Fascher, *op. cit.,* pp. 27–32. At Dodona (the ancient oracle of Zeus: cf. Homer, *Iliad* 16. 234f.), the *hypophēteis,* or oracle prophets, interpret the sacred signs and proclaim the will of the god.

6 L. Köhler, *Deuterojesaja (Jesaja 40–55) stilkritisch untersucht,* 1923, pp. 102–9; J. F. Ross, 'The Prophet as Yahweh's Messenger', in *Israel's Prophetic Heritage,* Anderson and Harrelson (edd.), 1962, pp. 98–107.

7 As well as the classic royal formula, there is the more rhetorical 'Hear the word of Yahweh'; also 'Thus has Yahweh said to me' and 'whispering of Yahweh'.

8 C. Westermann, *Basic Forms of Prophetic Speech,* Eng. tr., 1967, p. 102. (Henceforth cited as *B.F.P.S.*)

9 Cf. J. Lindblom, *Prophecy in Ancient Israel,* 1962, p. 35; J. Pedersen, *Israel, Its Life and Culture* I–II, 1926, pp. 157–70; O. Eissfeldt, *The Old Testament: An Introduction,* Eng. tr., 1965, pp. 77f.

10 H. W. Wolff, 'Hauptprobleme alttestamentlicher Prophetie', *Ev. Th.,* 1955, pp. 446–68; so also C. Westermann, *B.F.P.S.,* p. 63. Revelation could be received in a variety of ways, including dreams, visions and mechanical oracles. For message transmission in political and social life, cf. Gen. 32: 3ff. The three main stages are the commissioning of the messenger, the reception of the message and its final delivery.

11 Cf. J. P. Hyatt: 'as a messenger of God to the people of his time, the prophet was not a mechanical puppet but a strong individual': Commentary on Jeremiah, *Int. Bib.* 5, 1956, p. 782.

12 Jeremiah provides many instances: cf. 5: 31; 6: 13; 8: 10; 14: 13f.; 23: 14, 21, 25f., 32; 27: 9f., 14–16; 28: 15; 29: 8f., 31; also Ezek. 13 *passim;*

Zech. 13: 2–6; Deut. 13: 1–5. The false prophets proclaim 'their own deluding fancies' (Jer. 14: 14), and speak *shalom* where there is no *shalom*. The acid test is the historical outcome (28: 9). The falsity of the prophet shows up in his life (23: 14; 29: 23), his mercenary leanings (Micah 3: 5) and use of wine (Is. 28: 7–13): R. Rendtorff, *T.D.N.T.* VI, p. 806; J. Lindblom, *Prophecy*, pp. 210–15; but cf. R. E. Clements, *Prophecy and Tradition*, 1975, pp. 52ff. *Vid. infra*, n. 229. J. H. Hayes points to the institutional usage of foreign-nation oracles as a source of inauthentic oracles: 'The Usage of Oracles against Foreign Nations in Ancient Israel', *J.B.L.* 87, 1968, pp. 81–92.

13   Cf. 1 Kings 18, esp. v. 19: 'the four hundred and fifty prophets of Baal and the four hundred prophets of Asherah'; Mount Carmel was held sacred both by Phoenicians and Israelites: cf. O. Eissfeldt, *Der Gott Karmel*, 1953; also 2 Kings 10, esp. vv. 18–27. For further evidence of prophets in Phoenicia, cf. *A.N.E.T.*, pp. 25ff.; J. Lindblom, *Prophecy*, pp. 29ff.

14   E.g., 1 Kings 19: 1–18; Jer. 12: 1–6; 15: 10–21; 18: 18–23; and esp. 20: 7–12, 14–18. The experience is expressed both in judgment prophecy and in lamentation, which is related to the salvation oracle: *vid. infra*, pp. 14f. The motif of rejection is central to the notion of the suffering servant: esp. Is. 53 *passim*.

15   Cf. C. Westermann, *B.F.P.S.*, pp. 13–80.

16   R. B. Y. Scott, 'The Literary Structure of Isaiah's Oracles', *S.O.T.P.*, pp. 175–86.

17   Scott's fourth form, *exhortation*, is not discussed below since it is essentially a paraenetic procedure which prophets occasionally used: i.e., it is not a basic prophetic form.

18   Cf. C. Westermann, *B.F.P.S.*, pp. 142–63. Cf. the regular legal procedure of the city gate: a transgression has been committed against God's law and in breach of the covenant. Since no proceedings have been instituted, God sends his messenger, although unlike civil judgment the effect of God's judgment may not be felt immediately.

19   *Ibid.*, pp. 169–89. The accusation tends to have two parts: a generalised statement of transgression and a more concrete instance of it (cf. Amos 2: 1). Similarly, the announcement is frequently two-fold: the first part concerns God's intervention, often expressed in the first person; the second part sets out the results for the people concerned, who are put into the third person (cf. Hos. 13: 8). The messenger formula sometimes appears in abbreviated form simply as 'therefore...' (cf. Hos. 2: 6). Cf. Amos 3: 1–2; Hos. 2: 5ff.; Is. 8: 6ff.; Micah 3: 1f., 4; 2: 1–4; 3: 9–12; Jer. 5: 10–14; 7: 16ff., 20. For judgment against foreign nations, cf. J. H. Hayes, *J.B.L.* 87, pp. 81–92.

20   C. Westermann, *B.F.P.S.*, pp. 190–4.

21   Cf. Is. 5: 8–30; 28: 1–33: 1; Hab. 2: 6–20; Amos 5: 18–6: 8; Zech. 11: 17. The woe, like the announcement of judgment, is related to the curse; C. Westermann, *B.F.P.S.*, pp. 194–8. Its converse is the blessing or beatitude: cf. Gen. 9: 25f.; Num. 22: 12; 24: 9. Cf. S. H. Blank, 'The Curse, the Blasphemy, the Spell, and the Oath', *H.U.C.A.* 23, 1950–51, pp. 73–95.

22   C. Westermann, *B.F.P.S.*, p. 47.

23   J. Begrich, 'Das priesterliche Heilsorakel,', *Z.A.W.* 52, 1934, pp. 81–92. It

is so named because it was thought that between the complaint and confidence in God's response (cf. Ps. 6: 7f.) there stood the announcement of salvation given by a priest; and it is this priestly form which Deutero-Isaiah used as the basis for his salvation utterances. But other prophets can effect a marked disjunction from cultic assurance (cf. Hos. 6: 11b – 7: 2). The priestly prayer of confession in Hos. 6: 1–3 is met by an announcement of judgment (6: 4–10), for Israel lacks covenant loyalty (4: 6): cf. Jer. 14: 1–10. For an oracle of salvation in Jeremiah, cf. Jer. 31: 15–20, where 'out of the despair of extinction... God has brought into being a new son relationship through mercy': B. S. Childs, *Memory and Tradition in Israel,* 1962, p. 41.

24   Principally, Is. 41: 8–13, 14ff.; 43: 1–3a, 5; 44: 2–5; 48: 17ff.; 49: 7, 14f.; 51: 7f.; 54: 4–8.

25   The lament can also present an announcement of judgment in a powerful way (cf. Amos 5: 1ff.; Is. 1: 4–9). It can also be formulated as an accusation (Is. 1: 2f., 21ff.). When the lamentation is addressed to Jerusalem, an ancient independent form – the lament over a city – probably stands behind it: cf. C. Westermann, *B.F.P.S.,* p. 203.

26   Cf. Ps. 71: 11; Is. 49: 14.

27   C. Westermann, 'The Way of the Promise through the Old Testament', in *The Old Testament and Christian Faith,* Anderson (ed.), 1964, pp. 203ff.

28   For a concise discussion of the marks of apocalyptic and its relation to prophetic eschatology, cf. H. H. Rowley, *The Relevance of Apocalyptic,* 1944, pp. 23f., esp. n. 2. D. S. Russell, *The Method and Message of Jewish Apocalyptic,* 1964, pp. 92ff., agrees with Rowley in regarding apocalyptic as a continuation of prophecy, but this view has been challenged on the grounds that the dualism, determinism and pessimism of apocalyptic effectively disjoin it from prophecy: cf. P. Vielhauer, 'Apocalyptic', *N. T. Apocrypha* II (Eng. tr., ed. R. McL. Wilson, 1965), pp. 595ff. G. von Rad, *Theology of the Old Testament* II, Eng. tr., 1965, pp. 303ff., regards history as the criterion of differentiation and argues that while prophecy took the *magnalia* as determinative, apocalyptic was concerned not with the past or present but with the End time. However, the reference in the text above is simply to imagery. Apocalyptic indulged in detailed (even in extravagant, weird and grotesque) imagery, but this could be true also of prophecy. Perhaps the book of Revelation is a good example of this: cf. D. Hill, 'Prophecy and Prophets in the Revelation of St John', *N. T. S.* 18, 1971–72, pp. 401–6.

29   E.g., Torah, covenant, land, nation, king and kingdom, temple and priesthood, prophet; God as creator, preserver, saviour, judge, etc.

30   W. E. Rast, *Tradition History and the Old Testament,* 1972, p. 64; cf. B. W. Anderson, 'Exodus Typology in Second Isaiah', *Israel's Prophetic Heritage,* pp. 177–95.

31   W. E. Rast, *Tradition History,* p. 71.

32   Cf. O. Kaiser, *Isaiah 1-12,* Eng. tr., 1963, pp. 125–30, 156–62. Kaiser speaks of 'a prophetic hymn of thanksgiving transformed into a prophecy of salvation': pp. 125f.

33   Cf. J. Skinner, *Prophecy and Religion,* r.p. 1963, pp. 320–34. The new covenant, he says, is characterised by three features, inwardness,

individualism and the forgiveness of sins.

34 Cf. W. Eichrodt, *Ezekiel*, Eng. tr., 1970, Ezek. 37: 1–14; S. F. Winward, *A Guide to the Prophets*, 1968, pp. 160ff.

35 Is. 42: 1–4; 49: 1–6; 50: 4–9; 52: 13 – 53: 12; cf. C. Westermann, *Isaiah 40–66*, Eng. tr., 1969, *in loc.* For the whole subject, cf. C. R. North, *The Suffering Servant in Deutero-Isaiah*, r.p. 1963, *passim*; H. H. Rowley, *The Servant of the Lord*, 1965, *passim*; V. Taylor, *Jesus and his Sacrifice*, r.p. 1955, pp. 39–48.

36 Cf. N. W. Porteous, *Daniel*, 1965, Dan. 7: 13f.; cf. H. H. Rowley, *Darius the Mede and the Four World Empires in the Book of Daniel*, 1959. .

37 The Spirit, *ruach*, seizes a man and inspires him to outstanding feats (e.g., Judg. 3:10; 13: 25; 14: 6, 19; 15:14; 1 Sam. 11: 6; 16:13); the Spirit inspires the poet (2 Sam. 23: 2); and prophetic bands (1 Sam. 10:10); even, in a sense, the false prophet (1 Kings 22: 20ff.). Shrewd policy and wise counsel are ascribed to the Spirit (Gen. 41: 38), as well as skills in arts and crafts (Ex. 31: 3; 35: 31ff.). The Spirit was also associated with the act of anointing. Spiritual endowment had a supernatural origin and was to be used for the common good. Occasionally, a 'literary' prophet speaks of being filled with power and the Spirit (Micah 3: 8), although they usually refer to themselves as directly commissioned messengers of the Word. In Ezek. 37: 14, the life-giving work of the Spirit is presupposed in relation to the renewal of Israel, and the Spirit is prominent in future expectation (cf. Is. 11: 2ff.; 32: 14ff.; 42: 1; 61: 1ff.; Joel 2: 28f.). In religious devotion, the Spirit represents God in dynamic relation to man (e.g., Ps. 139: 7; 51: 10f.). In general, the Spirit is the divine Power immanent in human history and human lives, yet this immanence is inseparable from transcendence: the Spirit is the Immanent-Transcendence of God. Cf. F. Baumgärtel, *T.D.N.T.* VI, pp. 359–67.

38 R. B. Y. Scott, *S.O.T.P.*, p. 185; cf. Is. 8: 11; Jer. 20: 9.

39 Jer. 20: 9; cf. Is. 8: 11 –'the Lord spoke thus to me with his strong hand upon me'.

40 Cf. Amos 8: 1–3, which Scott terms 'a primary oracle of assonance': cf. Is. 5: 7; also Jer. 1: 11f., 13–16; Is. 8: 1; for names of children cf. Is. 7: 3, 14; 8: 3; Hos. 1: 4, 6, 9; cf. also Jer. 20: 3f.

41 R. B. Y. Scott, *S.O.T.P.*, p. 186.

42 Attempts have been made to distinguish the 'word of God' and the 'word of the prophet': cf. H. Wildberger, *Jahwewort und prophetische Rede bei Jeremia*, 1942. Such a distinction, however, is permitted neither by the messenger formula nor by style nor literary genre; it also ignores the importance of tradition: cf. C. Westermann, *B.F.P.S.*, pp. 48ff.

43 *Shubh* means 'to turn about', 'go back', denoting in this context a change in one's attitude to God and in the way one lives one's life: it involves turning from sin to God and a steadfast resolve not to commit sin again: cf. G. F. Moore, *Judaism* I, r.p. 1954, p. 509, and III, n. 219. For early examples, cf. 2 Sam. 12: 13; 1 Kings 21: 27.

44 Cf. G. F. Moore, *Judaism* I, p. 501, esp. n. 1, and III, n. 213a.

45 E.g., Neh. 9; Dan. 9; Baruch 1: 15ff.; many penitential psalms.

46 E.g., Ecclus. 5: 4–7; 17: 13ff.; 18: 20f.; 44: 16; Pr. of Man. v. 7; Jubilees 5: 17f.; Wisd. 11: 23.

47 E.g., Jer. 32: 18 recasts Ex. 20: 5f.; Jer. 7: 21f. seems to follow Amos 5: 25f.; Jer. 48: 45f. reinterprets Num. 21: 28f. (cf. 24: 17); with Jer. 50: 51, cf. Is. 13: 1–14, 23, 47 (cf. Hab. 1–2); with Zeph. 2: 15, cf. Is. 47: 8; and with Dan. 11: 30, cf. Num. 24: 24.

48 Cf. Dan. 2: 24; 4: 24 (M.T. 4: 21); 5: 26; an angel gives Daniel the interpretation in 7: 16; at Qumran, the interpretation was granted to the Teacher of Righteousness: 1 Qp Hab. 7: 1–5; cf. also *glossolalia* and interpretation in 1 Cor. 14. Cf. F. F. Bruce, 'The Book of Daniel and the Qumran Community', in *Neotestamentica et Semitica*, Ellis and Wilcox (edd.), 1969, pp. 225ff.

49 Cf. Dan. 9: 22, 25; cf. Jos. *Ant.* 10: 267; CD. 1: 10ff.

50 E.g., the unconditional judgment speech is no longer used, since Israel had 'paid double for all her sins' (Is. 40: 2).

51 The silence of the prophetic voice is associated on the one hand with the emergence of written scriptures and on the other with desolation: cf. Ps. 74: 9 (the destruction of the temple) and 1 Macc. 4: 46; 9: 27; 14: 41 (the Maccabean struggle); but in times of crisis some prophetic voices are raised: cf. R. Meyer, *T.D.N.T.* VI, pp. 815f.

52 For Hyrcanus, cf. 1 Macc. 16: 11–22; Jos. *Ant.* 13: 299. Such prophecy as does occur is usually found either in the context of political turbulence or eschatological interpretation, or both. For the former, cf. Jesus ben Ananias (Jos. *Bell.* 6: 300ff.), zealot prophets (*Bell.* 6: 283ff., 299), Pharisaic prophets (*Ant.* 17: 43ff.), Theudas (*Ant.* 20: 97f.), and R. Akiba at the time of the Bar Kochba revolt. For the second emphasis, cf. the Essenes and the Qumran community: *Bell.* 2: 159; *Ant.* 13: 311ff.; 15: 373ff.; 17: 345ff.; 1 Qp Hab. 7: 1–5; 1 QH 4: 27–37; 7: 26–33; cf. M. Black, *The Scrolls and Christian Origins*, 1961, pp. 125–9.

53 The subject has been widely studied: cf. S. Mowinckel, *He That Cometh*, Eng. tr., 1956; M. A. Chevallier, *L'Esprit et le Messie dans le bas-judaisme et le Nouveau Testament*, 1958; U. Kellermann, *Messias und Gesetz*, 1971; G. F. Moore, *Judaism* II, pp. 323–76.

54 His milieu was that of the first-century Palestinian baptist movement, which included among its many varieties the Qumran sectarians and other groups of a generally Essenic character, as well as the Hemero-baptists, the Sabaeans and various Samaritan sects. Cf. W. Brandt, *Die jüdischen Baptismen*, 1910; J. Thomas, *Le mouvement baptiste en Palestine et Syrie*, 1935; C. H. H. Scobie, *John the Baptist*, 1964, pp. 32–40.

55 The word *ischuroteros* means more than 'mightier' in the ordinary sense. It suggests one characterised by *gebhurah*, the majestic might of the royal Messiah, in whose presence even the royal messenger is unfit to perform the meanest tasks. Cf. Is. 9: 6; 11: 2, 4; Ps. Sol. 17: 44; M. Chevallier, *L'Esprit et le Messie*, p. 54. Such scriptural allusiveness suggests that John was steeped in scriptural tradition and interpretation.

56 Imminence, however, is to be understood not only in terms of time sequence but as the existential encounter with the *eschaton* which requires the individual *now* to confront the totality of God's claim upon him.

57 The presence of *hagiō* with *pneumati* is almost certainly a Christian interpretation of John's utterance. The problem of 'with fire', present in Matthew and Luke but absent from Mark, need not concern us here. Contrast M.

Dibelius, *Die urchristliche Überlieferung von Johannes dem Täufer*, 1911, pp. 55–9, with C. H. Kraeling, *John the Baptist*, 1951, p. 60.

58 Is. 29: 6; 30: 27f.; Ezek. 1: 4; cf. H. J. Flowers, " 'Εν πνεύματι ἀγίῳ καί πυρί", *Exp. T.* 64, 1952–53, pp. 155f.; E. Schweizer, 'With the Holy Ghost and Fire', *Exp. T.* 65, 1953–54, p. 29. For Persian parallels, cf. Yasna 31: 3; 36: 1, 3; 47: 6.

59 E.g., Amos 7: 4; Ezek. 38: 22; Is. 31: 9; Mal. 4: 1; En. 90: 24–27; Ps. Sol. 15: 6; 1 QS 2: 8; 1 Qp Hab. 2: 11ff. 'River of fire' imagery occurs in Judaism from Daniel onwards: Dan. 7: 9f.; 1 QH 3: 27–32; 2 (4) Esd. 13: 10.

60 Cf. R. Eisler, *The Messiah Jesus and John the Baptist*, Eng. tr., 1931, p. 278.

61 Cf. the retrospective application of the title 'Elijah' to John, which was probably the product of Christian *pesher* on Mal. 4: 5 and 3: 1; cf. Mark 1: 2, 6f. One wonders if John identified himself with the 'messenger of the covenant' (Mal. 3: 1), but the problem of John's self-consciousness is almost as acute as that of Jesus: cf. J. A. T. Robinson, 'Elijah, John and Jesus', in *Twelve N. T. Studies*, 1962. There is little evidence of Christian apologetic directed against the followers of John: cf. W. Wink, *John the Baptist in Gospel Tradition*, 1968, p. 110.

62 Cf. the figure of eschatological discrimination (Matt. 3: 12; Luke 3: 17), in which the messianic work effects an explicit discrimination: the wheat is garnered; the chaff is destroyed by fire.

63 On 'therefore' as an abbreviated messenger formula, *vid. supra*, n. 19.

64 Cf. H. L. Strack and P. Billerbeck, *Kommentar zum Neuen Testament aus Talmud und Midrasch* 1922–28, I, pp. 162ff., 598f. Relevant rabbinic passages include *Sanhedrin* 98a, *Yoma* 86b, *Jer. Ta'anit* 63d; cf. G. F. Moore, *Judaism* II, pp. 350f.

65 Much of this material was readily assimilated into Christian utterance and vice versa: cf. R. Bultmann, *H.S.T.*, p. 117.

66 Matthew's setting, viz., contention with Pharisees and Sadducees, is almost certainly secondary. Luke (Q?) implies that it is directed to the Jews; Mark speaks of *all* Judaea and *all* Jerusalem (1: 5)!

67 For the individualising of the prophetic message to Israel, cf. Is. 55: 7; Ezek. 18: 21f.; 33: 11; and the penitential psalms: e.g., Ps. 51; cf. G. F. Moore, *Judaism* II, pp. 501f., 509, 520f.

68 Cf. Mark's programmatic statement ascribed to Jesus: 1: 15. Matthew uses this formula to articulate the tradition of John's 'preaching a baptism of repentance for the forgiveness of sins' (Mark 1: 4; Luke 3: 3) in conjunction with his proclamation of the imminence of the Coming One.

69 Cf. Mark 1: 1–4; Luke 1: 5ff.; 3: 1ff.; 3: 18; cf. 1: 19; 16: 16; Matt. 11: 12f.; John 1: 6, 19ff.; cf. Acts 1: 22; 10: 37; 13: 24.

70 Cf. Matt. 11: 13; W. Trilling, 'Die Täufertradition bei Matthäus', *B. Z.* (N.S.) III, 2, 1959, p. 279; W. Wink, *John the Baptist*, pp. 30–3.

71 Cf. W. Trilling, *B. Z.* (N.F.) III, 2, p. 285.

72 Matthew still preserves a distinction between the message of John and Jesus: contrast 3: 3 and 4: 16, and cf. G. Bornkamm, *Jesus of Nazareth*, Eng. tr., 1960, pp. 51f.

73 W. Wink, *John the Baptist*, p. 47. At this point he is discussing the thesis of H. Conzelmann, *The Theology of Luke*, Eng. tr., 1961, pp. 21–7.

74 H. Conzelmann, *Luke*, p. 23. Conzelmann's handling of Luke 16: 16 is

severely criticised by P. Minear in *Studies in Luke-Acts*, Keck and Martyn (edd.), 1966, p. 122.

75   H. Flender, *St Luke, Theologian of Redemptive History*, Eng. tr., 1967, pp. 123f.

76   W. Wink, *John the Baptist*, p. 55.

77   N. Perrin, *Rediscovering the Teaching of Jesus*, 1967, p. 75; cf. M. Dibelius, *Johannes*, pp. 20–9. Luke's version smooths out the linguistic and theological difficulties in Matthew's text; it also reflects the later tendency to play down John's status for christological reasons. Matthew reflects a high estimate of the Baptist and the affinity of his work with that of Jesus. Although Matthew may well have edited the tradition here, he stands nearer to it than Luke.

78   Cf. E. Käsemann, *Essays on New Testament Themes*, Eng. tr., 1964, pp. 42f.; G. Bornkamm, *Jesus*, p. 51.

79   It demonstrates why Luke does not parallel this saying. It also suggests that Matthew may have kept close to a tradition which reflected Jesus' attitude to John rather than that of the early church to him; and that this tradition connected John with the kingdom of God. Mark does not record a parallel to Matt. 3: 2, but immediately after John's arrest he reports Jesus' proclamation of the imminence of the kingdom (Mark 1: 14f.). Matthew's ascription of the same utterance to John and Jesus is very striking (3: 2; 4: 17). At least in this respect, he seems to suggest, there was a close community of interest between John and his successor.

80   Cf. Luke 11: 20; 17: 20f.

81   Cf. Luke 21 *passim*, esp. vv. 25–31. Cf. H. Conzelmann, *Luke*, pp. 125–32.

82   Cf. Matt. 21: 11, 46; Mark 6: 15 par.; 8: 28 par.; Luke 7: 16; John 6: 14; 7: 40; also John 4: 19; 9: 17; Luke 24: 19.

83   Cf. G. Friedrich, *T.D.N.T.* VI, p. 848; G. Vermes, *Jesus the Jew*, 1973, pp. 88ff.

84   The reception of the Spirit (Mark 1: 9ff. par.) is perhaps the element most likely to reflect the historical experience: cf. J. Jeremias, *New Testament Theology* I. *The Proclamation of Jesus*, Eng. tr., 1971, pp. 51ff. While the experience may have been very important to Jesus, Christian midrash and christological apologetic made it the subject of an epiphany story or 'faith legend': cf. R. Bultmann, *H.S.T.*, pp. 247–53; M. Dibelius, *Tradition*, p. 274. Bultmann comments: 'It is characteristically different from calling stories like Is. 6: 1–13; Jer. 1: 5–19; Ezek. 1 and 2; Acts 9: 1–9; Luke 5: 1–11; Rev. 1: 9–20; John 21: 15–17; not only is there not so much as a word about the inner experience of Jesus, but there is also no word of commission to the person called, and no answer from him, things which we normally find in proper accounts of a call. Nor is the passage concerned with Jesus' special calling to preach repentance and salvation, but the real subject is his being the Messiah, or the Son of God, and that cannot be described as a "call". . . The legend tells of Jesus' consecration as Messiah, and so is basically not a biographical, but a faith legend': *H.S.T.*, pp. 247f. J. D. G. Dunn, who makes a brave effort to substantiate the historicity of the pericope, concludes: 'The case is hardly proved': *Jesus and the Spirit*, 1975, pp. 62–7, esp. 65.

85   Cf. R. Bultmann, *H.S.T.*, p. 118. Surprisingly, Bultmann does not adequately discuss Matt. 4: 17 independently of Mark 1: 15. Mark's version employs

specifically Christian terminology ('believe in the gospel') and is therefore secondary.

86 Cf. C. H. Dodd, 'Jesus as Teacher and Prophet', in *Mysterium Christi*, Bell and Deissmann (edd.), 1930, p. 62.

87 Its absence in Luke is to be explained largely in terms of his theology of the kingdom. Luke has his own distinctive summons to repentance in 13: 1–5. In Mark, the disciples' mission is a preaching of repentance (6: 12). Matthew prefaced the woes in the cities of Galilee with an editorial comment on their failure to repent (11: 20).

88 Matt. 4: 17; 10: 7; Mark 1: 15; cf. Matt. 3: 8; 9: 35; Luke 4: 43; 8: 1; 9: 2, 11.

89 The symbol 'kingdom of God' presupposes the nature and purpose of kingship in Israel and suggests God's active rule in his creation. The ambivalence of this concept is illustrated by the fact that scholars have advocated both wholly realised and wholly future views of the kingdom. Without engaging in a full discussion here, it may be observed that both of these positions are to be excluded as incompatible with the evidence of the gospels (*vid.* Chapter 3). The puzzle centres on the use of the language of imminence ('at hand') – literally the language of time sequence – to denote simultaneously a number of complementary but contrasting aspects, including eschatological urgency (cf. Matt. 24: 43f.; 25: 1–12; Luke 12: 35–40); the realisation of the kingdom in the present through prophetic action while the *eschaton* in a total sense yet remains in the future (cf. Luke 11: 20); the intangibility of the kingdom (cf. Luke 17: 20f.); and its meaning in terms of human self-understanding and relationships (cf. Luke 10: 25–37; Luke 15 *passim*). It is not surprising, in view of this complexity, that the prophetic announcement is supported by a wide range of prophetic communications and actions.

90 Mark 1: 15 shows a trace of Christian missionary phraseology, but otherwise its main feature is the degree to which it reflects Dan. 7: 22; cf. F. F. Bruce, 'The Book of Daniel', p. 227. In view of all the evidence of 'realised' language, this logion, even in its Markan form, suggests something of Jesus' own midrashic activity.

91 *Vid.* Chapter 2, p. 48.

92 Cf. Matt. 1: 22; 2: 15, 17, 23; 8: 17; 12: 17; 13: 35; 21: 4; 26: 54, 56; 27: 9.

93 Cf. R. Otto, *The Kingdom of God and the Son of Man*, 1938, pp. 333–81; J. D. G. Dunn, *Jesus*, pp. 55–60.

94 Cf. M. Black, 'The Beatitudes', *Exp. T.* 64, 1952–53, pp. 125f. The beatitudes – good examples of Semitic poetry – possibly consisted in the first instance of groups of four-line stanzas, 'each couplet containing two lines in synthetic parallelism, and the second couplet in synonymous parallelism, with the first': *op. cit.*, p. 125. The first stanza consisted of two beatitudes (Matt. 5: 3 and 5), which, as Zahn saw, were derived from Is. 61: 1 ('the good news to the poor'). A second stanza may well have comprised Matt. 5: 4 and Luke 6: 21b, again inspired by Is. 61: 2f. ('to comfort all who mourn'). Matt. 5: 6 may well represent a telescoping of two couplets, one concerning hunger and the other thirst; again the reference is to the poor of Is. 61: 1 who long for the 'righteousness' that the day of salvation brings (61: 2f.). The 'pure in heart' might well take up Isaiah's 'brokenhearted',

i.e., contrite. Also, Luke 6: 23 ('rejoice in that day and leap for joy': cf. Matt. 5: 12) expresses an Aramaism that suggests movement and dancing: this reflects Is. 61: 3.

95   The beatitude or blessing is a prophetic form related to the salvation oracle and occurs characteristically in a series: *vid. supra*, n. 21.

96   F. F. Bruce speaks of 'exegesis and fulfilment on which the personal impress of Jesus has been stamped as clearly as that of the Teacher of Righteousness has been stamped on the Qumran interpretation, and in which we are provided with the foundations of Christian theology': 'The Book of Daniel', p. 235.

97   Cf. D. Flusser, *Jesus,* 1969, p. 90. But it is important to link the beginning of the age of fulfilment with Jesus' prophetic or prophetic-like activity.

98   Luke cites only the first line of this couplet as the text of the homily at Nazareth where the theme is salvation (4: 18f.); *vid.* also the citation of Is. 35: 5f. in Luke 7: 22; Matt. 11: 5; cf. J. Jeremias, *The Parables of Jesus,* Eng. tr., 1954, pp. 93f., 151, n. 59. But, as is demonstrated below, Jesus also gave expression to the judgment of God.

99   Cf. C. Westermann, *B. F. P. S.,* p. 206.

100   Cf. also Matt. 18: 7; 23: 13–29; 24: 19; Luke 6: 24ff.; 11: 42–47; 21: 23; Mark 13: 17.

101   Matthew's version gives the full form; Luke truncates to avoid repetition.

102   R. Bultmann, *H. S. T.,* p. 112, regards these woes as a community formulation, but these sayings are completely appropriate to the point in the ministry of Jesus at which it became clear that the response of these cities towards him was no longer favourable and that they had thus brought upon themselves eschatological judgment: cf. the prophetic motif that to receive or reject a prophet is to receive or reject him who sent the prophet (so also with an apostle, and with Jesus): cf. Luke 10: 16; Matt. 10: 40ff.; John 13: 20.

103   The material may itself reflect a prophetic saying of Jesus: cf. R. Bultmann, *H. S. T.,* p. 114.

104   The woes discussed above express or imply an announcement of judgment against specific people or groups. Other woes, though specific, raise problems of their own: Mark 14: 21 par. raises that of the Son of man and the passion narrative; Matt. 24: 19 par. that of apocalyptic; and Matt. 18: 7 is part of a complicated passage on offences. Luke 6: 24ff. is essentially different in that it deals with general types: the rich, the well-fed, those who laugh complacently and win popular favour. These woes are the converse of the beatitudes and are probably commentary upon them originating in the Palestinian church: cf. R. Bultmann, *H. S. T.,* p. 112. They add little to the understanding of the beatitudes.

105   Cf. R. Bultmann, *H. S. T.,* pp. 37, 115f.

106   The interpretation of the sign of Jonah in terms of the death and resurrection of the Son of man (Matt. 12: 39f.) is clearly secondary. Luke may have understood it to refer either to the resurrection of the Son of man, like Jonah, from the dead; or to the coming of the Son of man from heaven, like Jonah from a distant country (11: 29f.). Both of these interpretations also appear secondary. Cf. R. Bultmann, *H. S. T.,* p. 117f.; W. Manson, *The Gospel of Luke,* 1930, p. 143.

107 For other sayings about 'this generation', cf. Matt. 12: 41f. (Luke 11: 31f.); Matt. 23: 34ff (Luke 11: 49ff.).

108 One welcomes J. D. G. Dunn's observation that it is misleading to suggest that the kingdom is realised simply by virtue of the presence of Jesus (e.g., 'where Jesus is, there is the kingdom'); rather, the kingdom was present for Jesus 'only because the eschatological Spirit was present in and through him': *Jesus*, p. 48. However, this is only one way of expressing the matter. Since the realisation of the kingdom can be presented without explicit reference to the Spirit (cf. Luke 11: 20!), it is preferable to relate it simply to Jesus' prophetic ministry.

109 The basic point is that acts of exorcism are open to interpretation (cf. Luke 11: 15, 18): cf. the question of true and false prophecy (cf. 20: 4). To arrive at a proper answer, insight is required – itself a gift of God through his Spirit (cf. John 14: 26; 1 John 4: 1ff.). Deliberately to reject the action of God, by caricaturing either the overt act done in his name or the inner promptings of his Spirit, is the gravest of sins (cf. Matt. 12: 31f.; Mark 3: 28f.; Luke 12: 10). Cf. also his actions in defiance of the sabbath law: e.g., Mark 2: 23 – 3: 6; the prophetic action of blessing: e.g., Matt. 19: 13–15; also, Matt. 10: 12f. (and the reverse of the blessing, Luke 9: 5); and several powerful symbols of acceptance and humility: e.g., the 'child in the midst' pericope: Matt. 18: 1–6; Mark 9: 33–7; Luke 9: 46ff.; and the 'footwashing' pericope: John 13: 1–20.

110 Cf. C. Westermann, *B.F.P.S.*, p. 202 and 'The Way', p. 206, incl. n. 14; also cf. Is. 8: 1–4; Jer. 16: 1–12; 18: 1–12; 19 *passim*; Hos. chs. 1 and 3; Ezek. 4: 1ff.

111 With Mark 11: 12ff., cf. Matt. 21: 18–20. The fact that Luke has a parable on a similar theme (13: 6–9) does not mean that the parable gave rise to the symbolic action (or vice versa): cf. D. Hill, *The Gospel of Matthew*, 1972, pp. 294f.

112 Mark 14: 3–9; cf. Matt. 26: 6–13; Luke 7: 36ff.; John 12: 1–8; cf. D. Hill, *Matthew*, pp. 333f.

113 Cf. J. Jeremias, *The Eucharistic Words of Jesus*, Eng. tr., 1966, esp. pp. 14–37; C. W. Dugmore, 'The Study of the Origins of the Eucharist: Retrospect and Revaluation', in *Studies in Church History* II, Cuming (ed.), 1965, pp. 1–18.

114 Cf. I. T. Ramsey, *Christian Discourse*, 1965, pp. 6–13.

115 Related to this category are parables which give assurance that the work of God as king goes on, despite its unobtrusiveness: the sower (Mark 4: 3–8), the patient husbandman (4: 26–9), the mustard seed (4: 30ff.) and the leaven (Matt. 13: 33; Luke 13: 20f.). The incomparable value of being truly part of God's kingdom is illustrated by the parables of the treasure and the pearl (Matt. 13: 44f.), and the central requirement of the king by the good Samaritan (Luke 10: 25–37). Another way of depicting this is to focus on the criteria of the last judgment (Matt. 25: 31–46).

116 Parables like the talents (Matt. 25: 14–30; Luke 19: 12–27) or the trusted servant (Matt. 24: 45–51; Luke 12: 42–6) convey Jesus' warning of judgment to specific groups such as the scribes. The salt that has become useless (Matt. 5: 13 par.) is a warning to Israel as a whole; the two houses built respectively on rock and sand (Matt. 7: 24–7; Luke 6: 47ff.) carry a warning

for all. For the whole question of the message of the parables, cf. J. Jeremias, *Parables*, pp. 89–158.

117 Cf. the anointing at Bethany and the last supper. Even parables on the theme of salvation sometimes contain an indication of disaster ahead: the days will come when the bridegroom will be taken away (Mark 2: 20 par.).

118 This is implicit even in the original form of the parable of the wicked husbandman, as far as this is recoverable: cf. Mark 12: 1–9; Matt. 21: 33–41; Luke 20: 9–16; J. Jeremias, *Parables*, pp. 55–60. C. H. Dodd, *Parables*, pp. 124–32; Gospel of Thomas 66.

119 A judgment saying against the existing temple and containing an element of riddle clearly made an impact on his contemporaries and was apparently quoted against him at his trial. Matt. 26: 61; 27: 40; Mark 14: 58; 15: 29; John 2: 19ff.

120 For this aspect of the good Samaritan, cf. G. Hebert, *The Christ of Faith and the Jesus of History*, 1962, pp. 61f.

121 Cf. the antitheses in the Sermon on the Mount (Matt. 5: 21–48): D. Daube, *The New Testament and Rabbinic Judaism*, 1956, pp. 55–62; W. D. Davies, *S. S. M.*, pp. 101ff., 427ff.; cf. also *Torah in the Messianic Age and/or the Age to Come*, 1952, esp. pp. 54–83; E. Käsemann, 'The Problem of the Historical Jesus', in *Essays*, pp. 37f.

122 Cf. Matt. 5: 12; 23: 30f., 34, 37; Luke 6: 23; 11: 49f.; 13: 33f.

123 Modern scholars who have argued that Jesus did lay weight on the servant songs include H. W. Wolff, *Jesaja 53 im Urchristentum*, (3rd ed.) 1952, pp. 55ff., 75ff.; R. H. Fuller, *The Mission and Achievement of Jesus*, 1954, pp. 55–64; W. Zimmerli and J. Jeremias, *The Servant of God*, Eng. tr., 1957, pp. 98–104; J. Jeremias, *T.D.N.T.* V, pp. 700–17; O. Cullmann, *The Christology of the New Testament*, Eng. tr., 1959, pp. 51–82, esp. pp. 60–9. One difficulty, however, is the scant evidence in the gospels themselves (see n. 124 below); also, modern scholarship has tended, perhaps accidentally, to isolate the servant songs from the total context of Deutero-Isaiah's theology in a way that was not true of either the Jewish understanding of these texts or indeed of Deutero-Isaiah's writings. Even the early church seems to have been slow to 'pesher' Is. 53 in terms of the cross as vicarious sacrifice. *Vid. infra*, Chapter 4, n. 87. Hence the case against Jesus' use of the servant motif in this way has been stated by, for example, M. D. Hooker, *Jesus and the Servant*, 1959, pp. 147–63; F. Hahn, *The Titles of Jesus in Christology*, Eng. tr., 1969, pp. 54–63; and C. K. Barrett, *Jesus and the Gospel Tradition*, 1967, pp. 35–67, esp. 39ff.

124 Matt. 8: 17 refers to Jesus' healing ministry and makes no reference to vicarious suffering; and Luke 22: 37 appears to be a (Christian?) commentary on the fact that Jesus was crucified between two malefactors rather than an interpretation of the redemptive efficacy of suffering: cf. C. K. Barrett, *Jesus*, p. 40.

125 Cf. N. Perrin, *Rediscovering the Teaching of Jesus*, pp. 154–206.

126 Cf. J. A. T. Robinson, *Jesus and his Coming*, 1957, pp. 36–82.

127 Cf. J. A. T. Robinson, *Jesus*, pp. 44f.; T. W. Manson, 'The Son of Man in Daniel, Enoch and the Gospels', *B.J.R.L.* 32, 1950, p. 174. Such an interpretation is consistent with a dominical tradition behind such sayings as Luke 17: 23f., Matt. 24: 26f., and above all Mark 14: 62.

128   Cf. C. K. Barrett, *Jesus*, pp. 41–5.

129   N. Perrin, *Rediscovering the Teaching of Jesus*, p. 203. I am not sure that Perrin is using 'form' here in a structural way: he seems to refer to content as well.

130   Incl. Is. 49: 3 and 53: 10ff.; cf. the 'faithful remnant'. Jesus' tendency to identify with the experience of Israel, or her representatives, through the existential use of scripture or scriptural symbols may perhaps shed light on his citation of Ps. 22 on the cross: *vide supra*, pp. 27f.

131   Cf. B. Gärtner, *The Temple and the Community in Qumran and the N.T.*, 1965, pp. 111ff.; M. Goguel, *Vie de Jésus*, 1932, pp. 491ff.

132   Is. 61: 1 affirms the activity of the Spirit of God. In Ezek. 37, the Spirit of God resurrects Israel (cf. vv. 11–14). The renewed temple (Ezek. chs. 40–46) is the major symbol of revivified Israel. Jesus identifies himself with such symbols of the new Israel. Did he then identify himself specifically with the death and resurrection of Israel (symbolised by the temple) through the power of the Spirit? Cf. also Hos. 6: 2; B. Gärtner, *The Temple*, pp. 16ff., 51ff.

133   Cf. M. D. Hooker, *The Son of Man in Mark*, 1967, pp. 11–30, 120ff., 169ff., 182–98.

134   It may be observed here, in view of recent attempts to reopen this perennial problem, that if nineteenth-century liberal protestants mistook their own mirror image for the portrait of Jesus, it is no more satisfactory today to take Christian pietism, protestant or catholic, as the mirror of Jesus' self-consciousness.

135   It is, of course, a detached logion in the tradition: *tauta* has no specific antecedent.

136   Cf. J. Jeremias, *The Central Message of the New Testament*, 1965, p. 18; *The Prayers of Jesus*, 1967, pp. 54–7; *N.T. Theology* I, pp. 61–8.

137   R. Bultmann, *H.S.T.*, p. 160.

138   Cf. 2 Sam. 7: 14; 1 Chr. 17: 13; Ps. 2: 7; 89: 26f.; 103: 13; Wisd. 2: 13,16,18; Ecclus. 4: 10; 23: 1,4; 51: 10; Test. Levi 18: 6; Test. Jud. 24: 2; Jub. 1: 24f.

139   Mishna, *Tamid* 5: 1; cf. G. Vermes, *Jesus*, p. 79.

140   Cf. H. Conzelmann, *An Outline of the Theology of the New Testament*, Eng. tr., 1969, p. 103; and cf. the discussion below.

141   Cf. Mark 14: 36; Matt. 26: 39; Luke 22: 42; 11: 2 (cf. Matt. 6: 9).

142   M. Dibelius, *Tradition*, pp. 279–83, and R. Bultmann, *H.S.T.*, p. 160, took it to be essentially hellenistic, although others have judged it to be semitic in expression. Cf. T. W. Manson, *Sayings*, p. 79; W. L. Knox, *Some Hellenistic Elements in Primitive Christianity*, 1944, p. 7. At any rate, in its present form it can hardly be other than a statement of early church christology. Although it bears a certain resemblance to a post-resurrection logion, Matt. 28: 18, there is no mention here of 'authority': *panta* refers to revelation. Nevertheless, one can hardly imagine Matthew or Luke interpreting this logion other than christologically, as the context suggests.

143   The *panta* may well reflect the inclusiveness of devotion: cf. Matt. 21: 22. *Paredothē* may be used of handing down a tradition, message or lesson. 'Everything' is passed down to Jesus as a father hands on the alphabet to his son or as God commits his message to his prophet.

144   J. Jeremias, *Message*, p. 25; *N.T. Theology* I, pp. 56–9. Jeremias stresses the

importance of the use of the definite article in a generic sense in semitic metaphor or parable.

145 J. Jeremias, *Message*, p. 25.

146 Cf. Wisd. 2: 13, 16ff.

147 Cf. J. D. G. Dunn, who protests against Jeremias' abstracting of 'the middle couplet' from Matt. 11: 27 and insists that 'the whole verse follows from vv. 25ff. and cannot be so easily dissected'; finally, 'No! v. 27 almost certainly stands or falls as a whole... The exclusiveness and absoluteness of the claim remains': *Jesus*, p. 32. One is aware of dogmatic presuppositions in this kind of argumentation.

148 For a study of 'knowledge' in Matt. 11: 27 and the Qumran scrolls, cf. W. D. Davies, *Christian Origins and Judaism*, 1962, pp. 119–44. On the probability of contemporary belief in Jesus' 'sonship', cf. G. Vermes, *Jesus*, p. 209.

149 J. Jeremias, *Message*, p. 30.

150 Cf. J. C. G. Greig, 'Abba and Amen: Their Relevance to Christology', *T.U.* 103, *Studia Evangelica* V, 1968, pp. 3–13.

151 In so far as 'uniqueness' may be attributed to Jesus, other than in a post-resurrection christological sense, it must be made clear that the uniqueness properly belongs to the faithful Israel, with which Jesus identifies and which, in the eyes of his followers at least, he personifies and appropriates.

152 J. Jeremias, *Message*, p. 27. On the contrary, I argue that Jesus' usage is foreshadowed in the inner logic of the covenant.

153 J. Jeremias, *Message*, p. 27.

154 W. D. Davies, *S.S.M.*, p. 432.

155 E.g., in his healing, exorcism, and avoidance of asceticism: cf. E. Käsemann, 'Primitive Christian Apocalyptic' in *New Testament Questions of Today*, Eng. tr., 1969, p. 112.

156 Cf. G. Vermes, *Jesus*, p. 79.

157 Cf. J. D. G. Dunn, *Jesus*, pp. 84–8. R. Otto argued that Jesus was a charismatic: *Kingdom*, pp. 333–81; but his most cogent arguments simply indicate the broad prophetic type.

158 Matt. 11: 9; Luke 7: 26.

159 Cf. C. K. Barrett, *The Holy Spirit and Gospel Tradition*, 1947, pp. 140–62; cf. pp. 113–21.

160 Jesus' use of the title Son of man is especially problematic. If he used it apocalyptically, the early church may then have applied it retrospectively to him; cf. H. E. Tödt, *The Son of Man in the Synoptic Tradition*, Eng. tr., 1965, p. 295. On the other hand, G. Vermes has argued that Jesus used it simply as a neutral speech form: cf. *Jesus*, p. 186, and Appendix E, in M. Black, *An Aramaic Approach to the Gospels and Acts*, (3rd ed.) 1967, pp. 310–28. Important but unproven solutions were put forward by T. W. Manson, *The Teaching of Jesus*, 1955, pp. 227f. and E. Lohmeyer, *Das Evangelium des Markus*, 1951, p. 6; and by many others. *Vid. infra*, n. 247.

161 C. Westermann, *B.F.P.S.*, p. 105.

162 Cf. J. D. G. Dunn, *Jesus*, p. 95.

163 Cf. R. Bultmann, *Theology of the N.T.*, pp. 33f.

164 Cf. J. Y. Campbell, 'ΚΟΙΝΩΝΙΑ and its Cognates in the New Testament', *J.B.L.* 51, 1932; also *Three New Testament Studies*, 1965, pp. 1–28.

165 Cf. J. Knox, *The Church and the Reality of Christ*, 1963.
166 Cf. K. H. Rengstorf, *T. D. N. T.* I, pp. 407-47, esp. 430-7; A. Fridrichsen, *The Apostle and his Message*, 1947, pp. 4-16; J. Munck, 'Paul, the Apostles and the Twelve', *St. Th.* 3, 1950, pp. 96-110; G. Klein, *Die Zwölf Apostel*, 1961, pp. 114-216; C. K. Barrett, 'The Apostles in and after the New Testament', *Svensk Exegetisk Arsbok* XXI, 1957, pp. 30-49; *The Signs of an Apostle*, 1970; R. Schnackenburg, 'Apostles Before and During Paul's Time', in *Apostolic History and the Gospel*, Gasque and Martin (edd.), 1970, pp. 287-303; J. H. Schütz, *Paul and the Anatomy of Apostolic Authority*, 1975. On false apostles, cf. C. K. Barrett, 'ΨΕΥΔΑΠΟΣΤΟΛΟΙ (2 Cor. 11: 13)', in *Mélanges B. Rigaux*, 1970, pp. 377-96.
167 The Jerusalem tradition seems to have laid emphasis upon witness to the risen Christ as a *sine qua non* of apostleship, and to this Paul assents (1 Cor. 9: 1; 15: 1-11) although such a definition may not have been accepted widely in the hellenistic churches: cf. R. Schnackenburg, 'Apostles', pp. 291f., 301. In Acts, the criteria for membership of 'the Twelve' are even more specific: 1: 21f. On the other hand, not all witnesses to the resurrection became apostles: cf. the 'more than five hundred brethren'.
168 *Vid.* Chapter 4, *passim.*
169 1 Cor. 15: 4-8; Acts 2: 32; 10: 40f.; 13: 30f., etc.
170 Cf. I. T. Ramsey, *Christian Discourse*, pp. 2ff.
171 Cf. H. Anderson, *Jesus and Christian Origins*, 1964, pp. 203f.
172 The tradition of the appearances is part of the witness of faith. To admit the reality of the disciples' experiences does not make the resurrection an empirical, this-worldly 'fact', as if it were a phenomenon observable by the outside world.
173 R. Gregor Smith, *Secular Christianity*, 1966, p. 108.
174 C. H. Dodd compares this part of the resurrection pericope to the ἀναγνώρισις motif in Greek drama: 'The Appearances of the Risen Christ: An Essay in Form-Criticism of the Gospels', in *Studies in the Gospels*, Nineham (ed.), 1957, pp. 14, 18, 34. The nature of the encounter and of the element of recognition should be understood, however, in the light of the discussion *supra*, pp. 29f.
175 The necessary linguistic flexibility could be found only in 'second order', interpretative or metaphorical language: cf. I. T. Ramsey, *Christian Discourse*, pp. 2ff.; W. Pannenberg, *Jesus - God and Man*, Eng. tr., 1968, p. 74.
176 This coalescing of memory and interpretation from the standpoint of the resurrection faith eventually gives to the gospel traditions the special characteristics that constitute the classical *formgeschichtliche* puzzles.
177 Cf. Luke 24: 44f.; B. Lindars, *N. T. Apologetic*, pp. 32-74; M. Black, 'The Christological Use of the Old Testament in the New Testament', *N. T. S.* 18, 1971-72, pp. 1-14, esp. pp. 5f.
178 The verb 'explore' is used advisedly: the eschatological implications of the resurrection faith are among the most 'openended' aspects of the early church's life, and an area in which prophetic contributions were expected.
179 Cf. J. D. G. Dunn, *Jesus*, pp. 128ff. But, *vid. supra*, n. 167.
180 For 1 Cor. 15: 3-8, *vid.* Chapter 4, pp. 113-16; in Acts, cf. 2: 24, 32; 3: 15; 5: 30ff.; and, in particular, 10: 40ff.; and 13: 30f. Even when full allowance is made for the literary nature of these sermons, the focal position of the

apostolic witness to the death and resurrection of Christ indicates the basic contribution they made to the articulation and development of the Christian faith.

181   According to C. H. Dodd's analysis, this concise form has five elements: the situation, the appearance of the Lord, the greeting, the recognition, and the word of command (or commissioning): 'The Appearances of the Risen Christ', p. 11.

182   Cf. C. H. Dodd, 'The Appearances of the Risen Christ', p. 33. There seems to have been a variety of such pericopae, for the gospel writers evidently made no effort to relate their accounts to the basic *paradosis* which Paul used (there are, of course, reflections of the same material such as the first appearance to Peter, but this is not documented in the gospels). Nevertheless, the gospel pericopae are constructed with severe restraint (cf. Dodd, p. 34) and close attention to form.

183   On the whole it is more likely that the longer, more detailed and more material narratives represent a development from visionary representation than vice versa: so H. Grass, *Ostergeschehen und Osterberichte*, 1956, r.p. 1962, pp. 89f.; *contra*, E. Käsemann, 'Is the Gospel Objective?', *Essays on N.T. Themes*, p. 49; J. D. G. Dunn, *Jesus*, pp. 120ff.

184   For a full discussion of this narrative, cf. E. Haenchen, *The Acts of the Apostles*, Eng. tr., 1971, pp. 14–49; Haenchen observes that Luke's composition 'at times appears almost to create *ex nihilo*': *op. cit.*, p. 49. Cf. also M. Dibelius, *Studies in the Acts of the Apostles*, Eng. tr., 1956, pp. 15, 106; E. Trocmé, *Le 'Livre des Actes' et l'histoire*, 1957, esp. pp. 202–6.

185   Cf. E. Haenchen, *Acts*, p. 189; M. Dibelius, *Acts*, p. 124. For a parallel in modern hasidic Judaism, cf. A. C. Bouquet, *Everyday Life in New Testament Times*, 1953, pp. 217f.

186   Such preaching probably developed within the hellenistic mission: cf. W. Schmithals, *Paul and James*, Eng. tr., 1965, pp. 16–37; for a contrary viewpoint, cf. J. D. G. Dunn, *Jesus*, pp. 152–6.

187   Cf. 1 Cor. 14: 3ff., 13ff., 20ff., 32.

188   Some have attempted to link this with the rise of gnostic thinking in church circles: cf. J. Moffatt, *The First Epistle of Paul to the Corinthians*, 1938, pp. 206–17; E. Käsemann, *N.T. Questions*, pp. 124ff.; W. Schmithals, *Gnosticism in Corinth*, Eng. tr., 1971. But while this phenomenon can be linked to mystical and intellectual Hellenism, it was probably more directly influenced by Jewish hasidic tendencies baptised, as it were, into early Christianity and developing distinctively in that ethos, perhaps in a broadly gnostic direction: 'the first tentative beginnings of what was later to develop into full-scale Gnosticism': R. McL. Wilson, 'How Gnostic were the Corinthians?' *N.T.S.* 19, 1972–73, p. 74. Indeed, its source may simply be the hellenistic Jewish exegetical tradition: cf. B. A. Pearson, *The 'Pneumatikos-Psychikos' Terminology in 1 Corinthians*, 1973.

189   Cf. 1 Cor. 12: 31; 14: 1; 12: 39; also R. Bultmann, *Theology of the N.T.* I, pp. 139ff., 158ff.

190   Cf. his apologetic treatment of his own visions and revelations (2 Cor. 12: 1–4).

191   Thus for Paul ' "to be in the Spirit" no more denotes the state of ecstasy than "to be in Christ" is a formula of mysticism': R. Bultmann, *Theology*

of the N.T. I, p. 335; cf. pp. 330–40. His refinement of the concept includes the development of its eschatological significance: cf. *arrabon* (2 Cor. 1: 22; 5: 5) and *aparche* (Rom. 8: 23); of its christological associations (cf. 2 Cor. 3: 17); of its ethical consequences (cf. Gal. 5: 22); of its personal intimacy (cf. Rom. 8: 14; Gal. 5: 18).

192 The claim may be held to be implicit in 1 Cor. 14.

193 He prefers to underline his own apostleship and to designate his fellow workers by terms such as *sunergos, adelphos, diakonos* and, indeed, *apostolos*: cf. E. E. Ellis, 'Paul and his Co-Workers', *N.T.S.* 17, 1970–71, p. 440.

194 Rom. 12: 6ff.; 1 Cor. 12: 28f.; cf. Eph. 2: 20; 3: 5; 4: 11.

195 The prophet has a three-fold role in 1 Cor. 14: to build up the church (*oikodome*), to proclaim the message of scripture to the contemporary situation (*paraclesis*), and to encourage the weak and strengthen others in face of the difficulties of discipleship (*paramuthia*): cf. E. Cothenet, 'Prophetisme et Ministère d'après le Nouveau Testament', *La Maison Dieu* 108, 1971, p. 50.

196 *Vid. infra*, Chapter 2, pp.

197 Cf. 1 Cor. 14: 21; 2 Cor. 6: 16ff.; sometimes the exegetical formula 'it is written' is used: cf. Rom. 14: 11; E. E. Ellis, *Paul's Use of the Old Testament*, 1957, pp. 107–12.

198 Cf. C. Roetzel, 'The Judgment Form in Paul's Letters', *J.B.L.* 88, 1969, pp. 305–12.

199 Cf. E. E. Ellis, 'The Role of the Christian Prophet in Acts', in *Apostolic History and the Gospel*, Gasque and Martin (edd.), 1970, pp. 55–67.

200 Those named include Agabus (Acts 11: 27f.); Barnabas, Symeon, Lucius, Menaen, Saul (13: 1); Judas Barsabbas and Silas (15: 22, 32); not to speak of Philip's 'four unmarried daughters who prophesied' (21: 9). Many might prophesy occasionally, but only those who were seen to have the *charisma* of prophecy as a relatively continuous endowment seem to have been designated as prophets: cf. J. Lindblom, *Geschichte und Offenbarungen*, 1968, p. 179.

201 Cf. Acts 11: 27ff.; 21: 10f.

202 M. E. Boring, 'How May We Identify Oracles of Christian Prophets in the Synoptic Tradition? Mark 3: 28–29 as a Test Case', *J.B.L.* 91, 1972, pp. 507f.

203 M. E. Boring, *J.B.L.* 91, p. 508.

204 *Ibid.* Predictive elements occur in prophecy and related forms: e.g., Agabus' eschatological utterances (Acts 11: 28; 21: 11); Paul's farewell discourse (20: 23, 25, 29f.); and the narrative of the storm at sea (27: 22).

205 For a complex tradition which includes prophetic insight and judgment, cf. Acts 5: 1–11.

206 D. Hill, *N.T.S.* 18, p. 410.

207 He is, in fact, steeped in Old Testament prophetic imagery and highly skilled in applying a Christian prophetic hermeneutic: cf. R. H. Preston and A. T. Hanson, *The Revelation of St John the Divine*, (5th ed.) 1962, pp. 36–44.

208 Cf. W. C. van Unnik, 'A Formula describing Prophecy', *N.T.S.* 9, 1962–63, pp. 86–94; G. B. Caird, *The Revelation of St John the Divine*, 1966, p. 26;

the revelation affords insight into the whole of history but esp. the present
and future: cf. M. Rissi, 'The Kerygma of the Revelation to John', *Int.* 22,
1968, pp. 5f. The commissioning to write a book makes this prophet
different from contemporary Christian prophets and is more like Old
Testament practice: the book, however, is not to be sealed up against a
wicked generation (cf. Is. 8: 1f., 16), but to read aloud in the community
(Rev. 1: 3), 'for the time is near'.

209   Cf. Dan. 7: 13; 10: 5f.; also 7: 9.
210   Cf. Ezek. 1: 28; Dan. 7: 15; 8: 17, 27; 10: 8ff.; cf. Is. 6: 5; Jer. 1: 6f.
211   *Vid. supra* pp. 13f.
212   Cf. Is. 41: 4; 44: 2, 6.
213   The description of the experience suggests parallels with Luke's description
      of Paul's 'conversion': Acts 9: 1-9; 22: 4-16; 26: 9-18. P. Carrington's
      interesting discussion of its elements – *The Meaning of Revelation*, 1931,
      pp. 78-86 – probably emphasises the trance situation to the detriment of
      audition.
214   Cf. Rev. 1: 3; 21: 5; 22: 6, 18f. His words are divinely guaranteed.
215   On the letters cf. R. H. Charles, *The Revelation of St John* (*I.C.C.*) I,
      1920, pp. 37-47; P. Carrington, *Revelation*, pp. 91-105.
216   Cf. Rev. 2: 4ff., 14ff., 20-23; 3: 1f., 15-18.
217   Cf. Rev. 2: 5, 16, 22; 3: 3, 19.
218   Rev. 2: 7, 11, 17, 26; 3: 5, 12, 21: the conditional element is, of course,
      related to the notion of response and judgment by 'works' (cf. 2: 13), but
      it is also connected with the coming of the Messiah: cf. P. Carrington,
      Revelation, pp. 96f.
219   Cf. Rev. 2: 7, 10, 17, 26ff.; 3: 5, 11f., 20f.
220   Cf. Jer. 31: 34 (cf. Ex. 3: 7); Hos. 2: 20; 13: 4f.; John 10: 14f.
221   D. Hill takes the phrase 'to have the witness of Jesus' to mean 'to possess,
      i.e., to receive and faithfully preserve, Jesus' witness' (cf. John 3: 32f.),
      although this includes witnessing to Jesus: *N.T.S.* 18, p. 411.
222   Cf. C. Westermann, *B.F.P.S.*, p. 194; cf. Judg. 5: 23.
223   Cf. *enikēsen* (5: 5); M. Rissi, *Int.* 22, pp. 7-10.
224   Rev. 15: 3f.; 13; 22: 1-5; cf. 21: 5; Ps. 86: 9; Jer. 16: 19.
225   Rev. 14: 6ff.; cf. 13: 4, 8.
226   Cf. Rev. 11: 10, 18; 18: 20, 24; 19: 10; 22: 9; cf. 1 Cor. 14: 5.
227   Cf. Paul's stress on *eleutheria* in Gal. 2: 4; 5: 1, 13; Rom. 8: 21; 2 Cor. 3: 17.
228   Cf. John 3: 8; 2 Cor. 3: 17.
229   Cf. 'true' and 'false' prophecy in Israel: *vid. supra*, n. 12. Unsatisfactory
      criteria of differentiation cloud the issue: e.g., that salvation oracles were
      the province of false prophets (!), that cult prophecy is necessarily false,
      and that unfulfilled prophecy was shown to be invalid. The true prophet
      stands in the tradition of Moses: cf. Deut. 18: 15, 18; 2 Kings 17: 13f.;
      I. Engnell, 'Prophets and Prophetism in the Old Testament', in *Critical
      Essays on the Old Testament*, 1970, p. 174. Thus, Amos 3: 15 etc. is tanta-
      mount to a call to return to the Mosaic tradition; cf. also Elijah in 1 Kings
      21 (*re* land, king, justice). In turn, prophetic insight and interpretation
      extended the meaning, application and understanding of traditional *torah*.
      In fact, this interconnection of the prophets and the Mosaic tradition
      prepared the way for the conjunction of 'law and prophets' in the

scriptural 'canon' of Israel: cf. R. E. Clements, *Prophecy*, p. 54.

230   Cf. Chapter 4 on *paradosis*.

231   1 Cor. 7: 10; 9: 14; 11: 23ff.; cf. D. L. Dungan, *The Sayings of Jesus in the Churches of Paul*, 1971, esp. pp. 3–40, 83–131.

232   E.g., through an oracle of salvation: cf. Rev. 3: 20; the background to such utterances is frequently prophetic apprehension of Old Testament meaning in the light of the event of Christ and gospel tradition (cf. also Rev. 1: 8; 16: 15; 21: 6) or prophetic apprehension of christological meaning in the light of the Old Testament and gospel tradition (cf. the I-sayings of the fourth gospel).

233   Eph. 5: 19 and Col. 3: 16 both imply that such singing serves instructional ends. Overtones of hymns may be detected in 1 Tim. 3: 16; Phil. 2: 6–11; Col. 1: 15–20; Eph. 5: 14 and elsewhere, although not always with complete certainty. 1 Peter has also provided scope for hymn hunters! As far as gospel tradition is concerned, the birth narratives in Luke appear to enshrine material of this type: *vid. infra*, n. 246.

234   Cf. Matt. 11: 27; Luke 10: 22, where it is possible to distinguish between the early Christian christology, not unlike Johannine christology, expressed in the final form of the saying and the simple analogy that lies behind it: *vid. supra*, pp. 25ff.

235   Cf. Son of man; *vid. infra*, n. 247. On the whole subject of prophetic forms in apocalyptic, cf. L. Hartman, *Prophecy Interpreted*, Eng. tr., 1966, pp. 23–141.

236   This point is recognised by some form critics: cf. M. Dibelius, *Tradition*, pp. 241f.

237   R. Bultmann, *H.S.T.*, pp. 127f., assumed that the church drew no distinction between sayings of Jesus and Christian prophetic utterances: all were sayings of the risen and contemporary Lord. His initial presuppositions and his exposition of supporting evidence – esp. Od. Sol. 42: 6, as interpreted by H. Gunkel and H. von Soden – have more recently been severely challenged: cf. D. Hill, 'On the Evidence for the Creative Role of Christian Prophets', *N.T.S.* 20, 1973–74, pp. 262–70; F. Neugebauer, 'Geistspruche und Jesus logien', *Z.N.W.* 53, 1962, pp. 218–28. Again, E. Käsemann, in his essay 'Sentences of Holy Law in the New Testament', *N.T. Questions*, pp. 66–81, argued that 'sentences of holy law' like 1 Cor. 3: 17 and Matt. 10: 32, embodying an eschatological version of the *ius talionis*, were products of Christian prophecy, but this claim has been challenged both on formal grounds (cf. K. Berger, 'Zu den sogenannten Sätzen heiligen Rechts', *N.T.S.* 17, 1970–71, pp. 10–40), and also in terms of general presuppositions (cf. D. Hill, *op. cit.*, pp. 270–4). The tendency to make sweeping ascriptions of ostensibly dominical logia to Christian prophetic creativity is thus to be regarded with considerable reserve. Cf. now J. D. G. Dunn, 'Prophetic "I"-Sayings and the Jesus Tradition: The Importance of Testing Prophetic Utterances within Early Christianity', *N.T.S.* 24, 1978, pp. 175–98.

238   1 Cor. 15: 1ff.; Gal. 1: 9; cf. 1 Cor. 11: 2, 23; 2 Cor. 11: 4f.; 2 Thess. 2: 15.

239   E.g., gnostic presuppositions which stressed the spiritual Christ to the detriment of the historical Jesus; or charismatic excess; or as an expression or reflection of synagogue opposition to Christian belief. The hypothesis

of gnostic influence is now increasingly under attack: cf. B. A. Pearson, *1 Corinthians; vid. supra,* n. 188.

240   *Vid. supra,* pp. 30f.

241   1 Cor. 13 *passim*; cf. Gal. 5: 22f.; Matt. 7: 15–23; on this score, certain types of action typical of the false prophet are indicated in Didache 11: 8; cf. Hermas, *Mand.* 11: 8.

242   Cf. Jesus' treatment of Is. 61: 1ff.; *vid. supra,* pp. 20f.; also Matt. 5: 21–48; 21: 33–44. Jesus does not appear to follow the formal pattern of explicit or overt midrashic (*pesher*) procedures, used so frequently by the Qumran sectarians, but rather the implicit or covert midrash, also used at Qumran (1Q 17, 18; 2Q 19, 20; 4Q), the essence of which was the interpretative paraphrasing of the Old Testament text. What Jesus has in common with the Teacher of Righteousness is his eschatological stance, his dialogue with the Eschaton (so to speak), which determines his exegesis and relates it to himself, his followers and the present time. In this respect, his stance is prophetic. For this whole subject, cf. E. E. Ellis, 'Midrash, Targum and New Testament Quotations', in *Neotestamentica et Semitica,* 1969, pp. 61–9. Further discussion is found *infra* in Chapter 2, pp.   ff; and C. H. Dodd, *According to the Scriptures,* 1952.

243   Cf. Luke 24: 13–35, where the two disciples are helped by their unknown friend to come to a new understanding of the scriptures before they recognise Jesus; cf. vv. 19–27 and v. 31.

244   Cf. Mark's introduction (1: 2f.) and Matthew's recurrent 'this was to fulfil what was spoken by the prophet...'. Here the evangelists are using *testimonia* in isolation from the midrash which originally gave them significance. The nativity stories and the Son of man tradition are discussed below. The passion narrative is also coloured by Christian midrash: cf. B. Lindars, *N.T. Apologetic,* pp. 75–137.

245   *Vid. supra,* pp. 29ff.

246   For the nativity story in Matthew as Christian midrashic *haggadah,* emanating from Jewish Christian circles, cf. D. Hill, *The Gospel of Matthew,* 1972, pp. 33, 76f., 81. The quotations are the nucleus and germ of the growth of the cycle: cf. K. Stendahl, *The School of St Matthew,* 1954, pp. 135f., 204. The stories are 'not primarily didactic but kerygmatic': W. D. Davies, *S.S.M.,* p. 67. This fact, with the activity of the Spirit (Matt. 1: 22), may suggest that the piety which shaped them embodied a prophetic strain. In Luke's composite infancy narratives (cf. A. R. C. Leaney, *A Commentary on the Gospel According to St Luke,* 1958, pp. 20–7), midrash is evident in the hymns of messianic joy (note their recurrent use of 'prophet'), angelophanies, oracles of salvation (1: 13f.; cf. 1: 30f., 67f.); 'prophet of the highest' (1: 76). Thus, at least one of Luke's sources was characteristically prophetic. Cf. B. Lindars, *N.T. Apologetic,* pp. 189–221.

247   Although the derivation of the term Son of man from Jewish apocalypticism is still a matter of debate (cf. N. Perrin, *Rediscovering the Teaching of Jesus,* pp. 164–99; A. J. B. Higgins, 'Is the Son of Man Problem Insoluble?', *Neotestamentica et Semitica,* pp. 80–7), the Son of man christology is clearly the product of Christian midrash: cf. N. Perrin, 'Mark XIV. 62: The End Product of A Christian Pesher Tradition?', *N.T.S.* 12, 1966, pp. 150–55. Basic texts included Ps. 110: 1; Ps. 8; and Dan. 7: 13; cf. Mark 12:

36b: W. O. Walker Jr., 'The Origin of the Son of Man Concept as Applied to Jesus', *J.B.L.* 91, 1972, pp. 482–90. The initial impetus for this Christian midrash may well have been complex: Jesus' own midrashic practice (*vid. supra*, pp. 23ff.), and recollections, misunderstandings or reinterpretations of his use of *bar nasha*: cf. the work of G. Vermes (cited *supra*, n. 160); also to be noted is the impact of the resurrection faith, with its eschatological implications, and finally the emergence of the Son of man figure in Christian prophecy in hellenistic Jewish circles (cf. Acts 7: 56): cf. H. Teeple, 'The Origin of the Son of Man Christology', *J.B.L.* 84, 1955, pp. 213–50. The areas involved may have included Jerusalem but, more characteristically, Syria and perhaps Galilee. We are justified, therefore, in relating the Son of man problem to Christian prophetic experience in dialogue with Christian midrash, probably on the basis of the Septuagint.

248   Cf. John on Patmos: R. H. Preston and A. T. Hanson, *Revelation*, pp. 36–43. Thus Rev. 1: 12–18 draws heavily upon Daniel, with Ezek. 43: 2, and the I-saying (1: 8) reflects Is. 41: 4; and all this scriptural material is applied to the interpretation of Christ. By John's time (perhaps c. A.D.95), the fact that synoptic tradition was already fixed may well have allowed greater freedom to the prophet-exegete. Thus his I-sayings, unmistakably attributed to the exalted Lord (3: 20; 16: 15), tend to suggest a reinterpretation both of Old Testament symbols and – quite clearly in places – gospel and other New Testament material (with Rev. 16: 15, cf. Rev. 3: 3; 1 Thess. 5: 2, 4 and the familiar gospel image in Matt. 22: 43; Luke 12: 39). It would be difficult to argue for influence in the opposite direction; but this tradition has possibly a later expression in 2 Pet. 3: 10. For the relation of Daniel to the eschatological discourses in Mark and Matthew, cf. L. Hartman, *Prophecy*, pp. 145–74.

249   The alleged individualism of John can be traced to this source: cf. C. F. D. Moule, 'The Individualism of the Fourth Gospel' in *Nov. T.* 5, 1962, pp. 171–90; A. Kragerud, *Die Lieblingsjünger im Johannesevangelium*, 1959, treats him as an inspired prophet.

250   A. C. MacPherson, cited by C. F. D. Moule, *Worship in the New Testament*, 1961, p. 67.

251   What *direct* influence can be allowed? Matt. 18: 5 is probably a Christian prophetic oracle attracted as commentary into a group of I-sayings in the tradition: cf. *Aboth.* 3: 2; 1 Cor. 5: 4; T. W. Manson, *Sayings of Jesus*, p. 211. Luke 11: 49ff. (cf. Matt. 23: 34ff.) is under strong suspicion of being the utterance of Christian prophecy which 'peshered' (possibly) an earlier saying of Jesus, but the most persuasive advocate of this case, perhaps too humbly, accepts the verdict 'not proven': E. E. Ellis, 'Luke XI, 49–51: An Oracle of a Christian Prophet?', *Exp. T.* 74, 1962–63, pp. 157f. Again, M. E. Boring, *J.B.L.* 91, pp. 511–21, has made out the case for these verses on the grounds that they represent an independent, eschatological logion characterised by three formal marks of Christian prophetic speech: *amen*, chiasmus, and legal form (p. 515), and probably represent 'something of a pesher on Isaiah 63: 3–11' (p. 517). But none of these marks, individually or together, establish the case, esp. as E. Käsemann's *ius talionis* argument has been found defective: *vid. supra*, n. 237; and chiasmus alone is a rhetorical form, by no means exclusive to prophecy. Another

possible suspect is Matt. 10: 5f. (an oracle of a Judaean prophet?). Perhaps behind Matthew 28: 18ff. there was a prophetic I-saying legitimising the hellenistic Jewish Christian mission. Nevertheless, a review of this evidence does not suggest a proliferation of Christian prophetic sayings on the lips of the Jesus of the synoptic gospels.

252 For the development of I-sayings in the context of Jewish-Christian hymnology, cf. the Odes of Solomon: J. R. Harris and A. Mingana, *The Odes and Psalms of Solomon* II, 1920, pp. 72–84; J. H. Charlesworth, *The Odes of Solomon*, 1973, pp. 109f. (Ode 28: 9–20), pp. 141f. (Ode 41: 8ff.), pp. 145ff. (Ode 42: 3–20), pp. 127f. (Ode 36: 3–8), pp. 116ff. (Ode 31: 6–13), pp. 75ff. (Ode 17: 6–16), pp. 41–4 (Ode 8: 8–19): cf. also the statement in the Preface: 'the Odes of Solomon is, I contend, the earliest Christian hymn-book'.

253 Three methods of assimilation are particularly important. One is by way of *attraction*: e.g., Matt. 18: 5; additionally, the prophetic utterance assimilated may show traces of other contributory processes, e.g., Christian *pesher* (cf. Luke 11: 49f.) or worship (Matt. 18: 20). A second is by *nucleation*: i.e., where the traditional saying has attracted to it a mass of related material and become practically submerged in it: cf. Mark 13: *vid.* H. Anderson, *The Gospel of Mark*, 1976, p. 290; usually a strong paraenetic concern governs such processes. A third way is through the *transmutation* of teaching material into a prophetic-type utterance to convey an immediate authority or assurance: cf. Matt. 16: 17–19; 18: 18f.; cf. 28: 18ff.

254 Cf. L. Hartman, *Prophecy*, pp. 245ff; and *vid. infra*, p. 116 (incl. n. 110).

Chapter 2. *Paraclesis* and homily

1 Cf. O. Schmitz, *T.D.N.T.* V, pp. 793–9; C. J. Bjerkelund, *Parakalô*, 1967.
2 *Vid. supra*, pp. 11f. (incl. n. 65).
3 This is not to ignore the distinctive contribution of the much older Hebrew tradition, which is fully discussed below.
4 E.g., Diogenes (404–323 B.C.) and Crates, the 'door-opener' (fl. 326 B.C.); Diogenes Laertius (4: 2) claims Antisthenes (446–366 B.C.) as the founder of the movement, but perhaps he is simply its precursor: cf. D. R. Dudley, *A History of Cynicism*, 1937, pp. 1–15; W. T. Stace, *A Critical History of Greek Philosophy*, 1920, pp. 158ff.
5 Diog. Laert. 4: 98.
6 Cf. P. Wendland, *Die hellenistisch-römische Kultur*, 1912, p. 75.
7 The son of a fishmonger and a 'hetaira', Bion was familiar with vulgar talk from the beginning, but on being sold into slavery he joined the household of a rhetorician and finally inherited his master's property. Realising his assets, he set out for Athens, went the round of the schools and then embarked on lecture tours of Greece, including Rhodes and Pella. For Bion's philosophy, cf. D. R. Dudley, *Cynicism*, pp. 65f. The sources for reconstructing Bion's message and his manner of preaching are fragmentary.
8 R. Leijs, 'Prédication des apôtres', *N.R.T.* 69, 1947, p. 610.
9 Cf. P. Wendland, *Kultur*, pp. 77f. Appropriate rhetorical devices include rhetorical questions, frequent interrogative formulae, short and incisive phrases, together with vivid, if commonplace, metaphors from everyday life, quotations, allegorical personification and stock figures.

10 Tr. D. R. Dudley, *Cynicism,* pp. 65f. Bion delighted in the use of personification (e.g., Poverty), simile (especially from the animal world), and metaphors, which he sometimes mixes to striking effect. The influence of the
rhetorical school is clear in the use of character sketches, *chreiai* or scenes
influenced by mime, in the careful use of rhythm, the balance of syllables,
parataxis, asyndeton and assonance. For further discussion of the diatribe,
cf. *Reallexikon für Antike und Christentum,* Bd. III, 1957, art. 'Diatribe:
(A) Nichtchristlich', by A. W. Capelle, coll. 990–97.

11 Other prominent Cynics included Menippus, Cercidas and Teles.

12 J. Higginbotham (ed.), *Greek and Latin Literature,* 1969, p. 225.

13 Roman satire consciously reflected the hellenistic diatribe: cf. Horace (incl.
his predecessors, Ennius and Lucilius), Persius, Petronius and Juvenal.

14 Zeno (333–261 B.C.) was a native of Citium, a Phoenician colony in Cyprus,
and was often called 'the Phoenician': Diog. Laert. 2: 114; 7: 3 etc. It is
sometimes claimed that his eastern connections encouraged not only his
cosmopolitanism but also his intense moral earnestness (cf. J. B. Lightfoot,
St Paul's Epistle to the Philippians, 1913, p. 273) and his popular preaching
(cf. W. B. Sedgwick, 'The Origins of the Sermon', *H.J.* 45, 1946, p. 158),
but this line of argument should not be pressed too far.

15 For a brief outline of Stoic philosophy, cf. A. H. Armstrong, *An Introduction to Ancient Philosophy,* (2nd ed.) 1949, pp. 119–29. Important contributions were made by Cleanthes (331–232 B.C.) and Chrysippus (282–
206 B.C.).

16 The life-style that follows from the basic Stoic mythology has as its lynch-
pin the conviction that man must conform to the laws of the universe
('nature') and to the rationality that is his own true nature. In a sense, he
cannot do anything but assent to the laws of necessity, but he should do
so voluntarily and rationally. Virtue is thus life according to reason. The
wise man is the good man; the foolish man is evil. There is, theoretically,
no intermediate position, but the Stoics were strikingly inconsistent in
admitting mild and rational emotions.

17 For a comparison of Seneca with Paul, cf. J. N. Sevenster, *Paul and Seneca,*
1961.

18 Epictetus of Hierapolis (*c.* A.D. 50–120), son of a slave woman and a slave
himself for a time, was a pupil of Musonius Rufus before setting up as a
teacher in Rome, moving finally to Nicopolis in Epirus when Domitian
banished all philosophers from Italy in A.D. 89. His discourses are preserved in the form of lecture notes by his pupil Arrian.

19 For a detailed study, cf. R. Bultmann, *Der Stil der paulinischen Predigt
und die kynisch-stoische Diatribe,* 1910.

20 R. Bultmann, *Der Stil,* p. 14.

21 Other rhetorical devices include the use of antithesis, *parallelismus memb-
rorum,* apostrophe and personification, similes, metaphors and analogies.
For a full discussion, cf. R. Bultmann, *Der Stil,* pp. 10–46.

22 Epictetus' diatribes usually have an explicit theme, which is frequently
philosophical: Providence (Epic. 1: 6; 1: 16; 3: 17); the nature of the Good
(2: 8); that Logic is necessary (1: 17; 2: 25). Sometimes they are concerned
to dispute with other philosophical schools, but their overriding concern is
with a life-style based on Stoic cosmological presuppositions (cf. 1: 3).

Most discourses are concerned directly with practice: how a man can always maintain his proper character (1: 2); how we should behave towards tyrants (1: 19); how we should struggle with difficulties (1: 24; 1: 30); how we ought to bear sickness (3: 10). Others deal with themes such as contentment (1: 12); anger (1: 28); courage tempered by caution (2: 1); tranquillity of mind (2: 2); anxiety (2: 13); inconsistency (2: 21); friendship (2: 22).

23 Bultmann perhaps overestimated Paul's dependence on the diatribe: cf. A. Bonhöffer, *Epiktet und das Neue Testament,* 1911, p. 179.

24 R. Bultmann, *Der Stil,* pp. 51f.

25 As in 2: 18.1 and 2: 18.7. Cf. R. Bultmann, *Der Stil,* pp. 46f.

26 The tradition of hellenistic preaching is to be set against the background of the continuing Greek rhetorical tradition, which goes back to Gorgias and the Attic Orators, and survived through many vicissitudes to inspire a noteworthy Roman counterpart and, in its Greek form, to influence Byzantine and oriental literature.

27 N. Morris, *The Jewish School,* 1937, pp. 37–41; D. Daube, 'Rabbinic Methods of Interpretation and Hellenistic Rhetoric', *H.U.C.A.* 22, 1949, pp. 239–64; L. Baeck, 'Greek and Jewish Preaching', in *The Pharisees and Other Essays,* 1947, pp. 109–22; cf. S. Lieberman, *Hellenism in Jewish Palestine* (I Cent. B.C.E. – IV Cent. C.E.), 1962, *passim*; J. N. Sevenster, *Do you know Greek?*, Eng. tr., 1968, esp. pp. 176–91; M. Hengel, *Judentum und Hellenismus,* 1969, esp. pp. 196–463 (Eng. tr., *Judaism and Hellenism,* 1974, 2 vols.); E. Schürer, *The History of the Jewish People in the Age of Jesus Christ* I, Vermes and Millar (edd.), 1973, pp. 143ff.

28 Cf. D. Daube, *H.U.C.A.* 22, pp. 239–64; *The New Testament and Rabbinic Judaism,* 1956, pt. II; S. Zeitlin, 'Hillel and the Hermeneutic Rules', *J.Q.R.* 54, 1963–64, pp. 161–73; W. H. Brownlee, 'Biblical Interpretation among the Sectaries of the Dead Sea Scrolls', *B.A.* 14, 1951, pp. 54–76; E. E. Ellis, *Paul's Use of the Old Testament,* 1957, p. 41.

29 A. Finkel, *The Pharisees and the Teacher of Nazareth,* 1964, p. 143. It is important, however, to pin-point what is meant by 'synagogue' prior to the catastrophe of A.D. 70. The synagogues of Judaea began simply as places of assembly which were used, in connection with the *Maamadot,* for the reading of the Torah: cf. H. Danby (ed.), *The Mishnah,* 1933, p. 794; S. Zeitlin, 'An Historical Study of the First Canonization of the Hebrew Liturgy', *J.Q.R.* 38, 1948, pp. 311ff. The reading of the prophetic books was then added as a commentary on the Torah and the scribes took the opportunity to apply their distinctive hermeneutic to the scriptures as a whole. Cf. Philo, *Fragm. Apud Euseb. Praep. Evang.* 8: 7, 12ff.; *De Sept.* 6; *Quod omnis probus liber,* 12; S. W. Baron, *A Social and Religious History of the Jews* II, 1952, pp. 280ff.

30 Cf. the early form of the Passover *Haggadah*: L. Finkelstein, 'The Oldest Midrash: Pre-rabbinic Ideals and Teachings in the Passover Haggadah', *H.T.R.* 31, 1938, pp. 291–317.

31 *Midrash* comes from *darash,* to search, probe or enquire; hence, the results of the examination, viz., commentary on scripture. By contrast, *mishnah* – root *shanah,* to repeat – is part of the interpretation of the written law and denotes the making and codification of laws, designed for repetition and learning by heart.

32 R. Bloch, 'Midrash', *D.B.S.* V, pp. 1265f. A. Robert has described midrashic procedure as a 'procédé anthologique': *D.B.S.* V, pp. 411–21. A. G. Wright, however, insists that midrash is properly a literary genre, designed to interpret a biblical text: 'The Literary Genre Midrash', *C.B.Q.* 28, 1966, p. 137; but R. le Déaut argued that midrash can belong to a variety of literary genres, and since it cannot be strictly defined it can only be described in terms of its presuppositions and methods: 'A propos d'une définition du midrash', *Biblica* 50, 1969, pp. 395–413 (Eng. tr., *Int.*, July 1971).

33 M. P. Miller, 'Targum, Midrash and the Use of the Old Testament in the New Testament', *J.S.J.* 2, 1971, p. 44.

34 I. Epstein in *Midrash Rabbah* I (Genesis), Freedman and Simon (edd.), 1939, p. xi.

35 E.g., Chronicles *passim* (incl. 2 Chr. 13: 22; the midrash of the prophet Iddo; cf. the midrash of the book of Kings: 24: 27); Ezek. 16; Is. 60–62 (based on Is. 40–55 and passages of the Torah); the servant songs; Prov. 1–9; Pss. 78, 132; cf. R. Bloch, *D.B.S.* V, pp. 1271–6.

36 M. D. Goulder, *Midrash and Lection in Matthew*, 1974, p. 29. However, even if one accepts G. Vermes' observation that the later post-biblical midrash is differentiated from the biblical only by the fact of the latter's canonisation (cf. 'Bible and Midrash: Early Old Testament Exegesis', in *Cambridge History of the Bible* I, 1970, p. 199), it will perhaps be allowed also that there is an intensity about the later meditation on the sacred texts which is also distinctive. Cf. M. P. Miller, *J.S.J.* 2, pp. 45f.

37 Cf. E. E. Ellis, 'Midrash, Targum and New Testament Quotations', in *Neotestamentica et Semitica*, pp. 62f.

38 Cf. M. Gertner, 'Midrashim in the New Testament', *J.S.S.* 7, 1962, p. 268.

39 Cf. G. Vermes, *Scripture and Tradition in Judaism*, 1961, p. 179.

40 Types identified include the following: implicit midrash designed to fill out the biblical story and at the same time eliminate possible offence (e.g., the Genesis Apocryphon) or to create a new story from biblical materials (e.g., Words of Moses, Prayer of Nabonidus); a collection of messianic texts (4Q Test.); as well as various types of paraphrase and targum fragments: cf. G. Vermes, *The Dead Sea Scrolls in English*, 1962, p. 214; M. P. Miller, *J.S.J.* 2, pp. 49ff.

41 *Contra* W. H. Brownlee: *The Dead Sea Habakkuk Midrash and the Targum of Jonathan* (Duke Div. Sch.) 1953, p. 12.

42 Cf. G. Vermes, 'A propos des commentaires bibliques découverts à Qumran', *La Bible et l'Orient*, 1955, pp. 95–103, cited by M. P. Miller, *J.S.J.* 2, p. 51; also W. H. Brownlee, *B.A.* 14, pp. 54–76.

43 1 Qp Hab. 7: 2; cf. 2: 2ff.; CD 1: 12.

44 This may be considered a special kind of extension of the contemporisation or actualising of scripture which is characteristic of midrash, but the extension is brought about by the intensity of the eschatological crisis within which the community lived and its midrashic procedures are therefore transformed and distinctive.

45 Frequently, word-play is involved: cf. F. F. Bruce, *Biblical Exegesis in the Qumran Texts*, 1960, pp. 32f.

46 The *locus classicus* is the *Habakkuk Commentary*: cf. F. M. Cross jnr., *The Ancient Library of Qumran and Modern Biblical Studies*, 1958, p. 84.

47   The idea of a single testimony book was mooted by J. Rendel Harris, *Testimonies* I, II, 1916–20: his acute observation of the evidence then available remains valuable but his conclusions are no longer acceptable and were criticised by C. H. Dodd in *According to the Scriptures, the Sub-Structure of N.T. Theology*, 1952, a work which antedated the publication of the *Habakkuk Commentary*. The school of exegesis suggested by Qumranic evidence prompted the hypothesis of an analogous Christian school behind St Matthew's gospel: cf. K. Stendahl, *The School of St Matthew*, 1954, although a distinctive individual hand is discernible in both Matthew and John. E. E. Ellis explored the application of Christian *pesher* in St Paul's writings: *Paul's Use of the Old Testament*, 1957. The problem is surveyed and discussed in B. Lindars, *New Testament Apologetic*, 1961, pp. 13–31; M. P. Miller, *J.S.J.* 2, pp. 54f.

48   Similarly, New Testament *testimonia* type texts probably presuppose a prior Christian midrash: cf. E. E. Ellis, *Neotestamentica et Semitica*, 1969, pp. 68f. In relation to further study of the phenomenon, M. P. Miller (*J.S.J.* 2, p. 55) has indicated three important possibilities: (i) textual variation may be related to the fluidity of the first-century Hebrew text; (ii) composite quotations, especially in the New Testament, may arise out of Jewish homiletical and midrashic techniques rather than from a testimony source as such; (iii) fixed sequences of quotations may be 'prophetic figures for use in liturgy'.

49   Cf. R. Bloch, *D.B.S.* V, pp. 1265ff.

50   The translation was carried out by the *meturgeman*; Aramaic was used in Palestine, Greek in the Diaspora.

51   Mostly somewhat late: cf. the Tanhuma and Pesiqtas; but some earlier examples do occur: e.g., Ber. R. 42: 1.

52   This type of homily is found particularly in relation to Jewish homiletic practice at festival time: cf. A. Finkel, *The Pharisees*, pp. 169f.

53   Cf. J. Mann, *The Bible as Read and Preached in the Old Synagogue* I, 1940, pp. 11f.; cf. S. Maybaum, *Die ältesten Phasen in der Entwicklung der jüdischen Predigt*, 1901, pp. 15ff. Maybaum suggested that the original pattern of the Palestinian midrashic homily had five parts: (A) the text derived from a pericope from the Pentateuch; (B) connection with the second text cited in the proem; (C) the second or proemial text from Prophets or Writings, with exposition; (D) connection with peroration; (E) peroration repeats text of Torah pericope. It is indeed a credible hypothesis that the homily developed as an exegesis of the reading of the Torah but later appeared to relate more directly to the *haftarah,* which was itself chosen to elucidate the Torah text (*op. cit.*, pp. 41f.). The collection of homilies in Exodus R. 15–52 appears to reflect this pattern. For a discussion of this whole subject, cf. P. Borgen, *Bread from Heaven*, 1965, pp. 51–8.

54   B. San 38b.

55   J. W. Bowker, 'Speeches in Acts: A Study in Proem and Yelammedenu Form', *N.T.S.* 14, 1967–68, p. 100.

56   The Eliezer passage, which has undergone several recensions, can be found in Ber. R. 42: 1; Tanh. on Gen. 14: 1; Gen. R. 41; Pirqe 1, 2; 1 A.D.N. 4 (15b); 2 A.D.N. 13 (15b); cf. A. Finkel, *The Pharisees*, pp. 149ff.

57 J. Mann, *The Bible*, p. 105.

58 One work deserving mention is M. Smith, *Tannaitic Parallels to the Gospels*, 1951, pp. 78–114. For a criticism of this work, cf. W. D. Davies, *S.S.M.*, pp. 6–9. Cf. also W. O. E. Oesterley and G. H. Box, *The Religion and Worship of the Synagogue*, 1925, pp. 95ff.

59 In this example, the introduction – 'my sons, let not a man be ashamed of his companion' – is antithetical to the main section of the argument (it is better to be ashamed than to suffer famine, a fast which the Lord has not seen); and this thought is developed antithetically – on the acceptable fast.

60 But not Daniel, and probably not Ruth, Lamentations or Canticles: cf. R. H. Charles, *Apocrypha and Pseudepigrapha of the O.T.* I, 1913, pp. 479–511.

61 The homiletic pattern as a prayer form is seen in 3 Macc. 2: 2–20 and 6: 2–15, in both of which 'pearl stringing' is used. 4 Macc. has been described as being 'of the nature of a sermon, whether actually delivered in a synagogue or not', although perhaps more fittingly considered as 'a lecture rather than a sermon': R. H. Charles, *Apocrypha* II, p. 654.

62 H. Thyen, *Der Stil der Judisch-Hellenistischen Homilie*, 1955, pp. 40–63, cf. 12ff., 18. For criticism of Thyen's work, cf. K. P. Donfried, *The Setting of Second Clement*, pp. 27f.

63 G. Vermes, *The Dead Sea Scrolls*, p. 95.

64 Cf. 1: 1; 2: 2, 14, with the recurring 'Now listen'.

65 The *Community Rule* or *Manual of Discipline* contains a homiletic outline on the theme of the spirits of truth and falsehood in man, and this has been inserted by the compiler as 'a model sermon' (Vermes) in a part of the work that seems to have been originally the 'prompt book' for a sermon (Gaster): cf. G. Vermes, *The Dead Sea Scrolls*, p. 71; T. H. Gaster, *The Scriptures of the Dead Sea Sect*, 1957, p. 43. As the theme indicates, the sermon structure is characterised by antithesis, with strong eschatological overtones. Notable use is made of cataloguing as a paraenetic method. Ultimately, an end is ordained for falsehood and truth shall prevail.

66 H. A. Wolfson, *Philo – Foundations of Religious Philosophy in Judaism Christianity and Islam* I, 1948, p. 98.

67 Philo himself refers in several places to the sermon or homily given for instructional purposes in the synagogues on the sabbath: *Opif.* 43: 128; *Mos.* 2: 39. 216; *Spec.* 2: 15. 61f.; *Hypoth.* 7: 13 (*Eus. Praep. Evang.* 8: 7. 359d–360a). Either Philo was himself a prominent synagogue preacher who subsequently gave literary expression to the spoken discourses, or he adopted the model of such homilies for much of his written work: cf. H. A. Wolfson, *Philo*, p. 96.

68 Philo's philosophy itself is drawn from many schools and, because of his exegetical procedure, it is never developed systematically – which leads H. A. Wolfson to the conclusion that 'Philo was a preacher with a flair for philosophy rather than primarily a philosopher': *Philo*, p. 98.

69 Cf. H. Thyen, *Der Stil*, pp. 8f.

70 Cf. P. Borgen, *Bread from Heaven*, pp. 28–58. Borgen's particular interest is in comparing the above passages with John 6: 31–58. Cf. also Philo, *De Congressu Quaerendae Eruditionis Gratia* 170–174, where 'pearl stringing' on this theme is discernible.

71   Why the Pentateuch alone? An improbable solution is that Philo knew
      only the Pentateuch (cf. W. L. Knox, 'A Note on Philo's Use of the O.T.',
      J.T.S. 41, 1940, pp. 30–4). F. H. Colson's reply that the Pentateuch had
      greater authority for Philo sheds little more light on the problem, *J.T.S.*
      41, pp. 237–51. P. Borgen put it down to 'a liturgical peculiarity in
      Alexandria': *Bread from Heaven,* p. 55, n. 3.

72   Cf. P. Borgen, *Bread from Heaven,* pp. 51f.

73   E.g., Jews or proselytes, sophisticated or simple: cf. E. R. Goodenough,
      'Philo's Exposition of the Law and his *De Vita Mosis*', *H.T.R.* 27, 1933,
      pp. 119–24.

74   This alleged discourse is to be found at the end of most editions of *De
      Praemiis et Poenis* (14: 79).

75   Cf. E. R. Goodenough, *An Introduction to Philo Judaeus,* 1940, (2nd ed.)
      1962, pp. 54f.

76   *Ibid.*, p. 54.

77   To Philo's 'literal' corresponds the 'literal' or 'historical' of the fathers, and
      the *pesat* of the rabbis; his 'physical' to the 'allegorical' (fathers), *remez*
      (rabbis); his 'ethical' to the 'moral' (fathers), *deras* (rabbis); his 'mystical'
      to the 'anagogical' (fathers), *sod* (rabbis); cf. R. Marcus, *Philo,* Suppl. I,
      Questions and Answers on Genesis, Loeb, 1953, pp. ixf. The allegorical
      method was well known in the ancient world and provided a means of
      interpreting Homer and other mythology, although Plato preferred the
      alternative course of eliminating the offending myths altogether. Cf.
      Republic, 2: 378D. In Jewish circles it was equally well known. The rabbis
      used it and it is prominent in the Wisdom of Solomon: cf. 10: 17, where
      the pillar of cloud and fire is allegorised into Wisdom (cf. Philo *Quis rer.
      div. haer.* 42; *Vit. Mosis* 1: 29); 18: 24, where the long robe of the high
      priest is the whole cosmos (cf. Philo, *Vit. Mosis* 3: 11–14; *De mon.* 2: 5f.;
      and Josephus, *Ant.* 3: 7). It was congenial to Philo in that it helped him to
      find Plato in Moses and to remove gross anthropomorphisms from the Old
      Testament. He refers slightingly to literalists at a number of points (e.g.,
      Quod Deus Immut. 1: 280; *De Sobrietate* 1: 397; *De Confus Ling.* 38). At
      other times he refers to the literal and the allegorical as possible and accept-
      able lines of interpretation: e.g., *De Spec. Leg.* 3: 32. He can even castigate
      the allegorisers for 'handling the matter in too easy and off-hand a manner'
      and 'exploring reality in its naked absoluteness': cf. *De Migr. Abr.* 16.

78   Cf. Matt. 4: 23; 9: 35; 12: 9; 13: 54; Mark 1: 21, 39; 3: 1; 6: 2; Luke 4: 15ff.;
      4: 44; 6: 6; 13: 10; cf. John 6: 59; 18: 20.

79   Cf. H. Conzelmann, *Luke,* pp. 31–8; H. Schürmann, 'Zur Traditions-
      geschichte der Nazareth-Pericope Lk. 4, 16–30' in *Mélanges B. Rigaux,*
      1970, pp. 187–205. The editorial manipulation of 4: 22ff. militates against
      the attempt, possible on formal grounds, to link vv. 25ff. with Is. 61: 1ff.
      within one homiletic pattern: i.e., following the *proem* text, the examples
      of 'pearl stringing' include the Elijah and Elisha passages and present an
      antithesis to the theme: viz., the time of God's salvation is at hand, but
      Gentiles may be preferred before Jews in the sight of God. The expected
      conclusion, linking the antithesis to Is. 61 and possibly to Gen. 35: 9, is lost
      in the violent reaction of the hearers. Do vv. 25ff. represent another homily?
      Yet they are very appropriate to the Nazareth setting.

80 J. Mann, *The Bible*, pp. 283ff.

81 *Vid. supra*, p. 21; and cf. S. Agouridès, 'La Tradition des Béatitudes chez Matthieu et Luc', in *Mélanges B. Rigaux*, 1970, pp. 9–27.

82 One is not suggesting that there is no answer to this question: only that it must be answered. Was the material of this homily used frequently on other occasions by Jesus himself? Was it so characteristic of his position that he and, later, his followers made it the basis of further midrash? Cf. M. D. Goulder, *Midrash*, pp. 460f.

83 J. W. Doeve, *Jewish Hermeneutics*, p. 158; see generally pp. 119–61.

84 Only a few need be mentioned here: R. Bultmann, *Das Evangelium nach Johannes*, 1954, p. 174; W. Marxsen, *Introduction to the New Testament*, Eng. tr., 1968, p. 32; G. Bornkamm, 'Die eucharistische Rede im Johannes-Evangelium', *Z. N. W.* 47, 1956, pp. 166–9.

85 Cf. G. Richter, 'Zur Formgeschichte und literarischen Einheit von Joh. 6: 31–58', *Z. N. W.* 60, 1969, pp. 21–55.

86 For a review of the evidence, cf. J. D. G. Dunn, 'John VI – A Eucharistic Discourse?', *N. T. S.* 17, 1971, pp. 328ff.

87 P. Borgen, 'The Unity of the Discourse in John VI', *Z. N. W.* 50, 1959, p. 277; 'Observations on the Midrashic Character of John 6', *Z. N. W.* 54, 1963, pp. 232–40; *Bread from Heaven*, 1965, pp. 59–98. Cf. also A. Finkel, *The Pharisees*, pp. 158f.; A. Guilding, *The Fourth Gospel and Jewish Worship*, 1960, pp. 58–68.

88 For 'bread' as 'teaching', cf. the parable of the leaven: Matt. 13: 33; Luke 13: 21; cf. also Matt. 16: 12; Luke 12: 15.

89 Cf. J. L. Martyn, *History and Theology in the Fourth Gospel*, 1968, pp. 45ff., who emphasises the concern of John's school with the continuing apologetic dialogue with Judaism; cf. *supra*, pp. 36f.

90 K. P. Donfried, *The Setting of Second Clement*, p. 32.

91 I. Abrahams, *Studies in Pharisaism and the Gospels* I, 1917, pp. 10f., pointed out that this discourse must have been given in the spring (cf. 6: 10, 'much grass'; 6: 9, 13, 'barley loaves') and that in the second year of the triennial cycle the lessons for the first weeks in Iyyar (April/May) were taken from Ex. 16, which contains the story of the manna. For an exposition of the fourth gospel in terms of the triennial cycle, cf. A. Guilding, *The Fourth Gospel, passim.* Nevertheless, the evidence for lectionary practice in Jesus' time is sadly deficient. 'Any theory of N.T. origins which relies on detailed knowledge of the lectionary cannot avoid this criticism of lack of direct information about the early lectionaries': J. W. Bowker, *N. T. S.* 14, p. 99, n. 2.

92 E.g., Jesus' preaching precipitates a crisis (Luke 4: 28f.; John 6: 60, 66); and the role he claims for himself in the purpose of God (Luke 4: 21; John 6: 35, 38 etc.) sharpens the contrast between his human and divine origins (Luke 4: 22b; John 6: 42; cf. Matt. 13: 54; Mark 6: 1–4).

93 *Ego eimi* (vv. 35, 41, 48, 51), which may be midrashic at least in part, identifies Jesus with an Old Testament word or concept (as John the Baptist was identified with 'a voice crying in the wilderness' and as the rabbis later connected Trajan with the vulture of Deut. 28: 49): cf. P. Borgen, *Z. N. W.* 54, pp. 238f. Jesus' expositions thus bring his hearers to the point of decision about him (cf. vv. 29, 35f, 40, 47, 49, 64: also, 20: 31). Hence he

speaks with *exousia* and not as the scribes, or, in Johannine terms, his words
are 'spirit and life' (6: 35).

94   I.e., *yelammedenu rabbenu*: 'let our teacher instruct us'; *vid. supra*, p. 44,
n. 52.

95   B. Shab. 128b; cf. M. Shab. 18: 3; also Luke 14: 1–6.

96   B. Yom. 35b. Cf. A. Finkel, *The Pharisees*, p. 171.

97   I. Abrahams, *Studies in Pharisaism*, pp. 10f. Mark and Luke add an interpretation of Ex. 31: 14 – i.e., that it was 'for you'.

98   Cf. also John 7: 22f., where the example is the action of circumcision on
the sabbath. Jesus' point in relation to sabbath teaching is well made in
v. 24: 'Do not judge by appearances, but judge with right judgment'.

99   M. Git. 9: 10; cf. A. Finkel, *The Pharisees*, p. 172; *vid. infra*, pp. 119ff.

100   Cf. A. Finkel, *The Pharisees*, pp. 159–69.

101   If it is assumed that the speeches of Acts are the free compositions of a
Gentile writer such as Luke, we might expect him to present here a typical
Christian address to a Jewish audience. It is unlikely that he would be un-
aware of the restraints and conventions of a synagogue setting.

102   J. W. Bowker, *N. T. S.* 14, pp. 101–4.

103   Cf. M. Wilcox, *The Semitisms of Acts*, 1965, pp. 21ff.

104   J. W. Bowker, *N. T. S.* 14, p. 104.

105   *Ibid.*

106   *Ibid.*

107   E. E. Ellis, 'Midrashic Features in the Speeches of Acts', in *Mélanges B.
Rigaux*, 1970, pp. 306ff.

108   Ps. 2: 7; Is. 55: 3; Ps. 16: 10; cf. E. Lövestam, *Son and Saviour*, Eng. tr.,
1961, pp. 8–87.

109   *Vid. supra*, pp. 44f.

110   Cf. the Deuteronomic history (e.g., Josh. 24: 1–18), and 1 and 2 Maccabees.

111   Again, a *proem* type homily is probably in the background: the speech 'can
certainly be analysed as a proem homily on Joel 2: 32, with a *seder* Deut.
29: 1–21 and a *haftarah* Is. 63: 9–19': J. W. Bowker, *N. T. S.* 14, p. 105; but
'the problem is to know whether it is a case of the material demanding the
pattern or of the pattern being imposed on the material. Where the lections
are not specified but have to be inferred, there must inevitably be a large
area of doubt': *op. cit.*, p. 106.

112   Cf. E. Trocmé, *Le 'Livre des Actes' et l'histoire*, 1957, *ad loc.*; E. Haenchen,
Z. N. W. 26, pp. 286–90; C. S. C. Williams, *A Commentary on Acts*, 1957,
pp. 100ff.; K. Lake, in *Beginnings* II, pp. 149f.; G. H. C. Macgregor, *Acts,
Int. Bib.* IX, 1954, pp. 91ff.; G. W. H. Lampe, in *Peake*, 1962, pp. 894f.

113   Cf. H. W. Beyer, *Die Apostelgeschichte*, 1947, p. 49.

114   Cf. J. W. Bowker, *N. T. S.* 14, p. 107.

115   Cf. similar recitals in Deut. 29, Josh. 24: 2–13; 1 Sam. 12: 6–13; Neh. 9:
6–31.

116   There is identification in vv. 2–22 with *hoi pateres hēmōn*, but in v. 39 they
refuse to obey Moses. A. F. J. Klijn follows Irenaeus (4: 15.1): *patres vestri*.
This eliminates many difficulties and links well with v. 51: cf. A. F. J. Klijn,
'Stephen's Speech – Acts VII. 2–53', *N. T. S.* 4, 1957–58, p. 27.

117   Cf. Ex. 33: 1 – 34: 9; Is. 63: 10; 65: 22–66: 5; Jer. 6: 10; 9: 26.

118   Cf. 1 QS 1: 21ff.; 3: 13ff.; A. F. J. Klijn, *N. T. S.* 4, pp. 28–31. The distinct-

iveness of the minority standpoint is illustrated by Stephen's rejection of the temple of Solomon, as distinct from the tabernacle (cf. 'habitation' in Ps. 132: 5; cf. 2 Sam. 6: 17; 7: 3, 5f.; 1 Chr. 15: 1): see also 1QS 8: 5f.; 11: 3–6. On this subject, cf. F. F. Bruce, *Commentary on the Book of Acts,* 1954, pp. 159f.; W. Manson, *Epistle to the Hebrews,* 1951, p. 34; C. F. D. Moule, 'Sanctuary and Sacrifice in the Church of the N.T.', *J.T.S.* (N.S.1), 1950, pp. 29ff.; M. Simon, 'Saint Stephen and the Jerusalem Temple', *J.E.H.* 2, 1951, pp. 128–31; A. F. J. Klijn, *N.T.S.* 4, pp. 29f.

119   Thus, an essential part of such missionary preaching was not simply to commend what I have called a minority viewpoint but to invite Jewish hearers to dissociate themselves from disobedient Israel and become part of the true temple which serves God in a spiritual way.

120   This adaptation probably involved abbreviation, reflected in slightly awkward transitions in vv. 43f. and 47f.; cf. E. Haenchen, *Z.N.W.* 26, pp. 289f.

121   It included exclusivist and expansionist, particularist and universalist tendencies co-existing in tension: cf. J. Bonsirven, *Le judaïsme palestinien au temps de Jésus-Christ* I, 1934, pp. 137ff.; M. Simon, *Verus Israel,* 1948, pp. 316–34.

122   Cf. B. Gärtner, *The Areopagus Speech and Natural Revelation,* 1955, p. 70.

123   *Ibid.,* p. 71.

124   *Ibid.,* p. 46; cf. F. W. Beare, 'New Testament Christianity and the Hellenistic World', in *The Communication of the Gospel in New Testament Times,* 1961, pp. 57–73. But stylistic features do not emerge strongly in the Areopagus speech.

125   Cf. Jos. *Bell.* 7: 45; G. F. Moore, *Judaism* I, p. 324.

126   The Athenians may have misunderstood *anastasis* as a hypostasis: cf. Chrysostom, *Com. in Acta, Hom.* 38. 1; J. H. Maclean, 'St Paul at Athens', *Exp. T.* 44, 1932–33, pp. 550–3.

127   Cf. H. Windisch, *Der Hebräerbrief,* (2nd ed.) 1931, pp. 98ff.

128   Calvin was correct in holding that the theme commences in the last section of chapter 10, not at the beginning of 11; cf. J. Moffatt, *Epistle to the Hebrews (I.C.C.),* 1924, p. 158. For a different analysis based on literary considerations, cf. A. Vanhoye, *La structure littéraire de L'Épitre aux Hébreux,* 1963, pp. 180ff., although he admits that vv. 10: 36–39 announce developments to come. G. W. Buchanan describes it as a 'transition passage': *To the Hebrews,* 1972, p. 176.

129   Cf. E. Grässer, *Der Glaube im Hebräerbrief,* 1965, pp. 41–63.

130   But it is no longer possible to identify *seder* or *haftarah* with any confidence. Rather, it seems to be a device of Christian preaching simply to illustrate a Christian point of view by means of a wide selection of scriptural examples, especially from the Torah. For the use of Hab. 2: 3f. (Septuagint), cf. F. F. Bruce, *Commentary on Hebrews,* 1964, pp. 271–5; G. W. Buchanan, *To the Hebrews,* p. 175.

131   Cf. C. K. Barrett, 'The Eschatology of the Epistle to the Hebrews', in *The Background of the New Testament and its Eschatology,* Davies and Daube (edd.), 1956, pp. 363–93.

132   1 Clement also contains striking examples of 'pearl stringing' and the recital technique: cf. the theme of 'rivalry' (cf. chs. 2f., 4–13). Throughout the epistle one can detect the hellenistic preacher, steeped in the Septuagint

and acquainted with some of Paul's letters and some gospel material, as he speaks to the contemporary situation: never more at home than when he is reeling off scriptural examples to reinforce his message, or urging the Christian virtues with earnest moralism.

133 The religion of Israel involves, of course, a prime concern for the history of the people, within which God's saving activity is held to be manifested; and the 'things concerning Jesus' stand in this religio-historical tradition: cf. G. E. Wright, *God Who Acts*, 1952.

134 On chapter 16, cf. J. I. H. McDonald, 'Was Romans XVI a separate letter?', *N.T.S.* 16, 1970, pp. 369-72. It is conceivable that a shorter form of Romans, excluding the latter epistolary material, circulated in some areas of the church as a doctrinal tract.

135 Cf. E. Käsemann, *An die Römer*, 1974, pp. 18-29; O. Kuss, *Der Römer Brief*, 1963, pp. 20-5.

136 Old patterns of thought die hard: Paul included a *proem* text (Hab. 2: 4) in his theme statement and applied it to passages from the Torah (e.g., Deut. 10: 17; cf. 2 Chr. 19: 7). Accordingly, its meaning underlies his thinking throughout the discourse, until finally he links it explicitly and triumphantly with Gen. 15: 6 (cf. Rom. 4: 3, 9, 22). There are also some fairly extensive examples of *haruzin* (3: 10-18; cf. 4: 7f.), taken mainly from the psalms but including Is. 59: 7f. At the appropriate point, he gives strong expression to the standpoint from which he 'peshers' the scriptures (3: 21-26). In view of Paul's presentation of it (cf. 1: 15), this discourse is probably typical of his preaching to Christian groups (like the Romans) with a strongly Jewish background.

137 Some commentators take Rom. 3: 21 as the beginning of an entirely new major section of the letter, so that the divisions become 1: 18 - 3: 20; 3: 21 - 8: 39. This seems to me a singularly ill-judged analysis. Not only does it ignore a more radical break at 5: 1 but it fails to recognise that Paul is developing his argument on the theme of 1: 16f. by means of the judgment-salvation antithesis, as is shown particularly by 2: 7-10. Rom. 3: 21-31, with its positive statement of the righteousness of God, is an integral part of this development: cf. W. Lüthi, *The Letter to the Romans*, Eng. tr., 1961, pp. 9-55.

138 E. Käsemann, *Perspectives on Paul*, Eng. tr., 1971, p. 79. The entire essay, 'The Faith of Abraham in Romans 4', pp. 79-101, is relevant here; also *An die Römer*, pp. 84-121; H. W. Schmidt, *Der Brief des Paulus an die Römer*, 1972, pp. 64-88.

139 E. Käsemann, *Perspectives*, p. 95.

140 J. W. Bowker, *N.T.S.* 14, p. 110, describes Rom. 4 as 'constructed in almost perfect *yelammedenu* style'. He holds that the series of questions in 3: 27 - 4: 1 presents 'a typical *yelammedenu* situation'; he points to Gen. 15: 6 as a crucial text (4: 3), the argument proceeding by *haruzin* until it returns to the text: 'that is why his faith was "reckoned to him as righteousness" ' (v. 22); and he suggests that this material resembles a Jewish missionary sermon, especially in the setting of the Diaspora. There may be some force in this argument, but it is not wholly adequate: (i) the alleged *yelammedenu* situation is brought about not by questions addressed to a teacher but by a series of rhetorical questions characteristic of the diatribe and recurring

throughout this discourse of Paul (cf. 2: 3f., 21ff.; 3: 1f., 5–9); (ii) *haruzin* exposition occurs also in 3: 10–18, on the theme of universal sinfulness and the impossibility of justification according to works of the law (cf. 3: 19f.): i.e., there is a close correspondence between the procedures of ch. 3 and ch. 4; (iii) the claim that Abraham's righteousness rested on faith (4: 3; cf. Gen. 15: 6) picks up and illustrates the general point made in the theme statement, 'he who through faith is righteous shall live' (1: 17; cf. Hab. 2: 4). Paul links Abraham and Hab. 2: 4 similarly in Gal. 3: 6–9, 11. Indeed, Paul may have been recalling familiar exposition and may have incorporated several versions of it in different letters (with Rom. 1: 16 – 4: 25, cf. Gal. 3–5); but the rabbinic form presupposed and modified is, for the most part, the *proem* rather than *yelammedenu* homily.

141 Stylistically this discourse abounds with the rhetorical figures which characterise living discourse. For the place of rhetoric in rabbinical training, cf. C. G. Montefiore and H. Lowe (edd.), *Rab. Anth.*, p. 681; cf. S. Lieberman, *Greek in Jewish Palestine*, 1942, pp. 15–67. Stylistic procedures derived from the diatribe include the sequence of word-play in 1: 23, 25, 27f.; the catalogue of vices in 1: 29ff., adorned with assonance and incorporating a closing cadence in the best classical style; the addressing of the imaginary opponent (2: 1, 3); the repeated use of short rhetorical questions, sometimes combined with a pointed *ad hominem* address. But Paul operates throughout as a hellenistic Jewish preacher, combining diatribal features with rabbinic exegesis and argumentation: cf. his scriptural quotations at 2: 24, 3: 10–18, and 4: 7f. His exegesis of the Abraham passage in chapter 4 is rabbinic in its methods, but the distinctively Christian standpoint is evident in the 'peshering' of the basic texts. On the whole subject, cf. R. Bultmann, *Der Stil*, pp. 66–74; H. I. Marrou, 'Diatribe: Christlich', *Reallexicon für Antike und Christentum*, Band III, 1957, pp. 997–1009.

142 C. H. Dodd, *The Epistle of Paul to the Romans*, 1932, pp. xxxf.

143 W. L. Knox, *Some Hellenistic Elements in Primitive Christianity* (Schweich Lectures 1942), 1944, p. 32.

144 Is Is. 29: 14 the *proem* text, or is it Job 5: 12f.?

145 Although the analyses of homiletic *Gattungen* offered here were arrived at independently, it is pleasing to discover a large measure of agreement with W. Wuellner, 'Haggadic Homily Genre in 1 Corinthians 1–3', *J.B.L.* 89, 1970, pp. 199–204.

146 W. Wuellner, *J.B.L.* 89, p. 201, writes: 'Thanks to the homily *Gattung* the role of the digression in 2: 1–5 can be appreciated both as to its structional and stylistic, as well as its substantive significance. The eschatological judgment conclusion is anything but a diatribal "digression" as Bultmann maintained.'

147 Is. 64: 4; 65: 17 may pick up the *haftarah*, although this, of course, is supposition.

148 Thus John Knox says that these chapters 'constitute a more or less independent element in the epistle and can be considered not only as a unit, but also with less reference to the rest of the letter than can any earlier section': *Int. Bib.* IX, *Romans*, p. 535.

149 Cf. W. L. Knox, *Hellenistic Elements*, p. 36. Knox describes this passage as 'entirely Philonic'; cf. Philo, *De. Virt.* 206ff.; *De Praem. et Poen.* 58ff. But

Paul's language has a directness and efficiency which Philo's lacks.

150 The unitary structure of these chapters is as self-evident as the diatribal style and rabbinic characteristics: cf. C. H. Dodd, *Romans,* pp. 148f. The theme differs from that of 1:16f. in that it is problematical, and its out-working reflects this in its exceptionally close argumentation and in its anguished intensity. Here above all in the epistles, we hear the authentic voice of Paul the preacher. Dodd, however, mechanises Paul's procedures anachronistically when he imagines him eagerly laying hold of a sermon laid aside for just such an eventuality and incorporating it in this epistle, 'to save a busy man's time and trouble in writing on the subject afresh': *op. cit.,* pp. 149f: only one step away from depicting him telling his secretary Phoebe to locate the sermon in the card index system under the heading: 'Jews – rejection of'. The recognition of the unitary structure and homiletic nature of these chapters requires neither the hypothesis of an interpolation nor of a previously written document. The theme is by its very nature one upon which Paul must have discoursed frequently, and its inner structures and delicate nuances were imprinted deeply upon his mind.

151 Several other passages should be noted in this context. Rom. 5:1–8:39 evinces homiletic structure: 5:1–5 might be regarded as the theme state-ment, adapted to the overall epistolary purpose; and the main sections would be 5:6–21; 6:1–7:25; and 8:1–39, all of which develop the argu-ment systematically and lead up to a glorious, rhetorical conclusion (8:35–39), reminiscent of Epictetus 1:18, 22. These chapters also abound in rhetorical devices: e.g., rhetorical questions (cf. Rom. 6:1; 7:7; 8:31), parallelism (cf. 5:9f.; 12:19), antitheses (cf. 8:10; 38f.), comparisons or analogies (cf. 6:16ff.; 7:2ff.); repetition (cf. *nomos* in 7:7–8:2). Never-theless, the identification of a self-contained homiletic structure is less convincing here than in 1:16–4:25 and 9:1–11:36. It is probably safer to describe 5:1–8:39 as mainly epistolary in form though employing homiletic and paraenetic elements. On the other hand, reflections of a Christian counterpart to the *yelammedenu* form may be found in Gal. 2:14–21. The issue is one of Christian *halachah*: should circumcised Christians eat with uncircumcised? (cf. 2:12f.). Paul's counter to Peter (given in direct speech: 2:14) resembles a debate between two schools. His case is that faith is central to justification, both for Jews and Gentiles, and he appeals (as in Rom. 3:20) to Ps. 143:2 (Gal. 2:16). The roots of Christian *halachah* must spring from the gospel itself, in a straightforward way (cf. 2:14, 16, 20f.). Additionally, it could be argued that a homiletic structure underlies Gal. 3–5.

152 A. C. Purdy describes the question of its literary form as 'one of the unsolved problems of New Testament research': *Hebrews, Int. Bib.* XI, p. 591; but the discussion has progressed since he wrote.

153 Three points may be made briefly: (a) The document as it stands is designed to be sent as a letter (cf. ch. 13), but no attempt has been made to impose epistolary form on the main part of the document or its introduction. Within church circles, it would be eminently suitable for reading aloud to the assembled group or congregation (cf. 1 Thess. 2:2; Col. 4:16). Parallels are not lacking for writings designed for epistolary use but without epistolary introductions: cf. 4 Maccabees, 1 John, 2 Clement, Barnabas. The specific purpose or occasion of the epistle need not be discussed here. (b) The sub-

stance of the document is homiletic: cf. *logos paraclēseōs* (13: 22), the phrase used to describe a synagogue address in Acts 13: 15. The expressly hortatory passages (cf. 2: 1ff.; 3: 7ff.; 5: 11 - 6: 20; 11 *passim*) are integral to the design of the material, not mere interpolations. The writer thinks of himself as a speaker rather than a writer (2: 5; 6: 9; 8: 1; 9: 5; 11: 32; cf. 12: 25; 13: 6) and of the recipients as hearers rather than readers (cf. 5: 11). Hebrews may therefore be fittingly thought of as 'an epistolary sermon which the preacher was prevented from delivering orally' (F. F. Bruce, *Hebrews,* in *Peake*, p. 1019) or 'a written sermon with an epistolary ending' (*ibid.*, p. 1008). (c) The document evinces a total unitary structure which includes several main constituents. The total unit has been secured not only by the progressive type of the argumentation but also by subtle authorship. The author gives advance notice of some of the theological themes he will subsequently develop. For example, the theme of Jesus as high priest, developed in 4: 14 - 5: 10, is adumbrated in 2: 17 and 3: 1, 'God's rest' (4: 1-13) in 3: 11 and 18; and the Melchizedek argument (7: 1 - 8: 7) in 5: 6, 10; and 6: 20. But without denying this essential unity, it is also necessary to see whether the author has made use of smaller and originally independent units to construct the total document. *Prima facie* this would appear to be the case.

154   A. C. Purdy, *Hebrews*, p. 592.

155   Cf. S. Kistemaker, *The Psalm Citations in the Epistle to the Hebrews*, 1961, pp. 102-16.

156   For the place of chiasmus in the New Testament generally, cf. N. W. Lund, *Chiasmus in the New Testament: A Study in Formgeschichte*, 1942. Hebrews, however, is omitted from consideration in this work.

157   Note the tenses. The life of Jesus is in the past; the inspiration he gives to believers is in the present; exhortation is for the present and future, but its basis is often in the past.

158   Cf. Heb. 5: 6, 10; 6: 20; 7: 11, 15, 17, 21, 28; cf. S. Kistemaker, *Psalm Citations*, pp. 116-24. This discourse includes another heavily 'peshered' psalm citation at 10: 5-10 (Ps. 40: 6ff.).

159   When all is said and done, Hebrews remains problematical. Some critics have properly underlined its essential unity, apart from ch. 13. G. W. Buchanan described chs. 1-12 as 'a homiletical midrash based on Psalm 110': *To the Hebrews,* p. xix, but this is to narrow the perspective excessively, as the work of S. Kistemaker, if not my own analysis, illustrates. The homiletical structures identified above, while probably reflecting separate and memorable homilies characteristic of the Christian teacher who inspired Hebrews (C. Spicq has described him as a professor of biblical studies! - *L'Epître aux Hebreux* I, 1953, p. 25), were skilfully combined in digest form to present a consistent and coherent theological statement. The final document and outline homilies it comprised were probably the work of the same teacher. There is, I suggest, no case for considering chs. 1-12 as one complete homily. The homiletic structures are discerned within the well-integrated document they have been used to create.

160   Apart from the recital type homily on 'faith and endurance' (Heb. 10: 32 - 12: 13), the remainder of the document is made up of sundry ethical exhortations, properly classed as *paraenesis*.

161 For a detailed comparison, *vid.* E. M. Sidebottom, *James, Jude and 2 Peter,* 1967, pp. 65–8; J. Moffatt, *Introduction to the Literature of the New Testament,* 1911, pp. 348ff.

162 B. Reicke, *The Epistles of James, Peter and Jude,* 1964, p. 190.

163 Epistolary convention affects only Jude 1–3, at which point the writer switches dramatically to the theme of the homily.

164 In its form, 2 Peter is differentiated from Jude in two ways: it is more consciously epistolary (1: 1f.; 3: 1); and it is testamentary: it takes the form of a farewell discourse of Peter (1: 14f.). In line with these factors, 2 Peter is more contrived stylistically, reflecting the baroque and extravagant Asianic school increasingly fashionable at this period (early second century).

165 This is not to say that 2 Peter is necessarily later than Jude or that it is dependent on Jude.

166 Cf. E. Käsemann, 'An Apologia for Primitive Christian Eschatology', in *Essays,* pp. 169–95, esp. 169f. 2 Peter is therefore doubly interesting in that it not only presents a kind of epistolary homily on a theme of its own but it shows, in comparison with Jude, how readily homiletic material can be adapted to meet a different situation. This presupposes, of course, a fair degree of common ground, represented in the case of Jude and 2 Peter by their concern with false teachers.

167 The epistolary opening (2 Pet. 1: 1f.) is followed by informal *didache,* showing the influence of rhetoric (1: 5ff.), with emphasis on recall (1: 12) and with testamentary overtones (1: 14f.).

168 Käsemann says that it 'provides support *via negationis* for the proof which is being built up'; *Essays,* p. 178.

169 Cf. J. Moffatt, *Introduction,* pp. 48ff., 315ff., 461ff.; L. E. Elliott-Binns, *James* in *Peake,* 1962, p. 1022.

170 C. L. Mitton, *The Epistle of James,* 1966, pp. 237f.

171 E. G. Selwyn's analysis, admittedly 'not easy', distinguishes three doctrinal sections separated by three hortatory sections, but this is perhaps no more than a general guide to the reader and does not amount to a proper formal analysis: cf. *The First Epistle of St Peter,* 1946, pp. 4ff. Thus his first doctrinal section has been described as a prayer-hymn (1: 3–12); his first hortatory section as pure *didache* (1: 13–21), together with a baptismal dedication (1: 22–25), and the beginnings of a festal song (2: 1–10): cf. H. Preisker in H. Windisch, *Kommentar z. Kath. Epp., H.N.T.,* 1951, pp. 156ff. Other parts have been identified as a hymn about Christ (2: 21–24), a revelation (3: 13 – 4: 7a) and an amended prayer (4: 7b–11). The document might therefore be a liturgical guide – perhaps even to be ascribed to the baptismal celebration at the Paschal vigil: cf. F. L. Cross, *1 Peter, a Paschal Liturgy,* 1954. Such a solution has met with criticism, cf. C. F. D. Moule, 'The Nature and Purpose of 1 Peter', *N.T.S.* 3, 1956, pp. 1ff., but it has at least the merit of indicating the diversity of material contained in this general epistle – which remains, perhaps, the best description of it: cf. E. G. Selwyn, *op. cit.,* p. 1; A. M. Hunter, *1 Peter* in *Int. Bib.* XII, 1957, p. 81. It presents an interesting similarity to Ephesians: cf. C. L. Mitton, 'The Relationship between 1 Peter and Ephesians', *J.T.S.* (N.S. 1), 1950, pp. 67ff.

172 Outside the New Testament, 2 Clement evinces many formal similarities to the homily, but the matter cannot be discussed in detail here: cf. C. C.

Richardson, *Early Christian Fathers* I, 1953, p. 183; *contra*, C. Stegemann, *Herkunft und Entstehung des sogennanten zweiten Klemensbriefes*, 1974, pp. 106–17. The matter is discussed also by K. P. Donfried, 'The Theology of Second Clement', *H. T. R.* 66, 1973, pp. 487–501; cf. *The Setting of Second Clement*, pp. 98–181.

173 W. Marxsen, *Der Evangelist Markus*, 1956. The main difference is that it consists throughout of paraenetic and traditional material, by means of which the reader is instructed with the help of editorial comment or addition. It lacks explicit homiletics, but it shares with the homily both kerygmatic and didactic purpose and structural features.

174 One is concerned here with the overall pattern rather than detailed analysis. Mark skilfully blends the various elements together, so that it is not always easy to be sure where one section ends and another begins (e.g., the introduction of part 2 and the main body). An analysis based solely on groupings of pericopae therefore differs from that given above: cf. V. Taylor, *The Gospel According to St Mark*, 1952, pp. 90–104.

175 Cf. C. H. Dodd, *The Johannine Epistles*, 1946, p. xxi; G. Johnston, *I, II, III John*, in *Peake*, 1962, p. 1035.

176 A. N. Wilder, *I John*, in *Int. Bib.* XII, 1957, p. 217.

177 Thus, while it is true that 1: 4, 2: 17 and 5: 12 mark natural pauses in its flow, it would be unwise to attempt to structure the discourse round these points without first ascertaining whether the inner logic and sequence of the discourse corresponds to such a pattern.

178 Cf. R. Bultmann, *Die drei Johannesbriefe*, 1967, pp. 21–30.

179 I.e., a consciously composed literary or rhetorical unit with characteristic rhythm, parallelism and structural regularity and balance. It was not necessarily sung, probably recited ecphonetically.

180 Cf. O. A. Piper, 'I John and the Didache of the Primitive Church', *J. B. L.* 66, 1947, pp. 449f.

181 R. Bultmann, *Die drei Johannesbriefe*, pp. 30–5.

182 The 'hymn of light', however, has two extended clauses (1: 7c and 9c) which are integral to the literary poem as it stands but which probably did not belong to the original utterance since the couplet appears to be basic. The purpose of the addition is to introduce the doctrine of the atonement upon which the author then comments in his first epistolary note (2: 1–3). A similar tendency is seen at 2: 5b, 6, which is a definitive statement interjected into the flow of the couplets. The interruption is continued in the following epistolary and didactic note (2: 7f.). The source is then resumed, a final comment being added at 2: 11b.

183 In another series of rhetorical units (2: 18f., 22f.), the writer takes the appearance of antichrists as symptomatic of the approach of the *eschaton*, and concludes with a rhetorical exhortation (24f.) which reiterates in simpler form the essence of the prologue (1: 1–3). It would appear that the writer is making use of familiar, stylised *didache*. With A. N. Wilder, I detect a transition point at 2: 28 rather than 3: 1; *Int. Bib.* XII, p. 251.

184 E. von Dobschütz, 'Johanneische Studien I', *Z. N. W.* 8, 1907, pp. 4ff. The couplets are 2: 29b and 3: 4; 3: 6a and 6b; 3: 7b and 8a; 3: 9a and 10b. All except 3: 7b and 8a begin with '*pas ho*' and participle; 7b and 8a do not have '*pas*'.

185 A. N. Wilder expresses agreement with the source theory here, on the grounds that 'the use of parallelism is so clear': *Int. Bib.* XII, p. 276. That there is 'balance of thought and form' in 4: 5f. is readily discernible, although in the existing material all the elements are not present. This points once again to the rather free use of source materials by the writer.

186 E.g., 7b, 8a (if there is any truth in my suggested 'hymn of love', this couplet is secondary and probably originates in catechetical teaching); 4: 15; 4: 20f. (cf. 2: 4).

187 5: 13, 15 (twice), 18, 19, 20. In v. 20, *dianoian*, 'understanding', and *alethinon* are also used.

188 There can be no doubt as to the essentially Christian nature of these utterances. The 'hymn of light', even in what I suspect to be its earlier form, contains a clear reference to the forgiveness of Christ (1: 9); there appears to be no good reason to doubt its authenticity as J. C. O'Neill does (*The Puzzle of 1 John,* 1966, p. 10). The equally mystical 'hymn of love' dwells upon the notion of God as love; the commentary relates it explicitly to the sending of the Son, and his incarnation and atonement (4: 9f.). Bultmann's contention that there is a theological discrepancy between the source material and the author of 1 John is weak: cf. O. Piper, *J. B. L.* 66, p. 447: 'One might be tempted to enquire whether any differences of christology existed between the "*Vorlage*" and the rest of the epistle'. Indeed, the whole tenor of the epistle is against such a presumption. A teacher does not highlight inadequate material unless he is going to launch a specific attack on it, which is not the case here; nor does he make inadequate material the basis of a pupil's handbook. But O'Neill's argument that the source derived from a Jewish sect which provided the background of the writer and his followers (now Christian) and also his opponents (who refused to become Christian) is ingenious and attractive, though perhaps not capable of complete proof: cf. *op. cit.*, pp. 6f., and *passim.*

189 Outside the New Testament, Melito's *Peri Pascha* provides an example of a thematic homily, developed cyclically and built up into a highly rhetorical work – a panegyric or encomium: cf. J. I. H. McDonald, 'Some Comments on the Form of Melito's Paschal Homily', *Studia Patristica* XII, 1975, pp. 104–12.

190 Cf. C. Mohrmann, 'Praedicare-Tractare Sermo: Essai sur la terminologie paleochrétienne', *La Maison Dieu* 39, 1954, pp. 105ff.

Chapter 3. *Paraenesis* and *catechesis*

1 Isocrates, *To Demonicus* 5.
2 1 Cor. 14: 19 (R.S.V.).
3 The 'protreptic discourses': Isocrates, *To Demonicus.*
4 Since we prefer not to use *didache* as a specific category, the problem of appropriate terminology is acute. *Paraineo* (advise, recommend) occurs in Acts 27: 9, 22 in a non-technical context but is a useful general term. *Katēcheo* (give information, Acts 21: 21, 24) means 'instruct' in 1 Cor. 14: 19; Gal. 6: 6; Rom. 2: 18; Acts 18: 25; cf. Luke 1: 4; but because of its association with later catechetics the term *catechesis* alone might prove misleading. We have therefore opted for a conjunction of both terms.

Other important terms include *nouthesia* ('instruction', 'admonition', 'warning') and *paideia* ('instruction', 'discipline', 'nurture') but they have a more specialised reference than is appropriate for the general chapter heading.

5   Concerns such as the care of the soul, the intellectual and moral personality, the vision of goodness; methods such as the dialogue.

6   A. H. Armstrong, *Ancient Philosophy*, p. 31.

7   There is an area of overlapping. *Paraenesis* can make use of diatribal features such as rhetorical questions and various rhetorical figures. On the other hand, the diatribe, which is longer and more fully developed, may utilise within its structure several shorter units that are essentially paraenetic.

8   Cf. Aristotle, *Rhetoric* 2: 21.

9   Its connotation is essentially local: a geographical or physiological location, or a place in a book, a passage.

10 Cf. Aristotle, *Rhetoric* 1: 2; 2: 23. Cicero, *De Orat.* 3: 27; *Topica, passim*; cf. Quintilian, 5: 10, 20.

11 Socrates, *Memorabilia* 3: 9.

12 E.g., about taking offence when your greeting is not returned: *ibid.*, 3: 13f.

13 Cf. D. G. Bradley, 'The "Topos" as a Form of Pauline Paraenesis', *J.B.L.* 72, 1953, pp. 238–46.

14 For a technical discussion of maxims and related rhetorical forms, cf. Aristotle, *Rhetoric* 2: 21.

15 Isocrates, *To Demonicus* 16.

16 *Ibid.* 14.

17 *Ibid.* 15.

18 *Ibid.* 27f.

19 Marcus Aurelius, *Meditations* 7: 32, cf. 33f. Also cf. Epictetus, *Encheiridion* 31.

20 Epictetus, *Encheiridion* 33.

21 The simile is frequently the central constituent in the *topos*, being drawn, for example, from seafaring, the stage, the army, the world of animals or nature, town or country life, medicine or surgery, and the human body. The background of such forms is to be found in Homer and the gnomic poets such as Theognis: cf. F. Hauck, *T.D.N.T.* V, p. 746. Plato tends to draw his material from the everyday world of typical happenings and human relations, or he uses myth. We find therefore the figure of the ship (*Laws.* 6: 758a), analogies from music (*Phaed.* 85e) and the animal world (*Apol.* 30e), and the mythical battle of the giants (*Soph.* 246a). His extended image of the charioteer and his horses is developed allegorically: the charioteer is reason, the black horse the sensual element in man and the white horse the rational or moral element (*Phaed.* 247–57). His figures are usually 'interwoven stylistically into the flow of speech; they are not independent stylistic unities, as in the Gospels'; Hauck, *ibid.* Aristotle categorises such figures as 'examples' which play a supporting or 'proof' role in rhetoric. They may be drawn from the sober world of historical event or from the realm of imagination, such as fables and Socratic illustrations.

22 Livy, 2: 32; for discussion of the parabolic usage involved, cf. E. Linnemann, *The Parables of Jesus,* Eng. tr., 1966, p. 21.

23 In the Greek tradition, the 'two ways' motif probably derives from the

antitheses of Heraclitus: cf. E. Norden, *Die antike Kunstprosa,* pp. 16ff., 508f. Hesiod gave poetical expression to it: cf. *Works and Days* 285, quoted by Xenophon, *Memorabilia* 2: 1. 20; and it occurs also in Xenophon: cf. Prodicus' tale, *op. cit.* 2: 1. 29. This ethical dualism is to be found elsewhere among the poets and also among the philosophers, including Aristotle, in whose writings the 'excess' and the 'defect' are set over against each other: for example, prodigality and stinginess: *Nicomachean Ethics* 4: 1121a. Pythagoras used the letter 'Y' to symbolise the 'two ways'; not, however, with the approval of Lactantius, who held such a symbol inadequate to express the total contradiction of good and evil, the one leading to light, the other to darkness: cf. *Div. Inst.* 6: 3ff. Plutarch, *De Iside et Osiride* 47, illustrates the interrelationship of Greek dualism and Iranian thought.

24 In the Orphic societies, ethics and eschatology combined to produce the concept of future retribution for vice, in which the basic types were sin against the gods and disrespect for parents: cf. E. von Dobschütz, *Christian Life in the Primitive Church,* Eng. tr., 1904, pp. 406f. On this basis, catalogues of vices are built up: injury to the stranger, murder, adultery, greed... Similarly, from Pythagorean circles come the catalogues, attributed to Lysis and cited by Iamblichus, which expound *akrasia* (intemperance) in terms of unlawful marriages, destructions, intoxications, unnatural pleasures and many other lusts; and *pleonexia* (greed) in terms of thefts, burglaries, parricides, sacrileges, poisonings...: *ibid.,* cf. Iamblichus, *De Vita Pythag.* 17: 18. Also quoted in K. E. Kirk, *The Vision of God,* 1931, p. 120.

25 Cf. E. Zeller, *Stoics, Epicureans and Sceptics,* Eng. tr., 1870, pp. 255–60.

26 Andronicus divided grief into twenty-five forms, fear into twelve or thirteen, desire into twenty-seven, and pleasure into five: cf. J. von Arnim, *Stoicorum Veterum Fragmenta,* 1921, pp. 96–100.

27 Aristotle, *Nicomachean Ethics* 2: 1108a.

28 Cf. A. Deissmann, *Light from the Ancient East,* Eng. tr., 1927, pp. 316f. Similarly, lists of vices lent spice to the more bawdy scenes in ancient comedy. In different vein, catalogues of virtues in inscriptions suggest their use as funeral honours. In general, cf. E. Kamlah, *Die Form der katalogischen Paränese im Neuen Testament,* 1964, pp. 139–48.

29 This has been the accepted terminology for the 'household codes' at least since K. Weidinger's work, *Die Haustafeln, Ein Stück urchristlicher Paränese,* 1928. Pioneer work has been done by A. Seeberg (1903) and M. Dibelius (1911). The findings of the German scholars were popularised in English by K. E. Kirk (1931), P. Carrington (1940) and E. G. Selwyn (1945). For a more recent review of the problem, cf. J. E. Crouch, *The Origin and Intention of the Colossian Haustafel,* 1972, pp. 18–36. The term was used by Luther in his Shorter Catechism and subsequently appeared as chapter headings in his Bible: cf. K. E. Kirk, *The Vision of God,* p. 120, n. 7.

30 Sophocles, *Antigone* 454f.

31 Xenophon, *Memorabilia* 4: 4.19–24; cf. Isocrates, *To Demonicus* 16; Diog. Laert. 8: 23; see also K. Weidinger, *Die Haustafeln,* pp. 27–31, 41f.

32 Epictetus, 2: 17. 31: cf. 3: 2. 4; 3: 7. 25ff.; also 1: 29. 39; 2: 10. 10f.; 2: 14. 8; cf. Musonius Rufus, *Pankratiđe* 5 (O. Hense, *C. Musonii Rufi Reliquiae,* 1905, p. 139): also *ibid.* 8.

33 Epictetus, 4: 30.

34 Cf. J. E. Crouch, *Colossian Haustafel*, pp. 45–56.

35 *Ibid.*, pp. 57–73; cf. O. J. F. Seitz, in *Interpreter's Dictionary of the Bible* III, 1962, art. 'Lists'.

36 Indeed, the Homeric examples, placed on the lips of vanquished warriors, include memorable utterances about the fate of the victors and, to that extent, approximate to *propheteia*: *Iliad* 16: 851ff.; 22: 359ff. Even more explicitly, Socrates in his last speech addresses those who have condemned him: cf. Plato, *Apol.* 39c.

37 Sophocles, *Oedipus at Colonus*, 1518–55.

38 Herodotus, 3: 65.

39 In addition to the above examples, cf. Xenophon, *Inst. Cyri* 8: 7; Ammianus Marcellinus, 25: 3. 15–23.

40 *Vid. supra*, pp. 43–8.

41 W. McKane, *Proverbs*, 1970, p. 413. McKane's view is a departure from the orthodox form-critical analysis of J. Schmidt, *Studien zur Stilistik der alttestamentlichen Spruchliteratur*, Alttestamentlich Abhandlungen 13, 1, 1936, pp. 1ff. *Vid.* McKane, *op. cit.*, pp. 1–10.

42 These proverbs are akin to the proverbial sentences found in the Egyptian book *Onchsheshoncy*: cf. W. McKane, *Proverbs*, pp. 117–50. They spring from the milieu of the countryside and country life, and possess a concreteness, practicality and earthiness that are to be expected from such a quarter. On the whole the more generalised the proverb is, the less open it is to interpretation. Another important source is the Assyrian teaching of *Ahikar*, over fifty parallels with Proverbs being noted by W. E. Oesterley, *The Book of Proverbs*, 1929. Characteristic themes in *Ahikar* are the need for discipline, moderation in speech, obedience to the king, prudence in business and personal relationships, the danger of bad company and respect for parents. Cf. McKane, *op. cit.*, pp. 156ff.

43 Cf. B. Gemser, *Spruche Solomons*, 1963, on 10: 11f.

44 E.g., Prov. 10: 14f., in which the *Stichwort* is 'ruin', and 10: 16f., where it is 'life'.

45 On 'speech' (Prov. 10: 18–21) and 'the fear of the Lord' (10: 27–30).

46 Cf. W. McKane, *Proverbs*, p. 3. The background of this form is the scribal teaching of Egypt. Prov. 22: 17 – 23: 11 is properly regarded as based upon the *Instruction of Amenemope*, cf. *A.N.E.T.*, pp. 420–25; W. McKane, *op. cit.*, pp. 102–17; while R. N. Whybray identified ten originally independent speeches on the Egyptian model underlying Prov. 1–9; *Wisdom in Proverbs*, 1965, pp. 33ff. (They are identified by introductory formulae at 1: 8ff.; 2: 1ff.; 4: 1ff.; 4: 20ff.; 5: 1ff.; 6: 20ff.; 7: 1ff.) In Egypt such teaching came from the milieu of the elitist scribal schools and entered Israel through the civil service established in the reigns of David and Solomon and developed further by their successors. There was an organised literary wisdom movement in Hezekiah's court (Prov. 25: 1): cf. R. B. Y. Scott, *Solomon and the Beginnings of Wisdom*, *V.T.* S. III, 1955, p. 273. These *hakamim*, however, were not distinct from the class of officials operating in Israel from David's day: cf. W. McKane, *Prophets and Wise Men*, 1965, p. 42.

47 Prov. 23: 19ff., R.S.V.

48 Other variations include the elaborate use of protases and apodoses in Prov.

2 and the more lyrical and hymnic style of 3: 13–20.

49   In the Testaments of the XII Patriarchs, the paraenetic forms are adapted
     to the testamentary motif, but the ethical themes are broadly similar to
     those of Proverbs or Sirach and at times reach for the ethical heights, as in
     the *topos* on forgiveness in Test. Gad 6: 3–7: cf. R. H. Charles, *Test. XII
     Patriarchs*, 1908, p. 155. Christian influence has been suspected here but
     not proved.

50   An agricultural milieu, in which harvests were periods of concentrated
     effort and every man's labour is essential.

51   W. McKane, *Proverbs* p. 415. But as the wisdom tradition became less
     attached to folklore and more consciously didactic, the imagery became
     definitive of the interpretation: cf. Prov. 10: 26 ('Like vinegar to the teeth
     and smoke to the eyes, so is the sluggard to those who send him'), where
     the success of the simile depends on the admissibility of the premise of the
     comparison – here the irritant qualities of vinegar and smoke. This in turn
     provides the clue to the interpretation of the corresponding part of the
     simile.

52   Cf. R. Bultmann, *H. S. T.*, 1963, p. 174.

53   The parable is characteristically in the indicative: this is the situation David
     has created by his action – a situation of human sin and divine judgment.

54   Other Old Testament parables are found in Judg. 9 (the trees); 2 Kings 14
     (the cedar and thistle); Is. 5 (the vineyard); Ezek. 17 (the vine and eagle).

55   *Vid.* M. D. Goulder, *Midrash*, pp. 66–9: 'A Hundred Rabbinic Parables';
     cf. also P. Fiebig, *Ältjüdische Gleichnisse und die Gleichnisse Jesu*, 1904;
     A. Feldman, *Parables and Similes of the Rabbis*, 1927; G. F. Moore,
     Judaism I, pp. 309f., 487–90; II, p. 384.

56   Cf. E. Linnemann, *Parables*, p. 20. The rabbis, unlike the Old Testament,
     tend to use personal relationships and situations in their parabolic teaching
     rather than nature parables: cf. M. D. Goulder, *Midrash*, pp. 51ff.

57   A good example is Ezekiel's allegory of the two eagles (Ezek. 17: 3–10),
     subsequently expounded with exact correspondences in vv. 12–21.

58   Test. Asher 1: 3–5, tr. from the text of de Jonge.

59   Prov. 4: 18f.; cf. 2: 1–15; also, Ps. 1: 6; Jer. 21: 8. Later examples include
     4 Macc. 14: 5; 1 En. 94: 1–4; 2 En. 30: 15.

60   The specific dualism receives its earliest expression in the passage from
     Test. Asher cited above; cf. R. H. Charles, *Test. XII Patriarchs*, pp. 16,
     161f. *Yetzer* itself simply means 'inclination', and is used in a neutral way
     in Sir. 15: 4f. In the Old Testament it can be directed to the good: Is. 26:
     3; 1 Chr. 29: 18, but more usually to evil: Gen. 6: 5; 8: 21; cf. 2 Esd. 4: 30f.
     cf. also Philo, *Quaest. in Ex.* 1: 23.

61   Cf. *Pirque Aboth*, 2: 1.

62   R. Jochanan ben Zakkai. Among other examples of the 'two ways', 1 En.
     94: 1–4; 2 En. 30: 15; Test. Levi 19: 1; Test. Judah 20: 1 may be singled
     out as particularly clear instances.

63   The Community Rule 3; cf. the War Rule, in which the imagery symbolises
     the cosmic conflict between the powers of Light and Darkness. For detailed
     discussion of 1 QS 3: 13 – 4: 26, cf. E. Kamlah, *Die Form*, pp. 39–50; cf.
     also J. Licht, 'An Analysis of the Treatise on the Two Spirits in DSD',
     Scripta Hierosolymitana 4, 1958, pp. 88–100.

64   K. E. Kirk, *The Vision of God*, pp. 123f.

65   Test. Asher 5:1-3, tr. from de Jonge's text; cf. also P. Winter, 'Ben Sira and
     the Teaching of "Two Ways" ', *V.T.* 5, 1955, pp. 315-18.

66   For discussion and analysis of types of catalogues in the *Corpus Hermeticum*,
     cf. E. Kamlah, *Die Form*, pp. 115-36.

67   Rendel Harris, *The Teaching of the Apostles*, 1888, pp. 82-6.

68   G. Vermes, *The Dead Sea Scrolls*, pp. 76f.; cf. Philo, *Sacr. Ab.* 11ff., 14f.;
     Virt. 182.

69   *Pirqe Aboth* 6:1,6. Cf. also the antithetical double catalogue in tractate
     Aboth in the Mishnah 4:9.

70   Sir. 7:18-35; 9:1-9; 33:24-31.

71   Philo, *De Dec.* 165ff.; cf. *De Posteritate Caini* 181.

72   Josephus, *Contra Ap.* 2.190-209.

73   Pseudo-Phocylides, 2:195-98, 209ff.; quoted in E. G. Selwyn, *1 Peter*, p.
     422. Schürer dated it prior to the first century B.C. The poem is nearer in
     form to the New Testament *Haustafeln* than the Stoic writers: J. E. Crouch
     Colossian Haustafel, p. 76. Similarly, the *Letter of Aristeas* shows much
     concern for family relationships and evinces some Stoic influence.

74   Philo uses it in *Leg. Alleg.* 1:56; 3:210; *De Cher.* 14; *De Sacr.* 43; *De Plant.*
     94; 100. He cites related lists of duties in *De Posteritate Caini* 181; and
     Quod Deus 17; 19; also *De Plant.* 146; *De Ebriet.* 17f.; *De Fuga* 3.

75   J. E. Crouch, *Colossian Haustafel*, pp. 79ff. He illustrates the point particular-
     ly from *De Spec. Leg.* 2:226f. The Stoics always tended to emphasise the
     duties of the individual; reciprocity, although sometimes admitted, is basically
     foreign to their position. Cf. also Philo, *Hypothetica* 7:14 (on the authenticity
     of this text, cf. J. E. Crouch, *op. cit.*, p. 81, n. 29); also Josephus, *Contra Ap.*
     2:190-209; to which reference was made *supra*; and 4 Macc. 2:10-13.

76   Cf. L. Ginzberg, *The Legends of the Jews*, r.p. 1955, vol. 5, n. 55; Strack and
     Billerbeck, III, pp. 36ff.; J. E. Crouch, *Colossian Haustafel*, pp. 92f. The
     'Derech-erez' regulations, which also preceded the Torah, were held similarly
     to apply to all men.

77   E.g., those of Jacob (Gen. 47:29 - 50:14), Joshua (Josh. 23:1 - 24:32),
     Samuel (1 Sam. 12) and David (1 Kings 2:1-9; 1 Chr. 28:1 - 29:28).

78   E.g., Deuteronomy (cf. chs. 1-4, 31-34); Testaments of the XII Patriarchs,
     esp. those attributed to the sons of Jacob; the Assumption of Moses; Jubilees.

79   E. Stauffer, *New Testament Theology*, Eng. tr., 1955, pp. 344ff.; cf. also J.
     Munck, 'Discours d'adieu dans le N.T. et dans la littérature biblique', in
     Mélanges M. Goguel, pp. 155-59.

80   Cf. 4 Esd. 14:18-36; S. Enoch 38; Apoc. Syr. Baruch 76:1-18.

81   E.g., Tobit 14:3ff.; 1 Macc. 2:49f.; 2 Macc. 6:30; Jub. 20:1ff.; Test. Levi
     1:2.

82   E.g., Tobit 14:3-11; 1 Macc. 2:51-68; 4 Esd. 14:18ff.; S. Enoch 2 and 55;
     Apoc. Syr. Baruch 77:1-26; 84:7; 85:7.

83   For documentation, cf. E. Stauffer, *N.T. Theology*.

84   The source critics attempted to link this passage with the circle of John's
     disciples, but at best it represents a Christian editing of Baptist tradition;
     cf. W. Wink, *John the Baptist*, p. 110.

85   Cf. Is. 58:6f.; Prov. 14:31; cf. Jos. *Ant.* 18:116f.

86   T. W. Manson, *The Sayings of Jesus*, p. 254; see also J. M. Robinson, *A New*

Quest of the Historical Jesus, 1959, pp. 116ff.; and, for a more balanced picture, G. Bornkamm, *Jesus of Nazareth*, pp. 44–52.

87 Cf. John's prophetic radicalism in relation to Herod Antipas (Mark 6: 18; Matt. 14: 4).

88 The 'offspring of vipers' may, however, have a theological significance – it is more than a term of reproach or abuse: cf. T. W. Manson, *The Sayings of Jesus*, p. 40.

89 Cf. Sir. 6: 2f.; 23: 25; Wisd. 4: 3ff.

90 Cf. C. H. H. Scobie, *John the Baptist*, pp. 60f.

91 The classical delineation of the teaching of Jesus on the basis of source criticism is probably that of T. W. Manson in his two books *The Teaching of Jesus*, 1931, and *The Sayings of Jesus*, 1937. The approach of form and redaction criticism to the same problem is well set out in N. Perrin, *Rediscovering the Teaching of Jesus*, 1967. For the criteria applied to traditional material in order to penetrate to Jesus' teaching, *vid.* N. Perrin, *op. cit.*, pp. 39–49; J. M. Robinson, 'The Formal Structure of Jesus' Message', in *Current Issues in New Testament Interpretation*, Klassen and Snyder (edd.), 1962; cf. R. H. Fuller, *A Critical Introduction to the N.T.*, 1966, pp. 96ff. *Vid.* also F. G. Downing, *The Church and Jesus*, 1968, pp. 93–131; R. S. Barbour, *Traditio-historical Criticism of the Gospels*, 1972, *passim*; M. Goulder, 'Jesus, The Man of Universal Destiny', in *The Myth of God Incarnate*, Hick (ed.), 1977, pp. 50–5. Some basic assumptions of the *formgeschichtliche Schule* were attacked, perhaps over-energetically, by H. Riesenfeld, *The Gospel Tradition and its Beginnings*, 1957, and B. Gerhardsson, *M.M. and T.T.* This Scandinavian school rightly took account of the phenomenon of the transmission of sacred tradition: *vid.* Chapter 4. In the approach adopted in this book – it may be termed structural or phenomenological – I accept with reservations the validity of all the perspectives indicated above but consider it essential to take much fuller account of the religious phenomena involved. As regards the form critics, they not only reject what I have called the principle of scepticism (*vid. supra*, p. 20) but also the theological assumptions which tend to occupy a cardinal position in their work: cf. O. Piper's criticism of Bornkamm's position as having for its focus 'a unitary God with Jesus as his first theologian': *Int.* 15, 1961, pp. 473ff.

92 E.g., Q, with its own theological or apologetic slant.

93 Cf. Mark 4, Luke 15. Thus, some collections were arranged according to parabolic type or theme.

94 Including 'pronouncement stories': cf. V. Taylor, *The Formation of the Gospel Tradition*, r.p. 1964, pp. 63–84; and 'dialogues' of various types: cf. T. W. Manson, *The Sayings of Jesus*, pp. 29f.

95 Cf. W. D. Davies, *S.S.M.*, pp. 1–13, esp. p. 13.

96 R. Bultmann, *H.S.T.*, pp. 69f., rightly distinguishes between constitutive motifs and those that are merely 'ornamental'. I should prefer to speak of motifs that are intrinsic to the form of the utterance as opposed to those that are not. Somewhat dogmatically, he takes the basic forms as 'principles (declamatory form)' – my 'gnomic' type; 'exhortations (imperative form)'; and 'questions'. This terminology does not appear adequately grounded in historical research into the early and pre-Israelite tradition, such as that carried out by McKane. I do not think Bultmann's subdivision of the

'principles' into 'material formulations' and 'personal formulations' possesses much significance. Nor do I always accept his general classification: 'whom God has joined together let no man separate' seems to me to belong to the instructional form, whereas Bultmann smuggles it into the 'personal formulations' of 'principles': *op. cit.*, p. 74.

97 Cf. Matt. 6: 19ff.; Luke 12: 33f. The study of the formal elements of Hebrew poetic expression – parallelism, rhythm and rhyme – was begun by Lowth in his *De Sacra Poesi Hebraeorum Praelectiones Academicae*, 1753; continued by J. Jebb, *Sacred Literature*, 1820; and much extended in relation to N.T. material by C. F. Burney, *The Poetry of Our Lord*, 1925. Cf. T. W. Manson, *The Teaching of Jesus*, pp. 50–6, 330; V. Taylor, *F. G. T.*, pp. 89–100.

98 Cf. Mark 9: 43–47 (Matt. 5: 29f.); Luke 17: 3f. (Matt. 18: 15, 22).

99 Cf. Luke 14: 8–10, 12–14.

100 For expanded gnomic forms, cf. Mark 4: 22 (and par.); 3: 24ff.; Luke 6: 43f.; and in particular Mark 10: 23ff.

101 E.g., hypocritical behaviour in relation to alms (Matt. 6: 2f.), prayer (6: 5f.), fasting (6: 16ff.), or right behaviour in terms of forgiveness (5: 23f.). Cf. also Luke 6: 39 – 'He also told them a parable: "Can a blind man lead a blind man...?"'

102 R. Bultmann needlessly isolates some questions as a separate main section of logia, on the grounds that they occur in Proverbs also, both as rhetorical and as catechetical questions: *H. S. T.*, pp. 72f. But these are merely variant forms of gnomic statement rather than a separate genre.

103 Some of the strophic balance tends to be lost in transmission and editing: cf. Luke 6: 37f., 41f. A less perfect example of this form occurs in Matt. 7: 15–20 (cf. Luke 6: 43ff.).

104 Matt. 6: 7–14 appears editorially inserted at this point, though deriving in the main from dominical tradition: cf. R. Bultmann, *H. S. T.* p. 133. When these are strung together under a general theme statement on piety and its dangers (6: 1), there emerges a complex that might be described structurally as an incipient homily, thus indicating the close relationship between homily and *paraenesis*. Another incipient homily is Matt. 6: 25–33, which is fundamentally paraenetic but in its total build-up approximates to the more elaborate homiletic structure.

105 The early formation of a community of disciples round Jesus is attested by all the gospels, and the pattern seems to have been at least partly perpetuated in the apostolic age. Thus K. Stendahl writes of Matthew: 'his Gospel more than the others is a product of a community and for a community': *Peake*, p. 769. A similar claim can be made for the Johannine teaching.

106 R. Bultmann, *H. S. T.*, p. 134ff.

107 Unlike Bultmann, I can find no good reason for disallowing Matt. 5: 38–39a, where the scriptural quotation approximates to a gnomic saying and, properly understood, carries an implied prohibition against excessive retaliation; and it is this which Jesus radicalises.

108 J. Sittler, *The Structure of Christian Ethics*, 1958, p. 5; cf. the discussion in E. L. Long Jr., *A Survey of Christian Ethics*, 1967, p. 126.

109 Cf. E. Linnemann, *Parables*, pp. 3–8. In briefest compass, the similitude focuses upon a typical situation or recurring event; the parable proper on

one case that is particularly significant; the illustration is primarily a narrative that exemplifies; the allegory is a narrative which hints throughout at a level of meaning other than the superficial meaning, a key being required to unlock the encoded message.

110 Jeremias, rightly suspicious (in my judgment) of the rigid categorisation of parables according to the above types, argued that the Semitic terms (*mashal, mathla*) applied in a general way to all sorts of topical figures; cf. J. Jeremias, *Parables,* pp. 17f.; but Eissfeldt's contention was that where *mashal* (the Hebrew equivalent of Greek *parabolē*) occurs it is used not as a comprehensive term but to denote a particular type of figure, although in different contexts it denotes different figures; cf. O. Eissfeldt, 'Das Maschal im A.T.', *B.Z.A.W.* 24, 1913, p. 33; also E. Linnemann, *Parables,* p. 131, n. 1.

111 The Hebrew *mashal* is normally used to denote the proverbs and aphorisms of the wisdom tradition. It can also denote a pithy taunt saying or byword (cf. Is. 14: 4) which sometimes shows a relationship to the lyrical 'woe' form adopted by the prophets from wisdom models: cf. Hab. 2: 6; also the vivid lament (Micah 2: 4).

112 E.g., in what way is the growth of the mustard seed relevant to my life and faith, to my understanding of my existence, or to my understanding of the reign of God? There is an element of wrestling with meaning: the answer may be found quickly or slowly.

113 Cf. C. H. Dodd, *Parables,* p. 16.

114 Cf. E. Linnemann, *Parables,* pp. 6f.

115 E.g., the great supper, Luke 14: 15–21; Matt. 22: 2–14.

116 Cf. E. Linnemann, *Parables,* pp. 88–97, where she also considers later church interpretations.

117 Paraenetic topics related to this theme may well have been numerous. The underlying Pharisaic topic may well have been 'birds of a feather flock together', while Jesus countered it with 'those that are well do not need a doctor, but those who are ill'.

118 Cf. I. T. Ramsey, *Christian Discourse,* pp. 6–11. Interestingly enough, Ramsey points out that 'the parable of the sower is given in the context of an imperative. "Hearken." "Behold." "Be on the look out for a challenge." ' (p. 9).

119 Cf. the parables of the wheat and the tares (Matt. 13: 24–30), the drag net (Matt. 13: 47f.), the ten virgins (Matt. 25: 1–13), the last judgment (Matt. 25: 31–46), the two houses (Matt. 7: 24–27; cf. Luke 6: 47ff.), and the rich man and Lazarus (Luke 16: 19–31); while other parables work on an explicit contrast of two people: the two sons (Matt. 21: 28–32), the two debtors (Luke 7: 41ff.) and, though less explicitly, the great supper (Matt. 22: 1–14; Luke 14: 16–24), the prodigal son (Luke 15: 11–32) and the Pharisee and the publican (Luke 18: 9–14).

120 E.g., Amos 5: 14 or Josh. 24: 15.

121 Cf. the image of the broad and narrow way (Matt. 7: 13f.); also, the antitheses of the Sermon approximate to the 'two ways' motif by contrasting the way of contemporary Judaistic practice and the way of radical obedience to God.

122 Cf. the prophetic practice of balancing beatitudes and woes, as Luke does.

123 The *Sitz im Leben* of this passage in Mark, as in its truncated parallel in

Matt. 15: 17, is controversy within the church as to what foods defile: 'thus he declared all foods clean' (Mark 7: 19b).

124   Cf. Mark 10: 29f., but once again the likelihood is that the catalogue was a Christian interpretation, as in Luke 21:16.

125   For this whole topic, cf. S. Wibbing, *Die Tugend- und Lasterkataloge im Neuen Testament*, 1959, pp. 87–94; W. D. Davies, *S.S.M.*, pp. 460f.

126   Matt. 15: 3ff.; cf. also the discussion on divorce, 19: 3–9.

127   This motif recurs in Luke 24: 42f.; John 13: 2ff.; Acts 10: 41.

128   Cf. E. Stauffer, *N.T. Theology*, pp. 344f.; also noted briefly in J. Munck, 'Discours d'adieu', p. 165; cf. *supra*, p. 79.

129   Cf. the notion that the church in the world 'sees' and 'knows' Christ although the world does not (John 14: 18–24); that the church is identified with Christ as it obeys his commands and follows his example (cf. 13: 12–17, 34 etc.); the coming of 'the ruler of this world' who has no power over Christ (14: 30; 16: 11; cf. 12: 31); the ultimate joy of the persecuted and grieving church (16: 22) – cf. the 'messianic woes': J. Munck, 'Discours d'adieu', pp. 166f.

130   Farewell features include Jesus' meeting with his own, who worship him; Jesus' commission to his disciples; and the assurance of his constant, if paradoxical, presence.

131   Cf. Jesus stands among them, blesses them (twice); identifies himself as the crucified one; and commissions them and transmits the Spirit. Another example is found in John 21: 15–23 ('tend my sheep'); the fate of Peter – v. 18; the fate of the beloved disciple – vv. 20–23); cf. Acts 1: 2ff.

132   Cf. J. Gnilka, 'Paränetische Traditionen im Epheserbrief', in *Mélanges B. Rigaux*, pp. 399ff.; A. Seeberg, *Der Katechismus der Urchristenheit*, 1903, r.p. 1966, pp. 211–24, incl. F. Hahn's Introduction to the 1966 edition, esp. pp. xviii–xxii.

133   Cf. R. Bultmann, *Theology of the N.T.* I, pp. 332f.

134   Cf. Rom. 13:14; Eph. 4: 24; cf. 6: 11, 13; Col. 3: 10 – the *induentes* motif.

135   Cf. 1 Pet. 2: 1f.; Rom. 13: 12; Eph. 4: 22, 25f.; Col. 3: 8; James 1: 21 – the *deponentes* motif. This put on/put off motif is taken by E. G. Selwyn to reflect a more developed form of baptismal catechesis: *The First Epistle of St Peter*, 1964, pp. 393–400. P. Carrington argued that an earlier form had been modelled on the Holiness Code (Lev. 17–26, esp. 17–19), which legislated for the initiation of a proselyte into Israel. This primitive Christian catechism, like the Holiness Code, insisted on baptism but, in place of circumcision and sacrifice, enjoined abstention from the three major sins of idolatry, murder and fornication: *The Primitive Christian Catechism*, 1940, pp. 14ff.; this represents the *abstinentes* motif.

136   Literally, 'in line with the goal I follow towards the prize' (Phil. 3:14).

137   E.g., 2 Thess. 1: 4; 2 Tim. 3: 11; 4: 3; Heb. 10–12; Eph. 6:18.

138   Cf. Rom. 2: 16. That Paul's *paraenesis* was deeply affected by this eschatological orientation is readily seen in 1 Cor. 6: 1ff.; 7: 26–31. On the other hand, he is quick to correct an exaggerated emphasis which would undermine responsible action in the present time (cf. 2 Thess. 3: 6–13, esp. v. 10).

139   At this point if at no other, there is some affinity between the Christian stance and the pessimism of the Graeco-Roman world, as expressed for example in Stoicism and Cynicism, and Gnosticism. But Judaism, with its

doctrine of Creation, and Christianity, with its gospel of the Creator's love for the world (cf. John 3:16), had the means of supplying a corrective to this total pessimism: cf. J. L. Houlden, *Ethics and the New Testament,* 1973, pp. 8f.

140   W. D. Davies, 'The Relevance of Moral Teaching in the Early Church', *Neotestamentica et Semitica,* 1969, p. 40. Such a position presupposes a casuistical element in early Christian teaching: cf. *S.S.M.*, p. 37.

141   Cf. the notion of 'imitating me as I imitate Christ': 1 Cor. 11:1; the 'grace of our Lord Jesus Christ' is the model in 2 Cor. 8:9, his patience under suffering in Phil. 2:5ff.; that of the atonement in 1 Cor. 8:11.

142   K. P. Donfried, *The Setting of Second Clement,* p. 111.

143   It is not suggested that the above distinctions represent absolute categories. There is a considerable area of overlap, and this convenient terminology simply identifies important tendencies in the *paraenesis* of the church.

144   For a full discussion of *paradosis,* cf. Chapter 4.

145   Cf. O. Cullmann, 'The Tradition', in *The Early Church,* pp. 64ff.

146   Cf. also the two negative statements in 1 Cor. 12:3.

147   Cf. Acts 16:30, to which the response is 'Believe in the Lord Jesus' (16:31). The question 'what shall we do?' (2:37) receives the reply 'Repent, and be baptised every one of you in the name of Jesus Christ' (2:38). It is not suggested, however, that *catechesis* necessarily adopts the question-and-answer form.

148   1 Cor. 15 might be described as a paracletic rather than a paraenetic topic: its development is discursive and extensive and lacks the concentrated paraenetic concern that characterises true *paraenesis.*

149   Cf. Clement's treatment of the resurrection (1 Clem. 24ff.). He first advances the basic symbol of scriptural teaching on the subject and above all the resurrection of Jesus himself (24:1). Supporting arguments are drawn from natural phenomena: the cycles of day and night, seedtime and harvest (24:3ff.); and the legend of the phoenix lends concrete illustration (25:1 – 26:1) before the final scriptural citations from Psalms and Job round off the topic.

150   Cf. D. L. Dungan, *The Sayings of Jesus,* p. 35; cf. B. Gerhardsson, *M.M.,* p. 318. *Vid. infra,* pp. 119–21.

151   Cf. B. Gerhardsson, *M.M.,* pp. 312ff.; D. L. Dungan, *The Sayings of Jesus,* pp. 81–135.

152   Cf. D. L. Dungan, *The Sayings of Jesus,* p. 98.

153   E.g., 'concerning the unmarried' (1 Cor. 7:25; cf. 12:1); this introductory form is common in hellenistic *paraenesis: vid. supra,* p. 71. Cf. also 1 Cor. 7:8, 10, 12.

154   In relation to the above examples, cf. 1 Cor. 7:26; 7:8, 10f., 12f.; 12:3; 15:3–8; 7:32f.; 11:3.

155   Cf. E. G. Selwyn, *1 Peter,* pp. 369–72.

156   1 Peter is a composite epistle which contains 'holiness' *paraenesis* in 1:13–21, not unlike 1 Thess. 4:1–8 in theme but with eschatological overtones (vv. 13, 17) and including a powerful statement of the atonement in the conclusion (vv. 18–21). This is a highly developed form of basic *paraenesis* and, characteristically, it is followed by a short *topos* on brotherly love (v. 22). I suspect that the next *topos* is in fact 1:23 – 2:3, on the subject

of 'the word of God' (v. 23ff.) or 'the gospel' (1: 25b; 2: 3), in which Is.
40: 6-9 is a major symbol, and the image of the 'new born babe' elucidates the proper attitude of the convert, after 'putting away' undesirable
practices (2: 1), to the message of the church. After the elevated song of
the church (2: 4-10; cf. H. Preisker, *op. cit.*, pp. 156ff. - in fact, he takes
2: 1-10 as a festal song in three strophes), there is another '*abstinentes*'
passage at 2: 11, followed by an appeal for responsible conduct to outsiders. Thereafter, the *paraenesis* is on the theme of subjection to the
authorities, which will be discussed in due course.

157 They are concerned with 'lusts' (1 Thess. 4: 5; 1 Pet. 1: 14), 'immorality'
(1 Thess. 4: 3, cf. 1 Cor. 5: 9), 'uncleanness' (1 Thess. 4: 7; cf. Eph. 4:19;
5: 5) and 'wanting more than one's share' (1 Thess. 4: 6; cf. Eph. 5: 5):
cf. E. G. Selwyn, *1 Peter*, pp. 372f., and Table I on pp. 370f. This separation motif can be linked with respect and active concern for one's neighbour (1 Thess. 4: 9; 1 Pet. 1: 22); but in 1 Thess. 4, the theme of 'brotherly
love' (*philadelphia*) occurs explicitly not in the basic paraenetic topic (4:
1-8) but in a subsequent general topic on the theme of *philadelphia*.

158 This, however, corresponds with Luke's version of the apostolic decree
(Acts 15: 29). Cf. E. G. Selwyn, *1 Peter*, p. 372, n. 1.

159 Selwyn's analysis is to be faulted on several counts. First, he pays no
attention to the form of the actual unit which occurs in the New Testament but discusses verbal parallelism wherever he finds it. Again, he is too
anxious to press what are after all fairly scattered and fragmented parallels
into positive codes, particularly baptismal codes, although there are practically no direct references to baptism in them and little evidence of the
formalism necessary to codification. Finally, the distinctive role he at times
ascribes to Silvanus appears to rest on subjective criteria. It is virtually impossible to separate out the *paradosis* from the interpretation which one
man is assumed to have given to part of it.

160 Cf. D. G. Bradley, *J.B.L.* 72, p. 246.

161 D. G. Bradley, *J.B.L.* 72, p. 244. In fact, Bradley is hardly justified in
dividing Rom. 13: 1-5 from vv. 6f. to form two separate *topoi*, one on the
subject of 'temporal authority' and the second on 'paying tribute'. It is, of
course, possible that such *topoi* were frequently used separately but the
writer has employed them in an extended *topos* on 'the right attitude to
civil authority', and the *Stichwörter* to which Bradley points belong to the
inner structure of the one extended unit. The structural pattern is typical
of a well-developed *topos*.

162 The wisdom tradition tends to derive the status and function of the civil
powers from God (cf. Prov. 8: 15f.; Wis. Sol. 6: 3; cf. Jos. *Bell.* 2: 140), but
the Jewish tradition and the gospels agree in subordinating their authority
to that of God: cf. Wis. Sol. 6: 1-11; Ps. 82 *passim*; Matt. 22: 21; Mark 12:
17; Luke 20: 25; Acts 5: 29. Hence it is likely that this topic derives from
Stoicism, and Stoic influence is fairly explicit in v. 1: *vid. supra*, Chapter 2,
pp. 41ff.; cf. J. C. O'Neill, *Paul's Letter to the Romans*, 1975, pp. 208f.

163 Cf. J. Kallas, 'Romans XIII 1-7: An Interpolation', *N.T.S.* 11, 1965, pp.
365-74. Early or mid second-century testimony to this passage is notably
absent: cf. also E. Barnikol, 'Römer 13: Der nichtpaulinische Ursprung
der absoluten Obrigkeitsbejahung von Römer 13: 1-7', *T.U.* 77, 1961,

pp. 65–133. One must, of course, guard against the unconscious desire of the modern scholar to rid himself of the difficulty of attributing this passage to Paul. For an attempt in the opposite direction, cf. O. Cullmann, *The State in the New Testament*, Eng. tr., 1957, pp. 50–70, esp. 56ff.

164 Many further examples of traditional or general topics occur throughout the epistle of James, but space does not permit us to discuss them here.

165 Cf. 1 Cor. 5: 2–5, 9, 11, 13.

166 Cf. *supra*, p. 71.

167 When the situation to which the *paraenesis* was addressed has ceased to be contemporary, the permanent value of the teaching can be preserved in a general paraenetic topic. Paul's situational teaching on food offered to idols has become generalised in Rom. 14: 15f., where it is simply part of a collection of wise sayings, almost certainly not the work of Paul: cf. J. C. O'Neill, *Romans*, pp. 220ff.

168 Cf. B. Gerhardsson, *M.M.*, p. 319. On the same theme, cf. C. H. Dodd, *Gospel and Law*, 1951, p. 49; W. D. Davies, *Paul and Rabbinic Judaism*, 1970, pp. 111ff. The New Testament debate on this subject is attended by considerable terminological and philosophical confusion, arising from the paradoxical nature of 'the command to love'. The basic point is that no-one can be commanded to have an emotion. If therefore an exegete stresses the notion of 'law' or 'command', he must then argue that *agape* is not so much an emotion, more a matter of will. But an important part of *agape* is that one does feel for others: cf. 'compassion'. It is the notion of 'law' or 'command' which must be modified. For Paul, the law of Christ operates not *qua* law but as a guide and criterion in relation to the situation, as an invitation to radical obedience to God, to radical openness to one's neighbour, and to a radical expression of *agape*.

169 J. Fletcher has focused attention on this issue in his books, *Situation Ethics*, 1966, and *Moral Responsibility*, 1967, as well as in other publications. He takes the view that there are only three approaches to making moral decisions: the legalistic, the antinomian and the situational (cf. *Situation Ethics*, p. 17); and he makes much of such New Testament material as corresponds to the last mentioned. His work, while stimulating, is open to criticism on several scores. For one thing, his selection of New Testament material is partial. The New Testament ethical procedures are much more varied than he allows: he tends to cite only what is convenient to his thesis. For another, he fails to analyse adequately the ethical criteria he uses to judge the rightness of action: e.g., consequences, motive, intrinsic rightness of action. (I acknowledge a debt here to helpful discussion with Ian C. M. Fairweather.)

170 A specific instance of the latter is found in 1 Cor. 16: 1–4. It follows the common opening formula: 'Now concerning the contribution for the saints' (16: 1). Instruction is given about systematic giving (v. 2) and about arrangements for the dispatch of the offerings to Jerusalem (v. 3f.). This particular topic moves at a purely practical level and no appeal is made here to any deeper theological principle: the latter is supplied in 2 Cor. 9, esp. 6–15.

171 Cf. Deut. 25: 4 (1 Cor. 9: 9); Matt. 10:10; Luke 10: 7 (1 Cor. 9: 14).

172 Cf. 1 Tim. 2 and 4 *passim*; 5: 23.

173 The 'two ways' section (Didache 1–5) differs so markedly from the second part as to suggest a different origin, perhaps a Jewish moral code on which

Barnabas drew; and this would be in line with an early date for the complete Didache (A.D. 60) suggested by J. P. Audet, *La didaché; instructions des apôtres*, 1958. This is in sharp distinction from the pessimistic view adopted by many English scholars: e.g., F. E. Vokes, *The Riddle of the Didache*, 1938, who detects Montanist influence in the second ('church order') part. This latter allegation is rightly rejected by C. C. Richardson, *Early Christian Fathers*, pp. 164f. who holds that this part 'was a late first century set of regulations about Church life', edited into the complete work about A.D. 150.

174 The Didache certainly shows traces of the growing institutionalisation and legalism in the church: cf. K. E. Kirk, *The Vision of God*, pp. 111-30. But, as in the case of prayer, the symbolism tends to redeem some of the apparent rigidity.

175 The tripartite division adopted by F. L. Cross, *1 Peter*, p. 9, seems completely arbitrary. He takes chs. 1-6 as the first part; 7-10 as 'a liturgical section'; the remainder as a 'church order'. But ch. 6 introduces the first of the topic forms which characterise the latter part of the work (cf. 6: 3), while ch. 14 is also 'liturgical'. Cross appears to have been influenced by a desire to find a liturgical manual of some kind. The sensible division would appear to be 1-5 and 6-16. The latter is entirely a church order which may originate about the time of the Pastorals.

176 Such extended figures have been described as standing 'between the Jewish and the Greek tradition': W. Straub, *Die Bildersprache des Apostels Paul*, 1937, cited in *T.D.N.T.* V, p. 760, n. 107.

177 For the full range of Pauline figures, cf. F. Hauck, *T.D.N.T.* V, p. 760.

178 Cf. the *Similitudes of Hermas*, esp. ch. 5.

179 E.g., the transmitted parable of the lost sheep is set by Matthew in the context of exhortation to church leaders to exercise faithful oversight of their flock (cf. Matt. 18: 14); and this kind of procedure – J. Jeremias calls it a shift of emphasis 'from the eschatological to the hortatory interpretation': *Parables*, p. 33 – could lead to some modification of the parables themselves: cf. Jeremias, *op. cit.*, pp. 31-6. In general, Matthew acts as the scribal interpreter of the parabolic tradition: cf. M. Goulder, *Midrash*, pp. 47-65.

180 For a discussion of the allegorisation of parable, cf. J. Jeremias, *Parables*, pp. 52-70; he takes 'the hellenistic environment', 'the Gentile mission', and 'the delay of the Parousia' as important factors in the process. Nevertheless, the ascription of the allegorising of this parable exclusively to early church interpreters is at least open to question: cf. C. F. D. Moule, 'Mark 4: 1-20 Yet Once More', *Neotestamentica et Semitica*, pp. 95-113.

181 Citing Ex. 33: 1-3, Barnabas explains: 'It is as if it had been said, "Put your trust in Jesus" ' (6: 10).

182 The allegorical can therefore be associated with the gnostic; its meaning is unfolded by him who possesses *gnosis*. Cf. Barnabas 6: 9; Hauck, *T.D.N.T.* V, p. 760.

183 Cf. E. Linnemann, *Parables*, p. 27; I. T. Ramsey, *Christian Discourse*, pp. 6f.

184 In the fourth gospel, Jesus speaks 'in parables', which in this context denotes hidden or abstruse discourse of the allegorical type; and this requires interpretation and understanding: cf. John 10: 6, where the reference is to the

'shepherd' discourse. Cf. also 16: 25 – 'I have said this to you in figures; the hour is coming when I will no longer speak to you in figures but tell you plainly of the Father' (i.e., at the *parousia*; but partly fulfilled at 16: 29).

185 Cf. Livy 2: 32, 8; Epictetus, *Dis.* 2: 10. 3; Dion. Hal. *Ant. Rom.* 3: 2. 5.

186 J. Daniélou, *Sacramentum futuri*, 1950, p. 4; cited by H. J. Schoeps, *Paul*, Eng. tr. 1961, p. 232.

187 H. J. Schoeps, *Paul*, p. 233. Cf. Philo and Qumran, but the former was concerned with the internal affairs of the soul. Paul also applies typology to Abraham (Rom. 4; Gal. 3: 16ff.) and the Passover (1 Cor. 5: 6–7). The close association of allegory and typology is illustrated by Gal. 4: 21–31. Cf. also Rom. 9–11.

188 Cf. Gal. 3: 23ff.; Phil. 3: 7; Rom. 12: 2.

189 Cf. Acts 15: 20, 29; 1 Thess. 4: 3, 5; 1 Pet. 1: 14f.; cf. P. Carrington, *Catechism*, pp. 16–21; E. G. Selwyn, *1 Peter*, pp. 369–75.

190 Cf. 1 Thess. 4: 7–12; 1 Pet. 1: 22.

191 Cf. P. Carrington, *Catechism*, pp. 32–7; E. G. Selwyn, *1 Peter*, pp. 386, 393–400; E. Kamlah, *Die Form*, pp. 34–8.

192 Cf. Odes of Solomon 7: 10; cf. 10: 10; 13: 2; 33: 10; Col. 3: 10; Eph. 4: 24; Gal. 3: 27.

193 E. G. Selwyn, *1 Peter*, p. 391, presents a Table on 'Baptism: its nature described', but with some exceptions (e.g., Rom. 6: 4) most passages refer to the conversion or the renewal of the individual rather than to the sacrament as such. Selwyn recognises four metaphors which describe such a change: rebirth, new creation, old man/new man, darkness/light (p. 392), but still persists with his hypothesis of a primitive baptismal catechism.

194 Cf. F. V. Filson, 'The Christian Teacher in the First Century', *J.B.L.* 60, 1941, p. 328.

195 For details, cf. E. G. Selwyn, *1 Peter*, pp. 376–82. For a detailed discussion of this motif in Ephesians, including parallels in Qumran texts and elsewhere, cf. J. Gnilka, 'Paränetische Traditionen im Epheserbrief', in *Mélanges B. Rigaux*, pp. 405ff.

196 E.g., Rom. 6: 6; Col. 3: 8ff.; Eph. 4: 22ff.; cf. Gal. 6: 15; 2 Cor. 5: 17.

197 It is incorporated with modifications in Barnabas – the ways of light and darkness – and is also known independently in a Latin translation. Cf. C. C. Richardson, *Early Christian Fathers*, p. 162.

198 Cf. K. E. Kirk, *The Vision of God*, p. 118.

199 E. Kamlah divides the catalogues into two types: (i) descriptive – 1 Cor. 6: 9f.; Gal. 5: 19–23; Rom. 1: 18–32; Rev. 21: 7f.; 22: 14f. and Matt. 5: 3–12; and (ii) those which operate within a paraenetic topic – 2 Cor. 6: 14 – 7: 1; 1 Cor. 5: 9–13; Rom. 13: 12ff.; and Col. 2: 20 – 3: 17; *Die Form*, pp. 11–34.

200 Also 1 Cor. 6: 9f.; Eph. 4: 31f. ('two ways'); 5: 3ff.; 1 Tim. 1: 9f.; 2 Tim. 3: 2ff. The catalogue thus occurs in genuine Pauline and pseudo-Pauline writings.

201 Cf. the parallel between 1 Cor. 6: 9f. and the 'vice' counters in a Roman gambling game, and that between Rom. 1: 29 and the confession of sin on the Day of Atonement.

202 Cf. K. E. Kirk, *The Vision of God*, p. 127.

203 It is unlikely that the gnostic form preceded the Christian: cf. R. McL. Wilson, *The Gnostic Problem*, 1958, pp. 176, 179; 'How Gnostic were the

Corinthians?' *N. T. S.* 19, 1972–73, pp. 65–74.

204 The balance and restraint which for the most part characterises the New Testament use of catalogues are not always preserved in the post-apostolic age, in which the prevailing legalistic formalism and the desire for dogmatic clarity at the expense of theological or ethical nicety found in the catalogue a useful instrument and means of expression. The 'way of death' set forth in the Didache as 'wicked and thoroughly blasphemous' is characterised by a catalogue of twenty-two vices very similar to Rom. 1: 29f. and, according to Rendel Harris, (*Teaching of the Apostles,* 1888, pp. 82–6), the sins confessed by the pious Jew on the Day of Atonement. Polycarp avails himself twice of catalogues of vices in his letter to the Philippians (2: 2; 4: 3), using the 'refraining from' type of introduction but hinting at a positive counterpart in both cases (2: 2f.; 4: 3a). Hermas has a whole array of catalogues, most of which, however, are well balanced: cf. *Mand.* 5: 2; 6: 2; 8: 3–5; *Sim.* 6: 5; 9: 15; cf. Aristeides, *Apol.* 15; Justin, *Apol.* 1: 14–17.

205 Col. 3: 18 – 4: 1; Eph. 5: 21 – 6: 9; 1 Pet. 2: 11 – 3: 7; cf. Titus 2: 1–10; 1 Tim. 2: 1–15; 5: 1–5, 17ff.; 6: 1f. They do not occur in the earlier and more authentic Pauline epistles. In early Christian literature, cf. Didache 4: 9ff.; Barnabas 19: 5, 7; 1 Clem. 1: 3; 21: 6–9; 38: 2; Ignatius, *Pol.* 4: 1 – 6: 1; Polycarp, *Phil.* 4: 2 – 6: 3.

206 *Vid. supra,* pp. 72f.

207 E.g., its relative independence of its context, its relatively concrete emphasis, its briefer exhortations, the concentration of *hapax legomena* in it, and the formal nature of its general *paraenesis*: cf. J. E. Crouch, *Colossian Haustafel,* pp. 10f.

208 Cf. the 'cosmological ecclesiology' of Eph. 1: 22f.

209 Frequently rendered, 'to every (fundamental) human (or social) institution'; i.e., state, household, family: cf. R.S.V., N.E.B. It has also been rendered 'to every institution ordained for men' (Hort; R.S.V. marg.). Such renderings are difficult to parallel. *Ktisis* means 'creation' or 'creature', thus giving the sense 'to every man' (Cranfield), 'to every human creature' (Kelly), 'to men of every sort' (Foerster) and introducing the whole passage: cf. W. Foerster, *T.D.N.T.* III, pp. 1034f.; C. B. E. Cranfield, *I Peter,* 1950, p. 57; J. N. D. Kelly, *The Epistles of Peter and of Jude,* 1969, pp. 108f.; E. Best, *I Peter,* 1971, p. 113f. It must be admitted that 1 Peter seems to take us to the brink of that total submission to the divinely ordained civil powers set out so uncompromisingly in Rom. 13: 1–7, where it probably reflects Stoic influence: *vid. supra,* p. 73. But cf. also Is. 5: 25–30; 45: 1; Dan. 2: 21, 37f.; 4: 17, 32; Wisd. 6: 3.

210 *Vid. supra,* pp. 70f. In 1 Tim. 2: 1–7 the *Haustafel* motif, though distinguishable, has given place to the church's ministry of prayer and intercession in an ecclesiastical *topos* with an evangelical concern. Titus 2: 1–10 is another ecclesiastical *topos* which subdivides the church group into 'older men', 'older women', 'young women', 'younger men', 'slaves' – and also 'yourself': Titus receives a personal admonition (v. 7) concerning his ministry (cf. 1 Pet. 5: 1–4; 1 Thess. 5: 12; Heb. 13: 7, 17. Cf. also the description of the bishop in 1 Tim. 3; Titus 1: 7ff.; relevant passages also occur in Clem. *Rom.* 1: 3; 21: 6). There may well be a sociological nuance in some of these divisions; the 'young men' of the hellenistic gymnasia were a recognised social group

(cf. 1 John 2:13f.). But, particularly in view of the personal admonition to Titus, it appears that the writer has simply identified what he considers to be significant age and status patterns in the Christian community.

211   J. E. Crouch, *Colossian Haustafel*, pp. 150f.

212   Cf. my discussion above of the farewell discourse in the Greek tradition (pp. 73f.) and in the Jewish (pp. 79f.).

213   The overtones of *propheteia* at the behest of the Spirit are noteworthy (Acts 20: 22f., 28).

214   There are eschatological implications here, as there are in the apostle's death which heralds the day of antichrist, characterised by false teaching and heresies (cf. the Pastorals).

215   On the death of the apostle, cf. 2 Tim. 4: 6ff.; his ministry, cf. 1 Tim. 1: 12–17; maintaining the tradition, cf. 1 Tim. 6: 20; false teachers, cf. 2 Tim. 3: 1–9; perseverance in following the apostle's example, cf. 2 Tim. 3: 10f., 14.

216   J. Munck, 'Discours d'adieu', p. 163.

217   Lit. 'my exodus': cf. v. 14 'the putting off of my tent'.

218   Cf. J. Munck, 'Discours d'adieu', pp. 163f.

219   Cf. Rom. 2: 18; 1 Cor. 14: 19; Gal. 6: 6 (= *didaskaloi* of 1 Cor. 12: 28; Eph. 4: 11); 2 Clem. 17: 1.

220   Cf. J. N. D. Kelly, *Early Christian Creeds*, 1950, pp. 40–52.

221   Cf. the 'two ways' material in Didache 1–6, teaching on the sacraments (7–10), and on eschatological matters, incl. prophecy (11–16); also Barnabas, *passim*; Irenaeus, *Adv. Haer.* 1: 19; Justin, *Apol.* 1: 61. On the whole subject, cf. J. Daniélou, *La catéchèse aux premiers siècles*, 1968, pp. 27ff.

222   Trinitarian formulae appear before long and have implications for *catechesis*: cf. Matt. 28: 19; Didache 7; Justin, *Apol.* 1: 61; Hippolytus, *Apostolic Tradition* 21.

223   Equally, catalogues of virtues and vices and the *Haustafeln* provided guidance for recent converts, as did topics of a general or specific nature. But in making this observation, one has practically said that almost all *paraenesis* was relevant to catechetical instruction.

224   Esp. in the western text: cf. O. Cullmann, *The Earliest Christian Confessions*, Eng. tr., 1949, p. 19f.

225   Cf. O. Piper, *J.B.L.* 64, p. 442. The style of 1 John lends itself at points to catechetical adaptation: e.g., 4: 13.

226   Cf. art. *catechesis I (early Christian), N.C.E.*, *in loc.*

227   Cf. *supra*, pp. 90ff., where traditional or basic *paraenesis* was seen to be of this character.

228   We must beware of regarding these abstractions or doctrinal propositions as themselves objective Truth unsullied by contagion with the human situation; as tends to be done, for example, by T. F. Torrance, *The School of Faith*, 1959, esp. pp. xxi–xxxi. As human statements, they bear witness to the Truth, which in a sense becomes Truth for a man only in the objectivity-subjectivity of address and response, encounter and commitment.

229   Also important in basic instruction is the acquisition of certain skills, such as the interpretation of scripture. Here homiletics in practice can also give guidance. There must be, however, a certain openness about the procedure – an openness to God, to the Spirit. Indoctrination into a closed system can

inhibit rather than assist the exploration of scriptural truth, since any
answer is predetermined by the conditioning.

Chapter 4. *Paradosis*

1 Plato, *Protagoras* 325e.
2 Xenophon, *Symposium* 3: 5.
3 Cf. Plato, *Republic* 607b.
4 Plato, *Philebus* 16c.
5 Cf. Critias, 113b, where the speaker carefully identifies the source of his
tradition.
6 Cf. R. O. P. Taylor, *The Groundwork of the Gospels*, 1946, p. 76. The
source material is collected in Spengel, *Rhetores Graeci*. Cf. M. Dibelius,
pp. 152–64.
7 R. O. P. Taylor, *Groundwork*, p. 85.
8 *Ibid.*, p. 87.
9 Cf. Diodorus Siculus, 5: 48.4, tr. C. H. Oldfather (Loeb).
10 B. Gerhardsson, *M.M.*, p. 19.
11 Cf. G. F. Moore, *Judaism* I, p. 251. For a discussion of the tradition about
the slaughtering of sacrificial animals, cf. M. Gaster, *The Samaritans*
(Schweich Lectures, 1923), 1925, pp. 69ff. There was apparently in the
Greek period a written record of this tradition, a book of *gezerot*, the
abolition of which Pharisaic-rabbinic Judaism celebrated.
12 E.g., in relation to the Day of Atonement, the directions in Lev. 16 are
wholly inadequate: it was priestly tradition which prescribed the appropriate priestly actions: cf. B. Gerhardsson, *M.M.*, pp. 251f.
13 Cf. J. Macdonald, *The Theology of the Samaritans*, 1964, p. 283; M. Gaster,
The Samaritans, p. 65.
14 Cf. M. Gaster, *The Samaritans*, pp. 69ff.
15 *Ibid.*, p. 66.
16 For a discussion of *pesher* in the Qumran community, *vid. supra*, Chapter 2.
17 For the affinities between Qumran and the Samaritans, cf. J. Macdonald,
Samaritans, p. 33.
18 Cf. M. Smith, 'A Comparison of Early Christian and Early Rabbinic Tradition', *J.B.L.* 82, 1963, pp. 169f. For B. Gerhardsson's reply, cf. *T.T.*, pp.
13ff.
19 *Vid. supra*, Chapter 2, pp. 43–6. Other important terms are *talmud*, complementary exposition; *gemara*, the fixed commentary complementary to
talmud; and *sebara*, the appreciation of doctrinal meaning.
20 Cf. the distinction implied in 'scribes and Pharisees' in the N.T.: cf. B.
Gerhardsson, *T.T.*, p. 21.
21 B. Gerhardsson, *T.T.*, p. 17; cf. *M.M.*, pp. 122–70.
22 B. Gerhardsson, *M.M.*, p. 93.
23 Cf. R. Bultmann, *H.S.T.*, p. 18.
24 Cf. Jos. *Ant.* 10: 51; cf. 13: 297, 409, and Philo, *Spec. Leg.* 4: 150.
25 The form of the text is probably derived from the Septuagint and therefore
from church teaching, but Taylor argues that the same point might well
have been established from the Hebrew text: V. Taylor, *Mark*, pp. 337f.
26 V. Taylor, *Mark*, p. 334.
27 Mark adds an appendix consisting of similar kinds of sayings, the hub of

which, v. 15, 'could belong to the oldest tradition' (cf. R. Bultmann, *H.S.T.*, p. 17) and 'is unquestionably genuine' (cf. V. Taylor, *Mark*, p. 342). Taylor notes that it states the basic principle, adopts as its form Semitic antithetical parallelism and is calculated to provoke thought by means of its parabolic nature. Matthew reports the offence taken by the Pharisees and Jesus' reply, which shows once again his rejection of the Pharisaic tradition as it was then held to operate (Matt. 15:12ff.). The form of the later verses (Mark 7:18b-23; Matt. 15:16-20) is conventional in Jewish and Greek *paraenesis* and adds little to the passage as a whole apart from underlining the notion that Jesus taught the disciples as a separate group – an inevitable implication, one would think, of having a disciples' group at all.

28 Cf. B. Gerhardsson, *M.M.*, p. 201.

29 Cf. B. Gerhardsson, *T.T.*, p. 25.

30 A. N. Wilder, 'Form History and the Oldest Tradition', in *Neotestamentica et Patristica*, 1962, p. 8.

31 M. Smith, *J.B.L.* 82, p. 176.

32 B. Gerhardsson, *T.T.*, p. 31. The reference in the last line is, of course, to E. Stauffer, *Die Botschaft Jesu damals und heute*, 1959, p. 10.

33 For a discussion of the tradition of the Lord's Prayer, cf. E. Lohmeyer, *The Lord's Prayer*, Eng. tr., 1965, esp. pp. 27f.; T. W. Manson, 'The Lord's Prayer', *B.J.R.L.* 38, 1955-56, pp. 99-113, 436-48; C. F. Evans, *The Lord's Prayer*, 1963, esp. p. 15; M. D. Goulder, *Midrash*, pp. 300f.; 'The Composition of the Lord's Prayer', *J.T.S.* 14 (N.S.1), 1963, pp. 32ff.

34 Mark 6:8-11; cf. Matt. 10:5-16; Luke 10:2-12. Bultmann encounters his familiar *formgeschichtliche* cul de sac in commenting on this passage: *H.S.T.*, p. 145. Apparently, any missionary charge must have emanated exclusively from the risen Lord. Yet behind the gospel redactions there stands the possibility of a phenomenologically appropriate prophetic mission on the part of the disciples in Jesus' lifetime.

35 Cf. Matt. 10:12-15; Luke 10:10ff.; Mark 6:11.

36 Cf. Mark 4:10 par.; 7:17; Matt. 15:15.

37 John 2:22; 12:16; 14:26; cf. Luke 24:25ff., 44-47.

38 Cf. B. Lindars, *N.T. Apologetic*, esp. pp. 32-74, 251-86.

39 Cf. J. Knox, *The Church and Christ*, esp. pp. 38-60.

40 Cf. H. Riesenfeld, *The Gospel Tradition and its Beginnings*, 1957, p. 22; B. Gerhardsson, *M.M.*, p. 244.

41 Cf. N. Perrin, *Rediscovering the Teaching of Jesus*, pp. 102-8.

42 Cf. H. Conzelmann, *The Theology of Luke*, 1960; E. Haenchen, *Acts of the Apostles*, 1971.

43 B. Gerhardsson, *M.M.*, p. 209.

44 *Ibid.*, p. 210.

45 *Ibid.*, p. 219.

46 Cf. Mark 16:7 and the Galilean hypotheses advanced by Lohmeyer, Lightfoot, Elliott-Binns and more recently Marxsen: *vid. infra*, n. 62.

47 B. Gerhardsson, *M.M.*, p. 217.

48 Cf. Is. 29:3; Ezek. 4:2; Ps. 137:9.

49 For a detailed critique of Gerhardsson's estimate of Jerusalem, cf. W. D. Davies, *S.S.M.*, pp. 469-72.

50 Cf. Gal. 1:11-17; 1 Cor. 9:1f.; 2 Cor. 12:12. W. D. Davies questions the

assumed consistency of Luke: the fact that he refers to apostles other than the Twelve (Acts 14: 4, 14) cannot simply be brushed aside: *S.S.M.*, p. 472.

51 Indeed, it may well be asked whether the Twelve could possibly qualify if Acts 1: 21f. is taken literally. The calling of the disciples was subsequent to Jesus' baptism, although some of them may have known at first hand of his association with John (cf. John 1: 35-42). The formula of Acts 1: 21f. appears to be notional or theological.

52 M. Smith, *J.B.L.* 82, p. 171. Curiously, Davies tends to minimise the significance of this fact: *S.S.M.*, p. 473.

53 It is a weakness of Davies' discussion of the Twelve that he cites Paul's attitude to 'the pillars' apparently as support for the authoritative position of the Twelve, whereas, in fact, the composition of 'the pillars' militates against the centrality of the Twelve: *S.S.M.*, pp. 472f.

54 Cf. R. A. Lipsius, *Acts of the Apostles (Apocryphal)*, *D.C.B.*, *in loc.* Cf. *A.N.C.L.* IX ii. 130ff. J. Foster, *After the Apostles*, 1951, p. 23, n. 37.

55 Cf. Justin, *Apol.* 1: 39; *Dial. with Trypho* 42.

56 But the Twelve may well have some importance for the transmission of *certain* traditions: *vid. infra.*

57 F. G. Downing, *The Church and Jesus*, 1968, p. 128; cf. *ibid.*, p. 42.

58 *Ibid.*, p. 128.

59 For the suggestion that 'Hebrews' spoke Aramaic or some other Semitic language, with possibly some additional knowledge of Greek, while the 'Hellenists' were primarily Greek speaking and non-Semitic in language, cf. C. F. D. Moule, 'Once More, Who were the Hellenists?' *Exp. T.* 70, 1959, pp. 100ff. But the cleavage appears to concern their respective attitudes to the Torah. The Torah-centred Christianity of the 'Hebrews' receives expression in the epistle of James. The paraenetic units focus upon or reflect the constant study of the scriptures (i.e., the Old Testament) and the development of a distinctive *pesher* tradition (cf. James 2: 18-26) incorporated in what are probably homiletic summaries (2: 14-26; 5: 7-11, 13-18). The basis on which this tradition operates is the recognition that Jesus is Lord and Christ (1: 1) and will come soon as Judge (5: 7, 9). For the authoritative, messianic interpretation of scripture, cf. 5: 12 (cf. Matt. 5: 37) and possibly 5: 17 (a reflection of Luke 4: 25?); it may also be detected at many points of the epistle. Jerusalem would prize the tradition which showed Jesus as the true teacher of the Torah (e.g., Matt. 5: 17 – 6: 18). These include the distinctive interpretation of the Mosaic law and the right attitude to worship (including temple worship: Matt. 5: 23), detachment from the world and undivided loyalty to and dependence upon God (Matt. 6: 19 – 7: 27), together with a strong emphasis on the practical expression of faith in life (Matt. 7: 21-27; cf. 25: 31-46). Such traditions were, of course, shared with the hellenistic churches; and it may well have been in a hellenistic milieu that 'Matthew' edited the traditions to produce the Sermon on the Mount as the messianic law prefaced by the beatitudes as the 'new commandments': cf. K. Stendahl, who compares it with the Qumranic Manual of Discipline: *School of St Matthew*; also *Peake*, 1962, pp. 775f.; W. D. Davies, *S.S.M.*, pp. 187ff. Luke also finds the material in currency in his churches but edits it in a different way.

60 Cf. the portrayal of Stephen in Acts, and esp. the charges brought against

him: Acts 6: 11, 13f.

61 Cf. C. H. H. Scobie, 'The Origin and Development of Samaritan Christianity', *N.T.S.* 19, 1973, pp. 401-9.

62 Cf. L. E. Elliott-Binns, *Galilean Christianity*, 1956, esp. pp. 43ff.; E. Lohmeyer, *Galiläa und Jerusalem*, 1936; R. H. Lightfoot, *Locality and Doctrine in the Gospels*, 1938. W. Marxsen, *Der Evangelist Markus*, pp. 33ff. finds the church in Galilee to be the *Sitz im Leben* of Mark's Galilean material. W. Schmithals, who states: 'Not Jerusalem but Galilee is the home of Christianity' (*Paul and James*, p. 33), goes on to stress the significance of Galilee as the centre of Christian mission.

63 The prominence given to Alexandria has suggested to some that Apollos' teaching was coloured by the allegorism of that city: cf. F. J. Foakes-Jackson, *Acts*, 1931, p. 174; to others that he was the writer of the epistle to the Hebrews (Luther; more recently, T. W. Manson, 'The Problem of the Epistle to the Hebrews', *B.J.R.L.* 32, 1949, pp. 1ff.). F. F. Bruce tentatively suggests a Galilean origin for his message: *Acts*, p. 382. Haenchen concludes that he was 'a missionary quite independent in his work and thought, whom Paul faced with considerable reserve': *Acts*, p. 556. The evidence of Acts 18: 24 – 19: 7 suggests an eschatological preacher of repentance in the tradition of John, possibly influenced also by the early teaching of Jesus. Luke's purpose is to induct him completely into apostolic Christianity.

64 Cf. B. Gerhardsson, *M.M.*, p. 251.

65 Manual of Discipline, 4: 8ff.

66 The church had perhaps received a considerable influx from these quarters in the period immediately before A.D. 70: cf. M. Smith, *J.B.L.* 82, pp. 175f.; P. Benoit, 'Qumran et le Nouveau Testament', *N.T.S.* 7, 1961, pp. 279ff.

67 It is a confident conclusion of the form critics that the passion narratives circulated as continuous entities from an early date though there is no unanimity as to their extent: cf. K. L. Schmidt, *Der Rahmen der Geschichte Jesu*, 1919, pp. 305ff.; M. Dibelius, *Tradition*, pp. 178ff.; R. Bultmann, *H.S.T.*, pp. 262ff.; V. Taylor, *F.G.T.*, pp. 44-62.

68 Antioch springs to mind at once as the centre of the wider mission (Acts 13: 1ff.). For what it is worth, Mark had connections there, although he was Jerusalem based (13: 13). Like Peter, he was a 'Hebrew' with close connections with the hellenistic mission.

69 E.g., further stories about Judas (Matt. 26: 14ff.; 27: 3-10) and Pilate (27: 19, 24f.); the earthquake and resurrection of the just (27: 51ff.).

70 Cf. H. Conzelmann, *Luke*, pp. 18-94.

71 Cf. V. Taylor, *Behind the Third Gospel*, 1926, pp. 33-75; cf. *F.G.T.*, pp. 51f.

72 Cf. J. A. T. Robinson, *N.T. Studies*, pp. 96ff.

73 Cf. V. Taylor, *F.G.T.*, pp. 53f., who notes affinities with Luke and opts for a hellenistic base; J. A. T. Robinson, *N.T. Studies*, pp. 98f., argues for a background in southern Palestine (although the gospel was published in a very different milieu); C. H. H. Scobie, *N.T.S.* 19, pp. 401-9, reviews the debate about the Samaritan affinities of the fourth gospel and takes it to be the product of the Galilean and Samaritan Christian communities which stood in a direct line with the Stephen–Philip mission.

74 Cf. Paul's interpretation of the Lord's supper, the Passion narrative in the fourth gospel in particular, and Melito's *Paschal Homily*. For a study of the

liturgical basis of Matthew, cf. M. Goulder, *Midrash.*

75 Much confusion attends the usual *formgeschichtliche* type statements of this point: cf. G. Bornkamm, *Jesus of Nazareth*, p. 25; M. Kähler, 'The so-called Hiṣtorical Jesus', pp. 60ff.; H. Zahrnt, *The Historical Jesus*, Eng. tr., 1963, p. 77. What should be stressed is the *qualitative*, not the *quantitative* aspect. The gospel, undiluted and unqualified, confronts us in each pericope.

76 Cf. W. C. van Unnik, *Tarsus or Jerusalem*, 1962, pp. 17–45, esp. pp. 44f.

77 This 'writing off' has an interesting parallel in the Talmud (b. Bab. Mes. 85a) where R. Zeira is said to have fasted 100 days in order to forget the Babylonian Talmud and prepare to learn the Palestinian Talmud instead: cf. B. Gerhardsson, *M. M.*, p. 168, n. 5.

78 O. Cullmann, *The Early Church*, p. 63.

79 Cf. A. Seeberg, *Der Katechismus*, pp. 43–58; A. M. Hunter, *Paul and his Predecessors*, pp. 15–18.

80 Cf. U. Wilckens, 'The Tradition-History of the Resurrection of Jesus', in *S. M. R.*, Moule (ed.), Eng. tr., 1968, p. 57.

81 Cf. H. Conzelmann, 'Zur Analyse der Bekenntnisformel 1 Kor. 15: 3–5', *Ev. Th.* 25, 1965, pp. 1–11.

82 Cf. G. Delling, 'The Significance of the Resurrection of Jesus for Faith in Jesus Christ', in *S. M. R.*, pp. 78f. Delling rightly stresses v. 11 as indicating that 1 Cor. 15: 3ff. represents a formula universally accepted in the church – not least in Jerusalem. This does not mean that the entire formula originated in Jerusalem. In Gal. 1: 18 Paul refers to a conference with Peter, not a two-week crash course in basic Christianity! *Contra*, B. Gerhardsson, *M. M.*, pp. 297ff. Despite G. D. Kilpatrick's case for taking *historēsai Kēphan* as 'to get information from Cephas' (*N. T. Essays*, Higgins (ed.), 1959, pp. 144f.), the meaning is not certain: cf. N.E.B.: 'to get to know Cephas'.

83 J. Jeremias, *The Eucharistic Words of Jesus*, Eng. tr., 1966, pp. 101ff. supported the view that traces of Aramaic forms point to a Jerusalem origin, but Aramaisms are notoriously difficult to detect with complete assurance and in any case permit only the most general conclusions to be drawn as to place of origin: the Syrian Christians, for example, were no doubt bilingual: cf. H. Conzelmann, *Ev. Th.* 25, pp. 5f. B. Gerhardsson pours scorn on attempts to refer the basic formula to the hellenistic church, but his difficulty arises from the fact that he assumes an apostolic college dwelling in remote isolation in Jerusalem. When this chimera has been removed, the hellenistic church is seen also to have apostolic leadership and counsel.

84 The model of 'the Messiah who died' would have been insupportable in a Jewish context without scriptural argument or 'proof': cf. Acts 17: 3 once again. There is no case for taking *kata tas graphas* with the preceding phrase: cf. M. D. Hooker, *Jesus and the Servant*, p. 119. 'The affirmation of expiation has its own weight and needs no further legitimation': F. Hahn, *Titles of Jesus*, p. 178. It is also unlikely that one prepositional phrase is qualified by another: *ibid.*, p. 216, n. 339.

85 Cf. G. F. Moore, *Judaism* I, pp. 547ff.; 2 Macc. 7: 32f., 37f.: 4 Macc. 6: 27ff.; cf. 17: 20ff. 'Here the sufferings and death of the righteous martyrs

are a vicarious expiation for the sins of their people': Moore, *op. cit.*, p. 549; cf. E. Lohse, *Märtyrer und Gottesknecht*, 1955, pp. 38ff., 78ff.

86   Cf. Rom. 3: 24f.; 4: 25; R. Bultmann, *Theology of the N.T.* I, p. 46.

87   It was apparently at a relatively late stage that a connection was made with the notion of vicarious suffering in Is. 53. Among those who accept the identification as pre-Pauline are J. Jeremias, *T.D.N.T.* V, p. 706; *Eucharistic Words of Jesus*, pp. 225–30; L. S. Thornton, 'The Body of Christ in the New Testament', in *The Apostolic Ministry*, Kirk (ed.), 1946, p. 71; cf. V. Taylor, 'The Origin of the Markan Passion-Sayings', *N.T.S.* 1, 1955, p. 161. The case against the identification of 1 Cor. 15: 3 and Is. 53 has been strongly presented by M. D. Hooker, *Jesus and the Servant*, pp. 117–20; with greater caution by F. Hahn, *Titles of Jesus*, pp. 55ff., 177f.; cf. also C. K. Barrett, *Commentary on 1 Corinthians*, pp. 338f.

88   I.e., 'according to the scriptures' is to be linked formally with 'was raised'; cf. F. Hahn, *Titles of Jesus*, p. 180. The reference to burial underlines the finality of the death. The appearance to Peter confirms God's action in raising Jesus. It also stamps vv. 3–5 as Petrine tradition.

89   U. Wilckens, 'Die Ursprung der Überlieferung der Erscheinungen der Auferstandenen', in *Dogma und Denkstrukturen*, Joest and Pannenberg (edd.), 1963, p. 74; also 'Tradition-History', pp. 59f.

90   E.g., that neither Paul nor the Hellenists knew anything about the tradition concerning Jesus. This view is, in fact, an *argumentum e silentio*: cf. G. Delling, 'Significance', p. 82. It also denies a major aspect of the role of the Twelve.

91   *Contra* W. Marxsen, *The Resurrection of Jesus of Nazareth*, Eng. tr., 1970, pp. 90ff. Even if they accepted beforehand that Jesus had appeared to Peter, his subsequent appearance to them has a validity of its own. To argue about the point at which they first believed in the resurrection of Jesus is unnecessarily pedantic.

92   This remains true even if we accept Marxsen's contention that the Twelve is a post-Easter grouping: *Resurrection of Jesus*, pp. 92f. They witnessed to what they had experienced: hence the importance of the appearance of Jesus to all of them.

93   J. D. G. Dunn, *Jesus and the Spirit*, pp. 143f.

94   Cf. E. von Dobschütz, *Ostern und Pfingsten*, 1903, pp. 31–43, and many commentators since, incl. C. K. Barrett, *A Commentary on the First Epistle to the Corinthians*, 1968, pp. 342f. The different presentations of Paul and Acts may be accounted for by contrasting views of apostleship, the highly schematised view of the resurrection–ascension period in Acts, and the close association which obtains in any case between the risen Christ and the giving of the Spirit (cf. John 20: 22).

95   Cf. J. D. G. Dunn, *Jesus and the Spirit*, pp. 144ff., who argues strongly against von Dobschütz but finally admits that 'the gift of the Spirit was not something quite so distinct and separate from the resurrection appearances as Luke implies'.

96   It might be associated with a resurrection appearance in Galilee, but no specific links are evident.

97   How significant is the figure Paul mentions? Does it mean any more than 'hundreds of people'? They are called 'brethren', not 'apostles'; hence the

appearances are not thought of by Paul exclusively in terms of the legitimation of apostleship. They also served as witness to the resurrection: an important point for Paul's argument in 1 Cor. 15.

98 O. Glombitza, 'Gnade – das entscheidende Wort', *Nov. T.* II, 1958, pp. 285f. takes 'fallen asleep' to mean that some apostles have given up their mission, but the phrase is a common euphemism for death: cf. C. K. Barrett, *1 Corinthians.*

99 For a discussion of the word *ektrōma*, cf. J. Schneider, *T.D.N.T.* II, p. 465f.; O. Glombitza, *Nov. T.* II, p. 287; J. Munck, 'Paulus Tamquam Abortivus' (1 Cor. 15: 8), in *N.T. Essays,* Higgins (ed.), pp. 182–7; C. K. Barrett, *1 Corinthians*, p. 344; J. D. G. Dunn, *Jesus and the Spirit*, pp. 101f.

100 J. Héring believes that the shared tradition consists of vv. 3 and 4: '15:3–4 may be identified with the "euangelion" (comparable to the Mishnah) and 15: 5–8 with the Pauline "logos" (as it were the Gemara)': *The First Epistle of Saint Paul to the Corinthians*, Eng. tr., 1962, p. 158. J. Jeremias includes v. 5 in it: *Eucharistic Words of Jesus*, pp. 101ff. The analysis given above suggests that 'he appeared to Peter' belonged to the common formula: cf. 'The Lord has risen indeed, and has appeared to Simon' (Luke 24: 34); and also that Paul combined this with another hellenistic Christian formula, 'he appeared to Peter, then to the twelve'. But the evidence of the gospels suggests that the priority of Peter's experience was not given equal weight in all the hellenistic churches.

101 Cf. C. K. Barrett, *1 Corinthians*, pp. 336f. *Contra* J. Héring, in the note above: the whole *paradosis* is Pauline *logos* (v. 1). But Héring's discussion of 15: 1–2 is valuable: *1 Corinthians*, pp. 157f.

102 The resemblance of this logion to Matt. 24: 30 or John 6: 39f. is too slight to carry conviction. The argument for the *agraphon* is fully worked out by J. Jeremias, *The Unknown Sayings of Jesus*, Eng. tr., (2nd ed.) 1964, pp. 80–3. He concedes that the saying has been amended by Paul in at least three places: 'the Lord himself', 'in Christ' and 'we' (v. 17). Probably then, 'the point only of the word of the historical Jesus is given, not the word itself': J. E. Frame, *I.C.C.*, 1912, p. 171.

103 Cf. M. Dibelius, *An die Thessalonicher I, II* (*H.N.T.*), 1925, p. 22.

104 Cf. B. Rigaux, *Saint Paul: Les Épîtres aux Thessaloniciens*, 1956, pp. 538f.: cf. also H. Anderson, *The Gospel of Mark*, 1976, p. 290.

105 Cf. J. G. Davies, 'The Genesis of Belief in an imminent Parousia', *J.T.S.* 14 (N.S. 1), 1963, pp. 104–7; E. Best, *Commentary on 1 Thessalonians*, 1972, pp. 189–93; J. D. G. Dunn, *Jesus and the Spirit*, p. 230.

106 B. Rigaux discusses the possibility: *op. cit.*, p. 538. Relevant passages include 2 Cor. 12: 1ff.; 13: 1; Gal. 1: 12; 2: 2; Eph. 3: 3; Acts 18: 9ff.; 20: 23; 21: 10f.; 27: 23; cf. 1 Cor. 15: 51. 'Paul aurait demandé dans la prière si les vivants devanceront les morts à la parousie, et le Seigneur lui aurait répondu "non" ' (Rigaux, p. 538).

107 Many commentators are excusably cautious, but an excess of caution is somewhat negative and unhelpful: e.g., A. L. Moore, *1 and 2 Thessalonians*, 1969, p. 69.

108 Cf. G. Kittel, *T.D.N.T.* IV, pp. 105f.; W. Foerster, *T.D.N.T.* III, pp. 1092f.

109 Cf. Micah 1: 3; Joel 2: 1; Ex. 19: 16ff.; Zech. 14: 5; Dan. 12: 2; Is. 26: 19a; 27: 12b, 13a. The 'peshering' of Daniel is perhaps most important.

110   Broadly speaking, Dan. 2: 31–45; 7: 7–27; 8: 9–26; 9: 24–27 and 11: 21 –
       12: 4 (13) correspond to Mark 13: 6–8, 12–16, 19–22 and 24–27; cf. L.
       Hartman, *Prophecy*, pp. 235ff.
111   Cf. Mark 13: 3f., where the reference is to the situation of the disciples;
       T. W. Manson, *Teaching*, pp. 17ff.
112   L. Hartman, *Prophecy*, p. 236.
113   Cf. L. Hartman, *Prophecy*, pp. 199f., 235.
114   Jesus may be connected to this realm of discourse in three ways: by his
       own 'peshering' of the scriptures (Daniel in particular) and the symbolism
       he derived from that source; by the 'secret' teaching which he gave the
       intimate circle of disciples (cf. Mark 13: 3); and by his explicit teaching on
       persecution (Matt. 5: 11f., 44; 23: 34 etc.).
115   *Vid. supra,* Chapter 1, pp. 16f., 35ff.
116   D. L. Dungan makes something of a meal of this problem – if the expression
       is not infelicitous! '. . . no sooner has Paul referred to this command of the
       Lord than he asserts in the most unequivocal language that he does not and
       will not obey it': *Sayings of Jesus*, p. 3. The sense in which 'commanded' is
       to be understood is discussed below. It has been suggested that one reason
       for Paul's attitude was that the Corinthians had not offered him financial
       support: cf. J. C. Hurd, *The Origin of 1 Corinthians*, 1965, pp. 203ff. There
       was clearly some problem at Corinth connected with Paul's handling of
       money: cf. 2 Cor. 12: 16ff.; 8: 20f.
117   An apostle teaches by his example: 1 Thess. 1: 6; 2 Thess. 3: 7, 9; cf. 1 Pet.
       2: 12: B. Gerhardsson, *M.M.*, pp. 185ff. The example-for-imitation set by
       Paul in 1 Cor. 9 is neither to take nor to refuse payment for ministry (and
       here only the apostolic ministry of Paul and Barnabas is under discussion)
       but to further the gospel.
118   B. Gerhardsson has indicated rabbinic parallels: *M.M.*, pp. 185ff., 318f.
119   F. W. Grosheide, *Commentary on 1 Corinthians*, 1953, p. 208; cf. B.
       Gerhardsson, *M.M.*, p. 318.
120   '. . . the labourer deserves his wages': cf. Matt. 10: 10. Commentators who
       relate 1 Cor. 9: 14 more or less directly to Luke 10: 7 include J. Moffatt,
       1938, p. 120; C. T. Craig, *Int. Bib.* X, 1953, p. 102; F. F. Bruce, 1971, p.
       85; J. Héring, 1962, connects it with Matt. 10: 10 (p. 80).
121   Cf. Luke 9: 1–5; 10: 1–12.
122   Cf. H. Conzelmann, *Theology of St Luke*, pp. 213f.
123   D. L. Dungan, *Sayings of Jesus*, p. 71.
124   *Misthou* probably does not refer here to salary but to hospitality: cf.
       'remain in the same house, eating and drinking what they provide . . . do
       not go from house to house' (Luke 10: 7) '. . . eat what is set before you'
       (v. 8).
125   The precise status of this quotation is hard to determine. If the Pastorals
       are given a relatively late date, Luke 10: 7 could be regarded as scripture,
       as some have done without worrying unduly about the dating: cf. E. K.
       Simpson, *The Pastoral Epistles*, 1954, p. 78. Or Jesus might be said to be
       using an Old Testament *apocryphon*, which is loosely described as scripture
       (it is not ascribed to Jesus in 1 Tim. 5: 17). Again, Deut. 25: 4 may alone
       be scripture; the second saying merely interprets it: cf. M. Dibelius and H.
       Conzelmann, *The Pastoral Epistles*, Eng. tr., 1972, p. 78f. It is possible, of

course, that the logion is purely proverbial. Similar sentiments, but not
identical forms, occur in Eur. *Rhesus* 191; Phocylides, *Fragm.* 17; cf.
C. Spicq, *Les Épîtres Pastorales* I, 1969, p. 543.

126   Cf. A. T. Hanson, *Studies in the Pastoral Epistles*, 1968, p. 112.

127   I.e., a church tradition concerning the maintenance of the ministry, not a
       collection of the logia of Jesus (*contra* D. Guthrie, *The Pastoral Epistles*,
       1957, pp. 105f.). That is why the same Old Testament quotation is used,
       and used in the same way, i.e., allegorically: cf. H. L. Strack and Billerbeck,
       Kommentar z. N.T. III, pp. 382–4. It is not the practice of the writer of 1
       Tim. to cite scripture except as part of a traditional hermeneutic.

128   D. Daube probably presses too far the notion that Paul was an innovator
       in his argument in favour of 'teaching for money': *N.T. and Rabbinic
       Judaism*, pp. 394ff.; cf. D. L. Dungan, *Sayings of Jesus*, p. 10, n. 1. Paul
       was recognising both the practice and its hermeneutical basis, although
       his own practice differed.

129   For a full discussion, cf. D. L. Dungan, *Sayings of Jesus*, pp. 51–66, 152–5.

130   Cf. E. Schweizer, *The Good News according to Mark*, 1971, pp. 129f.; H.
       Anderson, *Commentary on Mark*, p. 163.

131   Mark incorporates it in his narrative of the calling of the Twelve (Mark 3:
       14f.).

132   They received freely their commission and the message of the kingdom:
       cf. 2 Cor. 11: 7; *P. Aboth* 1: 13; D. Hill, *Gospel of Matthew*, pp. 185.

133   But Luke hedges it about with a prohibition about going from house to
       house (i.e., to get fresh hospitality each time!) – evidently a reflection of
       an abuse in early Christian circles: cf. Didache 11: 1–6; and 13 *passim*.

134   I cannot follow D. L. Dungan in his argument that Paul is necessarily refer-
       ring to Matthew's version (p. 79). No-one doubts that Paul is talking about
       food (1 Cor. 9: 4; cf. 9: 13), but so is Luke in 10: 7. Equally, no-one doubts
       that Paul on occasion did accept money (cf. Phil. 4: 15–18; 2 Cor. 11: 7–10),
       though this was not his usual practice (cf. 2 Cor. 2: 17). It does, however,
       tend to associate him with the Luke–Timothy tradition. Not that the issue
       of whether he was closer to Matthew or Luke is so very important: the
       traditions were not in dispute concerning basic principles.

135   Cf. J. S. Ruef, *Paul's First Letter to Corinth*, 1971, p. 56 (in a comment on
       1 Cor. 7: 10f.). He appeals, however, simply to E. Käsemann's 'Sätze heiligen
       Rechtes': *vid. supra*, Chapter 1, n. 237.

136   I.e., as a straightforward prohibition expressed with the precision of Jewish
       jurisprudence, that the husband should not divorce his wife (he alone could
       institute divorce proceedings), and that the wife should not separate from
       the husband: cf. D. Daube, *N.T. and Rabbinic Judaism*, p. 362. The paren-
       thesis Paul inserts (probably also reflecting a traditional position) indicates
       clearly that if the separation of the couple does take place neither party is
       free to re-marry (the case in point simply concerns the wife).

137   Cf. 1 Cor. 7: 6; D. Daube, 'Concessions to Sinfulness in Jewish Law', *J.J.S.*,
       1959, pp. 1–13.

138   Cf. 1 Cor. 7: 25–31. Paul's attitude is concessionary throughout: e.g., vv. 2,
       5, 7, 9, 38ff. His emphasis on mutuality within marriage is not to be taken
       as indicating that his underlying attitude to marriage is particularly positive:
       cf. D. L. Dungan, *Sayings of Jesus*, pp. 83–8.

139 H. Anderson, *Mark*, pp. 239, 241; cf. V. Taylor, *Gospel According to St Mark*, 1952, pp. 408ff.

140 Cf. D. L. Dungan, *Sayings of Jesus*, pp. 111f.

141 R. Bultmann, *H.S.T.*, p. 26f.

142 Cf. E. Schweizer, *Mark*, p. 204; G. F. Moore, *Judaism* II, p. 125; V. Taylor, *Mark*, p. 420; H. Anderson, *Mark*, p. 244.

143 D. L. Dungan describes the Graeco-Roman legal reference discussed in the note above as 'a dead give away at this point': *Sayings of Jesus*, p. 106. Here we have mission instructions for the future missionaries to the Gentiles. Mark's lack of interest in the details of the rabbinic interpretation of the Torah is also evident.

144 Matt. 5: 32 has: *parektos logou porneias,* a particularly rabbinic formula: *vid. infra,* n. 145; cf. D. Hill, *Matthew*, pp. 124f.; 280f.; A. Isaksson, *Marriage and Ministry in the New Temple*, Eng. tr., 1965, pp. 75–92, contains a critical discussion of the origin of the clause on unchastity and the possibility that it could be derived from Jesus' teaching.

145 Cf. H. Strack and P. Billerbeck, *Kommentar z. N.T.* I, pp. 312–21; R. H. Charles, *The Teaching of the New Testament on Divorce*, 1921, pp. 85ff.; T. W. Manson, *Teaching of Jesus*, pp. 136f.; V. Taylor, *Mark*, p. 417; M. D. Goulder, *Midrash and Lection*, pp. 290f.

146 G. F. Moore, *Judaism* II, p. 124, n. 4. But the notion that the man who marries a divorcee thereby commits adultery is foreign to Jewish law.

147 Parallels with Qumran suggest themselves here: e.g., CD. 4: 20f., which also appeals to Gen. 1: 27 against established interpretations of the Torah: cf. D. L. Dungan, *Sayings of Jesus*, pp. 116ff.; also A. Isaksson, *Marriage and Ministry*, pp. 57–63.

148 One of them (Matt. 5: 32) certainly does and, I maintain, the other probably does. I accept the general phenomenological appropriateness of these clauses to Jesus' teaching, but to ascribe either of them specifically to Jesus is to exceed the evidence. For example: D. L. Dungan argues that 'Matthew's clause *is not an exception but a necessary aspect of Jesus' answer given in vv. 4-6*': *Sayings of Jesus*, p. 113 (his italics); cf. H. L. Strack and P. Billerbeck, *Kommentar z. N.T.* I, p. 312; D. Hill, *Matthew*, p. 281. Re-marriage is incompatible with the view of marriage set forth in Jesus' interpretation of creation. Adultery, on the other hand, gives grounds for divorce since it has already destroyed the marital union. But Dungan's case breaks down when he spells out what he believes Jesus meant: 'There should be no divorce, unless the marital union is already destroyed *de facto*; then let it be destroyed *de jure* as well' (p. 114). This is no longer eschatological teaching: it is casuistry, and to that extent belongs to a different realm of discourse. It is therefore more likely to be secondary. But see the following notes.

149 Cf. W. D. Davies, *S.S.M.*, p. 398. Jesus may indeed have given 'more applied' teaching to those who responded to his message; but at most this would suggest the possibility that some of the casuistical material originated with him.

150 This is not a legal prescription: cf. V. Taylor, *Mark*, p. 419. The saying sums up Jesus' teaching on the indissolubility of marriage by forbidding the action of man in seeking dissolution of it. This appears to be secondary, since the climactic statement is 'so that they are no longer two but one flesh'. Did this

gnomic instructional form become attached to the tradition as a meaningful summary? For shorthand purposes, as it were, it characterises the whole tradition; and that is precisely how Paul uses it.

151 1 Corinthians may be dated 'in the spring of 54 or 55': cf. W. G. Kümmel, P. Feine and J. Behm (edd.), *Introduction to the New Testament*, Eng. tr., 1966, p. 205.

152 The abuses, connected in fact with social inequality, are demonstrated by the clannishness of the well-to-do at table (and the resentment of those excluded) and their over-indulgence: all of which show contempt for the church and a failure to remember (imitate) Jesus. Paul's response (cf. 1 Cor. 11: 22) reduces the observance to its essentials: cf. J. Héring, *1 Corinthians*, pp. 113f.; C. K. Barrett, *1 Corinthians*, pp. 260ff.

153 Cf. Acts 2: 23; this is not to deny that the story of Judas is part of the connotation – indeed, the story of the betrayal and the announcement of it by Jesus (cf. Mark 14: 17–21) are integral to the tradition.

154 Cf. the Passover thanksgiving: 'Praised be Thou, O Lord our God, king of the world, who causes bread to come forth from the earth'. The praise related to the wine was the thanksgiving after the meal: 'Let us praise the Lord, our God, to whom belongs that of which we have partaken': J. Jeremias, *Eucharistic Words of Jesus*, pp. 109f.

155 The words of interpretation (1 Cor. 11: 25a; Mark 14: 23a; Matt. 26: 27a; Luke 22: 20a) are taken by J. Jeremias to be the earliest part of the accounts of the last supper; indeed, their 'antiquity approaches that of the early kerygma (1 Cor. 15: 3b-5)': *Eucharistic Words of Jesus*, p. 100. The words of interpretation, however, were developed considerably in the early church (as the evangelists' accounts suggest), and this process had already begun prior to Paul's reception of the tradition.

156 While the background of Paul's discussion is clearly the common meals of the Corinthian *koinonia*, his instructions indicate at least the beginning of the separation of *agape* and sacrament: cf. J. Jeremias, *Eucharistic Words of Jesus*, pp. 121f.; 133ff. For the messianic banquet, cf. Is. 25: 6; 1 En. 72: 14; also Matt. 8: 11; Luke 22: 29f.

157 The relative freedom of the prophet in relation to the liturgy of the Lord's supper is illustrated by Didache 10: 7. The liturgies which came to be accepted in the churches may well have been influenced by prophetic activity, especially since the prophetic tradition was well adapted to dramatic and symbolic actions: cf. the prophetic 'marking out of a table in the Spirit' (Didache 11: 9) – symbolising the messianic banquet?

158 On the vexed question of the connection between 'the breaking of bread' and the Lord's supper, cf. J. Jeremias, *Eucharistic Words of Jesus*, pp. 119ff. Some passages in Acts (notably 27: 35f.) use 'the breaking of bread' to denote little more than the sharing of food – perhaps an embryonic sacrament, at least for Paul: cf. H. Lietzmann, *Mass and Lord's Supper: A Study in the History of the Liturgy*, Eng. tr., 1953, pp. 204–8. For a strongly non-liturgical interpretation, cf. J. D. G. Dunn, *Jesus and the Spirit*, pp. 184f., 405f. More attention, perhaps, needs to be paid to the context of the individual texts. After all, sacramental usage grows out of and remains related to everyday practice. Cf. also C. F. D. Moule, *Worship in the N. T.*, pp. 20ff.

159 In the longer version of Luke's account, the actions associated with the giving of the cup are abbreviated, as in 1 Cor. 11: 25. It may be, however, that Luke 22: 19b–20 is an insertion dependent on 1 Cor. 11: 23ff., since it is omitted by D and many old Latin MSS. The issue is fully discussed by the commentators. Luke clearly wishes to highlight the last supper as an anticipation of the messianic banquet: cf. 22: 15–18.

160 M. D. Goulder, *Midrash*, p. 172.

161 *Ibid.*, pp. 173f. But *vid. supra*, Chapter 2, n. 91.

162 M. D. Goulder, *Midrash*, p. 173.

163 *Ibid.*, p. 192.

164 Cf. G. H. C. Macgregor, *The Gospel of John*, 1928, pp. xiiif.; G. Ogg, in *History and Chronology in the New Testament*, Nineham (ed.), 1965, pp. 75–96.

165 Cf. J. Jeremias, *Eucharistic Words of Jesus*, pp. 26–36.

166 Cf. N. Perrin, *Rediscovering the Teaching of Jesus*, pp. 102–8.

167 Cf. *supra*, Chapter 3, where a final meal was seen to be part of the 'farewell speech' situation. Inevitably, the focus of such an occasion would be upon the impending death and how the disciples should regard it.

168 Cf. A. Jaubert, *La Date de la Cène*, 1957 (The Date of the Last Supper, Eng. tr., 1965); also *N. T. S.* 14, 1967–8, pp. 145–64.

169 But care is required in working out this hypothesis. E. Trocmé comments that Mlle Jaubert concludes her fine book 'with an astonishingly naive account of the course of the passion of Christ': *Jesus and his Contemporaries*, Eng. tr., 1973, p. 5.

170 Cf. E. Ruckstuhl, *Die Chronologie des Letzen Mahles und des Leidens Jesus*, 1963, *passim*; C. W. Dugmore, 'Origins of the Eucharist', pp. 1–18; A. R. C. Leaney, 'What was the Lord's Supper?' *Theology* 70, 1967, pp. 51–62; A. J. B. Higgins, *The Lord's Supper in the N. T.*, 1952, *passim*; Th. Preiss, *Life in Christ*, 1954, pp. 81ff. (anticipated Passover); for an earlier stage of the debate, cf. W. O. E. Oesterley, *The Jewish Background of the Christian Liturgy*, 1925, pp. 156–93 (not a Passover feast; emphasis on the *haburah* meal and the *kiddush*).

171 O. Cullmann, *The Early Church*, p. 67.

172 *Ibid.*, p. 68.

173 There are also difficulties in the view of W. D. Davies, *S. S. M.*, pp. 358ff. His emphasis on the person and words of Jesus as a New Torah (*op. cit.*, p. 363; cf. *Paul and Rabbinic Judaism*, 1955, pp. 147–76) goes beyond anything Paul writes and imparts a certain rigidity to his notion of tradition. When this fact is combined with his comparative neglect of Paul's paraenetic use of tradition, Davies' view is seen to lack the flexibility necessary for a wholly satisfactory account of the operation of *paradosis* in Paul.

174 Hence, gnostic *paradosis* is inauthentic when it transmits an understanding of life which is at variance with that given in Christ. When that happens, preservation of part of the tradition virtually intact is irrelevant to the authenticity of the total *logion*: cf. J. M. Robinson, 'The Formal Structure of Jesus' Message', in *Current Issues in N.T. Interpretation*, Klassen and Snyder (edd.), 1962.

Conclusion

1   Cf. E. Fuchs, *Studies in the Historical Jesus,* Eng. tr., 1964, pp. 84–103;
    G. Ebeling, *Word and Faith,* Eng. tr., 1963, pp. 305–32.
2   Cf. J. S. Glen, *The Recovery of the Teaching Ministry,* 1960, pp. 62–83.

SELECT BIBLIOGRAPHY

(Commentaries, dictionary articles and standard works of reference are not included)

Abrahams, I. *Studies in Pharisaism and the Gospels* I, Cambridge, 1917.

Agouridès, S. 'La Tradition des Béatitudes chez Matthieu et Luc', in *Mélanges B. Rigaux*, 1970.

Althaus, P. *The so-called Kerygma and the Historical Jesus*, Eng. tr., Edinburgh, London, 1959.

Anderson, B. W. 'Exodus Typology in Second Isaiah', in *Israel's Prophetic Heritage*, Anderson and Harrelson (edd.), 1962.

Anderson, B. W. (ed.) *The Old Testament and Christian Faith*, London, 1964.

Anderson, B. W. and Harrelson, W. (edd.) *Israel's Prophetic Heritage*, London, 1962.

Anderson, H. *Jesus and Christian Origins*, New York, Oxford, 1964.

Armstrong, A. H. *An Introduction to Ancient Philosophy*, London, 1947, (2nd ed.) 1949.

Audet, J. P. *La didaché; instructions des apôtres*, Paris, 1958.

Baeck, L. *The Pharisees and Other Essays*, New York, 1947.

Baillie, D. M. *God Was In Christ*, London, 1948.

Baird, W. 'What is the Kerygma? A Study of 1 Cor. 15: 3-8 and Gal. 1: 11-17', *J.B.L.* 76, 1957.

Baker, T. G. A. *What is the New Testament?*, London, 1969.

Barbour, R. S. *Traditio-historical Criticism of the Gospels*, London, 1972.

Barclay, W. 'A Comparison of Paul's Missionary Preaching and Preaching to the Church', in *Apostolic History and the Gospel*, Gasque and Martin (edd.), 1970.

Barnikol, E. 'Römer 13: Der nichtpaulinische Ursprung der absoluten Obrigkeitsbejahung von Römer 13: 1-7', *T.U.* 77, 1961.

Baron, S. W. *A Social and Religious History of the Jews* I-III, New York, 1952, 1958.

Barrett, C. K. *The Holy Spirit and Gospel Tradition*, London, 1947, 1966.

—— 'The Eschatology of the Epistle to the Hebrews', in *The Background of the New Testament and its Eschatology*, Davies and Daube (edd.), 1956.

—— 'The Apostles in and after the New Testament', *Svensk Exegetisk Arsbok* 21, 1957.

—— *Jesus and the Gospel Tradition*, London, 1967.

—— *The Signs of an Apostle,* London, 1967.

—— 'ΨΕΥΔΑΠΟΣΤΟΛΟΙ (2 Cor. 11:13)', in *Mélanges B. Rigaux,* 1970.

Bartsch, H. W. (ed.) *Kerygma and Myth,* Eng. tr., London, 1954.

Begrich J. 'Das priesterliche Heilsorakel', *Z.A.W.* 52, 1934.

Bell, G. K. A. and Deissmann, A. (edd.) *Mysterium Christi,* London, 1930.

Benoit, P. 'Qumran et le Nouveau Testament', *N.T.S.* 7, 1961.

Berger, K. 'Zu den sogenannten Sätzen heiligen Rechts', *N.T.S.* 17, 1970-71.

Bjerkelund, C. J. *Parakalô,* Oslo/Bergen/Tromsö, 1967.

Black, M. *An Aramaic Approach to the Gospels and Acts,* Oxford, 1946, (3rd ed.) 1967.

—— 'The Beatitudes', *Exp. T.* 64, 1952-53.

—— *The Scrolls and Christian Origins,* New York, Edinburgh, 1961.

—— 'The Christological Use of the Old Testament in the New Testament', *N.T.S.* 18, 1971-72.

Blank, S. H. 'The Curse, the Blasphemy, the Spell, and the Oath', *H.U.C.A.* 23, 1950-51.

Bonhöffer, A. *Epiktet und das Neue Testament,* Giessen, 1911.

Bonsirven, J. *Le judaisme palestinien au temps de Jésus-Christ* I-II, Paris, (2nd ed.) 1934-5.

Borgen, P. 'The Unity of the Discourse in John VI', *Z.N.W.* 50, 1959.

—— 'Observations on the Midrashic Character of John 6', *Z.N.W.* 54, 1963.

—— *Bread from Heaven,* Leiden, 1965.

Boring, M. 'How May We Identify Oracles of Christian Prophets in the Synoptic Tradition? Mark 3: 28-29 as a Test Case', *J.B.L.* 91, 1972.

Bornkamm, G. 'Die eucharistische Rede im Johannes-Evangelium', *Z.N.W.* 47, 1956.

—— *Jesus of Nazareth,* Eng. tr., London, 1960.

—— *Paul,* Eng. tr., London, 1971.

Bouquet, A. C. *Everyday Life in New Testament Times,* London, 1953.

Bowker, J. W. 'Speeches in Acts: A Study in Proem and Yelammedenu Form', *N.T.S.* 14, 1967-68.

Braaten, C. E. and Harrisville, R. A. (edd.) *Kerygma and History,* New York, 1962.

Bradley, D. G. 'The "Topos" as a Form of Pauline Paraenesis', *J.B.L.* 72, 1953.

Brandt, W. *Die jüdischen Baptismen,* Giessen, 1910.

Brownlee, W. H. 'Biblical Interpretation among the Sectaries of the Dead Sea Scrolls', *B.A.* 14, 1951.

—— *The Dead Sea Habakkuk Midrash and the Targum of Jonathan,* Duke Div. Sch., 1953.

Bruce, F. F. *Biblical Exegesis in the Qumran Texts,* London, 1960.

—— 'The Book of Daniel and the Qumran Community', in *Neotestamentica et Semitica,* Ellis and Wilcox (edd.), 1969.

Bultmann, R. *Der Stil der paulinischen Predigt und die kynisch-stoische Diatribe,* Göttingen, 1910.

—— *Der Geschichte der synoptischen Tradition,* Göttingen, 1921, (3rd ed.) 1958. (*History of the Synoptic Tradition,* Eng. tr., Oxford, 1963, 1968).

—— 'A New Approach to the Synoptic Problem', *J.R.* 6, 1926.

—— *Jesus and the Word,* Eng. tr., London, 1935, 1958.

—— *Theology of the New Testament*, I, II, Eng., tr., London, 1952, 1955.
—— *Glauben und Verstehen: Gesammelte Aufsätze*, 4 vols., Tübingen, 1952–67.
—— 'New Testament and Mythology', in *Kerygma and Myth* I, Bartch (ed.), 1954.
—— 'The Problem of Hermeneutics', in *Essays Philosophical and Theological*, Eng. tr., London, 1955.
—— 'Allgemeine Wahrheiten und christliche Verkündigung', *Z.T.K.* 54, 1957.
—— *Jesus Christ and Mythology*, London, 1960.
—— *Die drei Johannesbriefe*, Göttingen, 1967. (*The Johannine Epistles*, Eng. tr., Philadelphia, 1973.)
Burney, C. F. *The Poetry of Our Lord*, Oxford, 1925.
Buttrick, D. G. *et al.* (edd.) *Jesus and Man's Hope* I, Pittsburgh, 1970.

Campbell, J. Y. 'KOINΩNIA and its Cognates in the New Testament', *J.B.L.* 51, 1932.
—— *Three New Testament Studies*, Leiden, 1965.
Carrington, P. *The Meaning of Revelation*, London, 1931.
—— *The Primitive Christian Catechism*, Cambridge, 1940.
Charles, R. H. *The Teaching of the New Testament on Divorce*, Oxford, 1921.
Charlesworth, J. H. *The Odes of Solomon*, Oxford, 1973.
Chevallier, M. A. *L'Esprit et le Messie dans le bas-judaisme et le Nouveau Testament*, Paris, 1958.
Childs, B. S. *Memory and Tradition in Israel*, London, 1962.
Clements, R. E. *Prophecy and Tradition*, Oxford, 1975.
Conzelmann, H. *The Theology of Luke*, Eng. tr., London, 1960.
—— 'Zur Analyse der Bekenntnisformel 1 Kor. 15: 3–5', *Ev. Th.* 25, 1965.
—— *An Outline of the Theology of the New Testament*, Eng. tr., London, 1969.
Cothenet, E. 'Prophetisme et Ministère d'après le Nouveau Testament', *La Maison Dieu* 108, 1971.
Cross, F. L. *1 Peter, a Paschal Liturgy*, London, 1954.
Cross, F. M. Jr. *The Ancient Library of Qumran and Modern Biblical Studies*, London, 1958.
Crouch, J. E. *The Origin and Intention of the Colossian Haustafel*, Göttingen, 1972.
Cullmann, O. *The Earliest Christian Confessions*, Eng. tr., London, 1949.
—— *The Early Church*, Eng. tr., London, 1956.
—— *The State in the New Testament*, Eng. tr., London, 1957.
—— *The Christology of the New Testament*, Eng. tr., London, 1959, 1963.
Cuming, G. J. *Studies in Church History* II, London, 1965.

Dahl, N. A. 'The Problem of the Historical Jesus', in *Kerygma and History*, Braaten and Harrisville (edd.), 1962.
Danby, H. (ed.) *The Mishnah*, Oxford, 1933, 1964.
Daniélou, J. *Sacramentum Futuri*, Paris, 1950.
—— *La catéchèse aux premiers siècles*, Paris, 1968.
Daube, D. 'Rabbinic Methods of Interpretation and Hellenistic Rhetoric',

H.U.C.A. 22, 1949.

—— *The New Testament and Rabbinic Judaism*, London, 1956.

Davies, J. G. 'The Genesis of Belief in an Imminent Parousia', *J.T.S.* 14, (N.S.1), 1963.

Davies, W. D. *Paul and Rabbinic Judaism*, London, 1948, 1955, 1962, 1970.

—— *Torah in the Messianic Age and/or the Age to Come*, Philadelphia, 1952.

—— *Christian Origins and Judaism*, London, 1962.

—— *The Setting of the Sermon on the Mount*, Cambridge, 1964.

—— 'The Relevance of Moral Teaching in the Early Church', in *Neo-testamentica et Semitica*, Ellis and Wilcox (edd.), 1969.

Davies, W. D. and Daube, D. (edd.) *The Background of the New Testament and its Eschatology*, Cambridge, 1956.

le Déaut, R. 'A propos d'une définition du midrash', *Biblica* 50, 1969 (Eng. tr., *Int.*, July 1971).

Deissmann, A. *Light from the Ancient East*, Eng. tr., London, 1927.

Delling, G. 'The Significance of the Resurrection of Jesus for Faith in Jesus Christ', in *S.M.R.*, Moule (ed.), 1968.

Dibelius, M. *Die urchristliche Überlieferung von Johannes dem Täufer*, Göttingen, 1911.

—— *Die Formgeschichte des Evangeliums*, Tübingen, 1919, (3rd ed.) 1959 (Eng. tr., *From Tradition to Gospel*, London, 1934).

—— *Studies in the Acts of the Apostles*, Eng. tr., London, 1956, r.p. 1973.

—— *Jesus*, Eng. tr., London, 1963.

von Dobschütz, E. *Ostern und Pfingsten*, Leipzig, 1903.

—— *Christian Life in the Primitive Church*, Eng. tr., London, 1904.

—— 'Johanneische Studien I', *Z.N.W.* 8, 1907.

Dodd, C. H. 'Jesus as Teacher and Prophet', in *Mysterium Christi*, Bell and Deissmann (edd.), 1930.

—— *Parables of the Kingdom*, London, 1935, (3rd ed.) 1936.

—— *The Apostolic Preaching and its Developments*, London, 1936.

—— *Gospel and Law*, Cambridge, 1951.

—— *According to the Scriptures, the Sub-Structure of N.T. Theology*, London, 1952.

—— *The Interpretation of the Fourth Gospel*, Cambridge, 1953.

—— 'The Appearance of the Risen Christ: An Essay in the Form-Criticism of the Gospels', in *Studies in the Gospels*, Nineham (ed.), 1955.

—— 'The Primitive Catechism and the Sayings of Jesus', in *N.T. Essays*, Higgins (ed.), 1959.

—— *Historical Tradition in the Fourth Gospel*, Cambridge, 1963.

Doeve, J. W. *Jewish Hermeneutics in the Synoptic Gospels and Acts*, Assen, 1954.

Donfried, K. P. 'The Theology of Second Clement', *H.T.R.* 66, 1973.

—— *The Setting of Second Clement in Early Christianity*, Leiden, 1974.

Downing, F. G. *The Church and Jesus*, London, 1968.

Dudley, D. R. *A History of Cynicism*, London, 1937.

Dugmore, C. W. 'The Study of the Origins of the Eucharist: Retrospect and Revaluation', in *Studies in Church History* II, Cuming (ed.), 1965.

Dungan, D. L. *The Sayings of Jesus in the Churches of Paul*, Oxford, 1971.
Dunn, J. D. G. 'John VI – A Eucharistic Discourse?' *N.T.S.* 17, 1971.
—— 'New Wine in Old Wineskins: Prophet', *Exp. T.* 85, 1973.
—— *Jesus and the Spirit*, London, 1975.
—— 'Prophetic "I"-sayings and the Jesus Tradition: The Importance of
  Testing Prophetic Utterances within Early Christianity', *N.T.S.* 24, 1978.

Ebeling, G. *Word and Faith*, Eng. tr., London, 1963.
—— *Theology and Proclamation*, Eng. tr., London, 1966.
Eisler, R. *The Messiah Jesus and John the Baptist*, Eng. tr., London, 1931.
Eissfeldt, O. 'Das Maschal im A.T.', *B. Z. A. W.* 24, 1913.
—— *Der Gott Karmel*, Berlin, 1953.
—— *The Old Testament: An Introduction*, Eng. tr., Oxford, 1965.
Elliott-Binns, L. E. *Galilean Christianity*, London, 1956.
Ellis, E. E. *Paul's Use of the Old Testament*, Edinburgh, 1957.
—— 'Luke XI 49–51: An Oracle of a Christian Prophet?' *Exp. T.* 74, 1962–
  63.
—— 'Midrash, Targum and New Testament Quotations', in *Neotestamentica
  et Semitica*, Ellis and Wilcox (edd.), 1969.
—— 'Midrashic Features in the Speeches of Acts', in *Mélanges B. Rigaux*,
  1970.
—— 'The Role of the Christian Prophet in Acts', in *Apostolic History and
  the Gospel*, Gasque and Martin, 1970.
—— 'Paul and his Co-Workers', *N.T.S.* 17, 1970–71.
Ellis, E. E. and Wilcox, M. (edd.) *Neotestamentica et Semitica, Studies in
  Honour of Matthew Black*, Edinburgh, 1969.
Evans, C. F. 'The Kerygma', *J.T.S.* 7 (N.S. 1), 1956.
—— *The Lord's Prayer*, London, 1963.

Fascher E. ΠΡΟΦΗΤΗΣ, *Eine sprach- und religionsgeschichtliche Unter-
  suchung*, Giessen, 1927.
Feldman, A. *Parables and Similes of the Rabbis*, Cambridge, 1927.
Fiebig, P. *Altjüdische Gleichnisse und die Gleichnisse Jesu*, Tübingen,
  Leipzig, 1904.
Filson, F. V. 'The Christian Teacher in the First Century', *J.B.L.* 60, 1941.
Finkel, A. *The Pharisees and the Teacher of Nazareth*, Leiden, 1964.
Finkelstein, L. 'The Oldest Midrash: Pre-rabbinic Ideals and Teachings in
  the Passover Haggadah', *H.T.R.* 31, 1938.
Fitzmyer, J. A. 'The Use of Explicit O.T. Quotations in Qumran Literature
  and in the N.T.', *N.T.S.* 7, 1960–61.
Flacelière, R. *Greek Oracles*, Eng. tr., London, 1965.
Flender, H. *St Luke, Theologian of Redemptive History*, Eng. tr., London,
  1967.
Fletcher, J. *Situation Ethics*, London, 1966.
—— *Moral Responsibility*, London, 1967.
Flowers, H. J. ' 'Εν πνεύματι ἁγιώ καὶ πυρί', *Exp. T.* 64, 1952–53.
Flusser, D. *Jesus*, New York, 1969.
Foster, J. *After the Apostles*, London, 1951.
Freedman, H. and Simon, M. (edd.) *Midrash Rabbah*, 10 vols., London, 1939.

Fridrichsen, A. *The Apostle and his Message*, Uppsala, 1947.
Fridrichsen, A. *et al.* (edd.) *The Root of the Vine*, New York, 1953.
Fuchs, E. *Studies in the Historical Jesus*, Eng. tr., London, 1964.
Fuller, R. H. *The Mission and Achievement of Jesus*, London, 1954.

Gärtner, B. *The Areopagus Speech and Natural Revelation*, Uppsala, 1955.
—— *The Temple and the Community in Qumran and the N.T.*, Cambridge, 1965.
Gasque, W. W. and Martin, R. P. (edd.) *Apostolic History and the Gospel* (Festschrift to F. F. Bruce), Exeter, 1970.
Gaster, M. *The Samaritans* (Schweich Lectures, 1923), London, 1925.
Gaster, T. H. *The Scriptures of the Dead Sea Sect*, London, 1957.
Gerhardsson, B. *Memory and Manuscript, Oral Tradition and Written Transmission in Rabbinic Judaism and Early Christianity*, Lund, 1961.
—— *Tradition and Transmission in Early Christianity*, Lund, 1964.
Gertner, M. 'Midrashim in the New Testament', *J.S.S.* 7, 1962.
Glen, J. S. *The Recovery of the Teaching Ministry*, Edinburgh, 1960.
Glombitza, O. 'Gnade – das entscheidende Wort', *Nov. Test.* 2, 1958.
Gnilka, J. 'Paränetische Traditionen im Epheserbrief', in *Mélanges B. Rigaux*, 1970.
Goguel, M. *Vie de Jésus*, Paris, 1932.
Goguel, M. (Festschrift) *Aux sources de la tradition chrétienne*, Neuchâtel, 1950.
Goodenough, E. R. 'Philo's Exposition of the Law and his *De Vita Mosis*', *H.T.R.* 27, 1933.
—— *An Introduction to Philo Judaeus*, New Haven, Conn. 1940; (2nd ed.) Oxford, 1962.
Goulder, M. 'The Composition of the Lord's Prayer', *J.T.S.* 14 (N.S. 1), 1963.
—— *Midrash and Lection in Matthew*, London, 1974.
—— 'Jesus, the Man of Universal Destiny', in *The Myth of God Incarnate*, Hick (ed.), London, 1977.
Granfield, P. and Jungmann, J. A. *Kuriakon* (Festschrift Johannes Quasten), 2 vols., Munster, 1970.
Grass, H. *Ostergeschehen und Osterberichte*, Göttingen, 1956, r.p. 1962.
Grässer, E. *Der Glaube im Hebräerbrief*, Marburg, 1965.
Grasso, D. *Proclaiming God's Message: A Study in the Theology of Preaching*, Notre Dame, Ind., 1965.
Greig, J. C. G. 'Abba and Amen: Their Relevance to Christology', *Studia Evangelica* 5, Berlin, 1968.
Guilding, A. *The Fourth Gospel and Jewish Worship*, Oxford, 1960.

Haenchen, E. 'Quellenanalyse und Kompositionsanalyse in Acts 15', *Z.N.W.* 26, 1960.
Hahn, F. *The Titles of Jesus in Christology*, Eng. tr., London, 1969.
Hanson, R. P. C. *Tradition in the Early Church*, London, 1962.
Harris, J. Rendel, *Testimonies* I, II, Cambridge, 1916–20.
Harris, J. Rendel and Mingana, A. *The Odes and Psalms of Solomon* II, Manchester, 1920.

Hartman, L. *Prophecy Interpreted,* Eng. tr., Lund, 1966.

Hayes, J. H. 'The Usage of Oracles against Foreign Nations in Ancient Israel', *J.B.L.* 87, 1968.

Hebert, G. *The Christ of Faith and the Jesus of History,* London, 1962.

Henderson, I. *Myth in the New Testament,* London, 1952.

—— *Rudolf Bultmann,* London, 1965.

Hengel. M. *Judentum und Hellenismus,* Tübingen, 1969 (Eng. tr., *Judaism and Hellenism,* 2 vols., London, 1974).

Herzfeld, E. *Zoroaster and his World* I, Princeton, N.J., 1947.

Hick, J. (ed.) *The Myth of God Incarnate,* London, 1977.

Higgins, A. J. B. *The Lord's Supper in the New Testament,* London, 1952.

—— *The Tradition about Jesus: three studies,* Edinburgh, 1969.

—— 'Is the Son of Man Problem Insoluble?' in *Neotestamentica et Semitica,* Ellis and Wilcox, 1969.

Higgins, A. J. B. (ed.) *New Testament Essays: Studies in Memory of Thomas Walter Manson,* Manchester, 1959.

Hill, D. 'Prophecy and Prophets in the Revelation of St John', *N.T.S.* 18, 1971-72.

—— 'On the Evidence for the Creative Role of Christian Prophets', *N.T.S.* 20, 1973-74.

Hooker, M. *Jesus and the Servant,* London, 1959.

—— *The Son of Man in Mark,* London, 1967.

Hunter, A. M. *Paul and his Predecessors,* London, 1940,(2nd ed.) 1961.

—— *The Unity of the New Testament,* London, 1943.

—— *Interpreting the New Testament 1900-1950,* London, 1951.

Hurd, J. C. *The Origin of 1 Corinthians,* London, 1965.

Isaksson, A. *Marriage and Ministry in the New Temple,* Eng. tr., Lund, 1965.

Jaubert, A. *La Date de la Cène,* Gabalda, 1957 (Eng. tr., *The Date of the Last Supper,* New York, 1965).

Jeremias, J. 'Mc. 10: 13-16 Parr. und die Übung der Kindertaufe in der Urkirche', *Z.N.W.* 40, 1941.

—— *Die Abendsmahlworte Jesu,* Zürich, 1949 (Eng. tr., *The Eucharistic Words of Jesus,* London, 1966).

—— *The Parables of Jesus,* Eng. tr., London, 1954, 1963, 1972.

—— *Infant Baptism in the First Four Centuries,* Eng. tr., London, 1962.

—— *The Unknown Sayings of Jesus,* Eng. tr., London, (2nd ed.) 1964.

—— *The Central Message of the New Testament,* London, 1965.

—— *New Testament Theology* I, *The Proclamation of Jesus,* Eng. tr., London, 1971.

Jeremias, J. and Zimmerli, W. *The Servant of God,* Eng. tr., London, 1957.

Joest, W. and Pannenberg, W. (edd.) *Dogma und Denkstrukturen,* Göttingen, 1963.

Jüngel, E. *Paulus und Jesus,* Tübingen, 1962.

Jungmann, J. A. *Handing on the Faith: A Manual of Catechetics,* Freiburg, 1959.

Kähler, M. *Der sogenannte historische Jesus und der geschichtliche biblische*

Christus, Leipzig, 1892 (Eng. tr., *The so-called Historical Jesus and the historic Biblical Christ,* Philadelphia, 1964).

Kallas, J. 'Romans XIII 1–7: An Interpolation', *N.T.S.* 11, 1965.

Kamlah, E. *Die Form der katalogischen Paränese im Neuen Testament,* Tübingen, 1964.

Käsemann, E. 'Das Problem des historischen Jesus', *Z.T.K.* 51, 1954.

—— *Essays on New Testament Themes,* Eng. tr., London, 1964.

—— *The Testament of Jesus,* Eng. tr., London, 1968.

—— *New Testament Questions of Today,* Eng. tr., London, 1969.

—— *Perspectives on Paul,* Eng. tr., London, 1971.

Keck, L. E. and Martyn, J. L. (edd.) *Studies in Luke–Acts,* Nashville, Tenn., 1966.

Kelly, J. N. D. *Early Christian Creeds,* London, 1950.

Kirk, K. E. *The Vision of God,* London, 1931.

Kirk, K. E. (ed.) *The Apostolic Ministry,* London, 1946.

Kistemaker, S. *The Psalm Citations in the Epistle to the Hebrews,* Amsterdam, 1961.

Klassen, W. and Snyder, G. F. (edd.) *Current Issues in New Testament Interpretation; Essays in honour of Otto A. Piper,* London, 1962.

Klein, G. *Die Zwölf Apostel,* Göttingen, 1961.

Klijn, A. F. J. 'Stephen's Speech – Acts VII.2–53', *N.T.S.* 4, 1957–58.

Knox, J. *The Church and the Reality of Christ,* London, 1963.

Knox, W. L. *Some Hellenistic Elements in Primitive Christianity* (Schweich Lectures 1942), London, 1944.

Köhler, L. 'Deuterojesaja (Jesaja 40–55) stilkritisch untersucht', *B.Z.A.W.* 37, 1923.

Kraeling, C. H. *John the Baptist,* New York, 1951.

Kümmel, W. G. *Promise and Fulfilment,* Eng. tr., London, 1957; 1961.

Kümmel, W. G., Feine, P. and Behm, J. (edd.) *Introduction to the New Testament,* Eng. tr., London, 1966.

Lampe, G. W. H. 'The Holy Spirit in the Writings of St Luke', in *Studies in the Gospels,* Nineham (ed.), 1957.

Leaney, A. R. C. 'What was the Lord's Supper?' *Theology* 70, 1967.

Leijs, R. 'Prédication des apôtres', *N.R.T.* 69, 1947.

Licht, J. 'An Analysis of the Treatise on the Two Spirits in DSD', *Scripta Hierosolymitana* 4, 1958.

Lieberman, S. *Greek in Jewish Palestine,* New York, 1942.

—— *Hellenism in Jewish Palestine* (I Cent. B.C.E. – IV Cent. C.E.), New York, 1950, 1962.

Lightfoot, R. H. *History and Interpretation in the Gospels,* London, 1935.

—— *Locality and Doctrine in the Gospels,* London, 1938.

Lindars, B. *New Testament Apologetic,* London, 1961.

Lindblom, J. *Prophecy in Ancient Israel,* Oxford, 1962.

—— *Geschichte und Offenbarungen,* Lund, 1968.

Linnemann, E. *The Parables of Jesus,* Eng. tr., London, 1966.

Lohmeyer, E. *Galiläa und Jerusalem,* Göttingen, 1936.

—— *The Lord's Prayer,* Eng. tr., London, 1965.

Lohse, E. *Märtyrer und Gottesknecht,* Göttingen, 1955.

Long, E. L. Jr. *A Survey of Christian Ethics,* New York, 1967.

Lövestam, E. *Son and Saviour,* Eng. tr., Copenhagen, 1961.

Lund, N. W. *Chiasmus in the New Testament: A Study in Formgeschichte,* Chapel Hill, N.C., 1942.

Lundström, G. *The Kingdom of God in the Teaching of Jesus,* Eng. tr., Edinburgh, London, 1963.

Macdonald, J. *The Theology of the Samaritans,* London, 1964.

McDonald, J. I. H. 'Was Romans XVI a separate letter?' *N.T.S.* 16, 1970.

—— 'Some Comments on the Form of Melito's Paschal Homily', *Studia Patristica* 12, 1975.

McKane, W. *Prophets and Wise Men,* London, 1965.

Maclean, J. H. 'St Paul at Athens', *Exp. T.* 44, 1932–33.

Mann, J. *The Bible as Read and Preached in the Old Synagogue* I, II, New York, 1940, 1966.

Manson, T. W. *The Teaching of Jesus,* Cambridge, 1931, 1955.

—— *The Sayings of Jesus,* London, 1937, 1949.

—— 'The Problem of the Epistle to the Hebrews', *B.J.R.L.* 32, 1949.

—— 'The Son of Man in Daniel, Enoch and the Gospels', *B.J.R.L.* 32, 1950.

—— 'The Lord's Prayer', *B.J.R.L.* 38, 1955–56.

Martyn, J. L. *History and Theology in the Fourth Gospel,* New York, 1968.

Marxsen, W. *Der Evangelist Markus,* Göttingen, 1956.

—— *Introduction to the New Testament,* Eng. tr., London, 1968.

—— *The Resurrection of Jesus of Nazareth,* Eng. tr., London, 1968.

Miller, M. P. 'Targum, Midrash and the Use of the Old Testament in the New Testament', *J.S.J.* 2, no. 1, 1971.

Mitton, C. L. 'The Relationship between 1 Peter and Ephesians', *J.T.S.* 1 (N.S.1), 1950.

Moffatt, J. *Introduction to the Literature of the New Testament,* Edinburgh, 1911.

Mohrmann, C. 'Praedicare-Tractare Sermo: Essai sur la terminologie palaio-chrétienne', *La Maison Dieu* 39, 1954.

Moore G. F. *Judaism* I, II, III, Cambridge, Mass., 1927–30, r.p. 1954.

Morris, N. *The Jewish School,* London, 1937.

Moule, C. F. D. 'Sanctuary and Sacrifice in the Church of the New Testament', *J.T.S.* 1 (N.S.1), 1950.

—— 'The Use of Parables and Sayings as Illustrative Material in Early Christian Catechesis', *J.T.S.* (N.S. 3), 1952.

—— 'The Nature and Purpose of 1 Peter', *N.T.S.* 3, 1956.

—— 'Once More, Who were the Hellenists?' *Exp. T.* 70, 1959.

—— *Worship in the New Testament,* London, 1961.

—— *The Birth of the New Testament,* London, 1962.

—— 'The Individualism of the Fourth Gospel', *Nov. T.* 5, 1962.

—— 'Mark 4: 1–20 Yet Once More', in *Neotestamentica et Semitica,* Ellis and Wilcox (edd.), 1969.

Moule, C. F. D. (ed.) *The Significance of the Message of the Resurrection for Faith in Jesus Christ,* London, 1968.

Mowinckel, S. *He That Cometh,* Eng. tr., Oxford, 1956.

Munck, J. 'Paul, the Apostles and the Twelve', *St. Th.* 3, 1950.

—— 'Discours d'adieu dans le N.T. et dans la littérature biblique', in *Mélanges M. Goguel*, 1950.
—— 'Paulus Tamquam Abortivus', in *N.T. Essays*, Higgins (ed.), 1959.

Neill, S. *The Interpretation of the New Testament 1861–1961*, Oxford, 1964.
Neugebauer, F. 'Geistspruche und Jesuslogien', *Z.N.W.* 53, 1962.
Nineham, D. E. (ed.) *Studies in the Gospels: Essays in memory of R. H. Lightfoot*, Oxford, 1957.
—— *History and Chronology in the New Testament*, London, 1965.
Norden, E. *Die antike Kunstprosa*, Leipzig, Berlin, 1915, r.p. 1958.
North, C. R. *The Suffering Servant in Deutero-Isaiah*, London, 1948, r.p. 1963.

Oesterley, W. O. E., *The Jewish Background of the Christian Liturgy*, Oxford, 1925.
Oesterley, W. O. E. and Box, G. H. *The Religion and Worship of the Synagogue*, London, 1925.
O'Neill, J. C. *The Puzzle of 1 John*, London, 1966.
Otto, R. *The Kingdom of God and the Son of Man*, London, 1938.

Pannenberg, W. *Jesus – God and Man*, Eng. tr., London, 1968.
Parke, H. W. and Warmell, D. E. W. *The Delphic Oracle* II, Oxford, 1956.
Pearson, B. A. *The 'Pneumatikos–Psychikos' Terminology in 1 Corinthians*, S.B.L. Dissertation 12, 1973.
Pedersen, J. *Israel, Its Life and Culture*, I–II, London and Copenhagen, 1926; III–IV, *ibid.*, 1940, (2nd ed.) 1959.
Perrin, N. 'Mark XIV.62: The End Product of a Christian Pesher Tradition?' *N.T.S.* 12, 1966.
—— *Rediscovering the Teaching of Jesus*, London, 1967.
Piper, O. A. 'I John and the Didache of the Primitive Church', *J.B.L.* 66, 1947.
—— 'A Unitary God with Jesus as his First Theologian', *Int.* 15, 1961.
Pope, H. 'Prophecy and Prophets in New Testament Times', *I.T.Q.* 7, 1912.
Preiss, Th. *Life in Christ*, Eng. tr., London, 1957.

von Rad, G. *Theology of the Old Testament* I, II, Eng. tr., Edinburgh, 1962–65.
Ramsey, I. T. *Religious Language*, London, 1957.
—— *Christian Discourse*, London, 1965.
Rast, W. E. *Tradition History and the Old Testament*, Philadelphia, 1972.
Reicke, Bo. 'A Synopsis of Early Christian Preaching', in *The Root of the Vine*, Fridrichsen et al. (edd.), 1953.
Rétif, A. 'Qu'est-ce que le kérygme?' *N.R.T.* 71, 1949.
Richardson, C. C. *Early Christian Fathers* I, London, 1953.
Richter G. 'Zur Formgeschichte und literarischen Einheit von Joh. 6: 31–58', *Z.N.W.* 60, 1969.
Riesenfeld, H. *The Gospel Tradition and its Beginnings: A Study in the Limits of 'Formgeschichte'*, London, 1957 (also in *Studia Evangelica* 5, 1959, pp. 43–65).

—— *The Gospels Reconsidered: A Selection of Papers read at the International Congress on the Four Gospels in 1957*, Oxford, 1960.

—— *The Gospel Tradition*, Oxford, 1970.

Rigaux, B. (Festschrift) *Mélanges bibliques en hommage au R. P. Béda Rigaux*, Gembloux, 1970.

Rissi, M. 'The Kerygma of the Revelation to John', *Int.* 22, 1968.

Robinson, J. A. T. *Twelve New Testament Studies*, London, 1962.

—— *Jesus and His Coming*, London, 1957.

Robinson, J. M. *A New Quest of the Historical Jesus*, London, 1959.

—— 'The Formal Structure of Jesus' Message', in *Current Issues in New Testament Interpretation*, Klassen and Snyder (edd.), 1962.

—— 'On the "Gattung" of Mark (and John)', in *Jesus and Man's Hope*, D. G. Buttrick *et al.* (edd.)

Robinson, T. H. (ed.) *Studies in Old Testament Prophecy*, Edinburgh, 1950.

Roetzel, C. 'The Judgment Form in Paul's Letters', *J.B.L.* 88, 1969.

Ross, J. F. 'The Prophet as Yahweh's Messenger', in *Israel's Prophetic Heritage*, Anderson and Harrelson (edd.), 1962.

Rowley, H. H. *The Relevance of Apocalyptic*, London, 1944.

—— *The Servant of the Lord*, London, 1952, 1965.

—— *Darius the Mede and the Four World Empires in the Book of Daniel*, Cardiff, 1959.

Ruckstuhl, E. *Die Chronologie des Letzen Mahles und des Leidens Jesus*, Einsiedeln, 1963.

Russell, D. S. *The Method and Message of Jewish Apocalyptic*, London, 1964.

Schmidt, J. *Studien zur Stilistik der alttestamentlichen Spruchliteratur*, Alttestamentliche Abhandlungen 13, part 1, 1936.

Schmidt, K. L. *Der Rahmen der Geschichte Jesu*, Berlin, 1919.

Schmithals, W. *Paul and James*, Eng. tr., London, 1965.

—— *Gnosticism in Corinth*, Eng. tr., Nashville, Tenn., 1972.

Schnackenburg, R. 'Apostles Before and During Paul's Time', in *Apostolic History and the Gospel*, Gasque and Martin (edd.), 1970.

Schoeps, H. J. *Theologie und Geschichte des Judenchristentums*, Tübingen, 1949.

—— *Paul*, Eng. tr., London, 1961.

Schürer, E. *The History of the Jewish People in the Age of Jesus Christ* I, Vermes and Millar (edd.), Edinburgh, 1973.

Schürmann, H. 'Zur Traditionsgeschichte der Nazareth-Pericope Lk. 4, 16-30, in *Mélanges B. Rigaux*, 1970.

Schütz, J. H. *Paul and the Anatomy of Apostolic Authority*, Cambridge, 1975.

Schweitzer, A. *Von Reimarus zu Wrede*, Tübingen, 1906 (Eng. tr., *The Quest of the Historical Jesus*, London, 1910, (3rd ed.) 1954).

Schweizer, E. 'With the Holy Ghost and Fire', *Exp. T.* 65, 1953-54.

Scobie, C. H. H. *John the Baptist*, London, 1964.

—— 'The Origin and Development of Samaritan Christianity', *N.T.S.* 19, 1973.

Scott, E. F. *The Varieties of New Testament Religion,* New York, 1943.

Scott, R. B. Y. 'The Literary Structure of Isaiah's Oracles', in *S. O. T. P.,* T. H. Robinson (ed.), 1950.

—— *Solomon and the Beginnings of Wisdom, V. T.* Supplements III, 1955.

Sedgwick, W. B. 'The Origins of the Sermon', *H.J.* 45, 1946.

Seeberg, A. *Der Katechismus der Urchristenheit,* Leipzig, 1903, Munich, 1966.

—— *Die Didache des Judentums und der Urchristenheit,* Leipzig, 1908.

Selwyn, E. C. *The Christian Prophets,* London, 1900.

—— *The Oracles in the New Testament,* London, 1911.

—— *First Christian Ideas,* London, 1919.

Selwyn, E. G. *The First Epistle of St Peter,* (esp. Essay II pp. 365–466), London, 1946.

Sevenster, J. N. *Paul and Seneca,* Suppl. *Nov. T.* IV, Leiden, 1961.

—— *Do you know Greek?* Eng. tr., Suppl. *Nov. T.* XIX, Leiden, 1968.

Simon, M. 'Saint Stephen and the Jerusalem Temple', *J.E.H.* 2, 1951.

Sittler, J. *The Structure of Christian Ethics,* Baton Rouge, Louisiana, 1958.

Skinner, J. *Prophecy and Religion,* Cambridge, 1948, r.p. 1963.

Smith, M. *Tannaitic Parallels to the Gospels,* Philadelphia, 1951.

—— 'A Comparison of Early Christian and Early Rabbinic Tradition', *J.B.L.* 82, 1963.

Smith, R. Gregor, *Secular Christianity,* London, 1966.

Sparks, H. F. D. *The Formation of the New Testament,* London, 1952.

Stauffer, E. *New Testament Theology,* Eng. tr., London, 1955.

Stegemann, C. *Herkunft und Entstehung des sogennanten zweiten Klemensbriefes,* Bonn, 1974.

Stendahl, K. 'Kerygma und kerygmatisch', *T.L.Z.* 77, 1952.

—— *The School of St Matthew,* Uppsala, 1954, (2nd ed.) Lund, 1968.

Taylor, R. O. P. *The Groundwork of the Gospels,* Oxford, 1946.

Taylor, V. *The Formation of the Gospel Tradition,* London, 1933, r.p. 1964.

—— *Jesus and His Sacrifice,* London, 1937, r.p. 1955.

Teeple, H. 'The Origin of the Son of Man Christology', *J.B.L.* 84, 1965.

Templeton, D. A. 'A Critique of some Aspects of Kerygma as understood by R. Bultmann and C. H. Dodd' unpublished Ph.D. thesis, Univ. of Glasgow, 1967.

Thomas, J. *Le mouvement baptiste en Palestine et Syrie,* Gembloux, 1935.

Thornton, L. S. 'The Body of Christ in the New Testament', in *The Apostolic Ministry,* Kirk (ed.), 1946.

Thyen, H. *Der Stil der judisch-hellenistischen Homilie,* Göttingen, 1955.

Tödt, H. E. *The Son of Man in the Synoptic Tradition,* Eng. tr., London, 1965.

Torrance, T. F. *The School of Faith,* London, 1959.

Trilling, W. 'Die Täufertradition bei Matthaüs', *B.Z.* (N.F.) III, 2, 1959.

Trocmé, E. *Le 'Livre des Actes' et l'histoire,* Paris, 1957.

—— *La formation de l'évangile selon Marc,* Paris, 1963.

—— *Jesus and his Contemporaries,* Eng. tr., London, 1973.

Turner, C. H. 'Markan Usage', *J.T.S.* 25, 1924.
Tyrrell, G. *Christianity at the Crossroads*, London, 1909, (4th ed.) 1913.
van Unnik, W. C. *Tarsus or Jerusalem*, London, 1962.
—— 'A Formula describing Prophecy', *N.T.S.* 9, 1962–63.

Vanhoye, A. *La structure littéraire de l'Épitre aux Hébreux*, Paris, 1963.
Vermes, G. 'A propos des commentaires bibliques découverts à Qumran', *La Bible et l'Orient*, 1955.
—— *Scripture and Tradition in Judaism*, Leiden, 1961.
—— *The Dead Sea Scrolls in English*, Harmondsworth, 1962.
—— *Jesus the Jew*, London, 1973.
Vielhauer, P. 'Apocalyptic', in *N.T. Apocrypha* II, Hennecke and Schneemelcher (Eng. tr. ed. Wilson), 1965.
Vincent, J. J. 'Didactic Kerygma in the Synoptic Gospels', *S.J.T.* 10, 1957.
Vokes, F. E. *The Riddle of the Didache*, London, 1938.

Walker, W. O. Jr. 'The Origin of the Son of Man Concept as Applied to Jesus', *J.B.L.* 91, 1972.
Watt, W. M. *Muhammad, Prophet and Statesman*, London, 1961.
Weidinger, K. *Die Haustafeln, Ein Stück urchristlicher Paränese*, Leipzig, 1928.
Weiss, J. *Die Predigt Jesu vom Reiche Gottes*, Göttingen, (2nd ed.) 1900.
Wendland, P. *Die hellenistisch-römische Kultur*, Tübingen, 1912.
Westermann, C. 'The Way of the Promise through the Old Testament', in *The Old Testament and Christian Faith*, Andersen (ed.), 1964.
—— *Basic Forms of Prophetic Speech*, Eng. tr., London, 1967.
Whybray, R. N. *Wisdom in Proverbs*, London, 1965.
Wibbing, S. *Die Tugend- und Lasterkataloge im Neuen Testament*, Berlin, 1959.
Wilckens U. 'Die Ursprung der Überlieferung der Erscheinungen der Auferstandenen', in *Dogma und Denkstrukturen*, Joest and Pannenberg (edd.), 1963.
—— 'The Tradition-History of the Resurrection of Jesus' in *S.M.R.*, Moule (ed.), 1968.
Wilcox, M. *The Semitisms of Acts*, Oxford, 1965.
Wildberger, H. *Jahwewort und prophetische Rede bei Jeremia*, Zurich, 1942.
Wilder, A. N. *Eschatology and Ethics in the Teaching of Jesus*, New York, 1950.
—— 'Form History and the Oldest Tradition', in *Neotestamentica et Patristica*, Leiden, 1962.
—— *Early Christian Rhetoric*, London, 1964.
Wilson, R. McL. *The Gnostic Problem*, London, 1958.
—— *Gnosis in the New Testament*, Oxford, 1968.
—— 'How Gnostic were the Corinthians?' *N.T.S.* 19, 1972–73.
Wilson, R. McL. (ed.) *New Testament Apocrypha* (Eng. tr. of E. Hennecke and W. Schneemelcher, *N.T. Apokryphon*), London, 1963–65.
Wingren, G. *The Living Word*, Eng. tr., London, 1960.

Wink, W. *John the Baptist in Gospel Tradition*, Cambridge, 1968.

Wolff, H.W. 'Hauptprobleme alttestamentlicher Prophetie', *Ev. Th.* 15, 1955.

—— *Jesaja 53 im Urchristentum*, Berlin, (3rd ed.) 1952.

Wolfson, H. A. *Philo – Foundations of Religious Philosophy in Judaism, Christianity and Islam* I, II, Cambridge, Mass., 1948.

Wrede, W. *Das Messiasgeheimnis in der Evangelien*, Göttingen, 1901 (Eng. tr., *The Messianic Secret*, London, 1971).

Wright, A. G. 'The Literary Genre Midrash', *C.B.Q.* 28, 1966.

Wright, G. E. *God Who Acts*, London, 1952.

Wuellner, W. 'Haggadic Homily Genre in 1 Corinthians 1–3', *J.B.L.* 89, 1970.

Zaehner, R. C. *The Dawn and Twilight of Zoroastrianism*, London, 1961.

Zahrnt, H. *The Historical Jesus*, Eng. tr., London, 1963.

Zeitlin, S. 'An Historical Study of the First Canonization of the Hebrew Liturgy', *J.Q.R.* 38, 1948.

—— 'Hillel and the Hermeneutic Rules', *J.Q.R.* 54, 1963–64.

Zeller, E. *Stoics, Epicureans and Sceptics*, Eng. tr., London, 1870.

INDEX OF AUTHORS

219

INDEX OF SCRIPTURE PASSAGES